**RAND McNALLY**

# Traveler's World Atlas & Guide

# Quick Reference Contents

Second revised printing, 1994.
Library of Congress Cataloging-in-Publication Data
Rand McNally & Company.
    Traveler's world atlas and guide.
        p.  cm.
    At head of title: Rand McNally.
    Includes travel information, guide to selected cities, and country
profiles.
    Includes index.

    1. Atlases.  I. Title.  II. Title: Traveler's world atlas and
guide.  III. Title: Rand McNally traveler's world atlas & guide.
G1021.R487  1993  < G&M >
912—dc20                              93–11580
                                        CIP
                                        MAP

# Contents

# 4 Contents

# Contents 5

# Air Distances Between World Cities
*Given in statute miles*

| | Apia, Western Samoa | Azores Islands | Beijing, China | Berlin, Germany | Bombay, India | Buenos Aires, Argentina | Calcutta, India | Cape Town, South Africa | Cape Verde Islands | Chicago, U.S.A. | Darwin, Australia | Denver, U.S.A. | Gibraltar | Hong Kong |
|---|---|---|---|---|---|---|---|---|---|---|---|---|---|---|
| Apia | | 9644 | 5903 | 9743 | 8154 | 6931 | 7183 | 9064 | 10246 | 6557 | 3843 | 5653 | 10676 | 5591 |
| Azores Islands | 9644 | | 6565 | 2185 | 5967 | 5417 | 6549 | 5854 | 1499 | 3093 | 10209 | 3991 | 1249 | 7572 |
| Beijing | 5903 | 6565 | | 4567 | 2964 | 11974 | 2024 | 8045 | 7763 | 6592 | 3728 | 6348 | 6009 | 1226 |
| Berlin | 9743 | 2185 | 4567 | | 3910 | 7376 | 4376 | 5977 | 3194 | 4402 | 8036 | 5077 | 1453 | 5500 |
| Bombay | 8154 | 5967 | 2964 | 3910 | | 9273 | 1041 | 5134 | 6297 | 8054 | 4503 | 8383 | 4814 | 2673 |
| Buenos Aires | 6931 | 5417 | 11974 | 7376 | 9273 | | 10242 | 4270 | 4208 | 5596 | 9127 | 5928 | 5963 | 11463 |
| Calcutta | 7183 | 6549 | 2024 | 4376 | 1041 | 10242 | | 6026 | 7148 | 7981 | 3744 | 8050 | 5521 | 1534 |
| Cape Town | 9064 | 5854 | 8045 | 5977 | 5134 | 4270 | 6026 | | 4509 | 8449 | 6947 | 9327 | 5076 | 7372 |
| Cape Verde Is. | 10246 | 1499 | 7763 | 3194 | 6297 | 4208 | 7148 | 4509 | | 4066 | 10664 | 4975 | 1762 | 8539 |
| Chicago | 6557 | 3093 | 6592 | 4402 | 8054 | 5596 | 7981 | 8449 | 4066 | | 9346 | 920 | 4258 | 7790 |
| Darwin | 3843 | 10209 | 3728 | 8036 | 4503 | 9127 | 3744 | 6947 | 10664 | 9346 | | 8557 | 9265 | 2642 |
| Denver | 5653 | 3991 | 6348 | 5077 | 8383 | 5928 | 8050 | 9327 | 4975 | 920 | 8557 | | 5122 | 7465 |
| Gibraltar | 10676 | 1249 | 1226 | 1453 | 4814 | 5963 | 5521 | 5076 | 1762 | 4258 | 9265 | 5122 | | 6828 |
| Hong Kong | 5591 | 7572 | 1226 | 5500 | 2673 | 11463 | 1534 | 7372 | 8539 | 7790 | 2642 | 7465 | 6828 | |
| Honolulu | 2604 | 7180 | 5067 | 7305 | 8020 | 7558 | 7037 | 11532 | 8311 | 4244 | 5355 | 3338 | 8075 | 5537 |
| Istanbul | 10175 | 2975 | 4379 | 1078 | 2991 | 7568 | 3646 | 5219 | 3507 | 5476 | 7390 | 6154 | 1874 | 4980 |
| Juneau | 5415 | 4526 | 4522 | 4560 | 6866 | 7759 | 6326 | 10330 | 5911 | 2305 | 7105 | 1831 | 5273 | 5634 |
| London | 9789 | 1527 | 5054 | 574 | 4462 | 6918 | 4954 | 6005 | 2731 | 3950 | 8598 | 4688 | 1094 | 5981 |
| Los Angeles | 4828 | 4794 | 6250 | 5782 | 8701 | 6118 | 8148 | 9969 | 5772 | 1745 | 7835 | 831 | 5936 | 7240 |
| Manila | 4993 | 8250 | 1770 | 6128 | 3148 | 11042 | 2189 | 7525 | 9221 | 8128 | 1979 | 7661 | 7483 | 693 |
| Melbourne | 3113 | 12101 | 5667 | 9919 | 6097 | 7234 | 5547 | 6412 | 10856 | 9668 | 1964 | 8759 | 10798 | 4607 |
| Mexico City | 5449 | 4385 | 7733 | 6037 | 9722 | 4633 | 9495 | 8511 | 4857 | 1673 | 9081 | 1434 | 5629 | 8776 |
| Moscow | 9116 | 3165 | 3597 | 996 | 3131 | 8375 | 3447 | 6294 | 3982 | 4984 | 7046 | 5485 | 2413 | 4439 |
| New Orleans | 6085 | 3524 | 7314 | 5116 | 8865 | 4916 | 8803 | 8316 | 4194 | 833 | 9545 | 1082 | 4757 | 8480 |
| New York | 7242 | 2422 | 6823 | 3961 | 7794 | 5297 | 7921 | 7801 | 3355 | 713 | 9959 | 1631 | 3627 | 8051 |
| Nome | 5438 | 4954 | 3428 | 4342 | 5901 | 8848 | 5271 | 10107 | 6438 | 3314 | 6235 | 2925 | 5398 | 4547 |
| Oslo | 9247 | 2234 | 4360 | 515 | 4130 | 7613 | 4459 | 6494 | 3444 | 4040 | 8022 | 4653 | 1791 | 5337 |
| Panamá | 6514 | 3778 | 8906 | 5849 | 9742 | 3381 | 10114 | 7014 | 3734 | 2325 | 10352 | 2636 | 4926 | 10084 |
| Paris | 9990 | 1659 | 5101 | 542 | 4359 | 6877 | 4889 | 3841 | 2666 | 4133 | 8575 | 4885 | 964 | 5956 |
| Port Said | 10485 | 3391 | 4584 | 1747 | 2659 | 7362 | 3506 | 4590 | 3672 | 6103 | 7159 | 6819 | 2179 | 4975 |
| Quebec | 7406 | 2240 | 6423 | 3583 | 7371 | 5680 | 7481 | 7857 | 3355 | 878 | 9724 | 1752 | 3383 | 8650 |
| Reykjavik | 8678 | 1777 | 4603 | 1479 | 5191 | 7099 | 5409 | 7111 | 3248 | 2954 | 8631 | 3596 | 2047 | 6031 |
| Rio de Janeiro | 8120 | 4428 | 10768 | 6144 | 8257 | 1218 | 9376 | 3769 | 3040 | 5296 | 9960 | 5871 | 4775 | 10995 |
| Rome | 10475 | 2125 | 5047 | 734 | 3843 | 6929 | 4496 | 5249 | 2772 | 4808 | 8190 | 5561 | 1034 | 5768 |
| San Francisco | 4786 | 4872 | 5902 | 5657 | 8392 | 6474 | 7809 | 10241 | 5921 | 1858 | 7637 | 949 | 5936 | 6894 |
| Seattle | 5222 | 4501 | 5396 | 5041 | 7741 | 6913 | 7224 | 10199 | 5714 | 1737 | 7619 | 1021 | 5462 | 6471 |
| Shanghai | 5399 | 7229 | 662 | 5215 | 3133 | 12197 | 2112 | 8059 | 8443 | 7053 | 3142 | 6698 | 6646 | 772 |
| Singapore | 5850 | 8326 | 2774 | 6166 | 2429 | 9864 | 1791 | 6016 | 8700 | 9365 | 2075 | 9063 | 7231 | 1652 |
| Tokyo | 4656 | 7247 | 1307 | 5538 | 4188 | 11400 | 3186 | 9071 | 8589 | 6303 | 3367 | 5795 | 6988 | 1796 |
| Valparaíso | 6267 | 5678 | 11774 | 7795 | 10037 | 761 | 10993 | 4998 | 4649 | 5268 | 8961 | 5452 | 6408 | 11607 |
| Vienna | 10010 | 2291 | 4639 | 328 | 3718 | 7368 | 4259 | 5671 | 3147 | 4694 | 7974 | 5383 | 1386 | 5429 |
| Washington, D.C. | 7066 | 2667 | 6922 | 4167 | 7988 | 5216 | 8088 | 7894 | 3486 | 597 | 9923 | 1494 | 3822 | 8148 |
| Wellington | 2062 | 11269 | 6698 | 11265 | 7677 | 6260 | 7042 | 7019 | 10363 | 8349 | 3310 | 7516 | 12060 | 5853 |
| Winnipeg | 6283 | 3389 | 5907 | 4286 | 7644 | 6297 | 7424 | 9054 | 4556 | 714 | 8684 | 798 | 4435 | 7096 |
| Zanzibar | 9892 | 5323 | 5803 | 4309 | 2855 | 6421 | 3859 | 2346 | 4635 | 8358 | 6409 | 9221 | 4103 | 5414 |

| Honolulu, Hawaii, U.S.A. | Istanbul, Turkey | Juneau, Alaska, U.S.A. | London, United Kingdom | Los Angeles, U.S.A. | Manila, Philippines | Melbourne, Australia | Mexico City, Mexico | Moscow, Russia | New Orleans, U.S.A. | New York, U.S.A. | Nome, Alaska, U.S.A. | Oslo, Norway | Panamá, Panama | Paris, France | Port Said, Egypt | Quebec, Canada |
|---|---|---|---|---|---|---|---|---|---|---|---|---|---|---|---|---|
| 2604 | 10175 | 5415 | 9789 | 4828 | 4993 | 3113 | 5449 | 9116 | 6085 | 7242 | 5438 | 9247 | 6514 | 9990 | 10485 | 7406 |
| 7180 | 2975 | 4526 | 1527 | 4794 | 8250 | 12101 | 4385 | 3165 | 3524 | 2422 | 4954 | 2234 | 3778 | 1659 | 3391 | 2240 |
| 5067 | 4379 | 4522 | 5054 | 6250 | 1770 | 5667 | 7733 | 3597 | 7314 | 6823 | 3428 | 4360 | 8906 | 5101 | 4584 | 6423 |
| 7305 | 1078 | 4560 | 574 | 5782 | 6128 | 9919 | 6037 | 996 | 5116 | 3961 | 4342 | 515 | 5849 | 542 | 1747 | 3583 |
| 8020 | 2991 | 6866 | 4462 | 8701 | 3148 | 6097 | 9722 | 3131 | 8865 | 7794 | 5901 | 4130 | 9742 | 4359 | 2659 | 7371 |
| 7558 | 7568 | 7759 | 6918 | 6118 | 11042 | 7234 | 4633 | 8375 | 4916 | 5297 | 8848 | 7613 | 3381 | 6877 | 7362 | 5680 |
| 7037 | 3646 | 6326 | 4954 | 8148 | 2189 | 5547 | 9495 | 3447 | 8803 | 7921 | 5271 | 4459 | 10114 | 4889 | 3506 | 7481 |
| 11532 | 5219 | 10330 | 6005 | 9969 | 7525 | 6412 | 8511 | 6294 | 8316 | 7801 | 10107 | 6494 | 7014 | 5841 | 4590 | 7857 |
| 8311 | 3507 | 5911 | 2731 | 5772 | 9221 | 10856 | 4857 | 3982 | 4194 | 3355 | 6438 | 3444 | 3734 | 2666 | 3672 | 3355 |
| 4244 | 5476 | 2305 | 3950 | 1745 | 8128 | 9668 | 1673 | 4984 | 833 | 713 | 3314 | 4040 | 2325 | 4133 | 6103 | 878 |
| 5355 | 7390 | 7105 | 8598 | 7835 | 1979 | 1964 | 9081 | 7046 | 9545 | 9959 | 6235 | 8022 | 10352 | 8575 | 7159 | 9724 |
| 3338 | 6154 | 1831 | 4688 | 831 | 7661 | 8759 | 1434 | 5485 | 1082 | 1631 | 2925 | 4653 | 2636 | 4885 | 6819 | 1732 |
| 8075 | 1874 | 5273 | 1094 | 5936 | 7483 | 10798 | 5629 | 2413 | 4757 | 3627 | 5398 | 1791 | 4926 | 964 | 2179 | 3383 |
| 5537 | 4980 | 5634 | 5981 | 7240 | 693 | 4607 | 8776 | 4439 | 8480 | 8051 | 4547 | 5337 | 10084 | 5956 | 4975 | 7650 |
|  | 8104 | 2815 | 7226 | 2557 | 5296 | 5513 | 3781 | 7033 | 4207 | 4959 | 3004 | 6784 | 5245 | 7434 | 8738 | 5000 |
| 8104 |  | 5498 | 1551 | 6843 | 5659 | 9088 | 7102 | 1088 | 6171 | 5009 | 5101 | 1518 | 6750 | 1401 | 693 | 4644 |
| 2815 | 5498 |  | 4418 | 1842 | 5869 | 8035 | 3219 | 4534 | 2905 | 2854 | 1094 | 4045 | 4460 | 4628 | 6215 | 2660 |
| 7226 | 1551 | 4418 |  | 5439 | 6667 | 10501 | 5541 | 1549 | 4627 | 3459 | 4381 | 714 | 5278 | 213 | 2154 | 3101 |
| 2557 | 6843 | 1842 | 5439 |  | 7269 | 7931 | 1542 | 6068 | 1673 | 2451 | 2876 | 5325 | 3001 | 5601 | 7528 | 2579 |
| 5296 | 5659 | 5869 | 6667 | 7269 |  | 3941 | 8829 | 5130 | 8724 | 8493 | 4817 | 6016 | 10283 | 6673 | 5619 | 8124 |
| 5513 | 9088 | 8035 | 10501 | 7931 | 3941 |  | 8422 | 8963 | 9275 | 10355 | 7558 | 9926 | 9022 | 10396 | 8658 | 10497 |
| 3781 | 7102 | 3219 | 5541 | 1542 | 8829 | 8422 |  | 6688 | 934 | 2085 | 4309 | 5706 | 1495 | 5706 | 7671 | 2454 |
| 7033 | 1088 | 4534 | 1549 | 6068 | 5130 | 8963 | 6688 |  | 5756 | 4662 | 4036 | 1016 | 6711 | 1541 | 1710 | 4242 |
| 4207 | 6171 | 2905 | 4627 | 1673 | 8724 | 9275 | 934 | 5756 |  | 1171 | 3937 | 4795 | 1603 | 4788 | 6756 | 1534 |
| 4959 | 5009 | 2854 | 3459 | 2451 | 8493 | 10355 | 2085 | 4662 | 1171 |  | 3769 | 3672 | 2231 | 3622 | 5590 | 439 |
| 3004 | 5101 | 1094 | 4381 | 2876 | 4817 | 7558 | 4309 | 4036 | 3937 | 3769 |  | 3836 | 5541 | 4574 | 5745 | 3489 |
| 6784 | 1518 | 4045 | 714 | 5325 | 6016 | 9926 | 5706 | 1016 | 4795 | 3672 | 3836 |  | 5691 | 832 | 2211 | 3263 |
| 5245 | 6750 | 4460 | 5278 | 3001 | 10283 | 9022 | 1495 | 6711 | 1603 | 2231 | 5541 | 5691 |  | 5382 | 7146 | 2659 |
| 7434 | 1401 | 4628 | 213 | 5601 | 6673 | 10396 | 5706 | 1541 | 4788 | 3622 | 4574 | 832 | 5382 |  | 1975 | 3235 |
| 8738 | 693 | 6215 | 2154 | 7528 | 5619 | 8658 | 7671 | 1710 | 6756 | 5590 | 5745 | 2211 | 7146 | 1975 |  | 5250 |
| 5000 | 4644 | 2660 | 3101 | 2579 | 8124 | 10497 | 2454 | 4242 | 1534 | 439 | 3489 | 3263 | 2659 | 3235 | 5250 |  |
| 6084 | 2558 | 3268 | 1171 | 4306 | 6651 | 10544 | 4622 | 2056 | 3711 | 2576 | 3366 | 1083 | 4706 | 1380 | 3227 | 2189 |
| 8190 | 6395 | 7598 | 5772 | 6296 | 11254 | 8186 | 4770 | 7179 | 4796 | 4820 | 8586 | 6482 | 3294 | 5703 | 6244 | 5125 |
| 8022 | 854 | 5247 | 887 | 6326 | 6465 | 9934 | 6353 | 1474 | 5439 | 4273 | 5082 | 1243 | 5903 | 682 | 1317 | 3943 |
| 2392 | 6700 | 1525 | 5355 | 347 | 6963 | 7854 | 1885 | 5868 | 1926 | 2571 | 2547 | 5181 | 3322 | 5441 | 7394 | 2642 |
| 2678 | 6063 | 899 | 4782 | 959 | 6641 | 8186 | 2337 | 5199 | 2101 | 2408 | 1976 | 4591 | 3651 | 4993 | 6759 | 2353 |
| 4934 | 4959 | 4869 | 5710 | 6477 | 1152 | 5005 | 8039 | 4235 | 7720 | 7357 | 3784 | 5020 | 9324 | 5752 | 5132 | 6981 |
| 6710 | 5373 | 7235 | 6744 | 8767 | 1479 | 3761 | 10307 | 5238 | 10082 | 9630 | 6148 | 6246 | 11687 | 6671 | 5088 | 9097 |
| 3850 | 5556 | 4011 | 5938 | 5470 | 1863 | 5089 | 7035 | 4650 | 6858 | 6735 | 2983 | 5221 | 8423 | 6033 | 5842 | 6417 |
| 6793 | 8172 | 7271 | 7263 | 5527 | 10930 | 6998 | 4053 | 8792 | 4514 | 5094 | 8360 | 7914 | 2943 | 7251 | 8088 | 5504 |
| 7626 | 783 | 4895 | 772 | 6108 | 6120 | 9792 | 6306 | 1044 | 5385 | 4224 | 4657 | 850 | 6026 | 644 | 1429 | 3858 |
| 4829 | 5216 | 2834 | 3665 | 2300 | 8560 | 10173 | 1878 | 4883 | 966 | 205 | 3792 | 3870 | 2080 | 3828 | 5796 | 610 |
| 4708 | 10663 | 7475 | 11682 | 6714 | 5162 | 1595 | 6899 | 10279 | 7794 | 8946 | 7383 | 10974 | 7433 | 11791 | 10249 | 9228 |
| 3806 | 5361 | 1597 | 3918 | 1525 | 7414 | 9319 | 2097 | 4687 | 1418 | 1281 | 2599 | 3854 | 2998 | 4118 | 6032 | 1199 |
| 10869 | 3312 | 8795 | 4604 | 10021 | 5763 | 6802 | 9484 | 4270 | 8754 | 7698 | 8209 | 4803 | 8245 | 4396 | 2729 | 7443 |

# 10 Air Distances Between World Cities

| City | Reykjavik, Iceland | Rio de Janeiro, Brazil | Rome, Italy | San Francisco, U.S.A. | Seattle, U.S.A. | Shanghai, China | Singapore, Singapore | Tokyo, Japan | Valparaíso, Chile | Vienna, Austria | Washington, D.C., U.S.A. | Wellington, New Zealand | Winnipeg, Canada | Zanzibar, Tanzania |
|---|---|---|---|---|---|---|---|---|---|---|---|---|---|---|
| Apia | 8678 | 8120 | 10475 | 4786 | 5222 | 5399 | 5850 | 4656 | 6267 | 10010 | 7066 | 2062 | 6283 | 9892 |
| Azores Islands | 1777 | 4428 | 2125 | 4872 | 4501 | 7229 | 8326 | 7247 | 5678 | 2291 | 2667 | 11269 | 3389 | 5323 |
| Beijing | 4903 | 10768 | 5047 | 5902 | 5396 | 662 | 2774 | 1307 | 11774 | 4639 | 6922 | 6698 | 5907 | 5803 |
| Berlin | 1479 | 6114 | 734 | 5657 | 5041 | 5215 | 6166 | 5538 | 7795 | 328 | 4167 | 11265 | 4285 | 4309 |
| Bombay | 5191 | 8257 | 3843 | 8392 | 7741 | 3133 | 2429 | 4188 | 10037 | 3718 | 7988 | 7677 | 7644 | 2855 |
| Buenos Aires | 7099 | 1218 | 6929 | 6474 | 6913 | 12197 | 9864 | 11400 | 761 | 7368 | 5216 | 6260 | 6297 | 6421 |
| Calcutta | 5409 | 9376 | 4496 | 7809 | 7224 | 2112 | 1791 | 3186 | 10993 | 4259 | 8088 | 7042 | 7424 | 3859 |
| Cape Town | 7111 | 3769 | 5249 | 10241 | 10199 | 8059 | 6016 | 9071 | 4998 | 5671 | 7894 | 7019 | 9054 | 2346 |
| Cape Verde Is. | 3248 | 3040 | 2772 | 5921 | 5714 | 8443 | 8700 | 8589 | 4649 | 3147 | 3486 | 10363 | 4556 | 4635 |
| Chicago | 2954 | 5296 | 4808 | 1858 | 1737 | 7053 | 9365 | 6303 | 5268 | 4694 | 597 | 8349 | 714 | 8358 |
| Darwin | 8631 | 9960 | 8190 | 7637 | 7619 | 3142 | 2075 | 3367 | 8961 | 7974 | 9923 | 3310 | 8684 | 6409 |
| Denver | 3596 | 5871 | 5561 | 949 | 1021 | 6698 | 9063 | 5795 | 5452 | 5383 | 1494 | 7516 | 798 | 9921 |
| Gibraltar | 2047 | 4775 | 1034 | 5936 | 5462 | 6646 | 7231 | 6988 | 6408 | 1386 | 3822 | 12060 | 4435 | 4103 |
| Hong Kong | 6031 | 10995 | 5768 | 6894 | 6471 | 772 | 1652 | 1796 | 11607 | 5429 | 8148 | 5853 | 7096 | 5414 |
| Honolulu | 6084 | 8190 | 8022 | 2392 | 2678 | 4934 | 6710 | 3850 | 6793 | 7626 | 4829 | 4708 | 3806 | 10869 |
| Istanbul | 2558 | 6395 | 854 | 6700 | 6063 | 4959 | 5373 | 5556 | 8172 | 783 | 5216 | 10663 | 5361 | 3312 |
| Juneau | 3268 | 7598 | 5247 | 1525 | 899 | 4869 | 7235 | 4011 | 7271 | 4895 | 2834 | 7475 | 1597 | 8795 |
| London | 1171 | 5772 | 887 | 5355 | 4782 | 5710 | 6744 | 5938 | 7263 | 772 | 3665 | 11682 | 3918 | 4604 |
| Los Angeles | 4306 | 6296 | 6326 | 347 | 959 | 6477 | 8767 | 5470 | 5527 | 6108 | 2300 | 6714 | 1525 | 10021 |
| Manila | 6651 | 11254 | 6457 | 6963 | 6641 | 1152 | 1479 | 1863 | 10930 | 6120 | 8560 | 5162 | 7414 | 5763 |
| Melbourne | 10544 | 8186 | 9934 | 7854 | 8186 | 5005 | 3761 | 5089 | | 9792 | 10173 | 1595 | 9319 | 6802 |
| Mexico City | 4622 | 4770 | 6353 | 1885 | 2337 | 8039 | 10307 | 7035 | 4053 | 6306 | 1878 | 6899 | 2097 | 9484 |
| Moscow | 2056 | 7179 | 1474 | 5868 | 5199 | 4235 | 5238 | 4650 | 8792 | 1044 | 4883 | 10279 | 4687 | 4270 |
| New Orleans | 3711 | 4796 | 5439 | 1926 | 2101 | 7720 | 10082 | 6858 | 4514 | 5385 | 966 | 7794 | 1418 | 8754 |
| New York | 2576 | 4820 | 4273 | 2571 | 2408 | 7357 | 9630 | 6735 | 5094 | 4224 | 205 | 8946 | 1281 | 7698 |
| Nome | 3366 | 8586 | 5082 | 2547 | 1976 | 3784 | 6148 | 2983 | 8360 | 4657 | 3792 | 7383 | 2599 | 8209 |
| Oslo | 1083 | 6482 | 1243 | 5181 | 4591 | 5020 | 6246 | 5221 | 7914 | 859 | 3870 | 10974 | 3854 | 4803 |
| Panamá | 4706 | 3294 | 5903 | 3322 | 3651 | 9324 | 11687 | 8423 | 2943 | 6026 | 2080 | 7433 | 2998 | 8245 |
| Paris | 1380 | 5703 | 682 | 5441 | 4993 | 5752 | 6671 | 6033 | 7251 | 644 | 3828 | 11791 | 4118 | 4396 |
| Port Said | 3227 | 6244 | 1317 | 7394 | 6759 | 5132 | 5088 | 5842 | 8088 | 1429 | 5796 | 10249 | 6032 | 2729 |
| Quebec | 2189 | 5125 | 3943 | 2642 | 2353 | 6981 | 9097 | 6417 | 5504 | 3858 | 610 | 9228 | 1199 | 7443 |
| Reykjavik | | 6118 | 2044 | 4199 | 3614 | 5559 | 7160 | 5472 | 7225 | 1805 | 2800 | 10724 | 2804 | 5757 |
| Rio de Janeiro | 6118 | | 5684 | 6619 | 6891 | 11340 | 9774 | 11535 | 1855 | 6136 | 4797 | 7349 | 6010 | 5589 |
| Rome | 2044 | 5684 | | 6240 | 5659 | 5677 | 6232 | 6124 | 7420 | 463 | 4435 | 11524 | 4803 | 3712 |
| San Francisco | 4199 | 6619 | 6240 | | 678 | 6132 | 8479 | 5131 | 5876 | 5988 | 2442 | 6739 | 1504 | 9958 |
| Seattle | 3614 | 6891 | 5639 | 678 | | 5703 | 8057 | 4777 | 6230 | 5376 | 2329 | 7242 | 1150 | 9359 |
| Shanghai | 5559 | 11340 | 5677 | 6132 | 5703 | | 2377 | 1094 | 11650 | 5270 | 7442 | 6054 | 6350 | 5971 |
| Singapore | 7160 | 9774 | 6232 | 8479 | 8057 | 2377 | | 3304 | 10226 | 6036 | 9834 | 5292 | 8685 | 4480 |
| Tokyo | 5472 | 11535 | 6124 | 5131 | 4777 | 1094 | 3304 | | 10635 | 5679 | 6769 | 5760 | 5575 | 7040 |
| Valparaíso | 7225 | 1855 | 7420 | 5876 | 6230 | 11650 | 10226 | 10635 | | 7783 | 4977 | 5785 | 5931 | 7184 |
| Vienna | 1805 | 6136 | 463 | 5988 | 5376 | 5270 | 6036 | 5679 | 7783 | | 4429 | 11278 | 4604 | 3983 |
| Washington, D.C. | 2800 | 4797 | 4435 | 2442 | 2329 | 7442 | 9834 | 6769 | 4977 | 4429 | | 8745 | 1243 | 7884 |
| Wellington | 10724 | 7349 | 11524 | 6739 | 7242 | 6054 | 5292 | 5760 | 5785 | 11278 | 8745 | | 8230 | 8122 |
| Winnipeg | 2804 | 6010 | 4803 | 1504 | 1150 | 6350 | 8685 | 5575 | 5931 | 4604 | 1243 | 8230 | | 8416 |
| Zanzibar | 5757 | 5589 | 3712 | 9958 | 9359 | 5971 | 4480 | 7040 | 7184 | 3983 | 7884 | 8122 | 8416 | |

# Travel Information

Entry requirements and travel advisories are subject to change. Travelers are advised to contact a travel agent, the State Department, a passport office, and/or the embassy of the destination for definitive travel information. In Islamic countries, when appearing in public, women should cover their arms, legs, and, in some places, their heads. Holidays for which a date is not given change from year to year; contact the country's embassy for exact dates.

| Country | Algeria | Argentina | Australia |
|---|---|---|---|
| **Int'l Dialing Code** | 213 | 54 | 61 |
| **City Codes** | | Buenos Aires 1, Córdoba 51, La Plata 21, Mendoza 61, Rosario 41 | Adelaide 8, Brisbane 7, Canberra 62, Melbourne 3, Sydney 2 |
| **Consulate Phone** | (202) 265-2800 | (202) 939-6400 | (202) 797-3000 |
| **Climate** | Mild, wet winters with hot, dry summers along the coast; drier with cold winters and hot summers on high plateau. | Climate ranges from hot, subtropical lowlands of the north to cold and rainy in the south. January in Buenos Aires is like Washington, D.C. in July; July is like San Francisco in January. | Arid to semiarid; temperate in the south and east; tropical in the north; most of southern Australia has warm summers and mild winters (seasons are reversed from North America). |
| **Clothing** | Lightweight clothing for summer; lightweight winter clothing for November to April. A hat and sunglasses are essential. Not all rooms are warmly heated in the winter. | Lightweight cottons are advisable for the north; woolens are needed during the winters and year-round in the extreme south. Dress is more formal than in the U.S. Shorts are not universally acceptable. | Wear lightweight clothing year round in the temperate regions during the winter; warmer clothes and an overcoat are then required. Casual clothing is usually appropriate. |
| **Entry Requirements** | Passport, visa, ticket to leave, sufficient funds; cholera and other innoculations recommended | Passport, visa | Passport, visa, ticket to leave, sufficient funds |
| **Holidays** | New Year's Day, Jan. 1; Prophet's Ascension; Ramadan and Id al-Fitr; Labor Day, May 1; Id al Adha; Independence Day, July 5; Islamic New Year; Prophet's Birthday; Anniversary of the Revolution, Nov. 1 | New Year's Day, Jan. 1; Maundy Thursday; Good Friday; Labor Day, May 1; National Day, May 25; Flag Day, June 20; Independence Day, July 9; Anniversary of San Martin's Death, Aug. 17; Columbus Day, Oct. 12; Immaculate Conception, Dec. 8; Christmas Day, Dec. 25 | New Year's Day, Jan. 1; Australia Day, late Jan.; Good Friday; Holy Saturday; Easter Monday; ANZAC Day, Apr. 25; Queen's Birthday, June; Christmas Day, Dec. 25; Boxing Day, Dec. 26 |
| **Special Notes** | There is a shortage of hotel rooms in Algiers. Tapwater is not potable; bottled water is available. | Tapwater is safe. | |

| Country | Austria | Bahamas | Barbados |
|---|---|---|---|
| **Int'l Dialing Code** | 43 | 809 | 809 |
| **City Codes** | Graz 316, Linz 732, Wien (Vienna) 222 | | |
| **Consulate Phone** | (202) 483-4474 | (202) 319-2660 | (202) 939-9200 |
| **Climate** | Cold winters with frequent rain in the lowlands and snow in the mountains; cool summers with occasional showers. | Tropical marine. | Tropical. |
| **Clothing** | Clothing needs and tastes are about the same as the northeastern United States. Bring sweaters and light woolens during possible cool spells in the summer. Many restaurants in Vienna have dress codes. | Lightweight clothing is worn year-round. Beachwear should be confined to resort areas. Daytime dress is casual, evening clothes are more formal. | Light-weight clothing is worn year-round; rainwear is needed for the rainy season. Casual clothes are usually acceptable. |
| **Entry Requirements** | Passport | Proof of citizenship, ticket to leave | Passport, ticket to leave |
| **Holidays** | New Year's Day, Jan. 1; Epiphany, Jan. 6; Easter Monday; Labor Day, May 1; Ascension Day; Whitmonday; Corpus Christi; Assumption Day, Aug. 15; National Day, Oct. 26; All Saints' Day, Nov. 1; Feast of the Immaculate Conception, Dec. 8; Christmas Day, Dec. 25; St. Stephen's Day, Dec. 26 | New Year's Day, Jan. 1; Good Friday; Easter Monday; Whitmonday; Labor Day, early June; Independence Day, July 10; Emancipation Day, early Aug.; Discovery Day, Oct. 12; Christmas Day, Dec. 25; Boxing Day, Dec. 26 | New Year's Day, Jan. 1; Good Friday; Easter Monday; Labor Day, May 1; Whitmonday; Kadooment Day, early July; United Nations Day, early Oct.; Independence Day, November 30; Christmas Day, Dec. 25; Boxing Day, Dec. 26 |
| **Special Notes** | | Hurricane season is from June to November. Water is potable but saline, and many people use bottled water. Mosquitos and sandflies may be a problem. | Hurricane season is from June to October. |

| Belgium | Bermuda | Botswana | Brazil |
|---|---|---|---|
| 32 | 809 | 267 | 55 |
| Antwerpen 3, Bruxelles 2, Gent 91, Liège 41 | | Francistown 21, Gaborone 31 | Belo Horizonte 31, Brasília 61, Rio de Janeiro 21, São Paulo 11 |
| (202) 333-6900 | (202) 462-1340 | (202) 244-4990 | (202) 745-2700 |
| Mild winters with little snow; cool summers; rainy, humid, cloudy. | Subtropical; mild, humid; gales, winds are common during the frost-free but chilly winter | Semiarid with warm winters and hot summers. | In most of the country, days range from warm to hot; rainy season from November to February; cool winters in the extreme south; seasons are reversed from North America. |
| Clothing and shoe needs in Belgium are about the same as for the Pacific Northwest. Raincoat, umbrellas, and low-heeled, thick-soled walking shoes are necessary. | Warm-weather clothing is suitable April-November; moderately heavy clothing is needed during the winter. Swimwear should be worn only on the beach. Most restaurants have evening dress codes. | Lightweight clothing is worn, with spring clothing for cool evenings and winter months. | Spring or summer clothes are appropriate year-round. |
| Passport, ticket to leave, sufficient funds | Proof of citizenship, visa (for stays of more than 21 days), ticket to leave | Passport; yellow fever and hepatitis innoculations recommended | Passport, visa; yellow fever and other innoculations recommended |
| New Year's Day, Jan. 1; Easter Monday; Labor Day, May 1; Ascension Day; Whitmonday; National Day, July 21; Assumption Day, Aug. 15; All Saints' Day, Nov. 1; Armistice Day, Nov. 11; Christmas Day, Dec. 25 | New Year's Day, Jan. 1; Good Friday; Commonwealth Day, May 24; Bermuda Day, late May; Queen's Birthday, June; Cup Match Day, late July; Labor Day, early Sept.; Remembrance Day, Nov. 11; Christmas Day, Dec. 25; Boxing Day, Dec. 26 | New Year's Day, Jan. 1; Good Friday; Easter Monday; Ascension Day; President's Day, July 16; Botswana Day, Sept. 30; Public Holiday, Oct. 1; Christmas Day, Dec. 25; Boxing Day, Dec. 26 | New Year's Day, Jan. 1; Carnival, Feb./Mar.; Good Friday; Tiradentes Day, Apr. 21; Labor Day, May 1; Corpus Christi; Independence Day, Sept. 7; Nossa Senhora de Aparecida, Oct. 12; Proclamation of the Republic, Nov. 15; Christmas Day, Dec. 25 |
| Tapwater is potable. | | Tapwater is potable in the major towns. Do not swim in lakes or rivers. | Street crime is common in Brazil's larger cities. Tapwater is not safe for consumption. Carefully prepared and thoroughly cooked foods are safe for consumption. |

| Country | Bulgaria | Canada | Chile |
|---|---|---|---|
| Int'l Dialing Code | 359 | | 56 |
| City Codes | Plovdiv 32, Sofija 2, Varna 52 | | Concepción 41, Santiago 2, Valparaíso 32 |
| Consulate Phone | (202) 387-7969 | (202) 682-1740 | (202) 785-1746 |
| Climate | Cold, damp winters with considerable snowfall; hot, dry, summers. | Varies from temperate in the south to subarctic and arctic in the north. | Climate ranges from desert in the north to cool and damp in the south; summers are dry and hot with cool nights; winters are cold and rainy. Seasons are reversed from North America. |
| Clothing | Summer clothing should include sweaters for cool evenings. Warm clothing advisable for cold winters. Formal wear is seldom required. | Lightweight clothes for summer months with a sweater for cool evenings; heavy clothing for winter months. | Sweaters are useful for cool summer nights; a jacket or coat is needed in the winter. Shorts should not be worn outside resort areas. |
| Entry Requirements | Passport | Proof of citizenship | Passport, business visa or tourist card; difficult to enter and exit by car; innoculations recommended |
| Holidays | New Year's Day, Jan. 1; Independence Day, Mar. 3; Labor Days, May 1,2; Bulgarian Culture Day, May 24; Liberation Days, Sept. 9,10; October Revolution Day, Nov. 7 | New Year's Day, Jan. 1; Good Friday; Easter Monday; Victoria Day, mid-May; Dominion Day, July 1; Civic Holiday, early Aug.; Thanksgiving, Oct. 12; Remembrance Day, Nov. 11; Christmas Day, Dec. 25; Boxing Day, Dec. 26 | New Year's Day, Jan. 1; Good Friday; Labor Day, May 1; Battle of Iquique, May 21; Corpus Christi; St. Peter's and Paul's Day; Assumption Day, Aug. 15; National Liberation Day, Sept. 11; Independence Day, Sept. 18; Day of the Army, Sept. 10; Columbus Day, Oct. 12; All Saints Day, Nov. 1; Immaculate Conception, Dec. 8; Christmas Day, Dec. 25 |
| Special Notes | Tapwater is potable in the capital. Eating in larger restaurants is advised. | | Do not eat unwashed fruits and vegetables. Tapwater is generally potable except after occasional winter floods. It is prudent to gradually accustom the body to tap water by using bottled water initially. Smog is prevalent in Santiago. |

| China (excl. Taiwan) | Colombia | Costa Rica | Czech Republic |
|---|---|---|---|
| 86 | 57 | 506 | 42 |
| Beijing (Peking) 1, Fuzhou 591, Guangzhou (Canton) 20, Jinan 531, Nanjing 25, Shanghai 21 | Barranquilla 5, Bogotá 1, Cali 23, Medellin 4 | | Brno 5, Ostrava 69, Plzeň 19, Praha (Prague) 2 |
| (202) 328-2517 | (202) 387-8338 | (202) 234-2945 | (202) 363-6315 |
| Extremely diverse; tropical in the south to subarctic in the north. | Tropical along the coast and eastern plains; cooler in the highlands. | Tropical; rainy season from May to November; dry season from December to April. | Cool, pleasant summers; cold, cloudy, humid winters. |
| In the north, lightweight clothing is required for the summer and heavy woolens for the harsh winters. In the south, tropical clothing is suitable for summer and spring-like clothing is worn in the winter. Clothing should be casual but conservative. | Knits and lightweight woolens are suitable in Bogota. Tropical clothing is worn in the lowlands. | Spring-weight clothing, with a sweater for cool evenings is recommended. Beachwear should be confined to resorts. | Bring rainwear and light or heavy woolens depending on the season. Casual but conservative dress is appropriate. |
| Passport, visa; innoculations recommended | Passport, business visa or tourist card | Passport, business visa or tourist card, ticket to leave, sufficient funds | Passport |
| New Year's Day, Jan. 1; Chinese New Year, Jan. or Feb.; Labor Day, May 1; National Day, Oct. 1 | New Year's Day, Jan. 1; Epiphany, Jan. 6; St. Joseph's Day, Mar. 19; Maundy Thursday; Good Friday; Labor Day, May 1; Ascension Day; Corpus Christi; Feast of the Sacred Heart; St. Peter and Paul Day; Independence Day, July 20; Battle of Boyaca, Aug. 7; Assumption Day, Aug. 15; Columbus Day, Oct. 12; All Saints' Day, Nov. 1; Independence of Cartagena, Nov. 11; Immaculate Consumption, Dec. 8; Christmas Day, Dec. 25 | New Year's Day, Jan. 1; St. Joseph's Day, Mar. 19; Maundy Thursday; Good Friday; Anniversary of the Battle of Rivas, Apr. 11; Labor Day, May 1; Corpus Christi; Annexation of Guanacaste, July 5; Our Lady of the Angels, Aug. 2; Assumption Day, Aug. 15; Independence Day, Sept. 15; Columbus Day, Oct. 12; Immaculate Conception, Dec. 8; Christmas Day, Dec. 25 | New Year's Day, Jan. 1; Easter Monday; Christmas Day, Dec. 25; Boxing Day, Dec. 26. |
| Travel to most of Tibet and many other areas is restricted without special permission. Tours can be extremely strenuous. Use bottled water. | Because of sporadic guerilla activity, travel in certain areas may be hazardous. Tapwater is not always safe in large cities; food should be prepared carefully. | Drinking water in major San Jose hotels and restaurants is purified; outside the capital drinking water should be purified. | Tapwater is usually safe. |

| Country | Denmark | Dominican Republic | Egypt |
|---|---|---|---|
| **Int'l Dialing Code** | 45 | 809 | 20 |
| **City Codes** | Ålborg 8, Århus 6, København (Copenhagen) 3, Odense 7 | | Al-Iskandarīyah (Alexandria) 3, Al-Qāhirah (Cairo) 2, Aswān 97, Asyūṭ 88 |
| **Consulate Phone** | (202) 234-4300 | (202) 332-6280 | (202) 232-5400 |
| **Climate** | Humid and overcast; mild, windy winters; cool, sunny summers. | Tropical; little temperature variation. | Desert; hot, dry summers with moderate winters. |
| **Clothing** | Woolen clothes are worn most of the year. Lightweight clothes may be required in the summer. | Lightweight clothing suitable for hot, humid weather is appropriate in Santo Domingo year round. Restaurants may have evening dress codes. | Lightweight summer clothing is needed for the summer; light woolens for the winter and cool evenings. Casual dress is appropriate, but revealing clothing is not appreciated. |
| **Entry Requirements** | Passport, ticket to leave, sufficient funds | Passport, business visa or tourist card, ticket to leave | Passport, visa, sufficient funds; innoculations recommended |
| **Holidays** | New Year's Day, Jan. 1; Thurs.-Mon. surrounding Easter; Prayer Day; Ascension Day; Constitution Day, June 5; Christmas Day, Dec. 25; Boxing Day, Dec. 26 | New Year's Day, Jan. 1; Epiphany, Jan. 6; Our Lady of Altagracia, Jan. 21; Duarte, Jan. 26; Independence Day, February 27, Good Friday; Labor Day, May 1; Corpus Christi, May 25; Restoration of Independence Day, Aug. 16; Our Lady of Las Mercedes, Sept. 24; Christmas Day, Dec. 25 | Union Day, Feb. 22; Ramadan; Sinai Liberation Day, April 25; Labor Day, May 1; Evacuation Day, June 18; Islamic New Year; Revolution Day, July 23; Prophet's Birthday; Armed Forces Day, Oct. 6; Suez Day, Oct. 24; Victory Day, Dec. 23 |
| **Special Notes** | | Hurricane season is from June to November. Tapwater is not potable. | Water in Cairo and Alexandria is generally safe, but milk should be boiled. Negotiate the fare with taxi drivers before entering the taxi. |

| Fiji | Finland | France | French Polynesia |
|---|---|---|---|
| 679 | 358 | 33 | 689 |
| | Espoo 15, Helsinki 0, Tampere 31, Turku 21 | Bordeaux 56, Lyon 7, Marseille 91, Nice 93, Paris 1, Toulouse 61 | |
| (202) 337-8320 | (202) 363-2430 | (202) 944-6000 | (202) 944-6087 |
| Tropical with high humidity; rainfall is abundant in Suva; little temperature variation. | Cold winters; mild summers. Helsinki's winter climate is similar to Boston's. | Cool winters and mild summers inland; mild winters and hot summers along the Mediterranean. | Tropical, but moderate. |
| Lightweight clothing is appropriate; dress is generally casual. Swimwear should not be worn in towns. | Warm outdoor clothing for winter and light woolens for summer are necessary. | Clothing needs are similar to those in Washington, D.C. | Lightweight clothing is worn throughout the year. |
| Passport, ticket to leave, sufficient funds | Passport, ticket to leave, sufficient funds | Passport | Passport, visa |
| New Year's Day, Jan. 1; Good Friday; Holy Saturday; Easter Monday; Queen's Birthday, June; Bank Holiday, early Aug.; Prophet's Birthday; Fiji Day, early Oct.; Diwali (Festival of Lights); Prince of Wales's Birthday, Nov. 14; Christmas Day, Dec. 25; Boxing Day, Dec. 26 | New Year's Day, Jan. 1; Epiphany; Good Friday; Easter; Easter Monday; May Day Eve, Apr. 30; May Day, May 1; Ascension Day; Whitsunday; Whitmonday; Midsummer's Day; All Saints' Day; Independence Day, Dec. 6, Christmas Day, Dec. 25 | New Year's Day, Jan. 1; Easter Monday; Labor Day, May 1; Ascension Day; Whitmonday; Bastille Day, July 14; Assumption Day, Aug. 15; All Saints' Day, Nov. 1; Armistice Day, Nov. 11; Christmas Day, Dec. 25 | New Year's Day, Jan. 1; Good Friday; Easter Monday; Labor Day, May 1; Ascension Day; Whitmonday; Bastille Day, July 14; All Saints' Day, Nov. 11; Christmas, Dec. 25, 26 |
| Drinking water is safe in all cities and major tourist resorts. | Tapwater is potable. | | |

| Country | Germany | Greece | Guatemala |
|---|---|---|---|
| Int'l Dialing Code | 49 | 30 | 502 |
| City Codes | Berlin 30, Bonn 228, Essen 201, Frankfurt am Main 69, Hamburg 40, München (Munich) 89 | Athínai (Athens) 1, Iráklion 81, Lárisa 41, Piraiévs 1, Thessaloníki 31 | Guatemala 2, all other cities 9 |
| Consulate Phone | (202) 298-4000 | (202) 939-5800 | (202) 745-4952 |
| Climate | Cool, cloudy, wet winters and summers; high relative humidity. | Mild, wet winters; hot, dry, summers. | Hot and humid in the lowlands; cooler in the highlands. |
| Clothing | Germany is cooler than much of the United States, especially in summer. Light-weight summer clothing is seldom needed. Very warm clothing is needed in the winter. | Lightweight clothing from May-September; woolens from October-April. | Spring or summer-weight clothing is needed most of the year; woolens are practical November through February. |
| Entry Requirements | Passport, ticket to leave, sufficient funds | Passport | Passport, business visa or tourist card, innoculations recommended |
| Holidays | New Year's Day, Jan. 1; Good Friday; Easter Monday; Labor Day, May 1; Ascension Day; Whitmonday; Day of Unity, June 17; Repentance Day, Nov. 16; Christmas Day, Dec. 25; Boxing Day, Dec. 26. | New Year's Day, Jan. 1; Epiphany, Jan. 6; Independence Day, Mar. 25; Good Friday; Easter Monday; Labor Day, May 1; Pentecost; Assumption Day, Aug. 15; Ochi Day, Oct. 28; Christmas Day, Dec. 25 | New Year's Day, Jan. 1; Maundy Thursday; Good Friday; Holy Saturday; Labor Day, May 1; Army Day, June 30; Assumption Day, Aug. 15; Independence Day, Sept. 15; Revolution Day, Oct. 20; All Saints' Day, Nov. 1; Christmas Eve, Dec. 24, Christmas Day, Dec. 25; New Year's Eve, Dec. 31 |
| Special Notes | All water and food is safe. Telecommunications in former East Germany remain poor. | Drinking water is safe in Athens and most resorts. Wash fruit before eating. | Tapwater is not potable, and fruits and vegetables should be prepared carefully. |

| Hong Kong | Hungary | India | Indonesia |
|---|---|---|---|
| 852 | 36 | 91 | 62 |
| | Budapest 1, Debrecen 52, Győr 96, Miskolc 46 | Bangalore 812, Bombay 22, Calcutta 33, Madras 44, New Delhi 11 | Bandung 22, Jakarta 21, Medan 61, Semarang 24, Surabaya 31 |
| (202) 462-1340 | (202) 362-6730 | (202) 939-7000 | (202) 775-5200 |
| Cool, humid winters; hot, rainy summers. | Cold, cloudy, humid winters; warm, pleasant summers. | Varies from tropical monsoon in the south to temperate in the north. Summers are very hot in most of India. | Tropical; hot, humid; more moderate in the highlands; rainy season from November to April. |
| Cottons and rainwear are advisable for the summer; warmer clothes are needed for the winter. Sports clothes are good for daytime, evening clothes are more formal. | Lightweight clothing is needed for the summer and heavy woolens for the winter. | Summer clothing is suitable year round in the south. In the north, lightweight woolens are necessary from mid-December to mid-February. Women should wear modest, loose-fitting clothing. | Light-weight cotton clothes are worn year-round, often with two changes a day. Women should dress conservatively. |
| Passport, visa (for stays of more than 1 month), ticket to leave, sufficient funds | Passport | Passport, visa, ticket to leave; innoculations recommended | Passport, visa (for stays of more than 60 days); innoculations recommended |
| New Year's Day, Jan. 1; Chinese New Year, Jan. or Feb.; Good Friday; Easter Monday; Queen's Birthday, late June; Liberation Day, Aug.; Christmas Day, Dec. 25; Boxing Day, Dec. 26 | New Year's Day, Jan. 1; National (Liberation) Day, Apr. 4; Easter Monday; Labor Day, May 1; Constitution Day, Aug. 20; October Revolution Day, Nov. 7; Christmas Day, Dec. 25; Boxing Day, Dec. 26 | Republic Day, Jan. 26; Holi; Independence Day, Aug. 15; Dashara; Mahatma Gandhi's Birthday, Oct. 2; Diwali; Christmas Day, Dec. 25 | New Year's Day, Jan. 1; Good Friday; Ramadan and Id al-Fitr; Ascension Day; Hijra; Independence Day, Aug. 17; Prophet's Birthday; Christmas Day, Dec. 25 |
| | Tapwater in Budapest is potable. Avoid unpasteurized milk and food products that lack preservatives. | Political unrest makes travel to West Bengal, Jammu and Kashmir, and the Punjab potentially dangerous. Permits are required for many restricted areas. Tapwater is unsafe throughout India. In hotels and restaurants, drink only bottled or carbonated water and avoid ice cubes. | Increasing numbers of thefts have been reported on public transportation, especially in Jakarta and Bali. Sanitation is adequate to excellent in Indonesia's international hotels, but caution should be exercised outside major cities. |

| Country | Ireland | Israel | Italy |
|---|---|---|---|
| Int'l Dialing Code | 353 | 972 | 39 |
| City Codes | Cork 21, Dublin 1, Galway 91, Waterford 51 | Hefa (Haifa) 4, Ramat Gan 3, Tel Aviv-Yafo 3, Yerushalayim (Jerusalem) 2 | Firenze 55, Genova 10, Milano 2, Napoli 81, Palermo 91, Roma (Rome) 6, Venezia 41 |
| Consulate Phone | (202) 462-3939 | (202) 364-5500 | (202) 328-5500 |
| Climate | Humid and overcast; mild winters; cool summers. | Temperate; hot and dry in desert areas; cooler and more rainy in December through March. | Predominantly Mediterranean climate; alpine in the far north; hot and dry in the south. |
| Clothing | Medium to heavy-weight clothing is worn most of the year. | Clothing and shoe needs are about the same as for the American southwest. Dress at religious sites should be appropriately modest. | Woolens and sweaters are practical most of the year; cottons are recommended for the hot summers. |
| Entry Requirements | Passport, ticket to leave, sufficient funds | Passport | Passport |
| Holidays | New Year's Day, Jan. 1; St. Patrick's Day, Mar. 17; Good Friday; Easter Monday; Bank Holiday, early June; Bank Holiday, early August; Bank Holiday, late October; Christmas Day, Dec. 25; St. Stephen's Day, Dec. 26 | Purim; Passover; Independence Day; Yom Kippur; Rosh Hashana; Tabernacles; Hanukkah | New Year's Day, Jan. 1; Epiphany, Jan. 6; Easter Monday; Liberation Day, Apr. 25; Labor Day, May 1; Ascension Day; Anniversary of the Republic, June 2; Assumption Day, Aug. 15; All Saint's Day, Nov. 1; Immaculate Conception Day, Dec. 8; Christmas Day, Dec. 25; St. Stephen's Day, Dec. 26 |
| Special Notes | Tapwater is potable. | Travel to the West Bank and Gaza Strip is potentially dangerous. Tapwater is potable. All stores and banks are closed from sundown on Friday until sundown on Saturday. | Tapwater is safe. Meat, fruit, vegetables, and shellfish should be well-prepared. |

| Jamaica | Japan | Kenya | Korea, South |
|---|---|---|---|
| 809 | 81 | 254 | 82 |
| | Kyōto 75, Nagoya 52, Naha 988, Ōsaka 6, Sapporo 11, Tōkyō 3, Yokohama 45 | Kisumu 35, Mombasa 11, Nairobi 2, Nakuru 37 | Inch'ŏn 32, Pusan 51, Sŏul 2, Taegu 53 |
| (202) 452-0660 | (202) 939-6700 | (202) 387-6101 | (202) 939-5600 |
| Tropical; hot, humid; temperatures are more moderate in the interior highlands. | Varies from tropical in the south to cool temperate in the north. | Varies from tropical along the coast to arid in the interior. Rainy seasons are from March to June and from October to December. | Temperate, with rainfall heavier in summer than winter. |
| Summer clothes are suitable year round. The evenings can be chilly, especially from November to March, and light wraps or sweaters are recommended. Dress is informal, but swimsuits should be worn only at the beach. | Lightweight clothing is worn in the summer throughout the country. Medium to heavy-weight clothing is needed for the winter. Very heavy clothing is needed for the mountains. | Light and medium weight clothing is worn most of the year. Sweaters and light raincoats are needed during the rainy season. Some restaurants have evening dress codes. | Clothing requirements are similar to those of the eastern U.S. Dress is more conservative than in the U.S. |
| Proof of citizenship, business visa, ticket to leave, sufficient funds | Passport, visa, ticket to leave | Passport, visa, ticket to leave; cholera and other innoculations recommended | Passport, visa, ticket to leave |
| New Year's Day, Jan. 1; Ash Wednesday; Good Friday; Easter Monday; Labor Day, May 23; Independence Day, early August; National Heroes' Day, late Oct.; Christmas Day, Dec. 25; Boxing Day, Dec. 26 | New Year's Dec. 28-Jan. 3; Adult's Day, Jan. 15; National Foundation Day, Feb. 11; Vernal Equinox Day, Mar. 21; Constitution Day, May 3; Children's Day, May 5; Respect for the Aged Day, Sept. 15; Autumnal Equinox Day, Sept.; Health and Sports Day, Oct. 10; Culture Day, Nov. 3; Labor Thanksgiving Day, Nov. 23; Emperor's Birthday, Dec. 23 | New Year's Day, Jan. 1; Ramadan and Id al-Fitr; Good Friday; Easter Monday; Labor Day, May 1; Madaraka Day, June 1; Kenyatta Day, Oct. 20; Independence Day, Dec. 12; Christmas Day, Dec. 25; Boxing Day, Dec. 26 | New Year, Jan. 1-3; Lunar New Year, Jan. or Feb.; Independence Day, Mar. 1; Buddha's Birthday, May; Memorial Day, June 6; Constitution Day, July 17; Liberation Day, Aug. 15; Chusok (Thanksgiving), Aug. or Sept.; Armed Forces Day, Oct. 1; Foundation Day, Oct. 3; Korean Alphabet Day, Oct. 9; Christmas Day, Dec. 25 |
| Hurricane season is from June to November. Crime is becoming a serious problem in Kingston. Municipal water supplies are potable. Fruits and vegetables are safe. | Drinking water, fruits, and vegetables are safe. | Avoid tapwater and unwashed fruits outside the capital. Anti-malarial drugs are recommended. | Outside of the major hotels, water is generally not potable. |

| Country | Luxembourg | Malaysia | Malta |
|---|---|---|---|
| **Int'l Dialing Code** | 352 | 60 | 356 |
| **City Codes** | | Ipoh 5, Johor Baharu 7, Kajang 3, Kuala Lumpur 3 | |
| **Consulate Phone** | (202) 265-4171 | (202) 328-2700 | (202) 462-3611 |
| **Climate** | Mild winters; cool summers. | Tropical; hot summers and winters; heavy summer rainfall, moderate winter rainfall. | Mild rainy winter; hot, dry summers. |
| **Clothing** | Fall and light winter clothing is worn. Some restaurants have evening dress codes. | Lightweight clothing is suitable for the tropical climate, except in the highland resort areas. | City casual dress is appropriate. Lightweight apparel for the summer and woolens for thee winter are required. |
| **Entry Requirements** | Passport, ticket to leave, sufficient funds | Passport, ticket to leave, sufficient funds | Passport |
| **Holidays** | New Year's Day, Jan. 1; Easter Monday; May Day, May 1; Ascension Day; Whitmonday; National Day, June 23; Assumption Day, Aug. 15; All Saints' Day, Nov. 1; Christmas Day, Dec. 25; St. Stephen's Day, Dec. 26 | Ramadan and Id al-Fitr; Chinese New Year, Jan. or Feb.; Labor Day, May 1; Wesak Day, May 30; Monarch's Day, June 1; Id al-Adha; National Day, Aug. 31; Prophet's Birthday; Diwali; Christmas, Dec. 25 | New Year's Day, Jan. 1; Freedom Day, Mar. 31; Good Friday; Easter Monday; Labor Day, May 1; Assumption Day, Aug. 15; Republic Day, Dec. 13; Christmas Day, Dec. 25 |
| **Special Notes** | | Tapwater in the cities is considered safe. Malaria is a problem in rural areas. | Tapwater is very saline; bottled water is necessary and available. |

| Martinique | Mauritius | Mexico | Morocco |
|---|---|---|---|
| 596 | 230 | 52 | 212 |
|  |  | Acapulco 748, Cancún 988, Chihuahua 14, Ciudad de México 5, Monterrey 83, Puebla 22, Tijuana 66 |  |
| (202) 944-6087 | (202) 244-1491 | (202) 728-1600 | (202) 462-7979 |
| Tropical. | Warm, dry winters; hot, humid summers. Seasons are reversed from those in North America. | Varies from tropical to desert; cooler at higher elevations. Guadalajara and Mexico City are pleasant year-round. Monterey, the Yucatan Peninsula, and desert areas are very hot in the summer. | Mild winters; hot summers; moderate winter rainfall along the coast; interior dry all year; wide daily temperature variations. |
| Lightweight clothing and rainwear are advisable. Some restaurants have evening dress codes. | Lightweight cottons are worn with a sweater for cooler evenings. Woolens are needed for winter months. | Wear tropical clothing in desert areas and lowlands. In Mexico City and other mountainous areas, medium-weight clothing is comfortable. Shorts are worn only on the beaches. | Wear clothing suitable for the eastern central U.S., but more conservative. Bring a jacket or sweater for cool evenings. |
| Proof of citizenship, ticket to leave | Passport, ticket to leave | Proof of citizenship, business visa or tourist card; innoculations recommended | Passport |
| New Year's Day, Jan. 1; Mardi Gras, Feb.; Good Friday; Easter Monday; Labor Day, May 1; Ascension Day; Whitmonday; Bastille Day, July 14; Schoelcher Day, July 21; Assumption Day, Aug. 15; All Saints' Day, Nov. 1; Armistice Day, Nov. 11; Christmas Day, Dec. 25 | New Year's Day, Jan. 1; Cavadee; Mahashivaratri; Independence Day, Mar. 12; Ougadi; Ramadan and Id al-Fitr; Easter Monday; Labor Day, May 1; Assumption Day, Aug. 15; Ganesh Chaturthi, Sept. 14; Diwali; All Saints' Day, Nov. 1; Christmas Day, Dec. 25; Boxing Day, Dec. 26 | New Year's Day, Jan. 1; Constitution Day, Feb. 5; Birthday of Benito Juarez, Mar. 21; Maundy Thursday; Good Friday; Holy Saturday; Labor Day, May 1; Battle of Puebla, May 5; President's Message Day, Sept. 1; Independence Day, Sept. 16; Columbus Day, Oct. 12; Revolution Aniversary, Nov. 20; Christmas Day, Dec. 25 | New Year's Day, Jan. 1; Prophet's Ascension; Ramadan and Id al-Fitr; Feast of the Throne, Mar. 3; Labor Day, May 1; Id al-Adha; Islamic New Year; Ashura; Sahara Annexation Day, Aug. 14; Prophet's Birthday; Green March Day, Nov. 6; Independence Day, Nov. 18; Christmas Day, Dec. 25 |
| Hurricane season is from June to October. Drinking water is safe. | Tapwater is potable. Avoid uncooked vegetables. | Tapwater is not safe. Cooked food is safe to eat; raw vegetables often are not. Avoid ice cubes. | When outside the large cities and resorts, carry water purification tablets or a supply of purified drinking water. Eat only carefully prepared foods. |

| Country | Netherlands | New Zealand | Nigeria |
|---|---|---|---|
| Int'l Dialing Code | 31 | 64 | 234 |
| City Codes | Amsterdam 20, Rotterdam 10, 's-Gravenhage (The Hague) 70, Utrecht 30 | Auckland 9, Christchurch 3, Dunedin 24, Hamilton 71, Wellington 4 | Lagos 1 |
| Consulate Phone | (202) 244-5300 | (202) 328-4800 | (202) 822-1500 |
| Climate | Mild winters, cool summers. | Temperate; wet, windy, cool; warm summers; mild winters; seasons are reversed from North America. | Equatorial in the south, tropical in the center, arid in the north. |
| Clothing | Clothing needs are similar to those of Seattle, Washington. Some restaurants have evening dress codes. | Warm clothing is comfortable most of the year. Raincoats are essential. | Tropical wash-and-wear clothing and rainwear are recommended. Women should dress conservatively and slacks are not commonly worn. |
| Entry Requirements | Passport, ticket to leave | Passport, ticket to leave, sufficient funds | Passport, visa, ticket to leave, yellow fever innoculation; cholera innoculation recommended |
| Holidays | New Year's Day, Jan. 1; Good Friday; Easter Monday; Queen's Birthday, Apr. 30; Ascension Day; Whitmonday; Christmas Day, Dec. 25; Boxing Day, Dec. 26 | New Year's Day, Jan. 1; New Zealand Day, Feb. 6; Good Friday; Easter Monday; Queen's Birthday, June; Labor Day, late Oct.; Christmas Day, Dec. 25; Boxing Day, Dec. 26 | New Year's Day, Jan. 1; Ramadan and Id al-Fitr; Good Friday; Easter Monday; Worker's Day, May 1; Hijra; National Day, Oct. 1; Prophet's Birthday; Christmas Day, Dec. 25; Boxing Day, Dec. 26 |
| Special Notes | Tapwater is safe. | | Tapwater is not potable. Fruits and vegetables should be carefully prepared and meats cooked until well done. Take anti-malarial pills. |

| Norway | Peru | Philippines | Poland |
|---|---|---|---|
| 47 | 51 | 63 | 48 |
| Bergen 5, Stavanger 4, Trondheim 7 | Arequipa 54, Callao 14, Chiclayo 74, Cuzco 84, Lima 14, Trujillo 44 | Bacolod 34, Cebu 32, Davao 82, Iloilo 33, Manila 2 | Gdańsk 58, Katowice 32, Łódź 42, Poznań 61, Kraków 12, Warszawa (Warsaw) 22 |
| (202) 333-6000 | (202) 833-9860 | (202) 483-1414 | (202) 234-3800 |
| Temperate along coast, colder interior; rainy year-round on west coast. | Varies from tropical in the east to dry desert in the west; winters are damp; seasons are reversed from those in North America. | Hot and humid; cooler in mountainous areas. | Cold, cloudy, moderately severe winters with frequent precipitation; mild summers with frequent showers and thundershowers. |
| Lightweight clothing and light woolens are worn in the summer, and heavy clothing in the winter. | Medium-weight clothing is suitable in the winter; in summer, wear lightweight clothing. Fashions are similar to those in the U.S., but shorts should be worn only in resort areas. | Cotton and other lightweight clothing is worn all year. If traveling to the popular mountain resorts in northern Luzon, light sweaters are appropriate. Some resteraunts have evening dress codes. | Spring-weight clothing is worn in the summer and heavy clothing for the winter. Rainwear is advisable throughout the year. |
| Passport, ticket to leave, sufficient funds | Passport, business visa, ticket to leave; hepatitis innoculation recommended | Passport | Passport |
| New Year's Day, Jan. 1; Maundy Thursday; Good Friday; Easter Monday; May Day, May 1; Constitution Day, May 17; Ascension Day; Whitmonday; Christmas Day, Dec. 25; Boxing Day, Dec. 26 | New Year's Day, Jan. 1; Maundy Thursday; Good Friday; Labor Day, May 1; St. Peter and St. Paul's Day, June 29; Independence Days, July 28,29; Santa Rosa Day, Aug. 30; National Dignity Day, early Oct.; All Saints' Day, Nov. 1; Immaculate Conception, Dec. 8; December 24, Christmas Eve; Christmas Day, Dec. 25 | New Year's Day, Jan. 1; Maundy Thursday; Good Friday; Labor Day, May 1; Independence Day, June 12; Philippine-American Friendship Day, July 4; All Saint's Day, Nov. 1; Bonifacio Day, Nov. 30; Christmas Day, Dec. 25; Rizal Day, Dec. 30 | New Year's Day, Jan. 1; Easter Monday; Labor Day, May 1; Corpus Christi; National Day, July 22; All Saints' Day, Nov. 1; Christmas Day, Dec. 25; Boxing Day, Dec. 26 |
| Tapwater is potable. | Terrorism is prevalent in rural Peru, and a cholera epidemic makes fruits, vegetables and tapwater unsafe. | The Manila water supply is generally safe. Untreated or unboiled water should not be drunk outside the city. It is advisable to eat only fruits which can be peeled and to avoid fresh vegetables unless cleaned with safe water. | |

| Country | Portugal | Puerto Rico | Romania |
|---|---|---|---|
| **Int'l Dialing Code** | 351 | | 40 |
| **City Codes** | Coimbra 39, Lisboa (Lisbon) 1, Porto 2, Setúbal 65 | | Bucureşti (Bucharest) 1, Cluj-Napoca 951, Constanţa 916 |
| **Consulate Phone** | (202) 328-8610 | | (202) 232-4747 |
| **Climate** | Mild, damp winters; hot, dry summers; climate is more moderate along the coast. | Mild, little seasonal temperature variation. | Temperate; cold, cloudy winters with frequent snow and fog; sunny summers with frequent showers and thunderstorms. |
| **Clothing** | Wear summer clothing during the temperate sunny days and cool nights. Fall-weight clothing and a topcoat or warm raincoat are appropriate for winter. A rain hat or umbrella is recommended. Swimsuits should be confined to the beach. | Lightweight clothing is worn throughout the year with a sweater or jacket for cooler evenings. Some restaurants have evening dress codes. | Lightweight clothing is worn in the summer. Warm clothing is needed in the winter and throughout the year in the highlands. |
| **Entry Requirements** | Passport, visa | Proof of citizenship | Passport, visa; innoculations recommended |
| **Holidays** | New Year's Day, Jan. 1; Shrove Tuesday, Good Friday; Anniversary of the Revolution, Apr. 25; Labor Day, May 1; Portugal Day, June 10; Corpus Christi; Assumption Day, Aug. 15; Republic Day, Oct. 5; All Saints' Day, Nov. 1; Independence Day, Dec. 1; Immaculate Conception, Dec. 8; Christmas Day, Dec. 25. | New Year's Day, Jan. 1; Epiphany, Jan. 6; De Hostos' Birthday, Jan. 11; Martin Luther King's Birthday, Jan. 15; Presidents' Day, Feb.; Emancipation Day, Mar. 22; De Diego's Birthday, Apr. 16; Memorial Day, late May; Independence Day, July 4; Munoz Rivera's Birthday, July 17; Constitution Day, July 25; Barbosa's Birthday, July 27; Labor Day, early Sept.; Columbus Day, Oct.; Veteran's Day, Nov. 11; Discovery of Puerto Rico, Nov. 19; Thanksgiving, late Nov.; Christmas Day, Dec. 25 | New Year's Day, Jan. 1; Labor Day, May 1,2; Liberation Day, Aug. 23, 24 |
| **Special Notes** | Tapwater is potable year round in large cities and in outlying areas during rainy seasons. Bottled spring water is available. | Hurricane season is from June to November. | Hotel rooms are often poorly heated. Consumer goods are in short supply. |

| Russia | San Marino | Saudi Arabia | Singapore |
|--------|-----------|--------------|-----------|
| 7 | 39 | 966 | 65 |
| Moskva (Moscow) 095, Nižnij Novgorod (Gorky) 8312, St. Petersburg 812 | All points 549 | Al-Madīnah 4, Ar-Ridāḍ (Riyadh) 1, Jiddah 2, Makkah (Mecca) 2 | |
| (202) 628-7551 | | (202) 342-3800 | (202) 667-7555 |
| Mostly temperate to arctic continental; winters vary from cold in the west to frigid in Siberia; summers range from hot in the south to cool along the Arctic coast. | Mild to cool winters; warm, sunny summers. | Dry desert with hot days and cool nights. Winter months in the interior can be quite cool. | Tropical; hot, humid, rainy. |
| Clothing requirements the same as the nothern U.S., although the weather tends to be cooler. Public buildings, hotels, and homes are well heated. Hot weather occurs from June through August. | Woolens and sweaters are practical most of the year; cottons are recommended for hot summers. | Lightweight clothing is essential for the hot climate. However, during the winter months in the interior, warmer clothing is recommended. The coastal areas are more humid than the interior. Both men and women should dress conservatively. | Light cotton clothing is worn throughout the year. An umbrella is needed. Some restaurants have evening dress codes. |
| Passport, visa | Passport | Passport, visa, ticket to leave, cholera innoculation; sponsorship by a Saudi citizen or employer required | Passport, ticket to leave, sufficient funds |
| New Year's Day, Jan. 1; International Women's Day, Mar. 8; Labor Day, May 1,2; Victory Day, May 9; Constitution Day, Oct. 7 | New Year's Day, Jan. 1; Epiphany; Liberation Day, Feb. 5; Good Friday; Easter Monday; Labor Day, May 1; Ascension Day; Corpus Christi; Assumption Day, Aug. 15; National Day, Sept. 3; All Saints' Day, Nov. 1; All Souls' Day, Nov. 2; Immaculate Conception, Dec. 8., Christmas Day, Dec. 25, 26 | Ramadan and Id al-Fitr; Id al-Adha; Hijra; Prophet's Birthday | Chinese New Year, Jan. or Feb.; Ramadan and Id al-Fitr; Good Friday; Labor Day, May 1; Wesak Day, May; National Day, Aug. 9; Diwali; Christmas Day, Dec. 25 |
| Avoid tapwater, especially in St. Petersburg, and drink bottled water. Avoid cold foods, such as salads. | | Travel to Mecca and Medina is forbidden to non-Muslims. Do not photograph mosques or people at prayer. Women are not allowed to drive cars or bicycles. Alcoholic beverages are illegal. Eat and drink cautiously outside major hotels and restaurants. | |

| Country | South Africa | Spain | Sweden |
|---|---|---|---|
| **Int'l Dialing Code** | 27 | 34 | 46 |
| **City Codes** | Bloemfontein 51, Cape Town 21, Durban 31, Johannesburg 11, Pretoria 12 | Barcelona 3, Madrid 1, Sevilla 54, Valencia 6 | Göteborg 31, Malmö 40, Stockholm 8, Uppsala 18, Västerås 21 |
| **Consulate Phone** | (202) 232-4400 | (202) 265-0190 | (202) 944-5600 |
| **Climate** | Mostly semiarid; subtropical along coast; sunny days, cool nights. Seasons are reversed from those in North America. | Interior has hot, clear summers and cold winters; coast has moderate, cloudy summers and cool winters. | Temperate in the south with cold, cloudy winters and cool, partly cloudy summers; subarctic in the north |
| **Clothing** | Clothing suitable for central and southern California is appropriate for South Africa's mild climate. Many restaurants have evening dress codes. | Clothes suitable for the Washington, D.C., climate are recommended. Slacks are worn in public, but not shorts. Sweaters and raincoats are advisable. | Lightweight clothing is used in the summer, with heavy clothing for winter. |
| **Entry Requirements** | Passport, visa, ticket to leave, sufficient funds; cholera innoculation recommended | Passport; innoculations recommended | Passport, ticket to leave, sufficient funds |
| **Holidays** | New Year's Day, Jan. 1; Founder's Day, Apr. 6; Good Friday; Easter Monday; Ascension Day; Republic Day, May 31; Settler's Day, early Sept.; Kruger Day, Oct. 10; Day of the Covenant, Dec. 16; Christmas Day, Dec. 25; Boxing Day, Dec. 26 | New Year's Day, Jan. 1; Epiphany, Jan. 6; St. Joseph's Day, Mar. 19; Good Friday; May Day, May 1; Corpus Christi; St. John's Day, June 24; St. James' Day, July 25; Assumption Day, Aug. 15; National Day, Oct. 12; All Saints' Day, Nov. 1; Constitution Day,Dec. 6; Immaculate Conception, Dec. 8; Christmas Day, Dec. 25 | New Year's Day, Jan. 1; Good Friday; Easter Monday; Labor Day, May 1; Ascension Day; Whitmonday; Midsummer's Day, late June; All Saints' Day, early November; Christmas Day, Dec. 25; Boxing Day, Dec. 26 |
| **Special Notes** | The U.S. State Department warns that the political situation in South Africa is potentially dangerous. Drinking water is generally safe, but avoid bathing in lakes or streams. Anti-malarial pills are recommended in rural areas. | Drinking water in Madrid is safe. Use bottled water elsewhere. Peel all fruit. | Tapwater is potable, and dairy products pure. |

| Switzerland | Taiwan | Tanzania | Thailand |
|---|---|---|---|
| 41 | 886 | 255 | 66 |
| Basel 61, Bern 31, Genève 22, Lausanne 21, Lucerne 41, Zürich 1 | Kaohsiung 7, T'ainan 6, T'aipei 2 | Dar es Salaam 51, Dodoma 61, Mwanza 68, Tanga 53 | Chiang Mai 53, Krung Thep (Bangkok) 2, Nakhon Sawan 56, Ubon Ratchathani 45 |
| (202) 745-7900 | | (202) 939-6125 | (202) 483-7200 |
| Varies with altitude; cold, cloudy, snowy winters; cool to warm, cloudy, humid summers with occasional showers. | Chilly, damp winters; hot, humid summers; rainy season from June to August; often cloudy. | Varies from tropical along the coast to temperate in the highlands; rainy season from November to April; dry season from May to October. | Tropical; dry, cooler winters; warm, rainy, cloudy summers; southern isthmus is always hot and humid. |
| Light woolens may be worn in the summer and heavy winter clothing in the winter. | In winter, light jackets and sweaters are recommended; in summer, light-weight garments are essential. An umbrella is useful year-round. | Lightweight, tropical clothing is worn year-round, although in the cooler season, a light wrap is useful in the evenings. Conservative dress is required. Bring sunglasses and a hat. | Lightweight, washable clothing is comfortable and practical for Bankok's tropical climate. In northern Thailand, a jacket or sweater is needed during the cool season. Swimwear should be worn only on the beach. |
| Passport | Passport, visa, ticket to leave | Passport, visa, ticket to leave, cholera and yellow fever innoculations | Passport, ticket to leave; innoculations recommended |
| New Year's, Jan. 1,2; Good Friday; Easter Monday; Ascension Day; Whitmonday; Labor Day, May 1; National Day, Aug. 1; Christmas Day, Dec. 25; Boxing Day, Dec. 26 | Founding of the Republic, Jan. 1; Chinese New Year, Jan. or Feb.; Youth Day, Mar. 29; Tomb-sweeping Day, Apr. 5; Confucius's Birthday, Sept. 28; National Day, Oct. 10; Taiwan Restoration Day, Oct. 25; Chiang Kai-shek's Birthday, Oct. 31; Dr. Sun Yat-Sen's Birthday, Nov. 12; Constitution Day, Dec. 25 | Zanzibar Revolution Day, Jan. 12; CCM Day, Feb. 5; Good Friday; Easter Monday; Ramadan and Id al-Fitr; Union Day, Apr. 26; Peasants' Day, July 7; Hijra; Prophet's Birthday; Independence Day, Dec. 9; Christmas Day, Dec. 25 | New Year's Day, Jan. 1; Songkran Festival, Apr. 13; Coronation Day Anniversary, May 5; Visakhja Puja, May; Buddhist Lent, June or July; Queen's Birthday, Aug. 12; Chulalongkorn Day, Oct. 23; King's Birthday, Dec. 5; New Year's Eve, Dec. 31 |
| | Drinking water is safe at Taipei's major hotels, but when dining elsewhere, drink only hot or bottled water. High pollen counts and air pollution can contribute to asthma. | Tapwater is not potable. Water should be boiled and filtered and fruits and vegetables carefully prepared. Do not swim or paddle in lakes or streams. Anti-malarial drugs are recommended. Do not go barefoot. | Thailand has an extremely strict anti-narcotics law that provides for severe sentences, including the death penalty, for narcotics traffickers and users. Avoid tap water, raw milk, ice cream, uncooked meats, and unwashed raw fruits and vegetables. |

| Country | Trinidad and Tobago | Tunisia | Turkey |
|---|---|---|---|
| **Int'l Dialing Code** | 809 | 216 | 90 |
| **City Codes** | | Béja 8, Bizerte 2, El Kairouan 7, Sousse 3, Tunis 1 | Adana 711, Ankara 4, İstanbul 1, İzmir 51 |
| **Consulate Phone** | (202) 467-6490 | (202) 862-1850 | (202) 659-8200 |
| **Climate** | Tropical; dry season from January to May. | Temperate in the north with mild, rainy winters and hot, dry summers; desert in the south. | Mild, wet winters; hot, dry summers. Climate is more severe in the interior. |
| **Clothing** | Summerweight clothing is worn year round. Beachwear should be confined to the beach. Restaurants may have evening dress codes. | Wear lightweight clothes in the summer, light woolens and rainwear in the winter. Women should dress conservatively. | Summer requires lightweight clothing in the northern areas and tropical clothing in the south. Warm woolens are necessary for the winter months. |
| **Entry Requirements** | Passport, ticket to leave | Passport, ticket to leave, sufficient funds | Passport |
| **Holidays** | New Year's Day, Jan. 1; Ramadan and Id al-Fitr; Good Friday; Easter Monday; Whitmonday; Corpus Christi; Labor Day, June 19; Discovery Day, early Aug.; Independence Day, Aug. 31; Republic Day, Sept. 24; Diwali (Festival of Lights); Christmas Day, Dec. 25; Boxing Day, Dec. 26 | New Year's Day, Jan. 1; Anniversary of the Revolution, Jan. 18; Ramadan and Id al-Fitr; Independence Day, Mar. 20; Martyr's Day, Apr. 9; Labor Day, May 1; Id al-Adha; June 1, National Day; Youth Day, June 2; Islamic New Year; Ashura; Republic Day, July 25; Women's Day, Aug. 13; Prophet's Birthday; Evacuation Day, Oct. 15 | New Year's Day, Jan. 1; Ramadan and Id-al Fitr; National Sovereignty Day, Apr. 23; Spring Day, May 1; Youth Day, May 19; Constitution Day, May 27; Id al-Adha; Victory Day, Aug. 30; Republic Day, Oct. 29 |
| **Special Notes** | Hurricane season is from June to November. Tapwater is safe but do not drink water from an unknown source. Wash fruits and vegetables carefully. | Tunisia has no particular health hazards, but tapwater is not potable in certain seasons. | Tapwater should be avoided. |

| United Arab Emirates | United Kingdom | United States | Uruguay |
|---|---|---|---|
| 971 | 44 | 1 | 598 |
| Abū Ẓaby (Abu Dhabi) 2, Al-ʿAyn 3, Ash-Shāriqah 6, Dubayy 4, ʿUjmān 6 | Belfast 232, Birmingham 21, Cardiff 222, Glasgow 41, Liverpool 51, London 71 or 81, Manchester 61 | | Canelones 332, Mercedes 532, Montevideo 2, Paysandú 722 |
| (202) 338-6500 | (202) 462-1340 | | (202) 331-1313 |
| Desert; hot and dry; cooler in the eastern mountains and during the winter. | Temperate; mild winters; cool summers; cloudy with rainfall in all seasons. | Mostly temperate, but varies from tropical to arctic; arid to semiarid in west. | Warm temperate; winters are cool, but temperature seldom drops below freezing. Seasons are reversed from those in North America. |
| Lightweight attire is necessary during the summer. From mid-October through April, spring or fall clothing is suitable. Everyone should dress modestly. | Fall and winter clothing is needed from about September through April; spring and summer clothing is useful the rest of the year. Always bring a raincoat and umbrella. Some restaurants have dress codes. | Clothing ranges from very lightweight to very heavy, depending on the region and time of year. | Seasonal clothing, as in the U.S., is recommended. Warm clothing is essential in winter. Rainwear is useful. |
| Passport, visa, ticket to leave | Passport | Passport, visa | Passport, ticket to leave |
| New Year's Day, Jan. 1; Ramadan and Id al-Fitr; Id al-Adha; Hijra; National Day, Dec. 2; Christmas Day, Dec. 25 | New Year's Day, Jan. 1; Good Friday; Easter Monday; May Day, early May; Spring Bank Holiday, late May; Summer Bank Holiday, late August; Christmas Day, Dec. 25; Boxing Day, Dec. 26 | New Year's Day, Jan. 1; Martin Luther King's Birthday, Jan. 15; Presidents' Day, late Feb.; Memorial Day, late May; Independence Day, July 4; Labor Day, early Sept.; Columbus Day, early Oct.; Veteran's Day, Nov. 11; Thanksgiving Day, late Nov.; ChristmasDay, Dec. 25 | New Year's Day, Jan. 1; Epiphany, Jan. 6; Carnival; Holy Week; Landing of the 33 Patriots, Apr. 19; Labor Day, May 1; Battle of Las Piedras, May 18; Birth of Don Jose Artigas, June 19; Constitution Day, July 18; Independence Day, Aug. 25; Columbus Day, Oct. 12; All Souls' Day, Nov. 2; Immaculate Conception, Dec. 8; Christmas Day, Dec. 25 |
| Water is potable. | Traffic moves on the left on British roads. | | Water supply is well maintained. |

| Country | Venezuela | Yugoslavia | Zimbabwe |
|---|---|---|---|
| **Int'l Dialing Code** | 58 | 38 | 263 |
| **City Codes** | Barquisimeto 51, Caracas 2, Maracaibo 61, Valencia 41 | Beograd (Belgrade) 11, Novi Sad 21 | Bulawayo 9, Harare 4, Mutare 20 |
| **Consulate Phone** | (202) 342-2214 | (202) 462-6566 | (202) 332-7100 |
| **Climate** | Tropical; hot, humid; more moderate in the highlands; rainy season from may to November. | Temperate; hot, relatively dry summers with mild, rainy winters along the coast; warm summer with cold winters inland. | Tropical; moderated by altitude; rainy season from November to March. |
| **Clothing** | Spring-weight clothing is appropriate in Caracas. Elsewhere temperatures vary with altitude from tropics to freezing. Many restaurants have dress codes. Shorts should be worn only on the beach. | Lightweight clothing is worn in the summer and heavy clothing is required for the winter. | Light, summer apparel is appropriate from October to May. Fall or spring clothing is suitable the rest of the year. Some urban restaurants have evening dress codes. |
| **Entry Requirements** | Passport, business visa or tourist card, ticket to leave | Passport, visa | Passport, ticket to leave, sufficient funds, yellow fever innoculation |
| **Holidays** | New Year's Day, Jan. 1; Carnival; Maundy Thursday; Good Friday; Holy Saturday; Declaration of Independence Day, Apr. 19; Labor Day, May 1; Battle of Carabobo, June 24; Independence Day, July 5; Bolivar's Birthday, July 24; Columbus Day, Oct. 12; Christmas Eve, Dec. 24; Christmas Day, Dec. 25 | New Year, Jan. 1,2; Labor Day, May 1,2; Veterans' Day, July 4; Republic Day, Nov. 29, 30 | New Year's Day, Jan. 1; Good Friday; Easter Monday; Independence Day, Apr. 18; Worker's Day, early May; Africa Day; May 25; Heroes' Days, Aug. 11-12; Christmas Day, Dec. 25; Boxing Day, Dec. 26 |
| **Special Notes** | Tapwater should be boiled and vegetables carefully prepared. | Political instability makes travel to some areas potentially hazardous. | Sporadic violence is not uncommon; travel in rural areas is not advised. Tapwater is safe in all urban areas but not in rural regions. |

# City Maps

## Legend
For easy comparison of the major cities of the world, all the metropolitan maps are drawn at a consistent scale of 1:350,000. One inch on the map represents 5.5 miles on the earth's surface.

## Inhabited Localities
The symbol represents the number of inhabitants within the locality

| | |
|---|---|
| • | 0 – 10,000 |
| ○ | 10,000 – 25,000 |
| ⊙ | 25,000 – 100,000 |
| ⊡ | 100,000 – 250,000 |
| ▣ | 250,000 – 1,000,000 |
| ■ | > 1,000,000 |

The size of type indicates the relative economic and political importance of the locality

Écommoy      **St.-Denis**

Trouville

Lisieux      **PARIS**

Hollywood ■    **Section of a City,**
Westminster     **Neighborhood**
Northland ■    **Major Shopping Center**
Center

     **Urban Area** (area of continuous industrial, commercial, and residential development)

     **Major Industial Area**

     **Wooded Area**

## Political Boundaries
### International
(First-order political unit)

     **Demarcated, Undemar-cated, and Administrative**

     **Demarcation Line**

### Internal

     **State, Province, etc.**
(Second-order political unit)

     **County, Oblast, etc.**
(Third-order political unit)

     **Okrug, Kreis, etc.**
(Fourth-order political unit)

     **City or Municipality**
(may appear in combination with another boundary symbol)

## Capitals of Political Units

| | |
|---|---|
| **BUDAPEST** | **Independent Nation** |
| Recife | **State, Province, etc.** |
| White Plains | **County, Oblast, etc.** |
| Iserlohn | **Okrug, Kreis, etc.** |

## Transportation

### Road

 PASSAIC EXPWY. (I-80)    **Primary**

 BERLINER RING    **Secondary**

     **Tertiary**

### Railway

CANADIAN NATIONAL    **Primary**

     **Secondary**

     **Rapid Transit**

### Airport

 LONDON (HEATHROW) AIRPORT

### Rail or Air Terminal

■ *SÜD BAHNHOF*

REICHS-BRÜCKE    **Bridge**

GREAT ST. BERNARD TUNNEL    **Tunnel**

## Other Features

| | |
|---|---|
| SORBONNE ▲ | **Point of Interest** (Battlefield, museum temple, university, etc.) |
| STEPHANSDOM ⌖ | **Church, Monastery** |
| UXMAL ∴ | **Ruins** |
| WINDSOR CASTLE ¥ | **Castle** |
| ⌁ | **Lighthouse** |
| ASWÄN DAM \ | **Dam** |
| <> | **Lock** |
| Mt. Kenya 5199 △ | **Elevation Above Sea Level** |
| ★ | **Rock** |

Elevations are given in meters

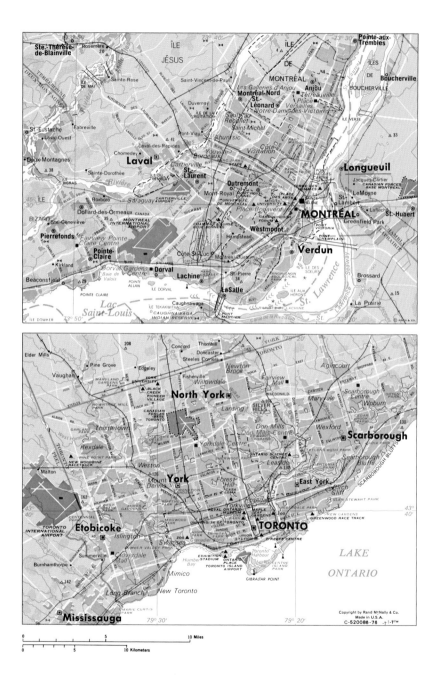

0        5                    10 Miles

0        5              10 Kilometers

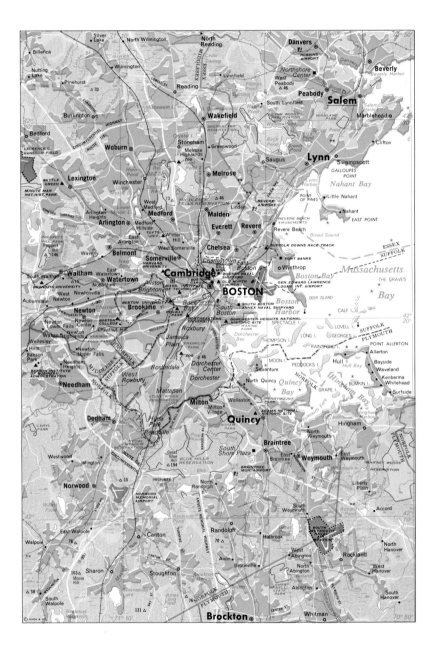

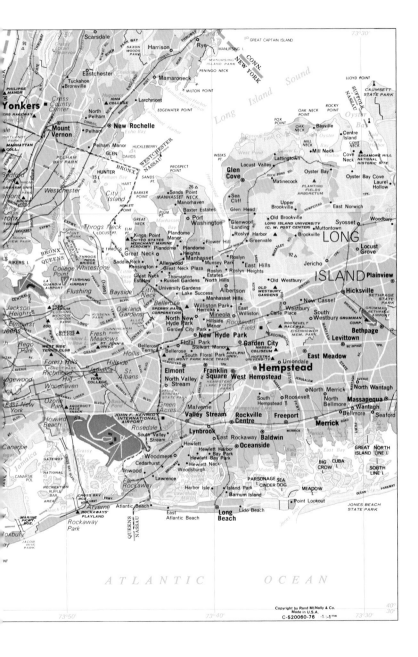

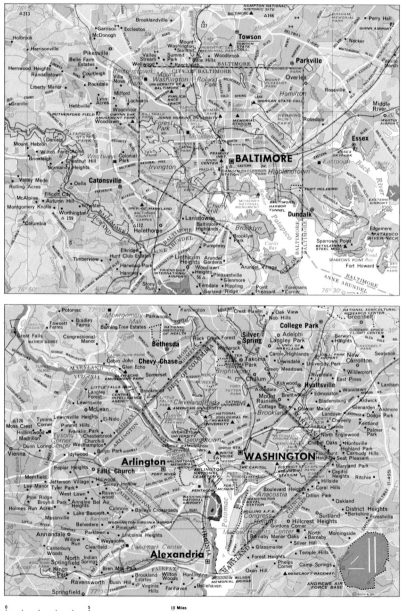

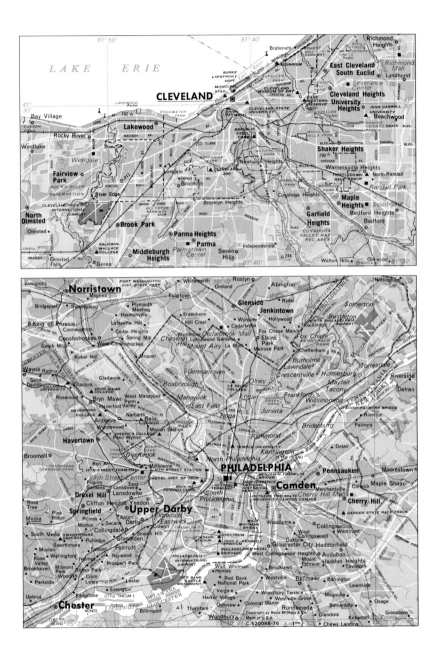

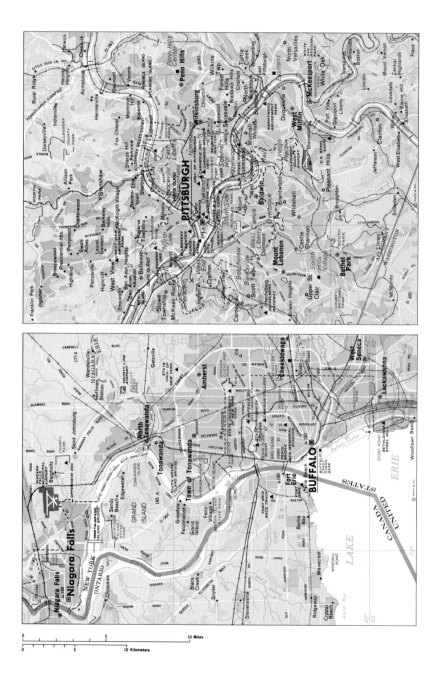

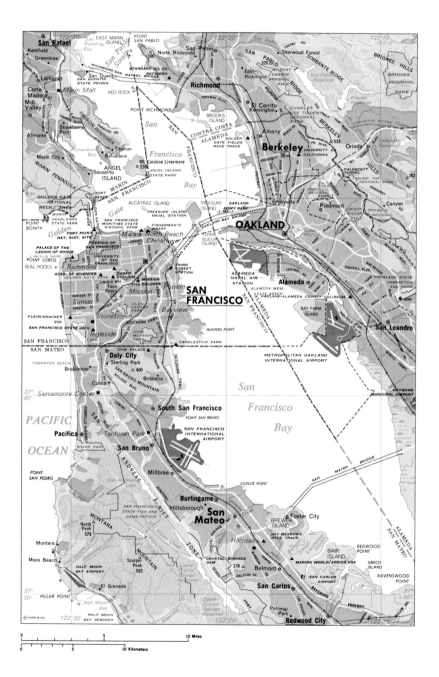

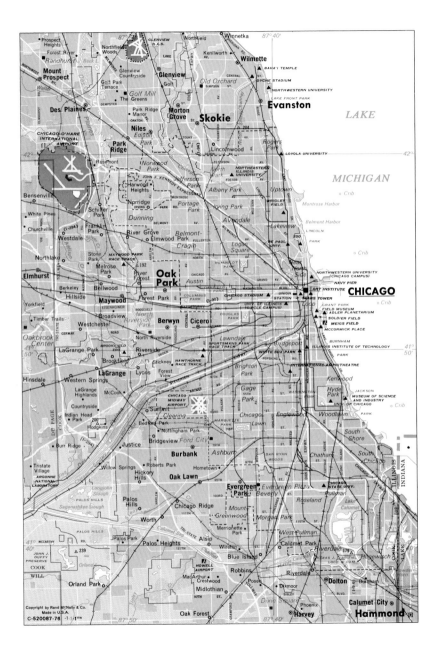

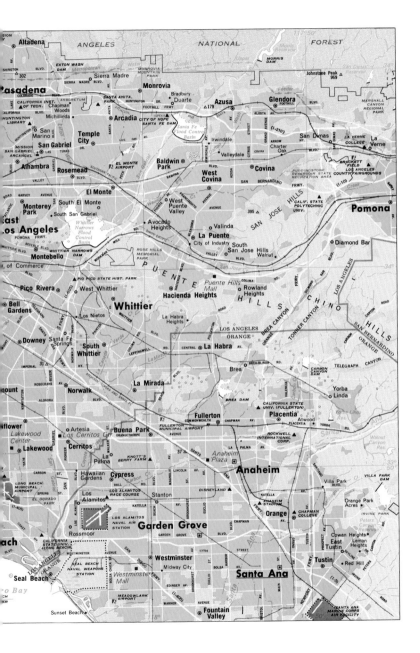

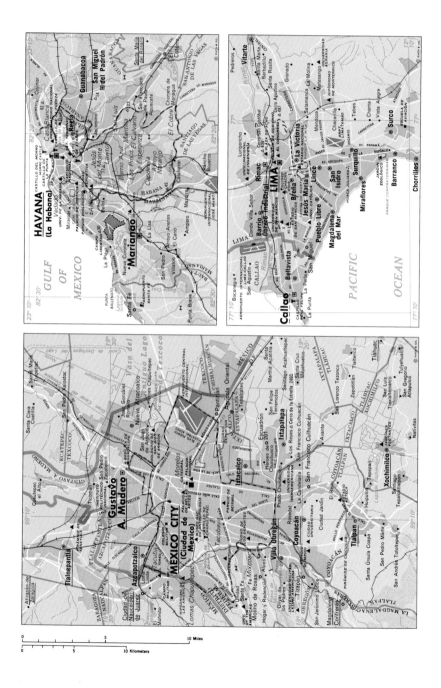

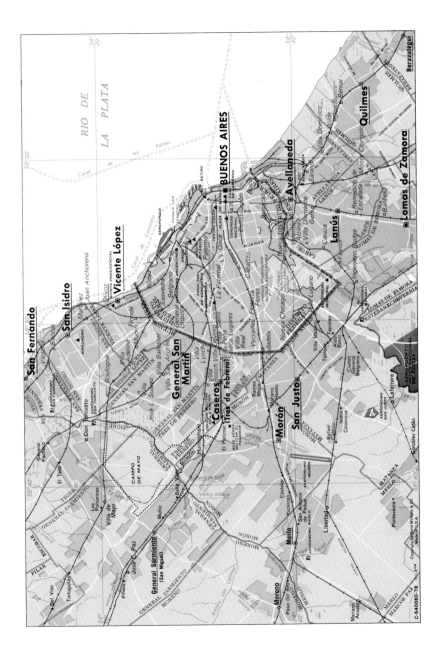

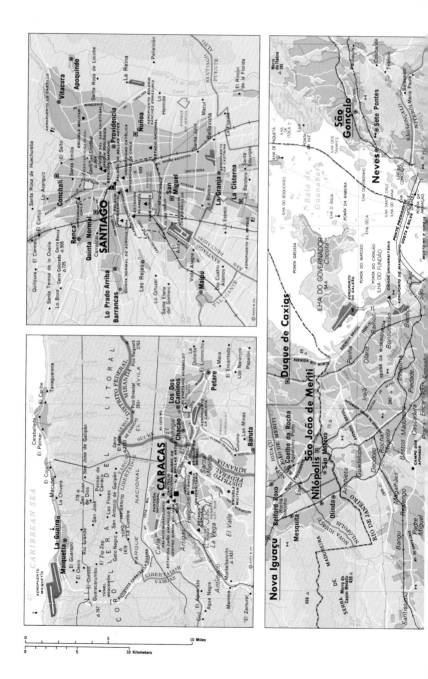

0    5    10 Miles

0    5    10 Kilometers

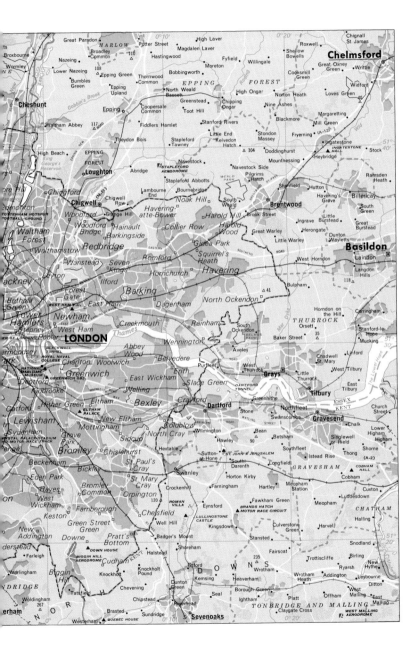

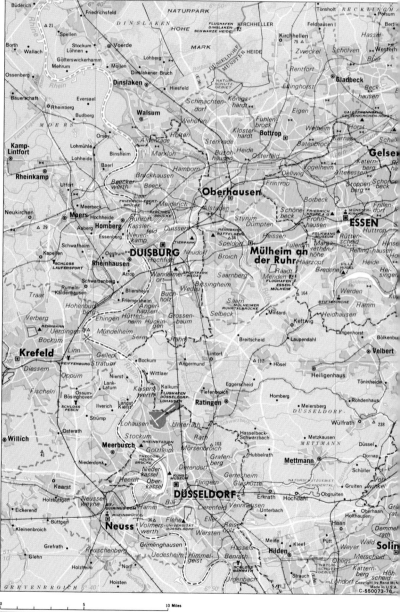

0          5          10 Miles

0          5          10 Kilometers

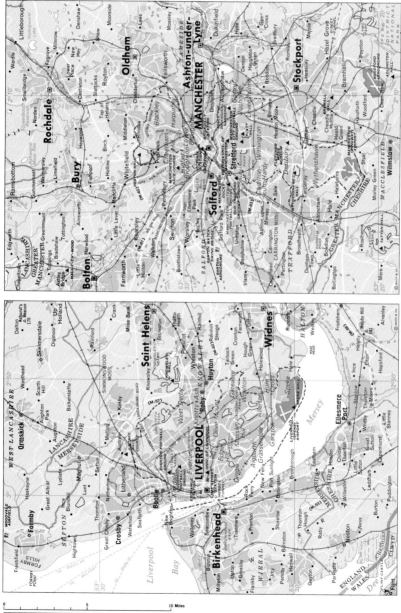

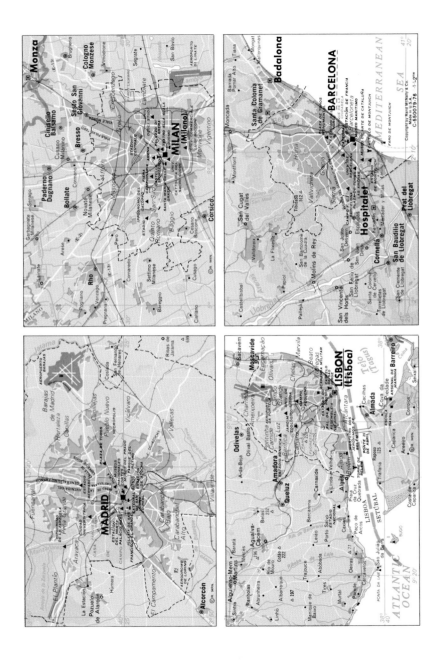

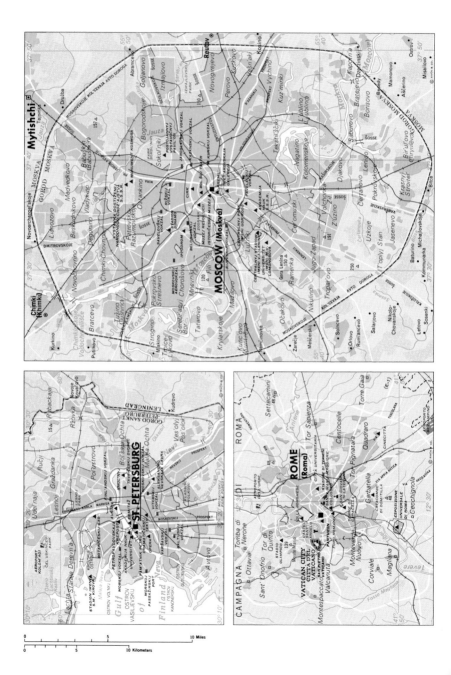

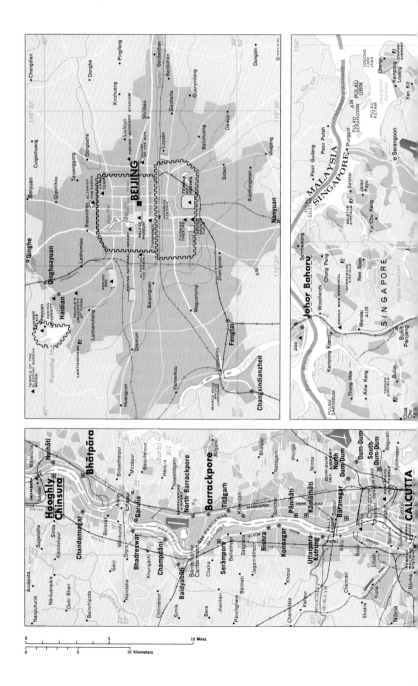

0       5            10 Miles

0       5            10 Kilometers

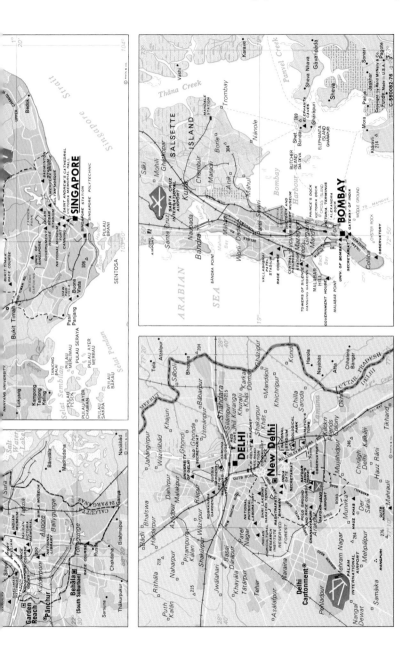

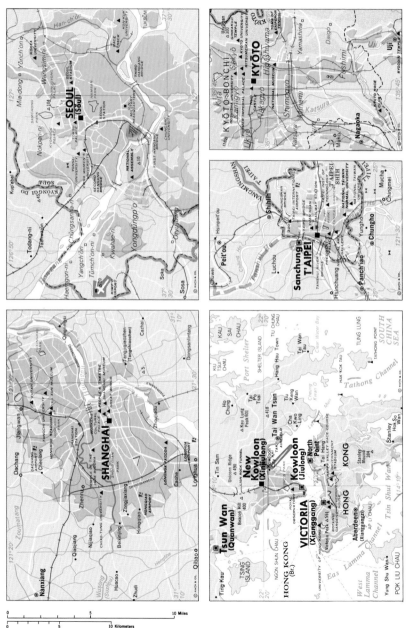

0       5       10 Miles
0       5       10 Kilometers

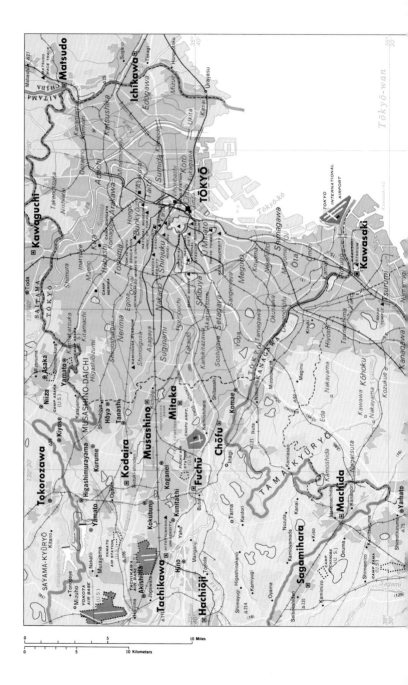

0       5       10 Miles

0       5       10 Kilometers

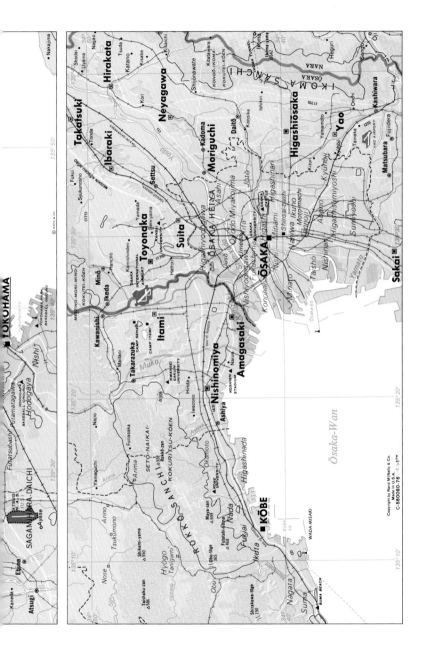

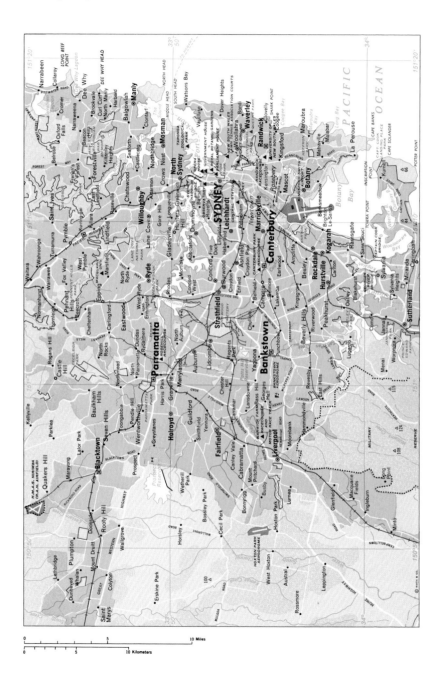

0 ___ 5 ___ 10 Miles

0 ___ 5 ___ 10 Kilometers

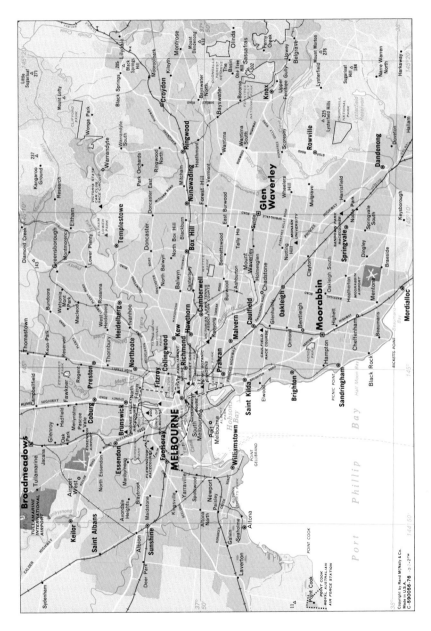

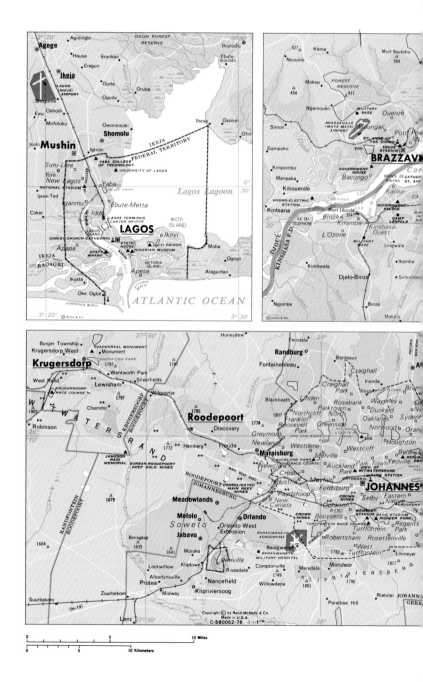

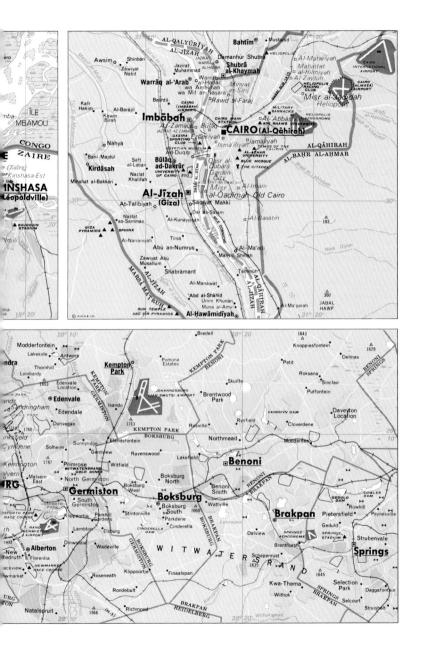

# Guide to Selected Cities

This alphabetical guide shows geographical and travel information for major international cities. The list includes metro area population figures, hotels, restaurants, additional information sources, and other details.

The population figures quoted represent the populations of entire metropolitan areas, which include one or more central cities, as well as socially and economically integrated surrounding areas.

## Amsterdam, Netherlands
**Population:** 1,860,000
**Altitude:** 5 ft. (1.5m.) below sea level
**Average Temp.:** Jan., 35°F. (2°C.); July, 64°F. (18°C.)
**Selected Hotels:**
Amsterdam Hilton, Apollolaan 138-140
De l'Europe, Nieuwe Doelenstraat 2-8
Grand Hotel Krasnapolsky, Dam 9
Marriott, Stadshouderskade 19-21
Okura Amsterdam, Ferd. Bolstraat 333
Sonesta, Kattengat 1
**Selected Restaurants:**
Bali, Christophe, De Boerderij, De Kersentuin, De Prinsenkelder, Dikker en Thijs, Excelsior, La Rive, Sama Sebo, 't Swarte Schaep
**Banking:** Hours are 9 A.M. to 4 P.M. Monday through Friday.
**Information Sources:**
Netherlands Board of Tourism
355 Lexington Avenue, 21st Floor
New York, New York 10017
212-370-7367

## Athens (Athínai), Greece
**Population:** 3,027,331
**Altitude:** 230 ft. (70m.)
**Average Temp.:** Jan., 52°F. (11°C.); July, 80°F. (27°C.)
**Selected Hotels:**
Amalia, 10 Amalias Ave.
Athenaeum Intercontinental, 89-93 Syngrou Ave.
Athens Hilton, 46 Vasilissis Sophias Ave.
Electra, 5 Hermou St.
Grande Bretagne, Constitution Sq.
Meridien, Constitution Sq.
Park, 10 Leoforos Alexandras Ave.
**Selected Restaurants:**
Cellar, Corfu, Dionyssos, Gerofinikas, Floca, L'Abreuvoir, Papakia, Stagecoach, Ta Nissia, Zonars
**Banking:** Hours are 8 A.M. to 2 P.M. Monday through Saturday.
**Information Sources:**
Greek National Tourist Organization
645 Fifth Avenue
New York, New York 10022
212-421-5777

## Atlanta, Georgia
**Population:** 2,833,511
**Altitude:** 1,050 feet
**Average Temp.:** Jan., 52°F. (11°C.); July, 85°F. (29°C.)

**Telephone Area Code:** 404
**Time Zone:** Eastern
**Selected Hotels:**
Atlanta Hilton & Towers, 255 Courtland St. NE, 659-2000
Atlanta Marriott Perimeter Center, 246 Perimeter Cente Pkwy. NE, 394-6500
Colony Square Hotel, 188 14th St. NE, 892-6000
Holiday Inn-Airport North, 1380 Virginia Ave., 762-8411
Hyatt Regency-Atlanta, 265 Peachtree St. NE, 577-1234
Omni Hotel at CNN Center, 100 CNN Center, 659-0000
Radisson Atlanta, 165 Courtland St., 659-6500
Westin Peachtree Plaza, 210 Peachtree St. NW, 659-1400
**Selected Restaurants:**
The Abbey, 163 Ponce de Leon Ave., 876-8831
Bugatti's, in the Omni Hotel at CNN Center, 659-0000
Cafe de la Paix, in the Atlanta Hilton & Towers, 659-2000
Coach and Six, 1776 Peachtree St. NW, 872-6666
La Grotta, 2637 Peachtree Rd. NE, 231-1368
Nikolai's Roof Restaurant, in the Atlanta Hilton & Towers, 659-2000
Pano's and Paul's, 1232 W. Paces Ferry Rd. NW, 261-3662
Terrace Garden Inn, 3405 Lenox Rd. NE, 261-9250
**Information Sources:**
Atlanta Convention & Visitors Bureau
233 Peachtree St. NE, Suite 2000
Atlanta, Georgia 30303 404-521-6600

## Beijing, China
**Population:** 7,320,000
**Altitude:** 165 ft. (50m.)
**Average Temp.:** Jan., 23°F. (-5°C.); July, 79°F. (26°C.)
**Selected Hotels:**
Although all travel arrangements are made by the China International Travel Service, here are the leading hotels and their telephone numbers:
Beijing-Toronto Hotel, 5002266
Great Wall Sheraton Hotel, 5005566
**Selected Restaurants:**
Beijing Orient Restaurant, Beijing Roast Duck Restaurant, Borom Piman, Champagne Room, Dynasty Grill Room, Yuen Tai
**Banking:** Hours vary from one branch to another of Bank of China - 9 A.M. to 5 P.M.

Information Sources:
China National Tourist Office
60 E. 42nd Street, Suite 3126
New York, New York 10165
212-867-0273

## Berlin, Germany

**Population:** 3,825,000
**Altitude:** 115 ft. (35m.)
**Average Temp.:** Jan., 31°F. (-1°C.); July, 66°F. (19°C.)
**Selected Hotels:**
Ambassor, Bayreuther Str. 42-43
Berlin Hotel Intercontinental, Budapester Str. 2
Bristol Hotel Kempinski, Kurfürstendamm 27
Palace Hotel, Europa Center
Schweizerhof, Budapester Str. 21-31
**Selected Restaurants:**
Alt Luxembourg, Alt Nürnberg, Bamberger Reiter, Blockhaus Nikolskoe, Chalet Corniche, Forsthaus Paulsborn, Frühsammers Restaurant an der Rehwiese, Hemingway's, Ponte Vecchio, Rockendorf's Restaurant
**Banking:**
Hours are from 8:30 A.M. to 1 P.M. and 2:30 P.M. to 4 P.M. weekdays (Thursday to 5:30 P.M.). Closed Saturday and Sunday.
**Information Sources:**
German National Tourist Office
747 Third Ave., 33rd Floor
New York, New York 10017
212-308-3300

## Boston, Massachusetts

**Population:** 4,171,643
**Altitude:** Sea level to 330 feet
**Average Temp.:** Jan., 29°F. (-2°C.); July, 72°F. (22°C.)
**Telephone Area Code:** 617
**Time Zone:** Eastern
**Selected Hotels:**
The Colonnade, 120 Huntington Ave., 424-7000
Copley Plaza Hotel, 138 St. James Ave., 267-5300
Hotel Meridien, 250 Franklin St., 451-1900
Logan Airport Hilton, 75 Service Rd., Logan International Airport, 569-9300
Omni Parker House, 60 School St., 227-8600
**Selected Restaurants:**
Anthony's Pier 4, 140 Northern Ave., 423-6363
The Cafe Budapest, 90 Exeter St., 266-1979
Copley's Restaurant, in the Copley Plaza Hotel, 267-5300
The Dining Room, in The Ritz-Carlton, Boston, 536-5700
Felicia's,145A Richmond St., up one flight, 523-9885
Genji, 327 Newbury St., 267-5656
Julien, in the Hotel Meridien, 451-1900
Locke-Ober Cafe, 3 Winter Pl., 542-1340
Parker's, in the Omni Parker House Hotel, 227-8600

Information Sources:
Greater Boston Convention & Visitors Bureau Inc.
Prudential Plaza West, Box 490
Boston, Massachusetts 02199
617-536-4100

## Brussels (Bruxelles), Belgium

**Population:** 2,385,000
**Altitude:** 53 ft. (16m.)
**Average Temp.:** Jan., 38°F. (3°C.); July, 66°F. (19°C.)
**Selected Hotels:**
Amigo, 1-3 Rue de l'Amigo
Atlanta, 7 Blvd. Adolphe Max
Brussels Europa, 107 Rue de la Loi
Brussels Hilton, 38 Blvd. de Waterloo
Metropole, 31 Place de Brouckère
Royal Windosr, 5-7 Rue Duquesnoy
Sheraton Brussels, 3 Place Rogier
**Selected Restaurants:**
Au Beurre Blanc, Bruneau, Comme Chez Soi, Dupont, En Plein Ciel, Francois, La Pomme Cannelle, La Truffe Noir, L'Ecailler Du Palais Royal, Villa Lorraine
**Banking:**
Hours are normally 9 A.M. to 1 P.M. and 2:30 P.M. to 3:30 P.M. Tuesday through Thursday; 9 A.M. to 1 P.M. and 2:30 to 4:30 P.M. Monday and Friday.
**Information Sources:**
Belgian Tourist Office
745 Fifth Avenue
New York, New York 10151
212-758-8130

## Buenos Aires, Argentina

**Population:** 10,750,000
**Altitude:** 65 ft. (20m.)
**Average Temp.:** Jan., 75°F. (24°C.); July, 51°F. (11°C.)
**Selected Hotels:**
Bauen Hotel, Callao 360
Libertador Hotel, Cordoba 698
Plaza, Calle Florida
Presidente, Cerrito 850, Ave. 9 de Julio
**Selected Restaurants:**
A Los Amigos, Au Bec Fin, Clark's, El Repecho de San Telmo, La Cabaña, La Chacra, Los Años Locos, Plaza Hotel Grill
**Banking:** Hours are 10 A.M. to 4 P.M. Monday through Friday.
**Information Sources:**
Argentina National Tourist Office
12 West 56th Street
New York, New York 10019
212-603-0443

## Cairo (Al-Qahirah), Egypt

**Population:** 9,300,000
**Altitude:** 65 ft. (20m.)
**Average Temp.:** Jan., 57°F. (14°C.); July, 82°F. (28°C.)
**Selected Hotels:**
El Salam, Abdel-Hamid Badawi St., Heliopolis
Holiday Inn Pyramids, Alexandria Desert Rd.

Mena House, in front of Pyramids of Giza
Nile Hilton, Tahrir Square
Cairo Marriott, Saray El Guezira, Zamalek
Cairo Meridien, Corniche El Nil, Garden City
Cairo-Sheraton, Gala Square, Giza
Sheraton Heliopolis, Oruba St.
Shepheards, Corniche El Nil, Garden City
**Selected Restaurants:**
Aladdin's, Al Rubayyat, Cairo Tower, El Haty, El
Nile Rotisserie, Estoril, Falafel, Kebabgy el
Gezirah, The Pharaohs, Semiramis Grill, Swiss
Air Restaurant, Vue des Pyramides
**Banking:** Hours are 8:30 A.M. to 1 P.M. Saturday
through Thursday; 10 A.M. to noon on Sunday.
Closed Friday.
**Information Sources:**
Egyptian Tourist Authority
630 Fifth Avenue
New York, New York 10111
212-246-6960

## Calcutta, India

**Population:** 11,100,000
**Altitude:** 20 ft. (6m.)
**Average Temp.:** Jan., 68°F. (20°C.); July, 84°F.
(29°C.)
**Selected Hotels:**
Airport Ashok, Calcutta Airport
Great Eastern, Old Court House St.
Oberoi Grand, 15 J. Nehru Rd.
Park Hotel, 17 Park St.
**Selected Restaurants:**
Amber, Blue Fox, Kwality, Moulin Rouge, Sky
Room, Trinca's, Waldorf
**Banking:** Hours are 10 A.M. to 2 P.M. Monday
through Friday; 10 A.M. to noon on Saturday.
**Information Sources:**
Government of India Tourist Office
30 Rockefeller Plaza
New York, New York 10112
212-586-4901

## Chicago, Illinois

**Population:** 8,065,633
**Altitude:** 579 to 672 feet
**Average Temp.:** Jan., 27°F. (-3°C.); July 75°F.
(24°C.)
**Telephone Area Code:** 312
**Time Zone:** Central
**Selected Hotels:**
Ambassador West Hotel, 1300 N. State Pkwy.,
787-7900
Barclay Chicago, 166 E. Superior, 787-6000
Chicago Marriott Hotel, 540 N. Michigan Ave.,
836-0100
Days Inn, 644 N. Lake Shore Dr., 943-9200
Fairmont Hotel, 200 N. Columbus Dr. at Illinois
Center, 565-8000
Holiday Inn, 350 N. Orleans St., 836-5000
Hotel Nikko, 320 N. Dearborn, 744-1900
Hyatt Regency O'Hare, 9300 W. Bryn Mawr Ave.,
Rosemont, 708-696-1234
Palmer House & Towers, 17 E. Monroe St.,
726-7500
Park Hyatt, 800 N. Michigan Ave., 280-2222
Tremont Hotel, 100 E. Chestnut St., 751-1900

The Whitehall, 105 E. Delaware Pl., 944-6300
**Selected Restaurants:**
Biggs Restaurant, 1150 N. Dearborn Pkwy.,
787-0900
Cape Cod Room, in the Drake Hotel, 787-2200
Gordon Restaurant, 500 N. Clark, 467-9780
House of Hunan, 535 N. Michigan Ave., 329-9494
Lawry's The Prime Rib, 100 E. Ontario St.,
787-5000
Nick's Fishmarket, 1 First National Plaza, Monroe
at Dearborn, 621-0200
Ninety-Fifth, 172 E. Chestnut, in the John Hancock
Center, 787-9596
Pizzeria Uno, 29 E. Ohio St., 321-1000
The Pump Room, Ambassador East Hotel, 1301
State Pkwy., 266-0360
Su Casa, 49 E. Ontario St., 943-4041
**Information Sources:**
Chicago Convention & Visitors Bureau
McCormick Place-on-the-Lake
Chicago, Illinois 60616
312-567-8500

## Dallas-Fort Worth, Texas

**Population:** 3,885,415
**Altitude:** 450 to 750 feet
**Average Temp.:** Jan., 44°F. (7°C.); July, 86°F.
(30°C.)
**Telephone Area Code:** (Dallas) 214, (Fort Worth)
817
**Time Zone:** Central
**Selected Hotels: DALLAS**
Adolphus Hotel, 1321 Commerce St., 742-8200
Fairmont Hotel, 1717 N. Akard St., 720-2020
Hyatt Regency-Dallas-Fort Worth Airport,
International Pkwy., 453-8400
Le Baron Hotel, 1055 Regal Row, 634-8550
Loew's Anatole Hotel, 2201 Stemmons Frwy.,
748-1200
Plaza of the Americas Hotel, 650 N. Pearl St.,
979-9000
Stouffer Dallas Hotel, 2222 N. Stemmons Frwy.,
631-2222
The Westin Hotel, 13340 Dallas Pkwy., 934-9494
**Selected Restaurants: DALLAS**
Le Relais, Plaza of the Americas Hotel, 979-9000
Il Sorrento, 8616 Turtle Creek Blvd., 352-8759
Old Warsaw, 2610 Maple Ave., 528-0032
Plum Blossom, in the Loew's Anatole Hotel,
748-1200
The Pyramid Room, Fairmont Hotel, 720-2020
**Information Sources: DALLAS**
Dallas Convention & Visitors Bureau
1201 Elm St., Suite 2000
Dallas, Texas 75270
214-746-6677
**Selected Hotels: FORT WORTH**
Green Oaks Inn, 6901 W. Freeway, 738-7311
Hyatt Regency Fort Worth, 815 Main St., 870-1234
La Quinta-Fort Worth West, 7888 I-30 W. at
Cherry Ln., 246-5511
Park Central Inn, 1010 Houston St., 336-2011
Quality Inn South, I-35 W. South at Seminary Exit,
923-8281
The Worthington, 200 Main St., 870-1000
**Selected Restaurants: FORT WORTH**
The Balcony, 6100 Camp Bowie Blvd., 731-3719

The Cattle Drive, 1900 Ben Ave., 534-4908
Crystal Cactus, in the Hyatt Regency Fort Worth,
  870-1234
Mac's House, 2400 Park Hill Dr., 921-4682
**Information Sources: FORT WORTH**
Fort Worth Convention & Visitors Bureau
100 E. 15th St., Suite 400
Fort Worth, Texas 76102
817-336-8791

## Denver, Colorado

**Population:** 1,848,319
**Altitude:** 5,130 to 5,470 feet
**Average Temp.:** Jan., 31°F. (-1°C.); July, 74°F.
(23°C.)
**Telephone Area Code:** 303
**Time Zone:** Mountain
**Selected Hotels:**
Brown Palace Hotel, 321 17th St., 297-3111
Burnsley Hotel, 1000 Grant St., 830-1000
Hotel Denver Downton, 1450 Glenarm Pl.,
  573-1450
Hyatt Regency Denver, 1750 Welton St., 295-1200
Radisson Hotel Denver, 1550 Court Pl., 893-3333
Stapleton Plaza Hotel and Fitness Center, 3333
  Quebec St., 321-3500
**Selected Restaurants:**
Churchill's, The Writers' Manor Hotel, 1730 S.
  Colorado Blvd., 756-8877
Ellyngton's, at the Brown Palace Hotel, 297-3111
Normandy French Restaurant, 1515 Madison St.,
  321-3311
Palace Arms, at the Brown Palace Hotel, 297-3111
Tante Louise, 4900 E. Colfax Ave., 355-4488
**Information Sources:**
Denver Metro Convention and Visitors Bureau
225 W. Colfax Avenue
Denver, Colorado 80202
303-892-1112

## Detroit, Michigan

**Population:** 4,665,236
**Altitude:** 573 to 672 feet
**Average Temp.:** Jan., 26°F. (-3°C.); July, 73°F.
(28°C.)
**Telephone Area Code:** 313
**Time Zone:** Eastern
**Selected Hotels:**
Holiday Inn Metro Airport, 31200 Industrial
  Expwy., 728-2800
Radisson Hotel Pontchartrain, 2 Washington Blvd.,
  965-0200
Hotel St. Regis, 3071 W. Grand Blvd., 873-3000
Hyatt Regency Dearborn, Fairlane Town Center
  Dr., Dearborn, 593-1234
Sheraton Southfield, 16400 J.L. Hudson Dr.,
  Southfield, 559-6500
Northfield Hilton, 5500 Crooks Rd., Troy,
  879-2100
The Westin Hotel, Renaissance Center, 568-8000
**Selected Restaurants:**
Captains, 260 Schweizer Place, 568-1862
Carl's Chop House, 3020 Grand River Ave.,
  833-0700
Caucus Club, 150 W. Congress St., 965-4970
Charley's Crab, 5498 Crooks Rd., Troy, 879-2060

Joe Muer's Sea Food, 2000 Gratiot Ave., 567-1088
London Chop House, 155 W. Congress St.,
  962-6735
Mario's Restaurant, 4222 2nd Ave., 833-9425
Pontchartrain Wine Cellars, 234 W. Larned St.,
  963-1785
Van Dyke Place, 649 Van Dyke Ave., 821-2620
**Information Sources:**
Metropolitan Detroit Convention & Visitors Bureau
100 Renaissance Center, Suite 1950
Detroit, Michigan 48243
313-259-4333

## Frankfurt am Main, Germany

**Population:** 1,855,000
**Altitude:** 325 ft. (99m.)
**Average Temp.:** Jan., 34°F. (1°C.); July, 67°F.
(19°C.)
**Selected Hotels:**
Steigenberger Frankfurter Hof, Kaiserplatz
Frankfurt Intercontinental, Wilhelm-Leuschner Str.
  43
Hessische Hof, Friedrich-Ebert Anlage 40
Parkhotel, Wiesenhüttenplatz 28-38
Schlosshotel Kronberg, in Kronberg at Hain Str. 25
Sheraton Rhein-Main, Airport
Steigenberger Airport Hotel
**Selected Restaurants:**
Bistrot 77, Börsenkeller, Da Franco, Erno's Bistro,
  Frankfurter Stubb, Humperdinck, Intercity,
  Restaurant Français, Weinhaus Brückenkeller
**Banking:** Hours 8:30 A.M. to 1 P.M. and 2:30 P.M.
  to 4 P.M., Monday through Friday; close at 5:30
  P.M. Thursday.
**Information Sources:**
German National Tourist Offices
747 Third Avenue, 33rd Floor
New York, New York 10017
212-308-3300

## Hong Kong (Victoria)

**Population:** 4,770,000
**Altitude:** 50 ft., (15m.)
**Average Temp.:** Jan., 59°F. (15°C.); July, 84°F.
(29°C.)
**Selected Hotels:**
Excelsior, Gloucester Rd., Causeway Bay
Furama Kempinski, 1 Connaught Rd. Central
Holiday Inn Harbour View, 70 Mody Rd., Kowloon
Hong Kong Hilton Hotel, 2 Queen's Rd. Central
Hyatt Regency Hong Kong, 67 Nathan Rd.,
  Kowloon
Lee Gardens, Hysan Ave., Causeway Bay
Mandarin Oriental, 5 Connaught Rd. Central
Omni Marco Polo, Harbour City, Kowloon
Miramar, 130 Nathan Rd., Kowloon
Peninsula, Salisbury Rd., Kowloon
Regal Meridien, 71 Mody Rd., Kowloon
Regent, Salisbury Rd., Kowloon
Royal Garden, 69 Mody Rd., Kowloon
Shangri-La, 64 Mody Rd., Kowloon
Sheraton Hong Kong, 20 Nathan Rd., Kowloon
**Selected Restaurants:**
Chesa, Gaddi's (Peninsula), Hilton's Eagle Nest,
  Hugo's (Hyatt), JK's, La Ronda, Mandarin Grill,
  Peacock, Peking Garden, Yung Kee

**Banking:** Hours are 9 A.M. to 3 P.M. Monday through Friday; 9 A.M. to noon on Saturday.
**Information Sources:**
Hong Kong Tourist Association
590 Fifth Avenue, 5th Floor
New York, New York 10036
212-869-5008

## Honolulu, Hawaii
**Population:** 836,231
**Altitude:** Sea level to 4,020 feet
**Average Temp.:** Jan., 72°F. (22°C.); July, 80°F. (27°C.)
**Telephone Area Code:** 808
**Time Zone:** Hawaiian (Two hours earlier than Pacific standard time)
**Selected Hotels:**
Halekulani, 2199 Kalia Rd., 923-2311
Hawaiian Regent, 2552 Kalakaua Ave., 922-6611
Hilton Hawaiian Village, 2005 Kalia Rd., 949-4321
Hyatt Regency Waikiki, 2424 Kalakaua Ave., 923-1234
The Ilikai, 1777 Ala Moana Blvd., 949-3811
Moana Surfrider, 2365 Kalakaua Ave., 922-3111
Outrigger Waikiki Hotel, 2335 Kalakaua Ave., 923-0711
Queen Kapiolani, 150 Kapahulu Ave., 922-1941
Royal Hawaiian, 2259 Kalakaua Ave., 923-7311
**Selected Restaurants:**
Furusato, 2500 Kalakaua Ave., 922-5502
Golden Dragon Room (Chinese), in the Hilton Hawaiian Village, 949-4321
Maile Room, in the Kahala Hilton, 734-2211
Michel's, in the Colony Surf Hotel, 2895 Kalakaua Ave., 923-6552
The Secret, in the Hawaiian Regent Hotel, 922-6611
The Willows, 901 Hausten St., 946-4808
**Information Sources:**
Hawaii Visitors Bureau Meetings & Convention Office
2270 Kalakaua Ave., Suite 801
Honolulu, Hawaii 96815
808-923-1811

## Istanbul, Turkey
**Population:** 7,550,000
**Altitude:** 30 ft. (9m.)
**Average Temp.:** Jan., 42°F. (6°C.); July, 74°F. (23°C.)
**Selected Hotels:**
Büyük Tarabya, Tarabya
Cinar Hotel, Yesilköy
Divan Hotel, Sisli
ETAP Hotel, Tepebasi
Istanbul Hilton, Harbiye
Macka Hotel, Tesvikiye
Marmara Hotel, Taksim Mey
Sheraton Hotel, Taksim
**Selected Restaurants:**
Abdullah Restaurant, Bebek Ambassadeurs, Divan Hotel Restaurant, Marmara Restaurant, Hotel Kalyon Restaurant, Konyali, Le Mangal (Sheraton Hotel), Liman (lunch), Orient Express, Restaurant 29, Ziya

**Banking:** Hours 9 A.M. to noon and 1:30 P.M. to 5:30 P.M. Monday through Friday.
**Information Sources:**
Turkish Government Tourist Office
821 United Nations Plaza
New York, New York 10017
212-687-2194

## Johannesburg, South Africa
**Population:** 3,650,000
**Altitude:** 5,750 ft. (1,753m.)
**Average Temp.:** Jan., 67°F., (19°C.); July, 51°F. (11°C.)
**Selected Hotels:**
Carlton, Main St.
Holiday Inn, Jan Smuts Airport
Milpark Holiday Inn, Empire Rd.
Rand International, 230 Bree St.
Rosebank, Tyrwhitt Ave.
Sandton Sun Hotel, Sandton
**Selected Restaurants:**
Bougainvillia, Chez Zimmerli, De Fistermann, El Gaucho, Jorissen at Devonshire, Le Francais, Leo, L'Escargot, Lien Wah Chinese, Linger Longer, Pot Luck, Rugantino, Scratch Caniels, Three Ships, Zoo Lake
**Banking:** Open at 9 A.M. and close at 3:30 P.M. except Wednesday, when closing hour is 1 P.M., and Saturday, when banks open at 8:30 A.M. and close at 11 A.M. On the last day of the month banks open at 8:30 A.M. and close at the normal hour for that day.
**Information Sources:**
South African Tourist Board
747 Third Avenue, 20th Floor
New York, New York 10017
212-838-8841

## Lisbon (Lisboa), Portugal
**Population:** 2,250,000
**Altitude:** 150 ft. (46m.)
**Average Temp.:** Jan., 51°F. (11°C.); July, 72°F. (22°C.)
**Selected Hotels:**
Alfa, Av. Columbano Bordalo Pinheiro
Altis, Rua Castilho 11
Avenida Palace, Rua 1.° de Dezembro 123
Diplomatico, Rua Castilho 74
Fénix, Praca Marquês de Pombal 8
Flórida, Rua Duque de Palmela 32
Lisbon-Sheraton, Rua Latino Coelho
Lisbon Penta, Av. Dos Combatentes
Mundial, Rua D. Duarte 4
Principe Real, Rua da Alegria 53
Ritz, Rua Rodrigo da Fonseca 88-A
Tivoli, Av. da Liberdade 185
**Selected Restaurants:**
Antonio Clara, Casa da Comida, Gambrinus, Michel's, Pabe, Ritz Hotel Grill, Solmar, Tagide, Tavares
**Banking:** Hours 8:30 A.M. to 11:45 A.M. and 1 P.M. to 2:45 P.M. Monday through Friday; closed Saturday.

Guide to Selected Cities **75**

**Information Sources:**
Portuguese National Tourist Office
590 Fifth Avenue, 4th Floor
New York, New York 10036
212-354-4403

## London, England
**Population:** 11,100,000
**Altitude:** 20 ft. (6m.)
**Average Temp.:** Jan., 40°F. (4°C.); July, 64°F. (18°C.)
**Selected Hotels:**
Berkeley, Wilton Pl., Knightsbridge
Britannia Inter-Continental, Grosvenor Sq.
Capital, Basil St., Knightsbridge
Churchill, Portman Sq.
Connaught, Carlos Pl., Mayfair
Dorchester, Park Lane
Grosvenor House, Park Lane
Hilton, Park Lane
Ritz, Piccadilly
Savoy, The Strand
Tower Thistle, St. Katherine's Way
Waldorf, Aldwych
**Selected Restaurants:**
Café Royal, La Gavroche, La Tante Claire, Mirabelle, Rules, Simpson's-in-the-Strand, Walton's
**Banking:** Hours in England are 9:30 A.M. to 3:30 P.M. Monday through Friday. Some banks are open Saturday.
**Information Sources:**
British Tourist Authority
40 West 57th Street, Suite 320
New York, New York 10019
212-581-4708

## Los Angeles, California
**Population:** 14,531,529
**Altitude:** Sea level to 5,074 feet
**Average Temp.:** Jan., 55°F. (13°C.); July, 73°F. (23°C.)
**Telephone Area Code:** 213
**Time Zone:** Pacific
**Selected Hotels:**
Beverly Hills Hotel, 9641 Sunset Blvd., (310) 276-2251
Biltmore Hotel, 506 S. Grand Ave., 624-1011
Century Plaza, 2025 Avenue of the Stars, (310) 277-2000
Holiday Inn-Hollywood, 1755 N. Highland Ave., 462-7181
Hyatt Los Angeles Airport, 6225 W. Century Blvd. (310) 670-9000
L'Ermitage, 9291 Burton Way, 278-3344
Le Parc Hotel De Luxe, 733 N. West Knoll Dr., (310) 855-8888
Los Angeles Airport Marriott, 5855 W. Century Blvd., (310) 641-5700
Los Angeles Hilton and Towers, 930 Wilshire Blvd., 629-4321
Sheraton Town Hotel, 2961 Wilshire Blvd., 382-7171
Sheraton-Universal, 333 Universal Terrace Pkwy., Universal City, (818) 980-1212

University Hilton, 3540 S. Figueroa St., 748-4141
The Westin Bonaventure Hotel, 404 S. Figueroa St., 624-1000
**Selected Restaurants:**
Bernard's, in the Biltmore Hotel, 612-1580
Lawry's Prime Rib, 55 N. La Cienega Blvd., 652-2827
Madame Wu's Garden, 2201 Wilshire Blvd., 828-5656
Perino's, 4101 Wilshire Blvd., 487-0000
Scandia, 9040 Sunset Blvd., West Hollywood, 278-3555
The Tower, 1150 S. Olive St., 746-1554
Yamato, in the Century Plaza Hotel, 277-1840
**Information Sources:**
Greater Los Angeles Visitors & Convention Bureau
515 S. Figueroa, 11th Floor
Los Angeles, California 90071
213-624-7300

## Madrid, Spain
**Population:** 4,650,000
**Altitude:** 2,100 ft. (640m.)
**Average Temp.:** Jan., 41°F. (5°C.); July, 76°F. (24°C.)
**Selected Hotels:**
Alameda, Av. Logrono 100
Castellana, Paseo de la Castellana 49
Eurobuilding, Padre Damian 23
Melia Madrid, Princesa 27
Miguel Angel, Miguel Angel 31
Mindanao, S. Francisco De Sales 15
Monte Real, Arroyo Fresno 17
Plaza, Plaza de España 8
Palace, Plaza de las Cortes 7
Princesa Plaza, Serano Jover 3
Villa Magna, Castellana 22
Wellington, Velazquez 8
**Selected Restaurants:**
Club 31, Cafe Chinitas, El Cenador del Prado, Cafe de Oriente, Jockey Club, Zalacain
**Banking:** Hours are 9 A.M. to 2 P.M. Monday through Saturday.
**Information Sources:**
Spanish National Tourist Office
665 Fifth Avenue
New York, New York 10022
212-759-8822

## Manila, Phillipines
**Population:** 6,800,000
**Altitude:** 10 ft. (3m.)
**Average Temp.:** Jan. 78°F. (26°C.); July, 82°F. (28°C.)
**Selected Hotels:**
Holiday Inn, 3001 Roxas Blvd., Pasay City
Hotel Intercontinental, Ayala Av., Makati
Hyatt Regency Manila, 2702 Roxas Blvd., Pasay City
Mandarin Oriental Manila, Makati Av., Makati
Manila Hotel, Rizal Park
Manila Peninsula, Ayala and Makati Av.
Philippine Plaza, Cultural Center Complex, Roxas Blvd.
Silahis International, 1990 Roxas Blvd.

**Selected Restaurants:**
Aristocrat, Au Bon Vivant, Barrio Fiesta,
Champagne Room in Manila Hotel,
Intercontinental Hotel Restaurant, Kamayan,
Maynila
**Banking:** Hours usually are 9 A.M. to 3 P.M.
Monday through Friday.
**Information Sources:**
Philippine Convention & Visitors Corp.
Philippine Center
556 Fifth Avenue
New York, New York 10036
212-575-7915

## Mexico City (Ciudad de México), Mexico
**Population:** 14,100,000
**Altitude:** 7,300 ft. (2,225m.)
**Average Temp.:** Jan., 54°F. (12°C.); July, 64°F.
(18°C.)
**Selected Hotels:**
Aristos, Paseo de la Reforma 276
Camino Real, Mariano Escobedo 700
Hotel El Presidenté Chapultepec, Campos Eliseos
218
Maria Isabel-Sheraton, Paseo de la Reforma 325
**Selected Restaurants:**
Anderson's, El Parador, Focolare, Fonda Santa
Anita, Hacienda de los Morales, La Cava,
Restaurant del Lago, Rivoli, San Angel Inn
**Banking:** Banks are open 9 A.M. to 1 P.M. Monday
through Friday; 9 A.M. to 12:30 P.M. on
Saturday.
**Information Sources:**
Mexican Government Tourism Office
405 Park Avenue, #1002
New York, New York 10022
212-755-7261

## Miami, Florida
**Population:** 3,192,582
**Altitude:** Sea level to 30 feet
**Average Temp.:** Jan., 69°F. (21°C.); July, 82°F.
(28°C.)
**Telephone Area Code:** 305
**Time Zone:** Eastern
**Selected Hotels:**
Doubletree, 2649 S. Bayshore Dr., 858-2500
Holiday Inn-Civic Center, 1170 NW. 11th St.,
324-0800
Best Western Marina Park Hotel, 340 Biscayne
Blvd., 371-4400
Marriott Airport Hotel, 1201 NW. LeJeune Rd.,
649-5000
Miami Lakes Inn, Athletic Club & Golf Resort,
Main St. & Bull Run Rd., Miami Lakes,
821-1150
Omni International Hotel, 1601 Biscayne Blvd.,
374-0000
Ramada Hotel-Miami International Airport, 3941
NW. 22nd St., 871-1700
**Selected Restaurants:**
Cafe Chauveron, 9561 E. Bay Harbor Dr.,
866-8779
Centro Vasco, 2235 SW. 8th St., 643-9606
Cye's Rivergate, 444 Brickell Ave., 358-9100

La Paloma, 10999 Biscayne Blvd., 891-0505
Raimondo, 4612 SW. LeJeune, 666-9355
**Information Sources:**
Greater Miami Convention and Visitors Bureau
701 Brickell Ave.
Miami, Florida 33131
305-539-3000

## Milan (Milano), Italy
**Population:** 3,750,000
**Altitude:** 400 ft. (122m.)
**Average Temp.:** Jan., 34°F. (1°C.); July, 73°F.
(23°C.)
**Selected Hotels:**
Dei Cavalieri, Piazza Missori 1
Excelsior Gallia, Piazza Duca d'Aosta 9
Grand Hotel Duomo, Via S. Raffaele 1
Grand Hotel et de Milan, Via Manzoni 29
Palace, Piazza della Repubblica 20
Principe Di Savoia, Piazza della Repubblica 17
Hilton, Via Galvani 12
**Selected Restaurants:**
Biffi Scala, Canoviano, Peck, St. Andrew's, Savini
**Banking:** Hours are 8:30 A.M. to 1 P.M. Monday
through Friday.
**Information Sources:**
Italian Government Travel Office
630 Fifth Avenue
New York, New York 10111
212-245-4822

## Montreal, Canada
**Population:** 2,921,357
**Altitude:** 50 ft. (15m.)
**Average Temp.:** Jan., 16°F. (-9°C.); July, 71°F.
(22°C.)
**Telephone Area Number:** 514
**Selected Hotels:**
Le Chateau Champlain, 1050 Ouest de
Lagauchetiere
Hotel Meridien-Montréal, 4 Complexe Desjardins
Montréal Aeroport Hilton International, 12505
Côte de Liesse Rd. in Dorval
Queen Elizabeth, 900 Blvd. Réné-Levesqne
Ritz-Carlton, 1228 Sherbrooke St. W
Ruby Foo's Hotel, 7655 Decaria Blvd.
**Selected Restaurants:**
Café de Paris, Chez la Mere Michel, Des Jardins,
Le Castillon in the Bonaventure Hilton
International, Le Neufchatel, Les Filles du Roy,
Les Halles
**Banking:**
Hours are generally from 10 A.M. to 3 P.M.
Monday through Thursday; 10 A.M. to 6 P.M. on
Friday. If Friday is a holiday, Friday hours are
observed on Thursday.
**Information Sources:**
Tourism Quebec
1001 Dorchester Square St.
Downtown Information Center
Montreal, Quebec
800-363-7777
514-873-2015

## Moscow (Moskva), Russia

**Population:** 13,100,000
**Altitude:** 395 ft. (120m.)
**Average Temp.:** Jan., 14°F. (-10°C.); July, 66°F.
(19°C.)
**Selected Hotels:**
Intourist, 3/5 Gorky St.
Metropole, 1 Marx Ave.
National, 14-1 Marx Ave.
Rossiya Hotel, 6 Razin St.
Ukraina, 2/1 Kutuzovsky Ave.
**Selected Restaurants:**
Aragvi, Arbat, Baku, Budapest, Peking, Praga,
    Seventh Heaven, Sofia, Slavyansky Bazaar,
    Uzbekistan
**Banking:** Banks are open from 9 A.M. to 1 P.M.
    Monday through Friday; days before holidays
    they close at noon.
**Information Sources:**
Intourist Information Office
630 Fifth Ave., Suite 868
New York, New York 10111
212-757-3884

## New Orleans, Louisiana

**Population:** 1,238,816
**Altitude:** 5 to 25 feet
**Average Temp.:** Jan., 55°F. (13°C.); July, 82°F.
(28°C.)
**Telephone Area Code:** 504
**Time Zone:** Central
**Selected Hotels:**
Fairmont Hotel, 123 Baronne St., 529-7111
Hyatt Regency New Orleans, 500 Poydras Plaza,
    561-1234
The Monteleone, 214 Royal St., 523-3341
New Orleans Hilton Riverside and Towers, Poydras
    St. at the Mississippi River, 561-0500
New Orleans Marriott, 555 Canal St., 581-1000
The Omni Royal Orleans Hotel, 621 St. Louis St.,
    529-5333
The Pontchartrain Hotel, 2031 St. Charles Ave.,
    524-0581
Royal Sonesta Hotel, 300 Bourbon St., 586-0300
**Selected Restaurants:**
Broussard's, 819 Conti St., 581-3866
Caribbean Room, in The Pontchartrain Hotel,
    524-0581
Commander's Palace Restaurant, 1403 Washington
    Ave., 899-8221
Galatoire's Restaurant, 209 Bourbon St., 525-2021
Louis XVI French Restaurant, 730 Bienville,
    581-7000
Masson's Restaurant Français, 7200 Pontchartrain
    Blvd., 283-2525
Sazerac Restaurant, in the Fairmont Hotel,
    529-7111
**Information Sources:**
Greater New Orleans Tourist & Convention
    Commission
1520 Sugar Bowl Dr.
New Orleans, Louisiana 70112
504-566-5011

## New York, New York

**Population:** 18,087,251
**Altitude:** Sea level to 410 feet
**Average Temp.:** Jan., 33°F. (-1°C.); July, 75°F.
(24°C.)
**Telephone Area Code:** 212
**Time Zone:** Eastern
**Selected Hotels:**
Carlyle, Madison Ave. at E. 76th St., 744-1600
The Helmsley Palace, 455 Madison Ave., 888-7000
The Hotel Pierre, 2 E. 61st St. at 5th Ave.,
    838-8000
The Plaza, 768 5th Ave., 759-3000
Regency, 540 Park Ave., 759-4100
Sherry-Netherland, 781 5th Ave., 355-2800
United Nations Plaza Hotel, 1 U.N. Plaza,
    355-3400
**Selected Restaurants:**
The Four Seasons, 99 E. 52nd St., 754-9494
La Cote Basque, 5 E. 55th St., 688-6525
Lutèce, 249 E. 50th St., 752-2225
Mitsukoshi, 461 Park Ave., 935-6444
"21" Club, 21 W. 52nd St., 582-7200
**Information Sources:**
New York Convention and Visitors Bureau, Inc.
Two Columbus Circle
New York City, New York 10019
212-397-8200

## Osaka, Japan

**Population:** 16,450,000
**Altitude:** 16 ft. (5m.)
**Average Temp.:** Jan., 40°F. (4°C.); July, 80°F.
(27°C.)
**Selected Hotels:**
Hotel Osaka Grand, 2-3-18 Nakanoshima, Kita-ku
International Hotel, 2-33 Honmachibashi, Chou-ku
Osaka Miyako Hotel, 6-1-55 Uehonmachi,
    Tennoji-ku
Osaka Royal Hotel, 5-3-68 Nakanashima, Kita-ku
Plaza, 2-2-49 Oyodo-Minami, Kita-ku
Toyo Hotel, 3-16-19 Toyosaki, Kita-ku
**Selected Restaurants:**
Chambord, Hanagoyomi, Kobe Misono, Little
    Pirates, Osaka Boteju, Osaka Joe's, Suehiro
    Honten
**Banking:** Hours are 9 A.M. to 3 P.M. Monday
    through Friday; 9 A.M. to noon on Saturday.
**Information Sources:**
Japan National Tourist Organization
630 Fifth Avenue
New York, New York 10111
212-757-5640

## Paris, France

**Population:** 9,775,000
**Altitude:** 140 ft. (43m.)
**Average Temp.:** Jan., 44°F. (7°C.); July, 76°F.
(24°C.)
**Selected Hotels:**
Le Bristol, 112 Rue du Faubourg St., Honoré
Crillon, 10 Place de la Concorde
George V, 31 Ave. George V
Intercontinental Paris, 3 Rue de Castiglione
Meridien Hotel, 81 Blvd. Gouvion-St. Cyr
Napoleon, 40 Ave. de Friedland

Paris Hilton, 18 Ave. de Suffren
Plaza Athenée, 25 Ave. Montaigne
Ritz, 15 Place Vendome, overlooking Place
Vendome
**Selected Restaurants:**
Drouant, Grand Vefour, La Maré, Lasserre,
Ledoyen, Le Vivarois, Lucas-Carton, Maxim's,
Pré Catelan, Taillevent, Tour d'Argent
**Banking:** From 9 A.M. to 4:30 P.M. Monday
through Friday; 9 A.M. to noon day before
holidays.
**Information Sources:**
French Government Tourist Office
610 Fifth Avenue
New York, New York 10020
212-757-1125

### Rio de Janeiro, Brazil

**Population:** 10,150,000
**Altitude:** 30 ft. (9m.)
**Average Temp.:** Jan., 79°F. (26°C.); July, 69°F.
(21°C.)
**Selected Hotels:**
Caesar Park, Ave. Vieira Souto 460
Copacabana Palace, Ave. Atlantica 1702
Everest Rio, Rua Prudente de Morais 1117
Leme Palace, Ave. Atlantica 656
Marina Palace, R. Delfim Moreira 630
Meridien Copacabana, Ave. Atlantica 1020
Miramar Palace, Ave. Atlantica 3668
Nacional Rio, Ave. Niemeyer 769
Rio Palace, Ave. Atlantica 4240
Sol Ipanema, Ave. Vieira Souto 320
Rio Sheraton, Ave. Niemeyer 121
**Selected Restaurants:**
Maxim's de Paris, La Streghe, Candido's,
Antiquarius, Chalé, La Tour, Mario's, Le Saint
Honoré, Petronio's, Club Gourmet, Nino, Rio's
**Banking:** Hours are 10 A.M. to 4:30 P.M. Monday
through Friday.
**Information Sources:**
Brazilian Tourism Office
551 Fifth Avenue
New York, New York 10176
212-286-9600

### Rome (Roma), Italy

**Population:** 3,175,000
**Altitude:** 80 ft. (24m.)
**Average Temp.:** Jan., 46°F. (8°C.); July, 75°F.
(24°C.)
**Selected Hotels:**
Ambasciatori Palace, Via Veneto 70
Bernini Bristol, Piazza Barberini 23
Cavalieri Hilton, Via Cadlolo 101
Eden, Via Ludovisi 49
Excelsior, Via Vittorio Veneto 125
Flora, Via Vittorio Veneto 191
Grand, Via V.E. Orlando 3
Hassler, Trinità dei Monti 6
Mediterraneo, Via Cavour 15
Parco dei Principi, Via G. Frescobaldi 5
Quirinale, Via Nazionale 7
Sheraton Roma, Viale del Pattinaggio

**Selected Restaurants:**
Albert Ciarla, Checchino dal 1887, La Rosetta, Le
Restaurant, Passetto, Patrizia e Roberto del
Pianeta Terra, Quinzi Gabrieli, Ranieri, Relais le
Jardin, San Souci
**Banking:** From 8:30 A.M. to 1:30 P.M. Monday
through Friday.
**Information Sources:**
Italian Government Travel Office
630 Fifth Avenue, #1565
New York, New York 10111
212-245-4822

### San Francisco, California

**Population:** 6,253,311
**Altitude:** Sea level to 934 feet
**Average Temp.:** Jan., 50°F. (10°C.); July, 59°F.
(15°C.)
**Telephone Area Code:** 415
**Time Zone:** Pacific
**Selected Hotels:**
The Fairmont Hotel, 950 Mason St., 772-5000
Four Seasons-Clift, 495 Geary St., 775-4700
Hilton Square, 333 O'Farrell St., 771-1400
The Holiday Inn Union Square, 480 Sutter St.,
398-8900
Huntington Hotel, 1075 California St., 474-5400
Hyatt on Union Square, 345 Stockton St., 398-1234
Hyatt Regency San Francisco, 5 Embarcardero
Center, 788-1234
Mark Hopkins Intercontinental, 999 California St.,
392-3434
Miyako Hotel, 1625 Post St., 922-3200
The Phoenix Inn, 601 Eddy St., 776-1380
Queen Anne, 1590 Sutter St., 441-2828
The Westin St. Francis, 335 Powell St., 397-7000
**Selected Restaurants:**
Amelio's 1630 Powell St., 397-4339
Blue Fox Restaurant, 659 Merchant St., 981-1177
Empress of China, 838 Grant Ave., 434-1345
Ernie's Restaurant, 847 Montgomery St., 397-5969
Fleur de Lys, 777 Sutter St., 673-7779
Fournou's Ovens, in The Stanford Court Hotel,
989-1910
**Information Sources:**
San Francisco Convention & Visitors Bureau
Convention Plaza 201 Third St., Suite 900
San Francisco, California 94103
415-974-6900

### Sao Paulo, Brazil

**Population:** 15,175,000
**Altitude:** 2,375 ft. (724m.)
**Average Temp.:** Jan., 71°F. (22°C.); July, 58°F.
(14°C.)
**Selected Hotels:**
Brasilton, Rua Martins Fontes 330
Caesar Park Hotel, Rua Augusta 1508
Eldorado, Ave. São Luis 234
Grande Hotel Ca D'Oro, Rua Augusta 129
Jaraguá, Viaduto Major Quedinho 40
Maksoud Plaza, Al. Campinas 150
Othon Palace, Rua Libero Badaró 190
Sao Paulo Center, Lgo. Sta. Ifigenia 40
Sao Paulo Hilton, Ave. Ipiranga 165

**Selected Restaurants:**
Abril em Portugal, Andrade, Baiúa, Bolinha, Chalet Suisse, La Casserole, Manhattan, Os Vikings, Presidente, Tarraço Italia, Via Veneto
**Banking:** Hours are 8 A.M. to 6:30 P.M. Monday through Friday.
**Information Sources:**
Brazilian Tourism Office
551 Fifth Avenue
New York, New York 10176
212-286-9600

## Singapore, Singapore
**Population:** 3,000,000
**Altitude:** 35 ft. (11m.)
**Average Temp.:** Jan., 79°F. (26°C.); July, 81°F. (27°C.)
**Selected Hotels:**
Dynasty Singapore, 320 Orchard Rd.
Goodwood Park, 22 Scotts Rd.
Hyatt Singapore, 10-12 Scotts Rd.
The Mandarin Singapore, 333 Orchard Rd.
The Marco Polo, Tanglin Circus
Shangri-La, 22 Orange Grove Rd.
Singapore Hilton, 581 Orchard Rd.
**Selected Restaurants:**
Aziza's, Casablanca, Compass Rose, Fourchettes, Harbour Grill, Moti Mahal, The Pinnacle
**Banking:** Hours are 10 A.M. to 3 P.M. Monday through Friday; 9:30 A.M. to 11:30 A.M. on Saturday.
**Information Sources:**
Singapore Tourist Promotion Board
590 Fifth Avenue, 12th Floor
New York, New York 10036
212-302-4861

## Stockholm, Sweden
**Population:** 1,449,972
**Altitude:** 55 ft. (17m.)
**Average Temp.:** Jan., 27°F. (-3°C.); July, 64°F. (18°C.)
**Selected Hotels:**
Birger Jarl, Tulegatan 8
Grand Hotel, Södra Blasieholmshamnen 8, opposite the Royal Palace
Strand, Nybrokajen 9
Diplomat, Strandvägen 7 C
Park, Karlavägen 43
Anglais, Humlegårdsgatan 23
Sheraton-Stockholm, Tegelbacken 6
**Selected Restaurants:**
Aurora, Den Glydene Freden, Fem Små Hus, Franska Matsalen, L'Escargot, Michel, Operakällaren, Riche, Solliden at Skansen, Stallmästaregarden
**Banking:** Hours from 9:30 A.M. to 3 P.M. on weekdays
**Information Sources:**
Swedish Tourist Board
655 Third Avenue
New York, New York 10017
212-949-2333

## Sydney, Australia
**Population:** 3,623,550
**Altitude:** 75 ft. (23m.)
**Average Temp.:** Jan., 71°F. (22°C.); July, 53°F. (12°C.)
**Selected Hotels:**
Boulevard Hotel, 90 William St.
Holiday Inn Menzies, 14-28 Carrington St.
Hyatt Kingsgate, Kings Cross Rd., Kings Cross
Regent of Sydney, 199 George St.
Sheraton Airport, 61-101 Phillip St.
Hilton International Sydney, 259 Pitt St.
**Selected Restaurants:**
Afrilanka, Beppi's, Chitose, Doyle's on the Beach, Harbor Restaurant, Jin Jiang, Kables, Le Trianon at King's Cross, San Francisco Grill
**Banking:**
Hours are 9:30 A.M. to 4 P.M. Monday through Thursday; 9:30 A.M. to 5 P.M. on Friday. Major branches are open for extended hours.
**Information Sources:**
Australian Tourist Commission
489 Fifth Avenue, 31st Floor
New York, New York 10017
212-687-6300

## Tel Aviv (Tel Aviv-Yafo), Israel
**Population:** 1,735,000
**Altitude:** 35 ft. (11m.)
**Average Temp.:** Jan., 57°F. (14°C.); July, 77°F. (25°C.)
**Selected Hotels:**
Carlton, 10 Hayarkon St.
Dan Tel Aviv, 99 Hayarkon St.
Diplomat, 145 Hayarkon St.
Hilton, Independence Park
Plaza, 155 Hayarkon St.
Ramada Continental, 121 Hayarkon St.
Sheraton, 115 Hayarkon St.
**Selected Restaurants:**
Alhambra, Casba, Taboon, Zion
**Banking:** Hours are 8:30 A.M. to 12:30 P.M. and 4 P.M. to 6 P.M. Sunday, Tuesday and Thursday; 8:30 A.M. to 12:30 P.M. Monday and Wednesday; and 8:30 A.M. to 12 noon Friday. Banks are closed on eves of holidays and on holidays.
**Information Sources:**
Israel Tourist Bureau
350 Fifth Avenue
New York, New York 10118
212-560-0650

## Tōkyō, Japan
**Population:** 27,700,000
**Altitude:** 20 ft. (6m.)
**Average Temp.:** Jan., 39°F. (4°C.); July, 77°F. (25°C.)
**Selected Hotels:**
Imperial Hotel, 1-1-1, Uchisaiwaicho, Chiyoda-ku
Hotel New Otani, 4-1, Kioicho, Chiyoda-ku
Hotel Okura, 2-10-4, Toranomon, Minato-ku
Keio Plaza Hotel, 2-2-1, Nishi-Shinjuku, Shinjuku-ku
Palace Hotel, 1-1-1, Marunouchi, Chiyoda-ku

The Tokyo Hilton, 6-6-2, Nishi-Shinjuku,
Shinjuku-ku
**Selected Restaurants:**
Attore, Bengawan Solo, Borsalino, Edo-Gin,
Fukudaya, Heichinrou, Inakaya, Ketel's, La Belle
Époque, L'Orangerie, Sabatini di Firenze,
Sasashu, Tokyo Joe's
**Banking:** Hours from 9 A.M. to 3 P.M. Monday
through Friday; 9 A.M. to noon on Saturday.
**Information Sources:**
Japan National Tourist Organization
650 Fifth Avenue
New York, New York 10111
212-757-5640

## Toronto, Canada
**Population:** 3,427,168
**Altitude:** 275 ft. (84m.)
**Average Temp.:** Jan., 23°F. (-5°C.); July, 69°F.
(21°C.)
**Telephone Area Number:** 416
**Selected Hotels:**
Four Seasons Motor Hotel, 21 Avenue Rd.
Holiday Inn-Downtown, 89 Chestnut St.
Park Plaza, 4 Avenue Rd.
Royal York, 100 Front St. W
Sheraton Centre, 123 Queen St.
Sutton Place, 955 Bay St.
**Selected Restaurants:**
Fisherman's Wharf, Imperial Room, Old Spaghetti
Factory, The Old Mill, Tanaka of Tokyo
**Banking:** Hours generally are from 10 A.M. to 3
P.M. Monday through Friday.
**Information Sources:**
Metropolitan Toronto Convention & Visitors Assn.
207 Quay West at Harbour Front
Toronto, Ontario M5J 1A7
416-368-9990

## Vienna (Wien), Austria
**Population:** 1,875,000
**Altitude:** 560 ft. (171m.)
**Average Temp.:** Jan., 30°F. (-1°C.); July, 68°F.
(20°C.)
**Selected Hotels:**
Ambassador, Neuer Markt 5
Bristol, Kärntner Ring 1, opposite Vienna Opera
Clima Villenhotel, Nussberggasse 2c
Imperial, Kärntner Ring 16
Parkhotel Schönbrunn, Hietzinger Haupstr. 12
Sacher, Philharmonikerstr. 4
Vienna Intercontinental, Johannesgasse 28
Hilton Wien, Am Stadtpark
**Selected Restaurants:**
Da Conte, Gottfried, Korso, Rotisserie Prinz Eugen
in the Hilton Hotel, Steirereck, Vier Jahreszeiten,
Zu den drei Husaren
**Banking:**
Hours are 8:00 A.M. to 12:30 P.M. and 1:30 P.M.
to 3:30 P.M. Monday, Tuesday, Wednesday, and
Friday; 1:30 P.M. to 5:30 P.M. on Thursday.

**Information Sources:**
Austrian National Tourist Office
500 Fifth Avenue
New York, New York 10110
212-944-6880

## Zurich, Switzerland
**Population:** 870,000
**Altitude:** 1,339 ft. (408m.)
**Average Temp.:** Jan., 31°F. (0°C.); July, 63°F.
(17°C.)
**Selected Hotels:**
Atlantis Sheraton, Doeltschiweg 234
Baur au Lac, Talstrasse 1
Bellerive au Lac, Utoquai 47
Carlton-Elite, Bahnhofstrasse 41
Dolder Grand, Kurhausstr. 65
Eden au Lac, Utoquai 45
Zum Storchen, Weinplatz 2
Zurich, Neumuhlequai 42
**Selected Restaurants:**
Agnes Amberg, Chez Max, Haus zum Ruden,
Kronenhalle, Rotisserie Lindenhofkeller, Veltliner
Keller, Zunfthaus zur Waage
**Banking:** Hours 8:30 A.M. to 4:30 P.M. Monday
through Friday; closed Saturday.
**Information Sources:**
Swiss National Tourist Office
608 Fifth Avenue
New York, New York 10020
212-757-5944

# World Travel Maps

## Inhabited Localities

The symbol represents the number of inhabitants within the locality

**At scales 1:6,000,000 to 1:12,000,000**

| | |
|---|---|
| • | 0–10,000 |
| ○ | 10,000–25,000 |
| ◉ | 25,000–100,000 |
| ◙ | 100,000–250,000 |
| ▣ | 250,000–1,000,000 |
| ■ | >1,000,000 |

**At 1:24,000,000 scale**

| | |
|---|---|
| • | 0–50,000 |
| ◉ | 50,000–100,000 |
| ◙ | 100,000–250,000 |
| ▣ | 250,000–1,000,000 |
| ■ | >1,000,000 |

**Urban Area** (area of continuous industrial, commercial, and residential development)

The size of type indicates the relative economic and political importance of the locality

Écommoy Lisieux **Rouen**

Trouville **Orléans** **PARIS**

### Capitals of Political Units

**BUDAPEST** Independent Nation

**Cayenne** Dependency (Colony, protectorate, etc.)

**Lasa** State, Province, etc.

### Alternate Names

**MOSKVA** / MOSCOW — English or second official language names are shown in reduced size lettering

**Volgograd** (Stalingrad) — Historical or other alternates in the local language are shown in parentheses

## Political Boundaries

**International** (First-order political unit)

Demarcated and Undemarcated

Indefinite or Undefined

Demarcation Line (used in Korea)

**Internal**

**State, Province, etc.** (Second-order political unit)

*MURCIA* **Historical Region** (No boundaries indicated)

## Transportation

Primary Road

Secondary Road

Navigable Canal

*Canal du Midi*

Tunnel

Ferry

## Hydrographic Features

Intermittent Stream

Rapids, Falls

Irrigation or Drainage Canal

Reef

*The Everglades* Swamp

Glacier
VATNAJÖKULL

*L. Victoria* Lake, Reservoir

*Tuz Gölü* Salt Lake

Intermittent Lake, Reservoir

Dry Lake Bed

## Topographic Features

| | | |
|---|---|---|
| Matterhorn 4478 | △ | Elevation Above Sea Level |
| 76 | ▽ | Elevation Below Sea Level |
| Mount Cook 3764 | ▲ | Highest Elevation in Country |
| Khyber Pass 1067 | ✕ | Mountain Pass |
| 133 | ▼ | Lowest Elevation in Country |

Elevations are given in meters, the Highest and Lowest Elevation in a continent are underlined

Sand Area

Lava

Salt Flat

ARCTIC OCEAN

GREENLAND
(Den.)

Beaufort Sea

VICTORIA
ISLAND

BAFFIN ISLAND

ICELAND

75°

RUSSIA

Arctic Circle

UNITED
STATES

Anchorage

Yellowknife

Hudson
Bay

Godthåb

UNITED
KINGDOM

60°

Bering Sea

ROCKY MTS

C A N A D A

Gulf of
Alaska

Winnipeg

NEWFOUNDLAND

IRELAND

LONDON

ALEUTIAN ISLANDS

Vancouver

NORTH
AMERICA

Montréal

FRANCE

45°

PACIFIC

SAN
FRANCISCO

UNITED STATES

CHICAGO

NEW YORK
Washington

ATLANTIC OCEAN

PORTUGAL SPAIN

LOS ANGELES

AÇORES AZORES
(Port.)

OCEAN

Mississippi

BERMUDA
(U.K.)

MOROCCO

30°

Tropic of Cancer

Houston

Gulf of Mexico

Miami

WESTERN
SAHARA

AL

HAWAIIAN ISLANDS
(U.S.)

MEXICO

CUBA

DOMINICAN
REPUBLIC

MAURI-
TANIA

A

15°

CIUDAD
DE MÉXICO

HAITI

PUERTO RICO
(U.S.)

SENEGAL

MALI

GUATEMALA

Caribbean Sea

HONDURAS

TRINIDAD AND
TOBAGO

GUINEA
SIERRA
LEONE

BURKINA
FASO

P

NICARAGUA

0°

Equator

O

PANAMA

VENEZUELA

GUYANA
FRENCH
GUIANA
SURINAME

Equator

L

ARCHIPIÉLAGO DE COLÓN
GALÁPAGOS ISLANDS
(Ec.)

ECUADOR

COLOMBIA

Y

Amazon

Belém

15°

N

AM.
SAMOA

ANDES

PERÚ

B R A Z I L

Recife

FIJI

E

SOUTH AMERICA

ATLANTIC OCEAN

TONGA

COOK
ISLANDS
(N.Z.)

FRENCH
POLYNESIA

S

BOLIVIA

Brasília

I

Tropic of Capricorn

PARAGUAY

RIO DE JANEIRO

30°

A

Asunción

SÃO PAULO

CHILE

PACIFIC

Santiago

URUGUAY
BUENOS AIRES

International Date Line

OCEAN

ARGENTINA

45°

FALKLAND ISLANDS
(U.K.)

60°

CABO DE HORNOS
CAPE HORN

Antarctic Circle

Bellingshausen Sea

Weddell Sea

75°

A    N    T    A    R

90° 180°  165°  150°  135°  120°  105°  90°   75°   60°   45°   30°   15°   0°

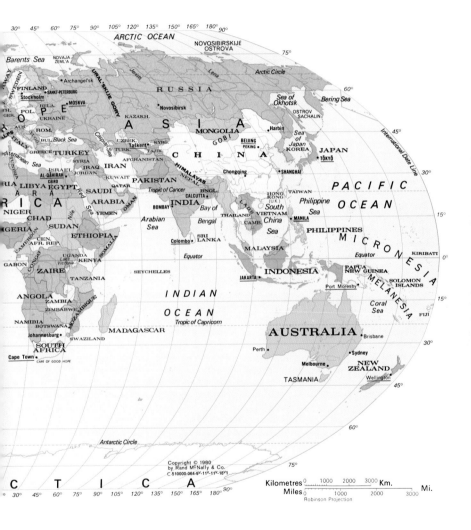

ARCTIC OCEAN

NOVOSIBIRSKIJE
OSTROVA

75°

Barents Sea

NOVAJA
ZEML'A

Jenisej

Lena

Arctic Circle

60°

SWEDEN

FINLAND

• Archangel'sk

RUSSIA

Sea of
Okhotsk

Bering Sea

Stockholm

SANKT-PETERBURG

• MOSKVA

• Novosibirsk

OSTROV
SACHALIN

EUROPE

BELA.

KAZAKH.

45°

POL

UKRAINE

ASIA

MONGOLIA

Harbin

Sea
of
Japan

JAPAN

International Date Line

GER.

AUS.

ROM.

UZBEK.

GOBI

BEIJING

KOREA

TÔKYÔ

ITALY

BUL.

Black Sea

Taškent

KYRG.

PEKING

30°

GREECE

TURKEY

Caspian Sea

TURK.

TAJIK.

CHINA

Mediterranean Sea

SYRIA

ISRAEL

IRAQ

IRAN

AFGHANISTAN

HIMALAYAS

Chongqing

• SHANGHAI

PACIFIC

AL-QÂHIRAH

JORDAN

NEPAL

CAIRO

KUWAIT

PAKISTAN

BNGL.

TAIWAN

OCEAN

LIBYA

EGYPT

QATAR

Tropic of Cancer

CALCUTTA

HONG
KONG

Philippine

15°

AFRICA

SAUDI
ARABIA

OMAN

INDIA

(U.K.)

South

Sea

NIGER

Red Sea

Nile

YEMEN

BOMBAY

Bay of

LAOS

VIETNAM

China

MANILA

CHAD

SUDAN

Arabian

Bengal

THAILAND

CAMB.

Sea

PHILIPPINES

NIGERIA

CEN.
AFR. REP.

ETHIOPIA

Sea

SRI
LANKA

MICRONESIA

CAMEROON

Colombo

MALAYSIA

Equator

KIRIBATI

GABON

CONGO

UGANDA

Lake
Victoria

KENYA

SEYCHELLES

Equator

0°

ZAIRE

TANZANIA

INDIAN

INDONESIA

PAPUA
NEW GUINEA

SOLOMON
ISLANDS

MELANESIA

ANGOLA

ZAMBIA

JAKARTA

Port Moresby

15°

ZIMBABWE

OCEAN

Coral
Sea

FIJI

NAMIBIA

MOZAMBIQUE

BOTSWANA

MADAGASCAR

Tropic of Capricorn

AUSTRALIA

• Brisbane

30°

Johannesburg •

SWAZILAND

SOUTH
AFRICA

Perth •

• Sydney

Cape Town •

CAPE OF GOOD HOPE

Melbourne •

NEW
ZEALAND

TASMANIA

Wellington

45°

60°

Antarctic Circle

75°

Copyright © 1980
by Rand M°Nally & Co.
C 510000-064-9ᵛ-11ᵛ-11ᵛ-18ᵛ1

CTICA

C        T        I        C        A

30°    45°    60°    75°    90°    105°   120°   135°   150°   165°   180°   90°

Kilometres  0    1000    2000    3000 Km.
Miles       0        1000        2000        3000        Mi.
Robinson Projection

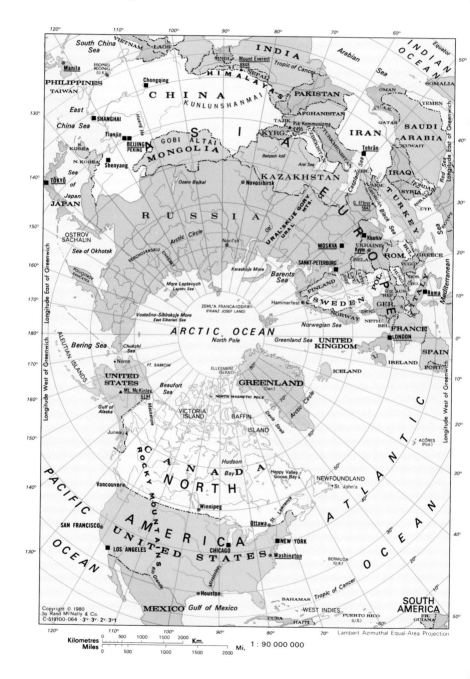

Copyright © 1980
by Rand McNally & Co.
C-519100-064 -3ᵛ-3ᵛ- 2ᵛ-3ᵛ⌐

Kilometres | 0  500  1000  1500  2000  Km.
Miles | 0  500  1000  1500  2000  Mi.

1 : 90 000 000

Lambert Azimuthal Equal-Area Projection

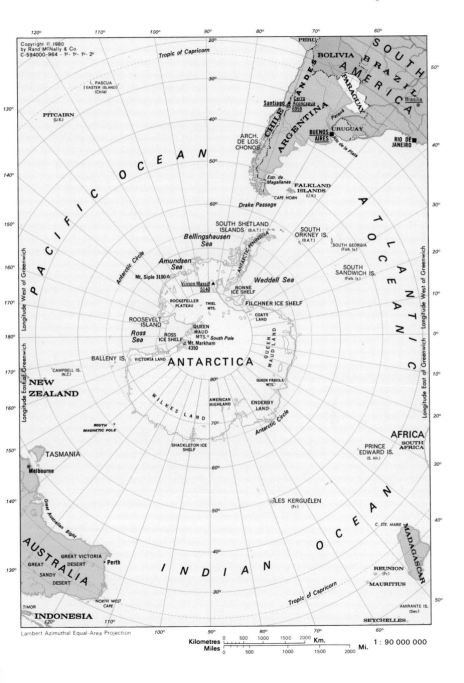

Lambert Azimuthal Equal-Area Projection

Kilometres

Miles

1 : 90 000 000

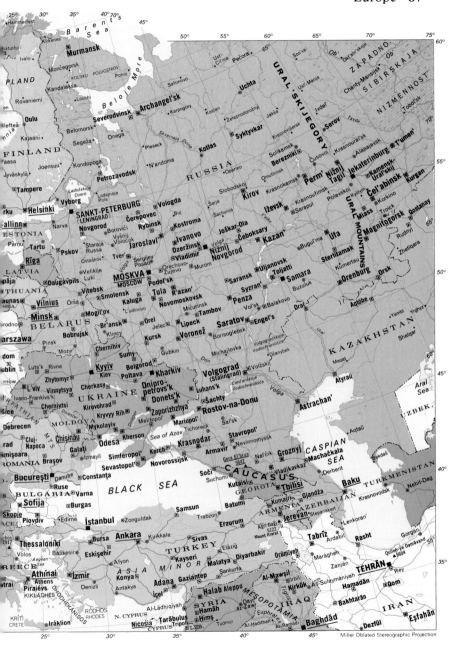

Miller Oblated Stereographic Projection

NORWEGIAN SEA

ATLANTIC

OCEAN

Arctic Circle

NORWAY

SWEDEN

FINLAND

RUSSIA

Gulf of Bothnia

Gulf of Finland

BALTIC SEA

Gulf of Riga

DENMARK

GERMANY

POLAND

ESTONIA

LATVIA

LITHUANIA

BELARUS

Skagerrak

Kattegat

NORTH SEA

NORDKAPP
NORTH CAPE

Hammerfest

Tromsø

Narvik

Bodø

Kiruna

Gällivare

Luleå

Oulu

Umeå

Östersund

Trondheim

Ålesund

Sundsvall

Gävle

Falun

Oslo

Uppsala

STOCKHOLM

Göteborg
Gothenburg

Helsinki
Helsingfors

SANKT-
PETERBURG

Turku
Åbo

Tampere

Vaasa
Vasa

Rovaniemi

KØBENHAVN
COPENHAGEN

Malmö

HAMBURG

Lübeck

Rostock

Szczecin
(Stettin)

Gdańsk
(Danzig)

Kaliningrad
(Königsberg)

Kaunas

Vilnius

Riga

Tallinn

Pskov

Vitebsk

GOTLAND

ÖLAND

BORNHOLM
(Den.)

AHVENANMAA
ÅLAND

Lambert Conformal Conic Projection

Kilometres 0  100  200  300 Km.

Miles 0  100  200  300 Mi.

1 : 13 000 000

Copyright © 1980
by Rand McNally & Co.
C-559500-064-5Y-8Y-7V-12V

Kilometres
Miles
1: 6 000 000

Launceston • Yeovil • Exeter • Portsmouth • Southampton • Havant • Crawley • Hastings • Folkestone • Gand • Gent
Newquay • Saint Austell • Weymouth • Lyme Bay • Torquay (Torbay) • Bournemouth • Worthing • Brighton • Calais • Saint-Omer • Roeselare • Kortrijk • BRUXELLE • BRUSSEL
Redruth • Truro • Plymouth • Boulogne-sur-Mer • Armentières • Roubaix • Nivelle
LAND'S END • Falmouth • LIZARD POINT

English Channel • La Manche

50°

Le Tréport • Rue • Lens • Valenciennes • Denain
Dieppe • Abbeville • Arras • Cambrai
GUERNSEY (U.K.) • St. Peter Port • Cherbourg • Saint-Valéry-en-Caux • CAUX • Neufchâtel-en-Bray • Péronne • Saint-Quentin • Hirs
CHANNEL ISLANDS • JERSEY (U.K.) • St. Helier • Barneville-Carteret • Valognes • Montivilliers • Bolbec • Marseille-en-Beauvaisis • Amiens
Baie de la Seine • Le Havre • Seine • Rouen • Beauvais • Noyon • Laon • Reth

49°

Saint-Pol-de-Léon • Perros-Guirec • Golfe de Saint-Malo • Carentan • Saint-Lô • Villers-Bocage • Troarn • Lisieux • Elbeuf • Compiègne • Creil • Soissons • Reims
ÎLE D'OUESSANT • Morlaix • St-Brieuc • Dinard • Saint-Malo • Villedieu • Avranches • Flers • Caen • Évreux • Mantes-la-Jolie • Versailles • Saint-Denis • Meaux • Château-Thierry • Châlons-sur-Marne
Brest • Guingamp • Dol-de-Bretagne • Domfront • Sées • L'Aigle • Dreux • Rambouillet • PARIS • Villeneuve-Saint-Georges • Esternay
Douarnenez • Châteaulin • Callac • Lamballe • Fougères • Mayenne • Alençon • Nogent-le-Rotrou • Chartres • Melun • Fontainebleau • Romilly-sur-Seine
POINTE DU RAZ • Crozon • Loudéac • Broons • Montfort • Sillé-le-Guillaume • Angerville • Montereau-faut-Yonne • Sens

48°

Quimper • Saint-Guénolé • Concarneau • Pontivy • Baud • Guichen • Rennes • Laval • Sarthe • Châteaudun • ORLÉANAIS • Château-Landon • Troy
Lorient • Auray • Vannes • Redon • Châteaubriant • Le Mans • Vendôme • Orléans • Atenay • Montargis • Châtillon-Coligny • Auxerre
Quiberon • Pontchâteau • Angers • ANJOU • Tours • Loire • Blois • Beaugency • La Ferté-Saint-Aubin • Tonnerre • Clamecy
BELLE ÎLE • Saint-Nazaire • Nantes • Loire • Vertou • Chalonnes-sur-Loire • Saumur • Château-du-Loire • Cher • Romorantin-Lanthenay • Cosne-sur-Loire • Corbigny

47°

Noirmoutier • Machecoul • Montaigu • Cholet • Thouars • Vienne • Sainte-Maure-de-Touraine • Vierzon • BERR • Bourges • Château-Chinon • Autu
Saint-Jean-de-Monts • Challans • Bressuire • Châtellerault • Saint-Amand-Mont-Rond • Nevers • Saint-Pierre-le-Moûtier • Montcea
Les Sables-d'Olonne • La Roche-sur-Yon • Luçon • Poitiers • Le Blanc • Châteauroux • Argenton-sur-Creuse • Chauvigny • Moulins • Paray-le-Monial • Charol

46°

ÎLE DE RÉ • Marans • Niort • Lussac-les-Châteaux • Guéret • Montluçon • Varennes-sur-Allier • Lapalisse
La Rochelle • Civray • Confolens • La Guerche-sur-l'Aubois • Chambon-sur-Voueize • Vichy • Roann
ÎLE D'OLÉRON • Rochefort • Ruffec • Lauriere • Aubusson • Auzances • Riom • Roann
Saintes • Charente • Saint-Junien • Bourg-Lastic • Puy de Sancy • Clermont-Ferrand • Lyon

ATLANTIC OCEAN

45°

POINTE DE LA COUBRE • Cognac • Angoulême • Limoges • Pierre-Buffière • Égletons • Puy de Sancy • Étienne
Royan • Châteauneuf-sur-Charente • Chálus • AVERGNE • MASSIF
Blaye-et-Sainte-Luce • Saint-Astier • Brive-la-Gaillarde • Dordogne • Murat • Yssingeaux • Langeac • Le P
Étang de Carcans • Coutras • Périgueux • Argentat • Saint-Chély-d'Apcher • Langoc
Mérignac • Ares • Bergerac • Gramat • Aurillac • CENTRAL

44°

Arcachon • La Teste-de-Buch • BORDEAUX • Dordogne • Cancon • Gourdon • Decazeville • Séverac-le-Château • La Canourgue • Grat
Étang de Cazaux • Langon • Cahors • Villefranche-de-Rouergue • Florac • Com
Mimizan • Captieux • Villeneuve-sur-Lot • Agen • Montauban • Rodez • Millau • Alès • Nîm
Morcenx • Tartas • Mont-de-Marsan • Castelsarrasin • Salles-Curan • Saint-Afrique • Saint-Hippolyte-du-Fort
Santander • Santona • Dax • ARMAGNAC • Fleurance • Gaillac • Albi • Millau • Lunel

43°

Santoña • Portugalete • Biarritz • Adour • Garlin • Auch • GASCOGNE • Toulouse • Castres • Montpellier • Sète
San Vicente de la Barquera • San Vicente de Baracaldo • San Sebastián • Bayonne • Vic-en-Bigorre • Boulogne-sur-Gesse • Muret • Mazamet • Saint-Pons • Béziers
Reinosa • Amurrio • Bilbao • Irún • Mauléon-Licharre • Pau • Saint-Gaudens • Carcassonne • Narbonne • Golfe
Herrera de Pisuerga • Villarcayo • Alsasua • Oloron-Sainte-Marie • Lourdes • Pamiers • Limoux • Perpignan
Osorno • Miranda de Ebro • Vitoria • Estella • Sabiñánigo • Bagnères-de-Bigorre • Tarascon • FRANCE • ESPAGNE • ANDORRA • Prades • Port-Vendres
Burgos • Briviesca • Logroño • Olite • Ebro • Jaca • PYRÉNÉES • Viella • Pico de Aneto 3404 • Llivia • FRANCE

Bay of Biscay

6° 5° 4° 3° 2° 1° 0° 1° 2° 3° 4°

Kilometres 0 50 100 150 Km.
Miles 0 50 100 150 Mi.
1: 6 000 000

Lambert Conformal Conic Projection

Bay of Biscay

43°

**El Ferrol
del Caudillo**
**La Coruña**

Cedeira
Vivero
Ribadeo
Mondoñedo
Luarca
Avilés
**Gijón**
Vimianzo
Grandas
Cangas
de Onís
**Oviedo**
**Santander**
Santoña
Portugalete
**San
Sebastián**
**San Vicente
de Baracaldo**
**Bilbao**

Betanzos
Ordenes
**Lugo**

G A L I C I A

A S T U R I A S

San Vicente
de la Barquera

C A N T Á B R I C A

Amurrio
Alsa

Padrón
**Santiago de
Compostela**

CORDILLERA

La Robla
Reinosa
Villarcayo
**Miranda
de Ebro**
**Vitoria**

Santa Eugenia
La Estrada
Monforte
de Lemos
**Ponferrada**
**León**
Guardo
Herrera de
Pisuerga
Osorno
Sedano
Haro
Briviesca
**Logroño**

**Pontevedra**
Astorga
La Bañeza
**Burgos**
Torrecilla en
Cameros
Calahorra

42°

**Vigo**
La Caniza
**Orense**
Puebla
de Trives
Telefo
2188
Valencia de
Don Juan
Asudillo
Palencia
Lerma
Agreda

La Guardia
Miño
Valença
Benavente
Medina
de Rioseco
**Valladolid**
Aranda
de Duero
El Burgo
de Osma
**Soria**

Viana do Castelo
Montalegre
Chaves
**Bragança**
Alcañices
Villalpando
Peñafiel
Duero
Almazán

41°

**Braga**
Vila Real
Mirandela
Toro
Tordesillas
Medina
del Campo
Riaza
Atienza

**Porto**
Douro
Vila Nova
de Foz Côa
Zamora
Fuentesaúco
Arévalo

**Vila Nova de Gaia**
São João
da Madeira
La Fregeneda
**Salamanca**
Peñaranda de
Bracamonte
**Segovia**
Lozoyuela
Jadraque
Molina de
Aragón

Aveiro
Albergaria-
a-Velha
Viseu
Pinhel
Ciudad
Rodrigo
La Fuente de
San Esteban
Colmenar
Viejo
**Guadalajara**

40°

Figueira
da Foz
**Coimbra**
Guarda
Estrela
1993
**Covilhã**
Belmonte
Guijuelo
Béjar
**Ávila**
**MADRID**
**Alcalá
de Henares**
Sacedón
**Cuen**

Pombal
Sertã
Castelo Branco
Hoyos
Plasencia
Pico de
Almanzor
2592
Navalcarnero
**Getafe**
Huete

**Leiria**
Torres
Novas
Vila Velha
de Ródão
Garrovillas
**Talavera
de la Reina**
Maqueda
**Aranjuez**
Tarancón

39°

Caldas
da Rainha
Azambuja
**Cáceres**
Navalmoral
de la Mata
Torrijos
Belvís de
la Jara
Mora
**Toledo**
Corral de
Almaguer
Motil
Palan

Vilafranca
de Xira
Santarém
Monforte
Valencia de
Alcántara
Montánchez
Trujillo
Logrosán
Villacañas
Alcázar
de San Juan
Quintanar
de la Orden

Cascais
**LISBOA** LISBON
Estremoz
Elvas
**Mérida**
Don
Benito
Herrera
del Duque
Piedrabuena
Daimiel
**Tomelloso**
La R

38°

Barreiro
**Setúbal**
Montemor-o-Novo
**Badajoz**
Cabeza
del Buey
**Ciudad
Real**
Manzanares
**Albacete**

Alcácer do Sal
Torrão
Évora
Alconchel
Almendralejo
Villafranca
de los Barros
Almadén
**Valdepeñas**
Alcaraz

Santiago do Cacém
Beja
Oliva de
la Frontera
Zafra
Barrancos
**Puertollano**

Odemira
Castro
Verde
Viana do
Alentejo
Fregenal
de la Sierra
Azuaga
Peñarroya-
Pueblonuevo
La Carolina
Orcera
Caravaca

37°

**Huelva**
Aracena
Constantina
**Córdoba**
Andújar
Bailén
**Linares**
Villacarrillo
La Sagra
2381

Portimão
Aliezur
Almodóvar
Calañas
Valverde
del Camino
Palma
del Río
Torredonjimeno
Fernán-Núñez
**Úbeda**
Mancha Real
Lo

CABO DE
SÃO VICENTE
Sagres
Albufeira
Faro
Ayamonte
Lepe
Bollullos par
del Condado
**Sevilla**
Carmona
Guadalquivir
**Écija**
Baena
**Jaén**
Baza
Vélez
Rubio
Huércal-
Overa

Golfo de
Cádiz
**Sanlúcar de
Barrameda**
Los Palacios
y Villafranca
Alcalá de
Guadaira
Osuna
Estepa
Lucena
**Granada**
Guadix
Sorbas

**El Puerto de Santa María**
**Cádiz**
**Jerez de
la Frontera**
**Morón de
la Frontera**
**Antequera**
Loja
Mulhacén
3478
**Almería**

San Fernando
Ronda
Alhaurín
el Grande
SISTEMAS
Motril
Adra
CABO DE

36°

Vejer de
la Frontera
Jimena de
la Frontera
Estepona
Torremolinos
**Málaga**

**Algeciras**
**Gibraltar** (U.K.)
Strait of Gibraltar

ATLANTIC

OCEAN

Conic Projection, Two Standard Parallels

**Tánger**
Tangier
**Ceuta** (Sp.)
Restinga
ISLA DE ALBORÁN
(Sp.)

Asilah
**Tétouan**
Souk-el-Arba-
des-Beni-Hassan

Larache
Al-Hoceima
**Melilla**
(Sp.)
Ghazaou

35°
**Ksar-el-
Kebir**
Bou
Bouhafsa
2120
R I F
**MOROCCO**
Aït Youssef
ou Ali
Selouane

Kilometres 0 50 100 150
Miles 0 50 100 150 Mi.
1: 6 000 000

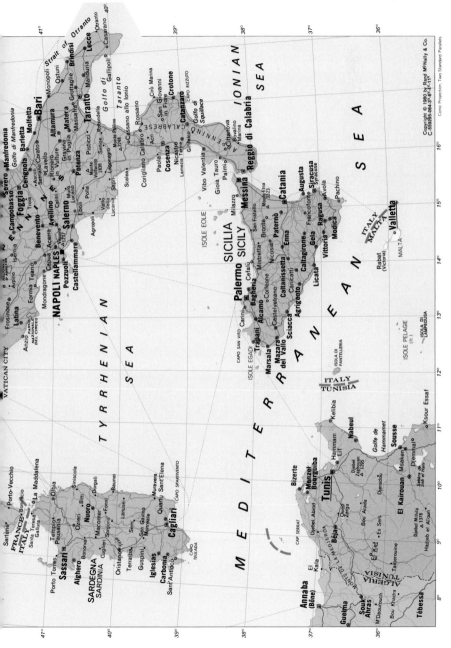

**100**

Copyright © 1980
by Rand McNally & Co.
C-579495-964 · 2v · 4v · 4v · 9v

Kilometres 0 50 100 150 Km.
Miles 0 50 100 150 Mi.
1: 6 000 000

33°  34°  35°  36°  37°  38°  39°  40°  41°  42°  43°  44°  45°

Ustje
zero  Lodejnoje Polje  Annenskij Most  Isakovo  60°
doga  Pavšozero  Levino  Ostrov  Ogibalovo  Kadnikovskij  Velikodvorskaja  Volockaja  Sergijevskaja  Pavolvo
virica  Alechovščina  Kožinskij  Zavod  Lipin Bor  Krutec  Suchon  Michajlovskij  Zelencovo
S'as'stroj  M'agozero  Krasnaja Gora  Ozero  Popovka  S'amža  Gora  Tot'ma  Starina
Kost'kovo  Bol'šaja Chundala  Beloje  Beloz'orsk  Žitjevo  Fominskoje  Kn'ažovo
Volchov  Radogošča  Pustin'  Sofronovo  Bičevinka  Ustje  Ceksino  Golub'  Jurenino  Nikol'skoje
lazevo  Tichvin  Čuny  Leonicha  Sokol  Šujskoje  Soligalič  Pankratovo
Boksitogorsk  Podborovje  Velikoje  Voskresenskoje  Moločnoje  Vologda  Vosja  Korcevo  Čuchloma  Kologriv
Budogošč  Somino  Babajevo  Šeksna  Kostroma  Korcevo  Bol'šaja Pas'ma
Nebolči  Sazonovo  Kaduj  Čerepovec  Fominskoje  Gr'azovec  Nikolo-Berezovec  Manturovo
l'šaja sera  Anciferovo  Chvojnaja  Imeni Žel'abova  Vanskoje  M'aksa  Baklanka  Buj  Loparovo  Ñeja
Malaja Višera  Zarubino  Ustreka  Vesjegonsk  DARVINSKIJ ZAPOVEDNIK  Pošechonje  Volodarsk  L'ubim  Galič  Kommunar
Okulovka  Vel'gija  Pestovo  Rybinskoje Vodochranilišče  Danilov  Severnoje  Voronjo  Makarjevo
Krestcy  Borovići  Lesnoje  Bol'šoje Ramenje  Ovinišče  Krasnyj Cholm  Rybinsk  Kostroma  Ostrovskoje  Gorčucha
Uglovka  Karel'skij Gorodok  Volga  Volga  Tutajev  Nekrasovskoje  Zavolžsk
Lyčkovo  Berezajka  Udoml'a  Sonkovo  Jaroslavl'  Jurjevec  Gorkovskoje
Bologoje  Bežeck  Vodochranilišče
nivo-Seliger  Trud  Vyšnij Voloček  Morkiny Gory  Uglič  Nerechta  Kinešma  Vičuga  Sokol'skoje  Puče?
ALDAJSKAJA  Firovo  Spirovo  Gavrilov-Jam  Furmanov  Okt'abr'skij  Gorodec
arevo  Ostaškov  Kalašnikovo  Kal'azino  Rostov  Petrovskoje  Ivanovo  Myt  NIŽNIJ
Peno  Kuvšinovo  Toržok  Vasiljevskij  Gora Tarchov  Cholm 294  Tejkovo  Šuja  Archipovka  Juža  NOVGOROD
eklino  Selizarovo  Moch  Kimry  Belyj Gorodok  Pereslavl'-Zalesskij  (GORKY)
Peno  Babino  Tver'  Dubna  Jurjev-  Gavrilov Posad  Kovrov  V'azniki  Dzeržinsk
VOZVYŠENNOST'  Suchoverkovo  Zaprudn'a  Pol'skij  Vladimir  Orgtrud  Stepancevo  Bogorodsk  Pavlovo
Nelidovo  Bachmutovo  Turginovo  Vysokovsk  Krasnozavodsk  Aleksandrov  Vača  Černucha
ZAPOVEDNIK  Ržev  Stepurino  Dmitrov  Sergijev Posad  Krasnoarmejsk  Sobinka  Murom  Kulebaki
Obuchova  Novos'olki  Sachovskaja  Volokolamsk  Solnečnogorsk  Kiržač  Krasnoje Echo  Vyksa  Ardatov
Žarkovskij  Tatarinka  Sereda  Istra  Mytišči  Balašicha  Orechovo-  Gus'-Chrustal'nyj  Košelicha
Vladimirskij Tupik  Syčovka  Ruza  MOSKVA  Zujevo  Rošal'  Melenki  Velikodvorskij  Jelat'ma
Cholm-  Novodugino  MOSCOW  Čerusti  Smilovo  MORDOVSKIJ
Žirkovskij  Gagarin  Možajsk  Aprelevka  L'ubercy  Domodedovo  Jegorjevsk  Velikodvorskij  Kasimov  Jermiš  ZAPOVEDNIK
Kasn'a  Naro-  Podol'sk  Voskresensk  Spas-Klepiki  Jelat'ma
algazovo  V'az'ma  Fominsk  Čechov  Kolomna  Beloomut  Murmino  Solotča  Poltevy
Peredel  Obninsk  Ozery  OKSKIJ ZAPOVEDNIK  Per'ki  Javas
arcevo  Safonovo  Klimov Zavod  Kondrovo  Serpuchov  Kašira  R'azan'  Spassk-R'azanskij  Čučkovo  At'urjevo
Koloďn'a  Mytišino  Ugra  Polotn'anyj  Jasnogorsk  Serebr'anyje  Mosolovo  Zubova  Torbejevo
Ozerišče  Jel'na  L'udkovo  Kaluga  Dugna  Venev  Prudy  Michajlov  Neznanovo  Poľana  Vyša
SKO  Spas-Demensk  Meščovsk  Peremyšl'  Leninskij  Tula  Sapožok  Sarai  Algasovo  Zemetčino
hislaviči  Jekimoviči  Voloje  Čerepet'  Škokino  Novomoskovsk  Ucholovo  Rasska?
Kirov  Šumici  Kozel'sk  Donskoj  Kimovsk  Skopin  R'ažsk  Moršansk
Roslavl'  Dubrovka  L'udinovo  Odojev  Bogorodick  Tovarkovskij  Gorn'ak  Starojurjevo  Basmakovo
Sum'ači  Dudorovskij  Chot'kovo  Budogošči  Meščenno  Aleksandro-Nevskij  Pervomajskij  Otjassy  Rudovka
ilbsfavič  D'at'kovo  Fokino  Jelenskij  Bolchov  Turdej  Dankov  Čaplygino  Tambov
Kletn'a  Mcensk  Korsakovo  Jefremov  Lebed'an'  Mičurinsk  Gorelovo  Rasskazovo
elynkovič  Br'ansk  Belyje Berega  Or'ol  Novosil'  Lamskoje  Kujman'  Lipeck  Belomestnaja Dvojn'a  Um'ot'
Suraž  Mglin  Sven'  Somovo  Kromy  Zmijovka  Izmalkovo  Syrskij  Gr'azi  Kotovsk  Inžavino
Klincy  Počep  Navl'a  Altuchovo  Dmitrovsk  Orlovskij  Livny  Jelec  Okt'abr'skoje  Usman'  Nižnaja Matrenka  Samaur  R'aksa-  Vysselki
Starodub  Trubč'ovsk  Belaja Ber'ozka  Železnogorsk  Maloarchangel'sk  Verchnij Lomovec  Talickij Čamlyk  Uvarovo
limovo  Sem'onovka  Znob'-Novgorodskoje  Sevsk  Fat'ož  Kolpny  Dolgoje  Urickoje  VORONEŽSKIJ ZAPOVEDNIK  Zerdevka  Šapkino  52°

33°  34°  35°  36°  37°  38°  39°  40°

Kilometres 0    200    400    600 Km.
Miles 0      200      400      600 Mi.     1 : 24 000 000

Lambert Conformal Conic Projection

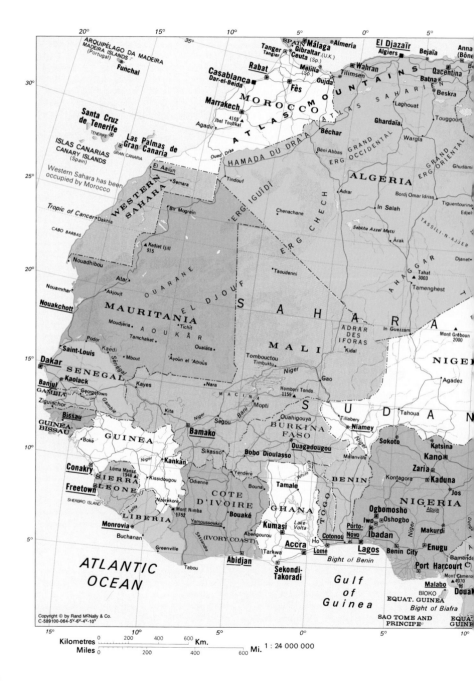

ARQUIPÉLAGO DA MADEIRA
MADEIRA ISLANDS
(Portugal)
Funchal

SPAIN
Tanger ■Málaga ■Almería
Tangier Gibraltar
Ceuta (U.K.)
(Sp.) Melilla
Casablanca Rabat
Dar-el-Beida ■ Oujda
Fès
Marrakech
Jbel Toubkal
Agadir 4165

Santa Cruz
de Tenerife
TENERIFE Las Palmas de
ISLAS CANARIAS Gran Canaria
CANARY ISLANDS GRAN CANARIA
(Spain)

Western Sahara has been
occupied by Morocco

El Djazaïr
Algiers Bejaïa Anna
(Bône
■Wahran Qacentina
Tilimsen Batna N Beskra
Laghouat Touggourt
Ghardaïa Wargla
Béchar Ghudami
El Aaiún HAMADA DU DRAA
Béni Abbas GRAND
ERG OCCIDENTAL
Tindouf ERG GRAND
Adrar ORIENTAL
Samara Chenachane Bordj Omar Idriss Tiguentourt
In Salah Edjel
Bir Mogrein Sebkha Azzel Metti TASSILI-N-AJJER
Kediet Ijill Árak
915 Djanet
Nouadhibou Taoudenni AHAGGAR
Atar Tahat
Nouamrhar Akjoujt Tamenghest 3003
Moudjéria Tichit ADRAR
Tamchaket AOUKÂR DES In Guezzam Mont Gréboun
Oualâta IFORAS 2000
Nouakchott MAURITANIA Kidal
Podor Kaédi Tombouctou
Saint-Louis Mbout Áyoûn el 'Atroûs Timbuktu Gao
Dakar SENEGAL Kayes Niger Agadez NIGE
Banjul Kaolack Nara Hombori Tondo
GAMBIA Georgetown 1155
Ziguinchor Kita MACIN Mopti
Bissau Ségou Bani Ouahigouya Tillabery Tahoua
GUINEA- Boké GUINEA Niger BURKINA Niamey
BISSAU Kankan FASO
Conakry Kissidougou Sikasso Bobo Dioulasso Ouagadougou Sokoto Katsina
SIERRA Odienne Bamako Malanville Kano
Freetown LEONE Nzérékoré Yendere Kontagora Zaria
SHERBRO ISLAND Mont Nimba Bouna Tamale BENIN Kaduna
LIBERIA 1752 COTE Ogbomosho Jos
Monrovia Yamoussoukro D'IVOIRE Bouaké GHANA TOGO NIGERIA
Buchanan Abengourou Kumasi Lake Iwo Oshogbo Abuja
Greenville (IVORY COAST) Volta Porto- Ibadan Makurdi
Tarkwa Ho Novo Benin City Enugu
Tabou Abidjan Accra Lomé Cotonou Lagos Port Harcourt
ATLANTIC Sekondi- Bight of Benin Malabo Doua
OCEAN Takoradi Gulf BIOKO
of EQUAT. GUINEA
Copyright © by Rand McNally & Co. Guinea Bight of Biafra
C-589100-064-5½-6½-4½-10½ SAO TOME AND EQUA
PRINCIPE GUINE

WESTERN SAHARA
Tropic of Cancer
Dakhla
CABO BARBAS
OUARANE
EL DJOUF
SAHARA
MALI
SUDAN

Kilometres 0 200 400 600 Km.
Miles 0 200 400 600 Mi. 1 : 24 000 000

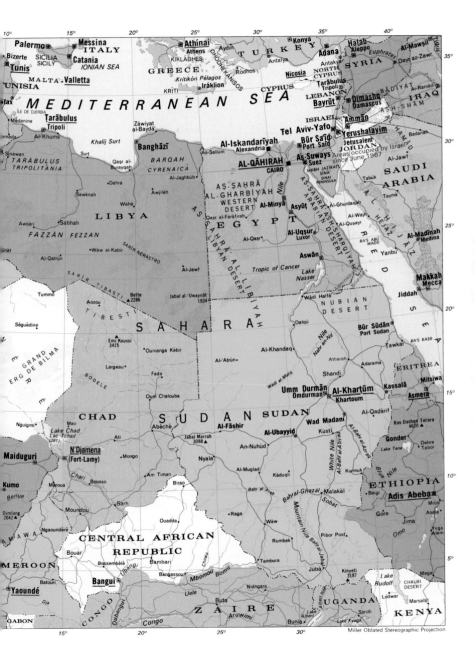

Palermo □
Messina
ITALY
Catania
Bizerte
SICILIA
SICILY
IONIAN SEA
Tunis ■
MALTA ■Valletta
TUNISIA
fax
ÎLE DE DJERBA
Médenine
Tarābulus
□Tripoli
Al-Khums
 amda
Sinawan
TARĀBULUS
TRIPOLITĀNIA
Awbārī •Sabhah
FAZZĀN FEZZAN
shāt
•Al-Qatrūn
Tummo
Séguédine

Athínai □
Aydin
GREECE
KIKLÁDHES
Kritikón Pélagos
KRÍTI •Iráklion

TURKEY
Antalya
Ródhos
DODEKÁNISOS
Konya
Adana
Halab
Aleppo
□Al-Mawşil
Euphrates
Dayr az-Zawr

MEDITERRANEAN SEA

Nicosia
NORTH
CYPRUS
CYPRUS
Tarābulus
Tripoli
LEBANON
Bayrūt ■

SYRIA

BĀDĪYAT
Al-Ramādi

□Dimashq
Damascus
ASH-SHĀM

IRAQ

Khalīj Surt
Zāwiyat
al-Bayḍā
□Banghāzī
Surt
Qaşr al-
Burayqah
BARQAH
CYRENAICA
Al-Jaghbūb
•Dahra
•Āwjilah

As-Sallūm
Al-Iskandarīyah
Alexandria

Bûr Sa'īd
Port Said

ISRAEL
Tel Aviv-Yafo ■
Yerushalayim
Jerusalem
Areas occupied by Israel
since June 1967

JORDAN

□'Amman

HAMĀD

•Badanah

Al-Jawf

SAUDI

AL-QĀHIRAH
CAIRO
AṢ-ṢAḤRĀ
AL-GHARBĪYAH
WESTERN
DESERT
Al-Minyā

As-Suways
Suez
SHIBH JAZĪRAT
SĪNĀ
SINAI
PENINSULA

Tabūk

Tayma

ARABIA

LIBYA

Sawknah
Waha
•Dahra

Qaşr al-Farāfirah

AṢ-ṢAḤRĀ

Asyūţ

Al-Ghurdaqah
Al-Wajh
AL HIJĀZ

Al-Qaşr
Al-Madīnah
Medina

Āl-Uqşur
Luxor

RA'S ABŪ
MĀDD

Yanbu'

AṢ-ṢAḤRĀ AL-LĪBĪYAH DESERT

SARĪR NERASTRO
•Wāw al-Kabīr

EGYPT

Aswān

Al-Jawf

Tropic of Cancer

Lake
Nasser

Makkah
Mecca

Jiddah

SARĪR TIBASTI
Bette
▲2286

Jabal al-'Uwaynāt
1934 ▲

Aozou

TIBESTI

SAHARA

Emi Koussi
3415 ▲

NUBIAN
DESERT

•Wādi Ḥalfā

Dalqū

Bûr Sūdān
Port Sudan

RA'S KASR

GRAND
ERG
DE BILMA

BODÉLÉ

•Ounianga Kébir

Largeau

•Fada

AṢ-ṢAḤRĀ

AL-ATRŪN

As-Sudd

Al-Khandaq

Abtarah
Atbarah

•Tawkar

Adarama

Shandi

ERITREA
Mitsiwa

Asmera

Nguigmi

Lake Chad
Lac Tchad
(281)

Mao
Ati

Abéché

CHAD

SUDAN

Umm Durmān
Omdurman
Al-Khartūm
Khartoum

Kassalā

Maiduguri

N'Djamena
(Fort-Lamy)

•Mongo

Jabal Marrah
3088 ▲

Al-Fāshir

Wad Madani

Al-Qaḍārif

Ras Dashen Terara
4620 ▲

Gonder

Debre
Tabor

Al-Ubayyiḍ

Kūsti

Kumo
Benue
Dimlang
2042 ▲

Maroua
Bousso

Chari

Am Timan

•Birao

An-Nuhūd

Kāduqlī

Nyala

Al-Muglad

Lake Tana

Ngaoundéré

Moundou

Sārh

Ouadda

•Raga

Bahr al-'Arab

Bahral-Ghazāl

Wāw

Mountain Nile Bahr al-Jabal

Malakāl

Sobat

•Beigi

Gore

ETHIOPIA

Adis Abeba

Mojo

Jima

Yirga
Alem

Asela

AIWA

Bouar

CENTRAL AFRICAN
REPUBLIC

Bossembélé

Bambari

Tambura

Rumbek

Pibor Post

Jūba

Kinyeti
3187 ▲

Lake
Rudolf

Mega

CHALBI
DESERT

Yaoundé ■

MEROON

Batouri

Dja

Bangui ■

Bangassou

Ubangi

Mbomu Bomu

Uele

Niangara

Buta

Lake
Albert

UGANDA

Lodwar

Marsabit

GABON

CONGO

ZAÏRE

Aruwimi

Lake
Kyoga

Soroti

KENYA

Congo

Bunia

*Soroti
*Mbale
NDA
*Eldoret
Mado
Gashi
SOMALIA
*Baraawe
*Afmadow
*Kirinyaga
5199
Lake
ictoria
Nakuru
KENYA
Bura
*Kismaayo
■Nairobi
SERENGETI
PLAIN
Kilimanjaro
5895
YATTA PLATEAU
*Lamu
*Shinyanga
wanza
Arusha
MASAI
STEPPE
*Voi
■Mombasa
*Singida
*Tabora
TANZANIA
Dodoma
Tanga
Zanzibar
PEMBA ISLAND
SEYCHELLES
• Victoria

*Kipembawe
*Iringa
Mikumi
*Morogoro
ZANZIBAR
■Dar es Salaam

AMIRANTE ISLANDS
(Sey.)
PLATTE ISLAND (Sey.)

Utete*
*Njombe
*Mahenge
Luwegu
Kilwa Kivinje
ALPHONSE ISLAND (Sey.)

ALDABRA ISLANDS
(Sey.)
PROVIDENCE ISLAND
(Sey.)

*Mzuzu
Manda
*Lindi
*Mtwara
ASTOVE ISLAND
(Sey.)
FARQUHAR GROUP
(Sey.)
AGALEGA ISLANDS
(Mauritius)

*Songea
Masasi
Rovuma
Lake
Nyasa
Lichinga
Montepuez
NJAZIDJA
Moroni• COMOROS
ÎLES GLORIEUSES
(Fr.)
CAP D'AMBRE
•Antsiranana

MALAWI
Lilongwe
Mandimba
*Maúa
Pemba
MAYOTTE
(Fr.)
*Dzaoudzi
NOSY BE
Andoany
*Iharana

Maromokotro
▲2876

TROMELIN
(Fr.)

Vila
Coutinho
Malema
Namapa
Analalava
*Antalaha

■Zomba
Blantyre
▲Sapitwa 3002
Nampula
Moçambique
Mahajanga
*Port-Bergé
*Maroantsetra

Tete
MOZAMBIQUE
Angoche
Marovoay
*Mananara
NOSY BARAHA

Quelimane
Pebane
Besalampy
Maevatanana
Tambohorano
Toamasina
■Antananarivo

Inyangani 2592
*Chinde
*Ankavandra
Belo
Antsirabe

Mutare
Monte Binga
▲2436
■Beira
MADAGASCAR
Morondava
Malaimbandy
*Ambositra
*Mahanoro

*Massangena
Nova Mambone
BASSAS DA INDIA
(Fr.)
Morombe
Beroroha
Fianarantsoa
Pic Boby
2658
*Manakara

PONTA SÃO SEBASTIÃO
PONTA DA BARRA FALSA
LE EUROPA
(Fr.)
Ankazobe
Toliara
*Betroka
Vangaindrano

*Inhambane
*Inharrime
Midongy
Atsimo
*Bekily
Androka
*Faradofay

*Xai-Xai
CAP SAINTE-MARIE

MAURITIUS
Port Louis•
Saint-Denis
RÉUNION
(Fr.)
MASCARENE
ISLANDS

Equator  0°

5°

10°

15°

Tropic of Capricorn  20°

25°

*INDIAN   OCEAN*
*INDIAN   OCEAN*

Copyright © 1980,1987
by Rand McNally & Co.
C-589200-064   -6ᵛᴵ -9ᵛᴵ -6ᵛ -17ᵛ

Kilometres
0   200   400   600  Km.
Miles
0   200   400   600  Mi.

1 : 24 000 000

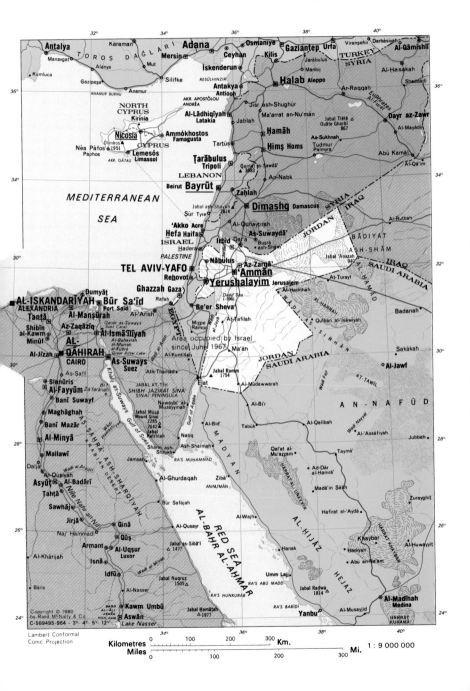

## The Middle East

Antalya • Karaman • **Adana** • Osmaniye • Viranşehir Darbāsiyah • **Al-Qāmishli**
Manavgat • Mersin • Ceyhan • Kilis • **Gaziantep** Urfa • Jarābulus • **TURKEY** • Al-Hasakah
Kumluca • Alanya • Mut • İskenderun • Manbij • **SYRIA** • Shaddādī
Gazipaşa • Silifke • RESÜLHINZIR • Antakya • Ar-Raqqah • Euphrates • **Dayr az-Zawr**
ANAMUR BURNU • Anamur • Antioch • Jisr ash-Shughūr • Ma'arrat an-Nu'mān • Jabal Tlété • Al-Mayādīn
**NORTH** • AKR. APOSTÓLOU • Al-Lādhiqīyah • Jablah • **Ḥamāh** • As-Sukhnah • Abū Kamāl
**CYPRUS** • ANDRÉA • Latakia • Tartūs • **Ḥimş** Homs • Tudmur Palmyra • Āl-Qa'im

MEDITERRANEAN SEA

**Ṭarābulus** • Qurnat as-Sawdā' 3083
Tripoli • An-Nabk

Beirut **Bayrūt** • **LEBANON**

Jabal ash-Shaykh 2814 • Zahlah • **Dimashq** Damascus • Ar-Rutbah
Şūr Tyre • Al-Qunayţirah • As-Suwaydā' • **JORDAN** • **IRAQ**
'Akko Acre • **Ḥefa** Haifa • Irbid Dar'a • Busra • **BĀDIYAT**
**ISRAEL** • Hadera • ash-Sham • **ASH-SHĀM**
**PALESTINE** • **Nābulus** • Az-Zarqā' • Jabal 'Anazah 940 • **SAUDI** • **IRAQ**
**TEL AVIV-YAFO** • **'Ammān** • Al-Hadīthah • Al-Ḥarrah • **ARABIA**
Rehovot • **Yerushalayim** Jerusalem • Al-Turayf
**Dumyāţ** • Ghazzah Gaza • Dead Sea (-396) • Badanah
**AL-ISKANDARĪYAH** • **Būr Sa'īd** • Rafah • **Be'er Sheva**
**ALEXANDRIA** • Port Said • Al-'Arīsh • Mizpe Ramon • Al-Tafilah • Qulban al-'Isāwiyah
**Ţanţā** • Az-Zaqāzīq • Al-Manşūrah • Ath-Thamad • Ma'ān • Sakākah
Shibīn • Al-Buḥayrah • **Al-Ismā'īlīyah** • Area occupied by Israel since June 1967 • **Al-Jawf**
al-Kawm • Al-Kubra • **JORDAN**
Minūf • **AL-** • Great Bitter Lake • Al-Kuntillah • **SAUDI ARABIA**
Al-Jīzah • **QĀHIRAH** • **As-Suways** • Jabal Ramm 1754
**CAIRO** • Suez • Elat • Al-Mudawwarah
Sinnūris • Khalīj as-Suways • JABAL AT-TIH • Al-Bi'r • **AN-NAFŪD**
**Al-Fayyūm** • SHIBH JAZĪRAT SĪNĀ' • Wadi Fajr • AT-TAWIL
Banī Suwayf • SINAI PENINSULA • Al-Qalībah
Maghāghah • Nuwaybi' al-Muzayyinah • Wadi Nayyal • Al-'Assāfiyah
Banī Mazār • Jabal Mūsā Mount Sinai 2285 • Tabūk • Jubbah
**Al-Minyā** • Jabal Katharīnah 2642 • Al-Bid' • Taymā'
Mallawī • Nabq • Ash-Sharmah • Qal'at al-Mu'azzam
Dairut • Sharm ash-Shaykh • Ad-Dār al-Hamrā'
**Asyūţ** • **Al-Badārī** • Jamsah • Ziba' • Madā'in Sāliḥ
Al-Qūsīyah • RAS MUHAMMAD • AN-NU'MĀN • Zurayghit
Ṭahṭā • Al-Ghurdaqah • Hafīrat al-'Aydā'
Sawhāj • Būr Safājah • Al-Wajh • AL-HIJĀZ
Jirjā • **Qinā** • Al-Qusayr • HARRAT AL-'UWAYRIḌ • Khaybar • Al-Huwayyit
Naj' Hammādī • **Qūş** • Jabal as-Sibā'ī 1477 • Hanak • Hadiyah
Armant • **Al-Uqşur** Luxor • Umm Lajj • Jabal Radwa 1814 • Abū Na'am • HEJAZ
Al-Khārijah • Isnā • Jabal Nuqrus 1505 • RAS ABŪ MADD
Bāris • Idfū • RAS HUNKURAB • RAS BARIDI • **Al-Madīnah** Medina
Al-Nasser • RED SEA AL-BAHR AL-AHMAR • Jabal Ḥamāṭah 1977 • Yanbu • Al-Musayjid • HARRAT KURAMĀ
Kawm Umbū • **Aswān** • Lake Nasser

Lambert Conformal Conic Projection

Kilometres 0 100 200 300 Km.
Miles 0 100 200 300 Mi.

1 : 9 000 000

The boundary between India and Pakistan through the disputed state of Jammu and Kashmir follows the "line of control" agreed upon by both countries in 1972.

Copyright © 1980,1987 by Rand McNally & Co.
C-569400-964 - 7ᵛ- 5ᵛ- 15ᵛ

Lambert Conformal Conic Projection
1 : 24 000 000

Kilometres 0 200 400 600 Km.
Miles 0 200 400 600 Mi.

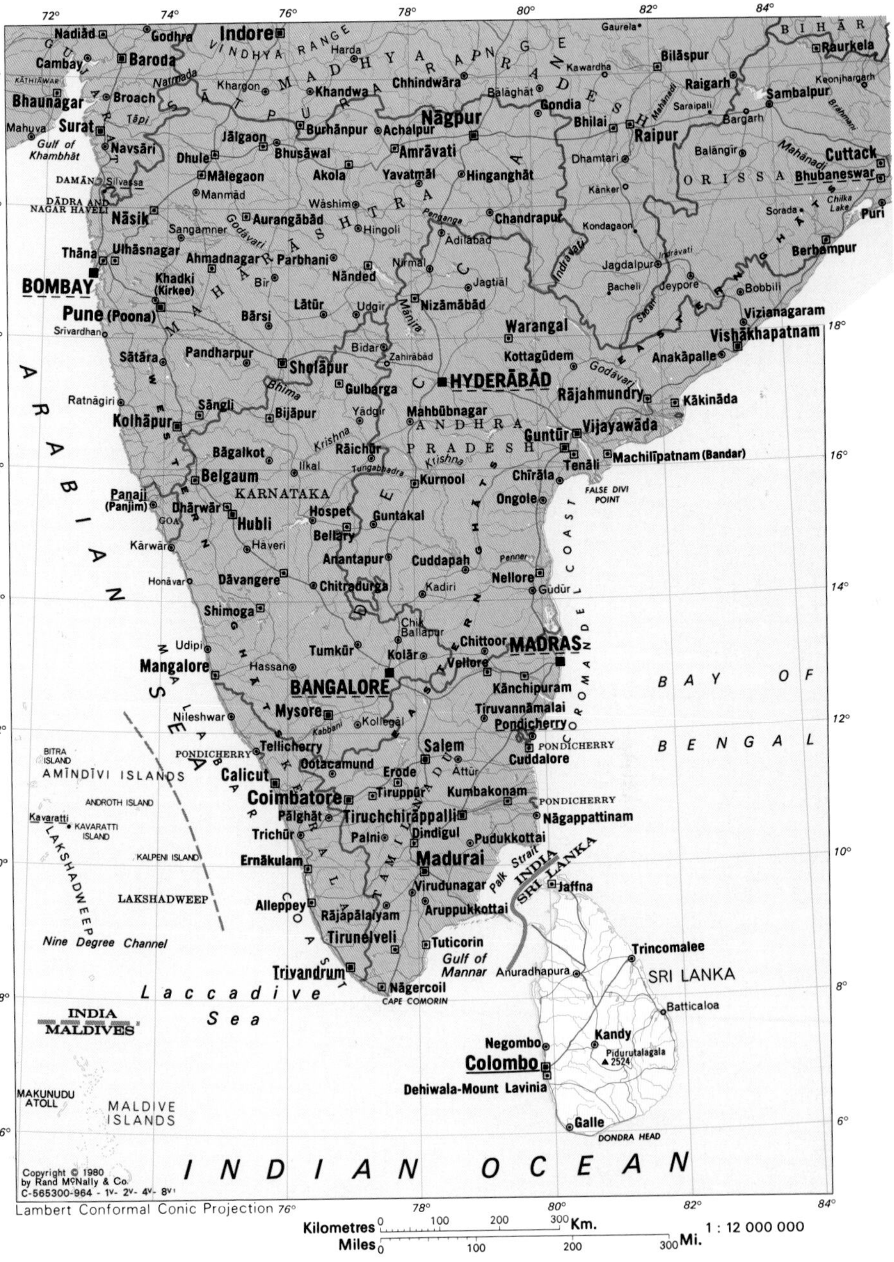

72° 74° 76° 78° 80° 82° 84°

BIHĀR

Nadiād • Godhra Indore VINDHYA RANGE Gaurela Raurkela
Cambay Baroda Harda MADHYA PRADESH Bilāspur
Bhaunagar KATHIAWAR Narmada Khargon Chhindwāra Kawardha Raigarh Kenojharngarh Sambalpur
Mahuva Broach Tāpti Khandwa Balāghat Gondia Bilai Saraipali Bargarh Brahmani
Surat Navsāri Jālgaon Burhānpur Achalpur Nāgpur Raipur Balāngir Mahānadi Cuttack
Gulf of Khambhāt Dhule Bhusāwal Amrāvati Dhamtari ORISSA Bhubaneswar
DAMĀN Silvassa Mālegaon Akola Yavatmāl Hinganghāt Kānker Sorada Chilka Lake Puri
DĀDRA AND NAGAR HAVELI Manmād Wāshim Chandrapur Kondagaon Berhampur
Nāsik Sangamner Godavari Hingoli Ādilābad Jagdalpur Indrāvati Jeypore Bobbili
Thāna Ulhāsnagar Aurangābād Parbhani Nirmal Bacheli Vizianagaram
BOMBAY Ahmadnagar Bir Nānded Jagtiāl Vishākhapatnam
Khadki (Kirkee) Lātūr Udgir Nizāmābād Warangal Anakāpalle
Pune (Poona) Bārsi Bidar Zahirābād Kottagūdem Godāvari Rājahmundry Kākināda
Srivardhan Pandharpur Sholāpur Gulbarga Mahbūbnagar HYDERĀBĀD Vijayawāda
Sātāra Bhima Yādgir ANDHRA Guntūr Machilīpatnam (Bandar)
Ratnāgiri Sāngli Bijāpur Krishna PRADESH Tenāli FALSE DIVI POINT
Kolhāpur Bāgalkot Rāichūr Kurnool Chīrāla
Panaji (Panjim) Belgaum Ilkal Tungabhadra Ongole
Dhārwār GOA KARNATAKA Hospet Guntakal
Kārwār Hubli Haveri Bellary Cuddapah Penner Nellore
Honāvar Dāvangere Chitradurga Kadiri Gudūr
Shimoga Chik Ballāpur BAY OF BENGAL
Udipi Tumkūr Kolār Chittoor MADRAS
Mangalore Hassan Kabbani BANGALORE Vellore Kānchipuram
Nileshwar Kolleggal Mysore Tiruvannāmalai CORMANDEL COAST
Tellicherry PONDICHERRY Pondicherry
BITRA ISLAND Ootacamund Salem PONDICHERRY
AMĪNDIVI ISLANDS Calicut Erode Cuddalore
Kavaratti KAVARATTI ISLAND Coimbatore Attūr
ANDROTH ISLAND Pālghāt Tiruppūr Kumbakonam PONDICHERRY
KALPENI ISLAND Trichūr Tiruchchirāppalli Nāgappattinam
LAKSHADWEEP Ernākulam Palni Dindigul Pudukkottai
Nine Degree Channel Alleppey Madurai INDIA SRI LANKA
INDIA Virudunagar Aruppukkottai Jaffna
MALDIVES Rājapālaiyam Palk Strait
MAKUNUDU ATOLL Tirunelveli Tuticorin
MALDIVE ISLANDS Trivandrum Gulf of Mannar Trincomalee
Nāgercoil Anuradhapura SRI LANKA
CAPE COMORIN Batticaloa
Laccadive Sea Negombo Kandy Pidurutalagala ▲2524
Colombo
Dehiwala-Mount Lavinia Galle DONDRA HEAD

ARABIAN SEA

INDIAN OCEAN

Copyright © 1980
by Rand McNally & Co.
C-565300-964 - 1V - 2V - 4V - 8V

Lambert Conformal Conic Projection

Kilometres 0 100 200 300 Km.
Miles 0 100 200 300 Mi.
1 : 12 000 000

**112**

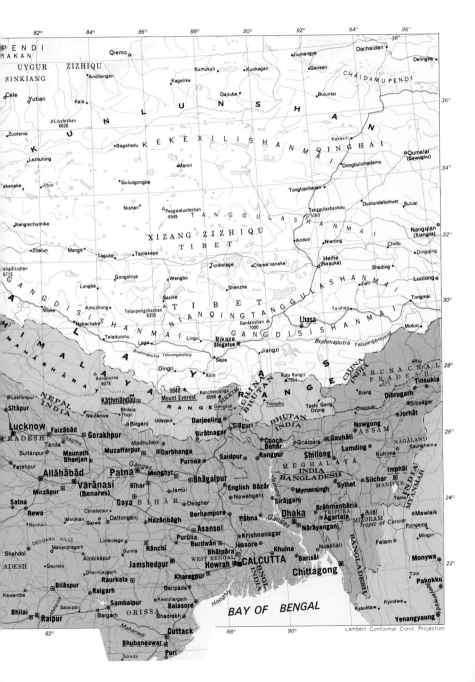

PENDI
MAKAN

UYGUR ZIZHIQU
SINKIANG

Qiemo

Jiumanya

Dachaidan

Delingha

38°

Kumukuli

Kuokegan

Gansen

CHAIDAMU PENDI

Cele

Andilangan

Kagelike

Dajiuba

Buluntai

Qumalai
(Sewugou)

36°

Yutian

Kala

Liushishan
6626

KUNLUNSHAN

KEKEXILISHANMAI

Kekexili

QINGHAI

Zuotema

Lazhulong

Bagehadu

Manni

Dongbulizhadamu

34°

akenake

Jituo

Guluogongba

Tongtianheyan

Tanggulashankou
5180

Duolundabohuer

Sulusi

Kangnichumike

Nishan

Pengwaluoteshan
6549

TANGGULASHANMAI

Anduo

Nierong

Chidu

Dingqing

32°

angdisishan
6715

Zhalun

Mange

Taguke

Taolakepa

XIZANG ZIZHIQU
TIBET

Tuobalage

Chawa'nanake

Heihe
(Naquka)

Shading

Luolong

Longka

Gongshiya

Wengbo

Shenzha

Jiali

Taizhao

Tongmai

30°

G
A
N
G
D
I
S
I
S
H
A
N
M
A
I

Nloke

Nakechake

Amuzhong

Teladuomu

Telaopengshashan
6355

Saxike

Lingu

TIBET

NIANQINGTANGGULASHANMAI

Ganlanshan
7000

GANGDISISHANMAI

Lhasa

Brahmaputra Yaluzangbujiang

Motuo

H
I
M
A
L
A
Y
A

MAHĀBHĀRAT

Brahmaputra Yaluzangbujiang

Dingri

Xilin

Rikaze
Shigatse

Sajia

Jiangzi

CHINA
INDIA

ARUNACHAL
PRADESH

Tinsukia

28°

Lakhimpur

NEPAL
INDIA

Annapurna
8078

8848
Mount Everest

Kānchenjunga
8598

SIKKIM

Kula Kangri
7554

CHINA
BHUTAN

RANGE

Riu

Riang

Dibrugarh

Sibsagar

Sitāpur

Nautanwa

Bhīkha
Thori

Udaypur

Birganj

RANGE

Gangtok

Thimphu

Tashi Gang
Dzong

Charduar

Jorhāt

Lucknow

Faizābād

Gorakhpur

Madhubani

Darjeeling

Siliguri

BHUTAN
INDIA

Nowgong

ASSAM

Lumding

NĀGALAND

26°

PRADESH

Sultānpur

Tānda

Bhagtra

Muzaffarpur

Darbhanga

Purnea

Saidpur

Cooch
Behār

Goālpara

Gauhāti

Kohima

Kaungbein

Fatehpur

Maunath
Bhanjan

Ganges

Rangpur

Shillong

MEGHALAYA

Imphāl

INDIA
MANIPUR
MYANMAR

24°

Allāhābad

Patna

Monghyr

Bhāgalpur

English Bāzār

Nawābganj

BANGLADESH

Sylhet

Silchar

Mirzāpur

Vārānasi
(Benares)

Bihār

Jamui

Deoghar

Mymensingh

Sirājganj

Brāhmanbāria

Agartala

Tamu

Mawlaik

Satna

Gaya

BIHĀR

Chhatarpur

Daltonganj

Garwa

Berhampore

Pābna

Ganges

Dhaka

Nārāyanganj

TRIPURA

Aijal

MIZORAM

Pyingaing

Rewa

Beohari

Waidhan

Hazāribāgh

Lohārdaga

Asansol

Purūlia

Krishnanagar

Jessore

Khulna

Noākhāli

Falam

Mingin

Shahdol

Manendragarh

Gumia

Rānchi

Burdwān

Bhātpāra

Barisāl

Monywa

22°

ADESH

Gaurela

Ambikāpur

Dharmjaygarh

Jamshedpur

WEST BENGAL

Howrah

CALCUTTA

BANGLADESH

Kawardha

Bilāspur

Raigarh

Kharagpur

Chittagong

BENGAL
INDIA

Pakokku

Bhilai

Saraipali

Sambalpur

Keonjhargarh

Balasore

Hooghly

Kyauktaw

Kyindwe

Yenangyaung

Raipur

Bargarh

ORISSA

Bhadrakh

BAY OF BENGAL

Tilin

82°

Mahānadi

88°

90°

Lambert Conformal Conic Projection

Cuttack

Bhubaneswar
Puri

Sorada

82°          84°          86°          88°          90°          92°          94°          96°

Kilometres 0 200 400 600 Km.

Miles 0 200 400 600 Mi.

1 : 24 000 000

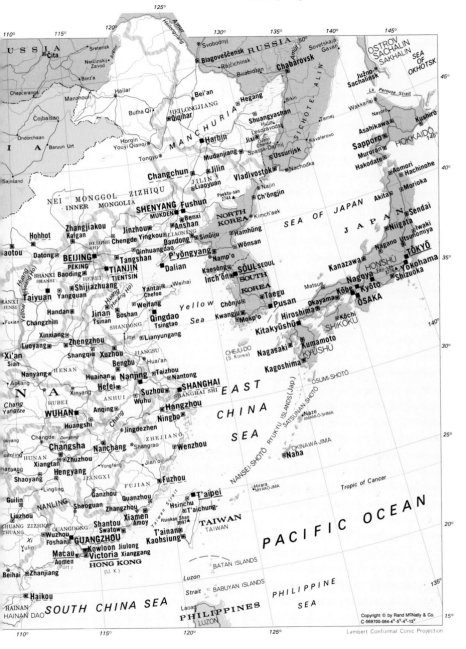

Lambert Conformal Conic Projection

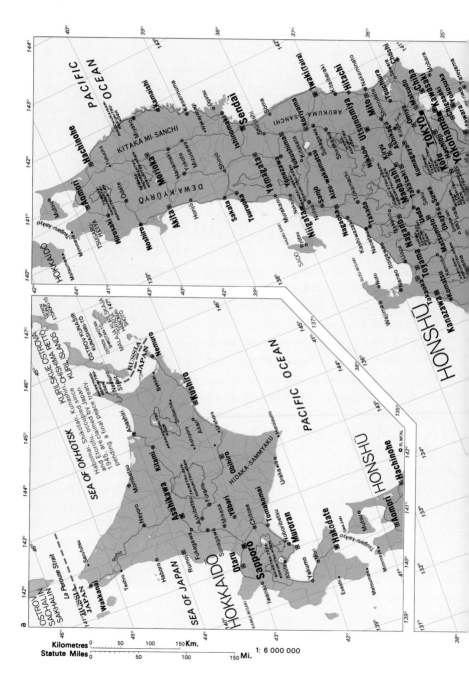

**a**

OSTROV
SACHALIN
SAKHALIN

La Perouse Strait

141° RUSSIA
JAPAN

SEA OF OKHOTSK

OSTROVA
KURILSKIE OSTROVA
KURIL'SKIE CHISHIMA RETTO
KURIL ISLANDS

RUSSIA
JAPAN

Russia. Shikotan, occupied Japan
and Etorofu, ceded by treaty.
Habomai, claimed since
1945, are claimed by
pending a final peace
treaty.

Wakkanai

HOKKAIDO

Asahikawa

Kitami

Nemuro

Kushiro

HIDAKA-SAMMYAKU

Obihiro

Otaru

Sapporo

Muroran

Tomakomai

Noboribetsu

Hakodate

SEA OF JAPAN

PACIFIC OCEAN

HONSHŪ

Aomori

Hachinohe

Tsugaru kaikyo

Kilometres 0   50   100   150 Km.
Statute Miles 0        50        100        150 Mi.

1: 6 000 000

PACIFIC OCEAN

Hachinohe

Aomori

Hirosaki

Noshiro

Akita

TSUGARU

HOKKAIDO

Mutsu

Tsugaru kaikyo

KITAKA MI-SANCHI

Kamaishi

Morioka

DEWA KYŪRYŌ

Honjo

Sakata

Tsuruoka

Kesennuma

Sendai

Ishinomaki

ABUKUMA-SANCHI

Yamagata

Yonezawa

Fukushima

Aizu-wakamatsu

Niigata

Nagaoka

Takada

Toyama

Nagano

Matsumoto

Suwa

Iwaki (Taira)

Hitachi

Mito

Utsunomiya

Nikko

Maebashi

Ueda

Takasaki

Chiba

TOKYO

Yokohama

Kawasaki

Ōmiya

HONSHŪ

KANTŌ

Kanazawa

Komatsu

Takaoka

Noto

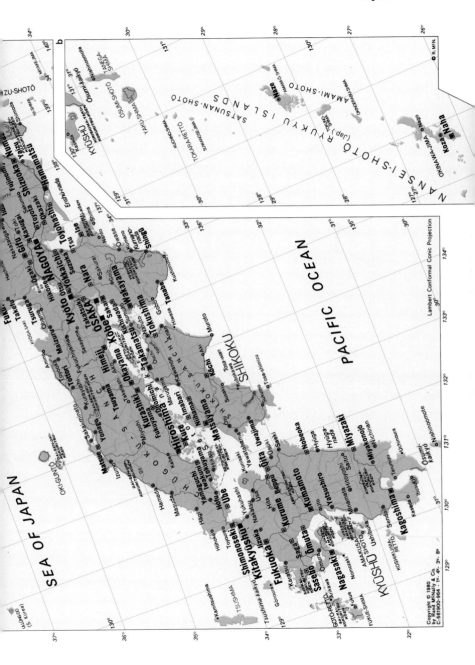

SEA OF JAPAN

PACIFIC OCEAN

KYUSHU

SHIKOKU

NANSEI-SHOTO RYUKYU ISLANDS

SATSUNAN-SHOTO (Jap.)

AMAMI-SHOTO

TOKARA-RETTO

OSUMI-SHOTO

OKINAWA-JIMA

Koza Naha

Naze

Nishinoomote

ZU-SHOTO

OKI-GUNTO

GOTO-RETTO

TSUSHIMA

Lambert Conformal Conic Projection

Copyright © 1980
by Rand McNally & Co.
C-561900-964 - IV - 4v - 3v - 8V

NAGOYA
OSAKA
Kyoto
Kobe
Hiroshima
Fukuoka
Nagasaki
Kagoshima
Kumamoto
Miyazaki
Kochi
Takamatsu
Tokushima
Matsuyama
Wakayama
Nara
Tsu
Gifu
Shizuoka
Hamamatsu
Numazu
Fukui
Tsuruga
Maizuru
Tottori
Matsue
Yonago
Okayama
Kurashiki
Himeji
Ise
Yokkaichi
Suzuka
Ube
Yamaguchi
Shimonoseki
Kitakyushu
Sasebo
Omuta
Kurume
Oita
Beppu
Saga
Yatsushiro
Nobeoka
Imabari
Niihama
Uwajima

Kilometres 0  200  400  600 Km.

Miles 0  200  400  600 Mi.

1 : 24 000 000

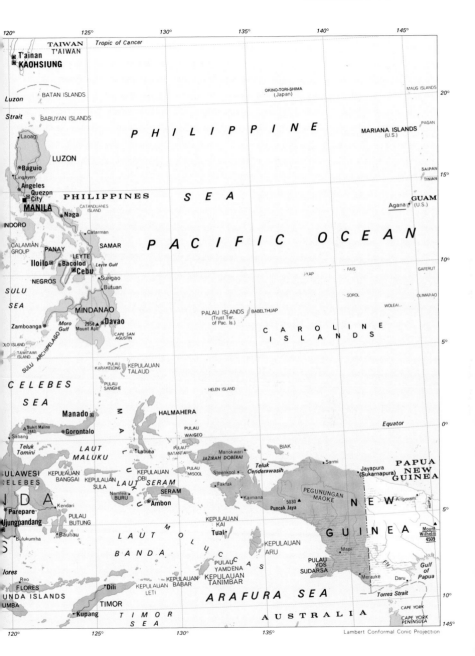

TAIWAN
T'AIWAN
T'ainan
KAOHSIUNG

Tropic of Cancer

OKINO-TORI-SHIMA
(Japan)

MAUG ISLANDS

*Luzon*   BATAN ISLANDS

PAGAN

*Strait*   BABUYAN ISLANDS

MARIANA ISLANDS
(U.S.)

P H I L I P P I N E

Laoag

LUZON

Baguio
Lingayen
Angeles
Quezon
City
MANILA   Naga

SAIPAN
TINIAN

S E A

PHILIPPINES

CATANDUANES
ISLAND

GUAM
Agana   (U.S.)

INDORO

Catarman

P A C I F I C   O C E A N

CALAMIAN
GROUP   PANAY   SAMAR

Iloilo   Bacolod   LEYTE
Cebu   Leyte Gulf

YAP   FAIS   GAFERUT

NEGROS
Surigao
Butuan

SULU
SEA   MINDANAO
Zamboanga   Moro   2954   Davao
Gulf   Mount Apo
CAPE SAN
AGUSTIN

SOROL   OLIMARAO

WOLEAI

PALAU ISLANDS   BABELTHUAP
(Trust Ter.
of Pac. Is.)

C A R O L I N E
I S L A N D S

OLO ISLAND
TAWITAWI
ISLAND
SULU ARCHIPELAGO

PULAU
KARAKELONG   KEPULAUAN
TALAUD

HELEN ISLAND

C E L E B E S

S E A

PULAU
SANGIHE

Manado   HALMAHERA

Bukit Malino
2443   Gorontalo
Sabang

Equator

PULAU
WAIGEO

Teluk
Tomini   LAUT
MALUKU

PULAU
BATANTA   Labuha   Manokwari   BIAK
JAZIRAH DOBERAI
PULAU
MISOOL   Teluk
Cenderawasih   Sarmi
Steenkool   Jayapura   PAPUA
(Sukarnapura)   NEW
GUINEA

ULAWESI
CELEBES   KEPULAUAN
BANGGAI   KEPULAUAN
SULA   LAUT   KEPULAUAN
OBI   Fakfak
SERAM   Arigoram

NDA   Kendari   SERAM
Namlea   Ambon   Kaimana   PEGUNUNGAN
MAOKE   N E W
BURU   5030   Puncak Jaya

Parepare
Ujungpandang   PULAU
BUTUNG

Bulukumba   Baubau   Tual   G U I N E A
Mount
Wilhelm
4509

KEPULAUAN
KAI

LAUT   Mapi

BANDA   KEPULAUAN
ARU

PULAU
YOS
SUDARSA

Gulf
of
Papua

lores
Reo
FLORES
UNDA ISLANDS
UMBA   Kupang   PULAU
YAMDENA   KEPULAUAN
TANIMBAR   Mapi
Merauke   Daru

KEPULAUAN BABAR
LETI

Dili

TIMOR

T I M O R
S E A

A R A F U R A   S E A

Torres Strait

CAPE YORK

A U S T R A L I A   CAPE YORK
PENINSULA

Lambert Conformal Conic Projection

Kilometres
0    200   400   600 Km.

Statute Miles
0         200        400      600 Mi.

1 : 24 000 000

a    *S e a*

135°        140°        145°        150°        155°

Daru    Gulf of    **Port**    D'ENTRECASTEAUX    TROBRIAND    VELLA    Giro.    SANTA
Papua    **Moresby**    ISLANDS    LAVELLA    NEW    ISABEL
WESSEL ISLANDS    OWEN STANLEY RANGE    **PAPUA**    GEORGIA
CAPE    **NEW GUINEA**    WOODLARK    **SOLOMON**
YORK    **NEW GUINEA**    ISLAND    **ISLANDS**    Honiara 160°
CAPE ARNHEM    CAPE    Solomon Sea    Mt. Popomanaseu
YORK    LOUISIADE ARCHIPELAGO    2331
GROOTE    Gulf    PENINSULA    TAGULA    ROSSEL    10°
EYLANDT    of    ISLAND    ISLAND
Limmen Bight    Carpentaria    PENINSULA    RENNELL

BARKLY TABLELAND    MORNINGTON    Cooktown    C o r a l
ISLAND
Mitchell    S e a    15°
nnant    Normanton    Ravenshoe    **Cairns**    WILLIS GROUP
eek    (Austl.)
HINCHINBROOK    GREAT BARRIER REEF    TREGOSSE ISLETS
ISLAND    (Austl.)
**GREAT**    Flinders    Hughenden    **Townsville**    ÎLES
Mount    Cloncurry    CUMBERLAND    CHESTERFIELD    ÎLE DE SABLE
Isa    ISLAND    (N. Cal.)    (N. Cal.)    20°
Georgina    **DIVIDING**    Winton    Mackay
RANGES    **QUEENSLAND**    SWAIN
Hay    SIMPSON    **GREAT ARTESIAN**    Emerald    REEFS    CAYE DE
A L I A    DESERT    **RANGE**    Blackall    Rockhampton    SAUMAREZ    L'OBSERVATOIRE
CURTIS I.    REEF    (N. Cal.)
Finke    Theodore    Tropic of Capricorn
**BASIN**    Quilpie    Bundaberg    CATO
ISLAND    25°
AUSTRALIA    GREY    Charleville    Mount Kiangarow    FRASER ISLAND
Lake Eyre    RANGE    1135    Maryborough    **PACIFIC**
North    Paroo    Saint George    **Toowoomba**    **Brisbane**
(Dry Salt Lake)    STURT    Warrego    **Ipswich**    **OCEAN**    165°
Lake Eyre    DESERT    Milparinka    Tenterfield    Lismore    MIDDLETON REEF
South    Walgett    Round Mountain
Lake    Woomera    Bourke    1608    Grafton
Torrens    Saint Mary    **Broken**    Darling    Tamworth    LORD HOWE ISLAND
Lake    Peak    **Hill**    Macquarie    Port    (N.S.W.)
Gairdner    1165    Nyngan    Macquarie    30°
SAWLER RANGES    Peterborough    **NEW SOUTH WALES**    Dubbo
EYRE PENINSULA    Port Pirie    Orange    **Newcastle**
Port    Spencer    Murray    Mildura    **SYDNEY**
ncoln    Gulf    Hay    **Wollongong**
CAPE    Gulf    Saint    **Adelaide**    **DIVIDING**
ATASTROPHE    Vincent    Wagga    **Canberra**
Wagga    **Albury**    A.C.T.    T a s m a n
NGAROO    Encounter    Bordertown    Murray    **RANGE**
LAND    Bay    **Bendigo**    Mount
Murray    Kosciusko
Mount Gambier    **VICTORIA**    2228    S e a    35°
Portland    **Geelong**    **MELBOURNE**    CAPE HOWE
Warrnambool    **GREAT**
CAPE OTWAY    SOUTH POINT    NINETY MILE BEACH
V    KING ISLAND    Bass Strait    FLINDERS ISLAND
Barks Strait
Smithton    Burnie    **Launceston**
Mount Ossa    1617    TASMANIA
35°    SOUTH    **Hobart**    SOUTH
WEST    EAST
CAPE    CAPE
140°        145°        150°        155°        160° Lambert Conformal Conic Projection

40°

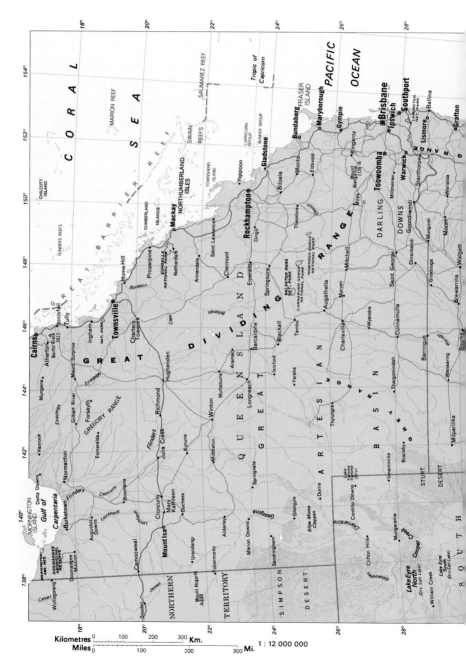

Kilometres 0 100 200 300 Km.
Miles 0 100 200 300 Mi.   1 : 12 000 000

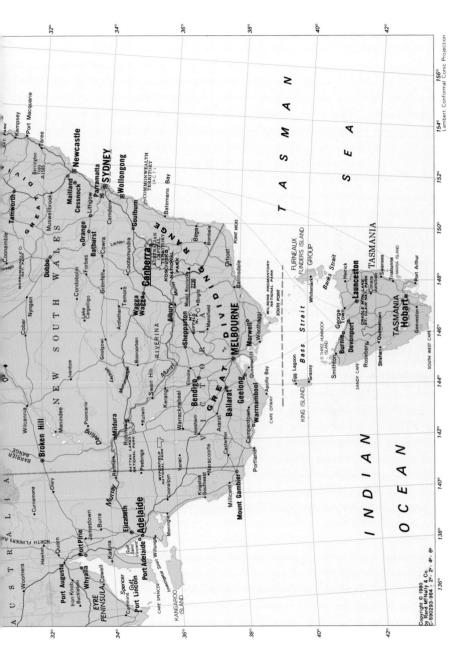

Lambert Conformal Conic Projection

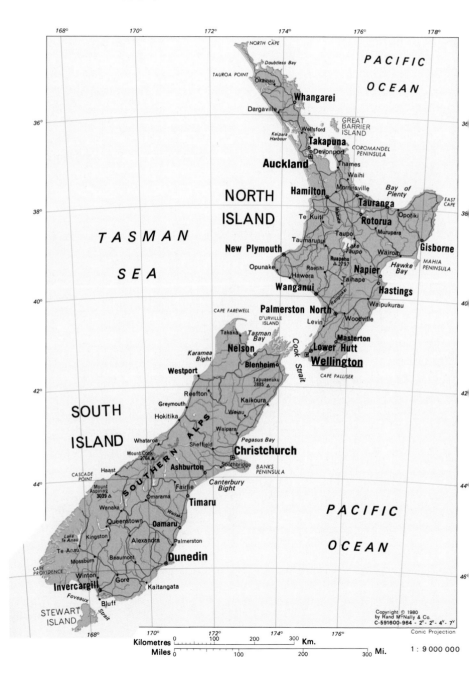

STEWART
ISLAND

Conic Projection

Kilometres

Miles

1 : 9 000 000

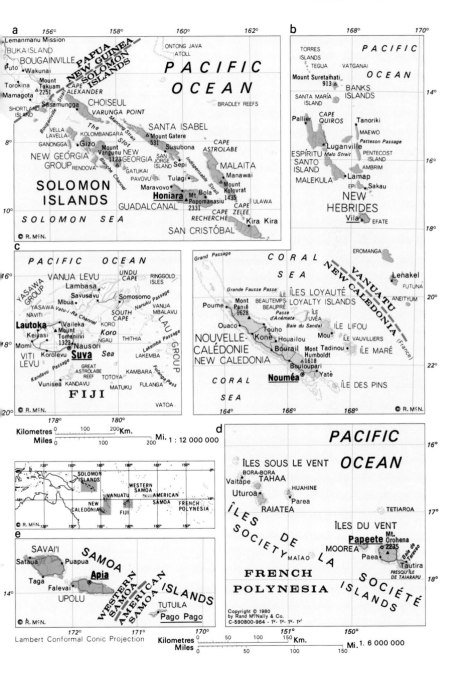

**a**

Lemanmanu Mission
BUKA ISLAND
BOUGAINVILLE
PAPUA NEW GUINEA
SOLOMON ISLANDS
Puto • Wakunai
Torokina
Mount Takuam △2251
Mamagota
SHORTLAND ISLAND
CAPE ALEXANDER
Sasamungga
CHOISEUL
VARUNGA POINT
VELLA LAVELLA
KOLOMBANGARA
GANONGGA • Gizo
NEW GEORGIA GROUP
Mount Vangunu △1123
NEW GEORGIA
RENDOVA
GATUKAI
SOLOMON ISLANDS
PAVUONI
Maravovo
GUADALCANAL
SOLOMON SEA

ONTONG JAVA ATOLL
PACIFIC OCEAN
BRADLEY REEFS
SANTA ISABEL
△Mount Gatere 531
Susubona
SAN JORGE ISLAND
Sepi
Tulagi
△Mount Kotovrat
Honiara
△Mt Bola Popomanasiu 2331 1435
CAPE ASTROLABE
MALAITA
• Manawai
ULAWA
CAPE ZELEE
CAPE RECHERCHE
Kira Kira
SAN CRISTÓBAL

© R. McN.

**b**

TORRES ISLANDS
• TEGUA
VATGANAI
Mount Suretamati 913 △
SANTA MARÍA ISLAND
Pallier
CAPE QUIROS
ESPÍRITU SANTO ISLAND
Malo Strait
MALEKULA
Luganville
PACIFIC OCEAN
BANKS ISLANDS
Tanoriki
MAEWO
Patteson Passage
PENTECOST ISLAND
AMBRIM
• Lamap
EPI • Sakau
NEW HEBRIDES
Vila • EFATE

14°
16°
18°

**c**

PACIFIC OCEAN
YASAWA GROUP
VANUA LEVU
Lambasa
Savusavu
Mbua
YASAWA
NAVITI
Vatu-i-Ra Channel
SOUTH CAPE
KORO
Lautoka
• Vaileka
△Mount Tomaniivi 1323
Keiyasi
Momi
VITI LEVU
Korolevu
Nausori
Suva
Kandavu Passage
Vunisea KANDAVU
GREAT ASTROLABE REEF
FIJI
UNDU CAPE
RINGGOLD ISLES
Somosomo
Nanuku Passage
VANUA MBALAVU
THITHIA
NGAU
Koro Sea
LAU GROUP
Lakemba Passage
LAKEMBA
KAMBARA
TOTOYA
MATUKU
FULANGA
Fulanga Pass
VATOA

16°
18°
20°

178° 180°

Grand Passage
Grande Fausse Passe
Mont Panié 1628 △
Poume •
BEAUTEMPS-BEAUPRÉ
Passe d'Anémata
ÎLE UVÉA
Baie du Sandal
Ouaco
Touho
Koné • Houailou
• Bourail
Mont Tadinou △1618
Humboldt
Bouloupari
Nouméa
Yaté
CORAL SEA
NOUVELLE-CALÉDONIE
NEW CALEDONIA
CORAL SEA
EROMANGA
ÎLES LOYAUTÉ
LOYALTY ISLANDS
ÎLE LIFOU
ÎLE VAUVILLIERS
ÎLE MARÉ
ÎLE DES PINS
NEW CALEDONIA VANUATU (France)
Lenakel
FUTUNA
ANEITYUM

20°
22°

164° 166° 168°

© R. McN.

Kilometres 0 100 200 Km.
Miles 0 100 200 Mi. 1 : 12 000 000

SOLOMON ISLANDS
WESTERN SAMOA
VANUATU
AMERICAN SAMOA
NEW CALEDONIA
FIJI
FRENCH POLYNESIA
© R. McN.

**e**

SAVAI'I
Sataua
Puapua
Taga
Falevai
SAMOA
Apia
UPOLU
WESTERN SAMOA
AMERICAN SAMOA
SAMOA ISLANDS
TUTUILA
Pago Pago
© R. McN.

14°

172° 171°

Lambert Conformal Conic Projection

**d**

PACIFIC OCEAN
ÎLES SOUS LE VENT
BORA-BORA
Vaitape
TAHAA
HUAHINE
Uturoa
• Parea
RAIATEA
ÎLES DU VENT
Papeete
Mt. Orohena △2235
MOOREA
Paea
MATAIO
Tautira
PRESQU'ÎLE DE TAIARAPU
Baie de Taravao
ÎLES DE LA SOCIETY
FRENCH POLYNESIA
SOCIÉTÉ ISLANDS
TETIAROA

Copyright © 1980
by Rand McNally & Co.
C-590800-964 - 1ᵛ - 1ᵛ - 1ᵛ - 1ᵛⁱ

16°
17°
18°

151° 150°

Kilometres 0 50 100 150 Km.
Miles 0 50 100 150 Mi. 1 : 6 000 000

San Diego
Tijuana
Mexicali
Ensenada
Yuma
San Luis
Rio Colorado
ARIZONA
Casa
Grande
Tucson
Silver
City
WHITE SANDS
NATIONAL
MONUMENT
Alamogordo
Artesia
Hobbs
NEW MEXICO
Carlsbad
Andrews

El Golfo de
Santa Clara
López
Collada
Lukeville
ORGAN PIPE CACTUS
NATIONAL MONUMENT
SAGUARO
NATIONAL
MONUMENT
Lordsburg
Las Cruces
CARLSBAD CAVERNS
NATIONAL PARK

PARQUE NACIONAL
SIERRA DE SAN
PEDRO MARTIR
Puerto
Peñasco
El Cózon
CHIRICAHUA
NATIONAL
MONUMENT
Bisbee
Nogales
Douglas
Anthony
Ciudad Juárez
El Paso
Guadalupe
Peak
2667
Kermit
Odes

Vicente
Guerrero
San Felipe
El Desemboque
Caborca
Altar
Santa
Ana
Cananea
Ascensión
Guadalupe
Sierra
Blanca
Van
Horn
Pecos

Rosario
SIERRA SAN PEDRO MARTIR
Golfo
de
Puerto
Libertad
Benjamín
Hill
Arizpe
Nacozari
Nueva
Casas
Grandes
Villa
Ahumada
Fort Stockton
Alpine
Sanderson

ISLA ÁNGEL
DE LA
GUARDA
El Desemboque
Carbó
Moctezuma
Mata Ortiz
Buenaventura
El
Sueco
San Antonio
de Bravo
Presidio
BIG BEND
NATIONAL
PARK

Punta
Prieta
ISLA
TIBURÓN
Kino
Hermosillo
Ures
Las Varas
Sahuaripa
Cerro Puerto
de Lajas
2578
El
Sauz
Maclovio
Herrera
NACIONAL SIE
DEL CARE

ISLA CEDROS
Bahía
Sebastián
Vizcaíno
El Arco
Tasñota
Suaqui
Grande
Yécora
Ciudad
Guerrero
Dolores
Chihuahua
Aldama
Julimes
Tacubaya
El Carricito

Guaymas
Ocampo
Cuauhtémoc
Delicias
Saucillo

PUNTA
ABREOJOS
San Ignacio
Santa Rosalía
Ciudad
Obregón
Esperanza
Creel
PARQUE
NACIONAL
BARRANCA
DEL COBRE
Valle de
Zaragoza
Ciudad
Camargo
La Esmeralda

Mulegé
Navojoa
Huatabampo
Yávaros
San Francisco
del Oro
Hidalgo
del Parral
Ciudad
Jiménez
Cerrillo

Comondú
Santo
Domingo
Loreto
ISLA
CARMEN
Los Mochis
San Blas
Guasave
Cerro Agua
Grande de Gastelum
Cerro Mohinora
3992
Cerro Agua
Caliente
3315
San
Bernardo
Las Nieves
Ceballos
Barcelona
San Pe
de las Colon

ISLA SANTA
MAGDALENA
San Luis
Gonzaga
ISLA
SAN JOSÉ
El Médano
ISLA DE SANTA
MARGARITA
Culiacán
Altata
Quilá
Peñcos
Los
Herreras
Tameapa
Copalquin
La Zarca
Abasolo
Pedricena
Gómez
Palacio
Torreón
Parras de
la Fuen
Juan Euge
Acacio

Todos Santos
ISLA
CERRALVO
La Paz
El Avión
Coacoyole
Tayoltita
Francisco
Madero
Miguel
Auza
Durango

Tropic of Cancer
El Quelite
Ciudad
Nombre
de Dios
Vicente
Guerrero
Rio
Grande

San José
del Cabo
Agua
Caliente
Cerro
Candelaria
3080

CABO
SAN LUCAS
Mazatlán
Rosario
Fresnillo
Zacatecas

Teacapán
Jerez de
García Salinas
Cerro Lechuguilla
2480

Tecuala
Rosamorada
Santiago
Ixcuintla
Aguascaliente
Cerro
El Viejo
2740
Jalpa

PACIFIC
ISLA MARÍA MADRE
ISLA MARÍA MAGDALENA
ISLA MARÍA CLEOFAS
ISLAS
MARÍAS
Tepic
Ahuacatlán
El Vigía
Jalostotitlán

Puerto
Vallarta
Guadalajara
Atotonilc
Alto

OCEAN
CABO CORRIENTES
Mascota
Cocula
Ocotlán
Zamora
de Chapala
Hidalg

ISLAS
REVILLAGIGEDO
(Mex.)
ISLA
SOCORRO
Autlán de
Navarro
Sayula
PARQUE NACIONAL
VOLCÁN DE COLIMA
Colima
PARQUE NACION
PICO DE TANCÍT
Ciudad
Guzmán
Apatzingán

Manzanillo
Pomaro

Kilometres 0  100  200  300  Km.
Miles 0  100  200  300  Mi.
1 : 13 300 000

BAHAMAS

CAT ISLAND

Tropic of Cancer

LONG
ISLAND

Crooked Passage

Sound Island

CROOKED
ISLAND

MAYAGUANA

TURKS AND
CAICOS ISLANDS
(U.K.)

LITTLE
INAGUA

CAICOS
ISLANDS

TURKS
ISLANDS
Grand
Turk

GREAT
INAGUA

Matthew
Town

ATLANTIC

OCEAN

Sagua de
Tánamo

HAITI

I N D I E S

Guantánamo

Cap-
Haitien

Montecristi

POINTE DU
CHEVAL BLANC

Gonaïves

San Francisco
de Macoris

Golfe de
la Gonâve

Santiago

Concepcion de la Vega

PUERTO RICO
(U.S.)

VIRGIN
ISLANDS
(U.S.) (U.K.)

ANGUILLA
(U.K.)

ILE DE LA
GONÂVE

Pico Duarte 3175

HISPANIOLA

Higüey

Arecibo

San Juan

Charlotte
Amalie

LEEWARD ISLANDS

Jérémie

Azua

San Pedro
de Macoris

Mayagüez

Caguas

BARBUDA

Port-au-
Prince

Santo
Domingo

Ponce

SAINT
CROIX

SAINT CHRISTOPHER
(SAINT KITTS)

ANTIGUA

Les
Cayes

Chaîne de
la Selle
2674

DOMINICAN
REPUBLIC

ST. KITTS AND NEVIS

MONTSERRAT
(U.K.)

GRANDE-
TERRE

A N T I L L E S

Pointe-à-Pitre

GUADELOUPE

BASSE-TERRE

L E S S E R   A N T I L L E S

DOMINICA

Roseau

B E A N   S E A

Montagne
Pelée 1397

Fort-de-France

60°

MARTINIQUE
(Fr.)

Castries

SAINT LUCIA

SAINT
VINCENT

Kingstown

Bridgetown

BARBADOS

ARUBA
(Neth.)

NETHERLANDS
ANTILLES

Oranjestad

BONAIRE

GRENADA

Saint George's

CABO DE LA VELA

PENÍNSULA DE
LA GUAJIRA

CURAÇAO

Willemstad

LA BLANQUILLA
(Ven.)

WINDWARD ISLANDS

Barran-
quilla

Santa
Marta

Ríohacha

PENÍNSULA
DE PARAGUANÁ

Golfo de
Venezuela

Punto Fijo

Coro

ISLAS LOS ROQUES
(Ven.)

ISLA DE
MARGARITA

ISLA LA TORTUGA
(Ven.)

Porlamar

TOBAGO

Port of Spain

Ciénaga

COLOMBIA

Pico Cristóbal
Colón

San Juan de
los Cayos

San Luis

Puerto Cumarebo

Pedregal

Cumaná

Carúpano

TRINIDAD
AND
TOBAGO

San
Fernando

Cartagena

VENEZUELA

Puerto
Cabello

PARQ.
HENRY
PITTIER

CARACAS

Puerto la
Cruz

Güiria

TRINIDAD

Arjona

Maracaibo

San Felipe

Maiquetía

Barcelona

Maturin

San Jacinto

Valencia

Maracay

PARQ. NAC.
GUATOPO

San Mateo

DELTA

San Onofre

Cabimas

Barqui-
simeto

PARQ. NAC.
EL ÁVILA

DEL

Sincelejo

Codazzi

Ciudad
Ojeda

Acarigua

de los Morros

San Juan

Altagracia
de Orituco

Zaraza

Cantaura

Tucupita

ORINOCO

Magangué

Lago de
Maracaibo

Trujillo

San José
de Guanipa

Barrancas

El Banco

Río Ariguaisa

Calabozo

Valle de
la Pascua

El
Tigre

Ciudad
Guayana

Planeta Rica

San Carlos
del Zulia

Valera

CORDILLERA DE MÉRIDA

Villa de
Bruzual

Arismendi

Upata

El Palmar

Nechí

Ericontrados

Barinas

LLANOS

Ciudad Bolívar

Cáceres

Ocaña

Gamarra

Mérida
Pico Bolívar
5002

Libertad

Puerto de
Nutrias

San Fernando
de Apure

Orinoco

Mapire

802

Cerro Bolívar

Caroní

El Mantéco

60°

Cúcuta

San Cristóbal

Apure

Achaguas

Maripa

64°

74°              72°              70°              68°              66°

64°

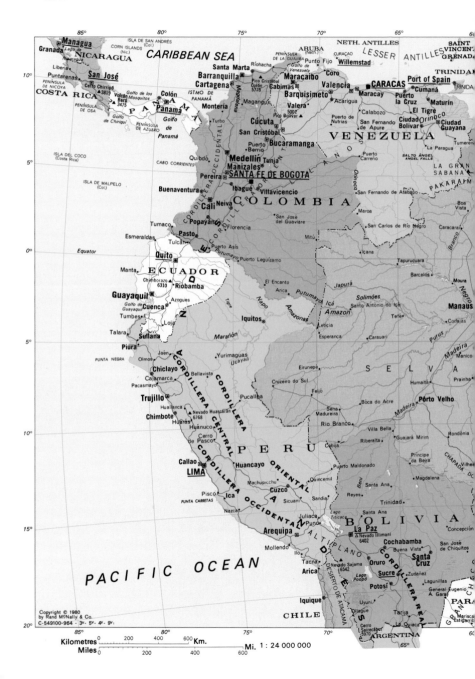

PACIFIC OCEAN

CARIBBEAN SEA

Copyright © 1980
by Rand McNally & Co.
C-549100-964 - 3v- 5v- 4v- 9v-

Kilometres 0 200 400 600 Km.
Miles 0 200 400 600 Mi. 1 : 24 000 000

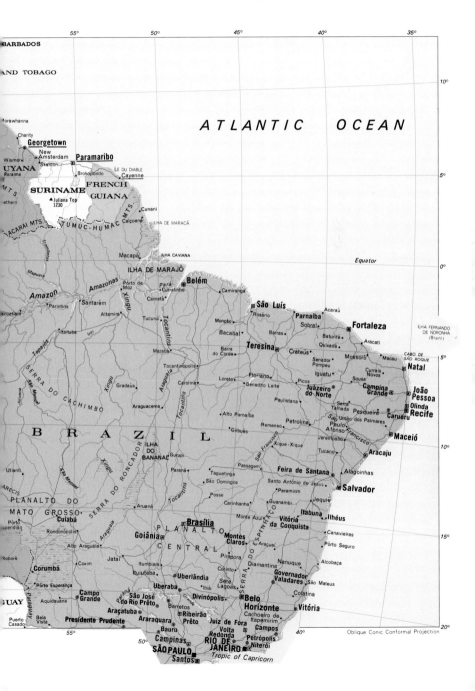

BARBADOS

AND TOBAGO

10°

Morawhanna

Charity

ATLANTIC OCEAN

Georgetown
Wismar
New
Amsterdam
Skeldon
Paramaribo
ÎLE DU DIABLE
Cayenne
UYANA
Roraima
Brokopondo
5°
ethem
SURINAME
FRENCH GUIANA
Juliana Top
1230
ACARAI MTS.
TUMUC-HUMAC MTS.
Cunani
Calcoené
ILHA DE MARACÁ

Mepuera

Amazon
Amazonas
Pôrto de
Moz
Pará
Curralinho
Macapá
ILHA CAVIANA
ILHA DE MARAJÓ
Belém
Camiranga
Equator
0°

Parintins
Santarém
Altamira
Xingu
Tucuruí
Cametá
São Luís
Rosário
Monção
Acaraú
Parnaíba
Sobral
Fortaleza
ILHA FERNANDO
DE NORONHA
(Brazil)
accoatiara
Itaituba
Iriri
Marabá
Bacabal
Barras
Baturité
Quixadá
Aracati
Macau
CABO DE
SÃO ROQUE
Tapajós
Senador
Pompeu
Natal
5°
SERRA DO CACHIMBO
Tocantinópolis
Barra
do Corda
Teresina
Crateús
Mossoró
Currais
Novos
São Manuel
Gradaús
Carolina
Loreto
Floriano
Picos
Iguatu
Sousa
Campina
Grande
João
Pessoa
Benedito Leite
Juàzeiro
do Norte
Serra
Talhada
Pesqueira
Olinda
Recife
Araguacema
Paulistana
Caruaru
BRAZIL
Alto Parnaíba
Remanso
Petrolina
União dos Palmares
São
Paulo
Afonso
Maceió
10°
ILHA
DO
BANANAL
Gilbués
Xique-Xique
Jeremoabo
Tucano
Utiariti
Gurupi
Aracaju
ARECIS
Paranã
Passagem
Feira de Santana
Alagoinhas
PLANALTO DO
Taguatinga
São Domingos
Santo António de Jesus
Salvador
MATO GROSSO
Posse
Carinhanha
Guanambi
Paramirim
Jequié
Itabuna
Ilhéus
Roboré
Aruanã
Monte Azul
Vitória
da Conquista
15°
Corumbá
Coxim
Jataí
Itumbiara
Cuiabá
Brasília
Goiânia
PLANALTO
CENTRAL
Montes
Claros
Araçuaí
Canavieiras
Pôrto Seguro
Rondonópolis
Pirapora
Corinto
Diamantina
Nanuque
Alcobaça
Alto Araguaia
Pôrto
speridiag
Ituiutaba
Sete
Lagoas
São Mateus
Cofatina
Campo
Grande
Uberlândia
Ibiá
Governador
Valadares
Aquidauana
São José
do Rio Prêto
Uberaba
Divinópolis
Belo
Horizonte
Vitória
Bela
Vista
Presidente Prudente
Araçatuba
Barretos
Araraquara
Ribeirão
Prêto
Juiz de Fora
Cachoeiro de
Itapemirim
Campos
Petrópolis
Niterói
Puerto
Casado
Bauru
Campinas
Volta
Redonda
RIO DE
JANEIRO
SÃO PAULO
Santos
Tropic of Capricorn
20°
UAY
GUAY

Oblique Conic Conformal Projection

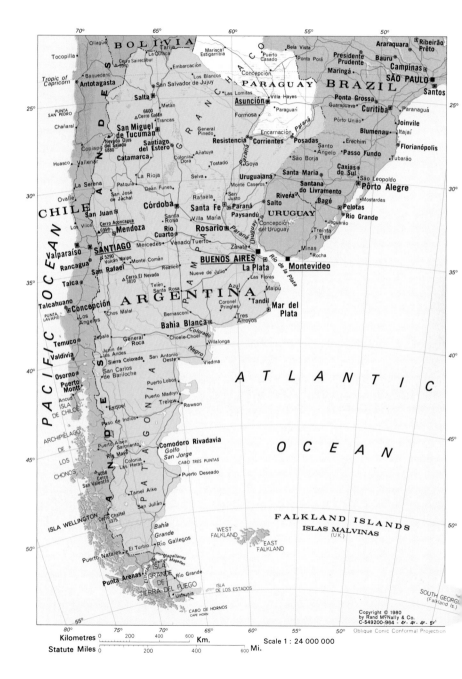

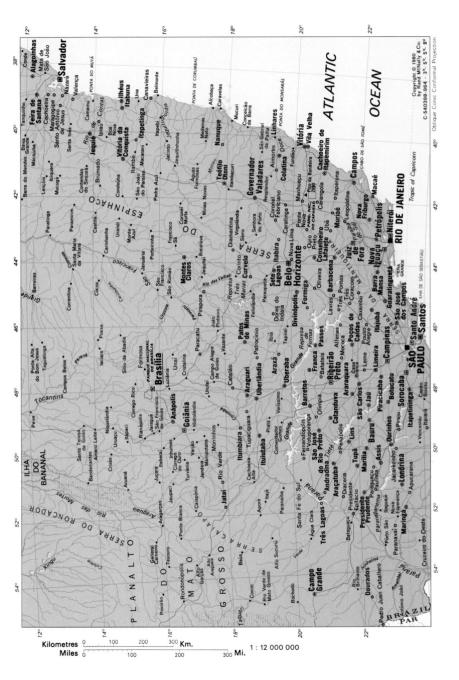

Kilometres 0 100 200 300 Km.

Miles 0 100 200 300 Mi.

1 : 12 000 000

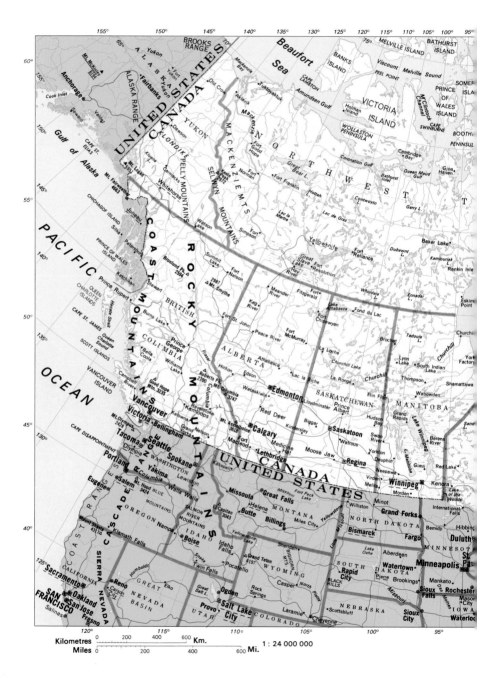

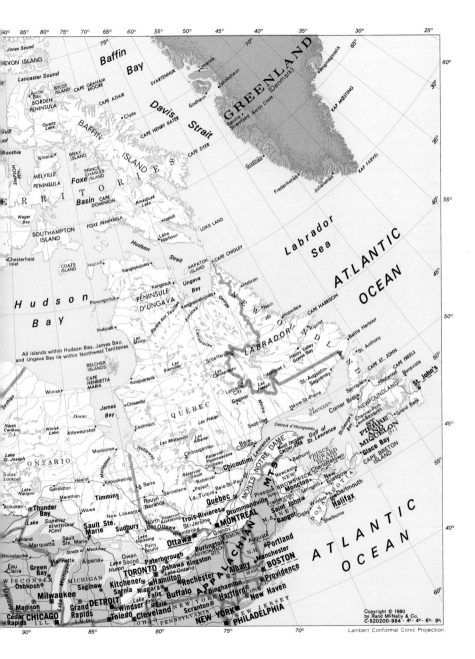

Lambert Conformal Conic Projection

Kilometres 0 200 400 600 Km.
Miles 0 200 400 600 Mi.   1 : 24 000 000

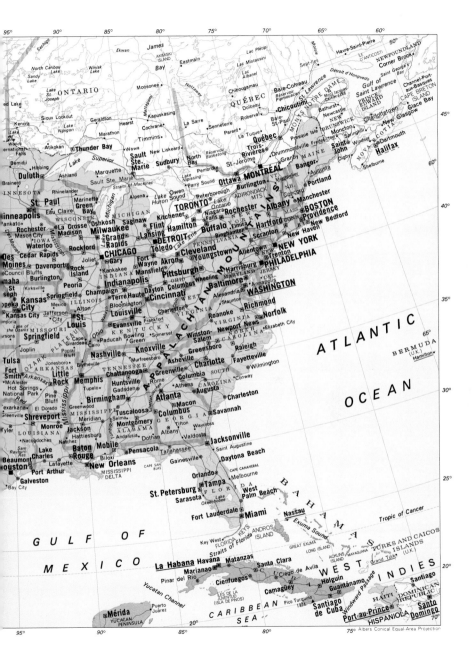

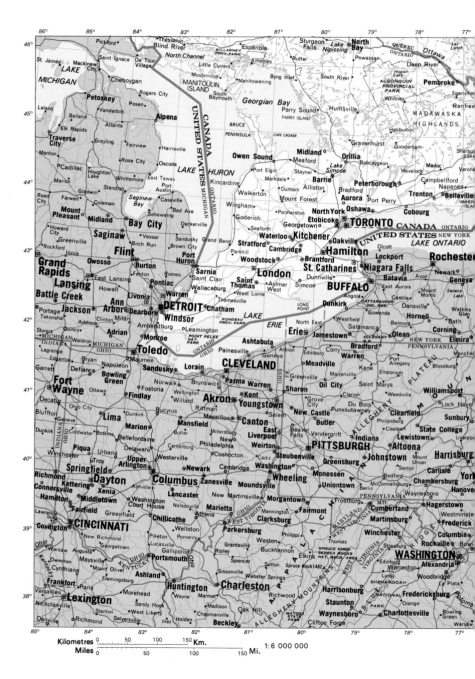

Kilometres  0  50  100  150  Km.

Miles  0  50  100  150  Mi.

1: 6 000 000

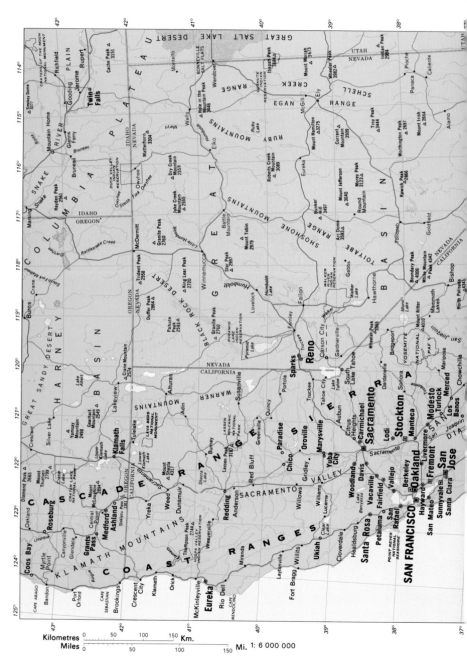

Kilometres 0 50 100 150 Km.
Miles 0 50 100 150 Mi. 1: 6 000 000

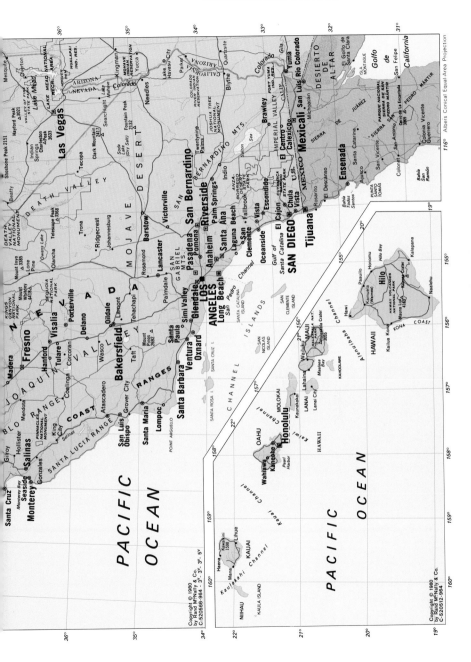

PACIFIC OCEAN

PACIFIC OCEAN

Albers Conical Equal-Area Projection

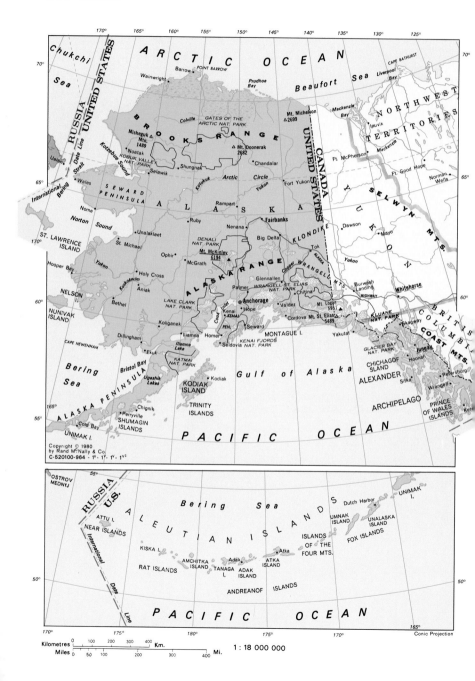

Kilometres 0 100 200 300 400 Km.

Miles 0 50 100 200 300 400 Mi.

1 : 18 000 000

Conic Projection

## THE CONTINENTS

| Continent | Area | Estimated Population | Population Density | Mean Elevation | Highest Elevation | Lowest Elevation |
|---|---|---|---|---|---|---|
| Africa | 11,700,000 sq. mi. (30,300,000 sq. km.) | 694,000,000 | 59/sq. mi. (23/sq. km.) | 1,900 ft. (600 m.) | Kilimanjaro, Tanzania, 19,340 ft. (5,895 m.) | Lac Assal, Djibouti, -502 ft. (-153 m.) |
| Antarctica | 5,400,000 sq. mi. (14,000,000 sq. km.) | . . . | . . . | 6,000 ft. (1,800 m.) | Vinson Massif, 16,864 ft. (5,140 m.) | Sea level |
| Asia | 17,300,000 sq. mi. (44,900,000 sq. km.) | 3,331,500,000 | 193/sq. mi. (74/sq. km.) | 3,000 ft. (900 m.) | Mt. Everest, China (Tibet)-Nepal, 29,028 ft. (8,848 m.) | Dead Sea, Israel-Jordan, -1,299 ft. (-396 m.) |
| Australia | 2,966,155 sq. mi. (7,682,300 sq. km.) | 17,420,000 | 5.8/sq. mi. (2.2/sq. km.) | 1,000 ft. (300 m.) | Mt. Kosciusko, New South Wales, 7,310 ft. (2,228 m.) | Lake Eyre, South Australia, -52 ft. (-16 m.) |
| Europe | 3,800,000 sq. mi. (9,900,000 sq. km.) | 695,200,000 | 183/sq. mi. (70/sq. km.) | 1,000 ft. (300 m.) | Gora El'brus, Russia, 18,510 ft. (5,642 m.) | Caspian Sea, -92 ft. (-28 m.) |
| North America | 9,500,000 sq. mi. (24,700,000 sq. km.) | 436,300,000 | 46/sq. mi. (18/sq. km.) | 2,000 ft. (600 m.) | Mt. McKinley, U.S. (Alaska), 20,320 ft. (6,194 m.) | Death Valley, U.S. (Calif.), -282 ft. (-86 m.) |
| Oceania, incl. Australia | 3,300,000 sq. mi. (8,500,000 sq. km.) | 27,300,000 | 8.3/sq. mi. (3.2/sq. km.) | | Mt. Wilhelm, Papua New Guinea, 14,793 ft. (4,509 m.) | Lake Eyre, South Australia, -52 ft. (-16 m.) |
| South America | 6,900,000 sq. mi. (17,800,000 sq. km.) | 306,700,000 | 44/sq. mi. (17/sq. km.) | 1,800 ft. (550 m.) | Cerro Aconcagua, Argentina, 22,831 ft. (6,959 m.) | Salinas Chicas, Argentina, -138 ft. (-42 m.) |
| WORLD | 57,900,000 sq. mi. (150,100,000 sq. km.) | 5,491,000,000 | 93/sq. mi. (36/sq. km.) | . . . | Mt. Everest, China (Tibet)-Nepal, 29,028 ft. (8,848 m.) | Dead Sea, Israel-Jordan, -1,299 ft. (-396m.) |

## Principal Mountains

| Mountains | Location | Feet | Meters | Mountains | Location | Feet | Meters |
|---|---|---|---|---|---|---|---|
| Aconcagua, Cerro | Argentina | 22,831 | 6,959 | Kinabalu, Gunong | Malaysia | 13,455 | 4,101 |
| Adams, Mt. | U.S. | 12,276 | 3,742 | Kirinyaga (Mt. | | | |
| Annapurna | Nepal | 26,503 | 8,078 | Kenya) | Kenya | 17,057 | 5,199 |
| Apo, Mt. | Philippines | 9,692 | 2,954 | Kommunizma, Pik | Tajikistan | 24,590 | 7,495 |
| Barú, Volcán | Panama | 11,401 | 3,475 | Kosciusko, Mt. | Australia | 7,310 | 2,228 |
| Blanc, Mont | France-Italy | 15,771 | 4,807 | Koussi, Emi | Chad | 11,204 | 3,415 |
| Bolívar, Pico | Venezuela | 16,411 | 5,002 | Kula Kangri | Bhutan | 24,783 | 7,554 |
| Boundary Pk. | U.S. | 13,143 | 4,006 | Las Minas, Cerro | Honduras | 9,400 | 2,865 |
| Ağrı Dağı (Mt. | | | | Lassen Pk. | U.S. | 10,457 | 3,187 |
| Ararat) | Turkey | 16,854 | 5,137 | Logan, Mt. | Canada | 19,524 | 5,951 |
| Cameroun, Mont | Cameroon | 13,353 | 4,070 | Makālu | China-Nepal | 27,825 | 8,481 |
| Chimborazo | Ecuador | 20,702 | 6,310 | Marcy, Mt. | U.S. | 5,344 | 1,629 |
| Chirripó, Cerro | Costa Rica | 12,530 | 3,819 | Margherita Pk. | Uganda-Zaire | 16,762 | 5,109 |
| Citlaltépetl, Volcán | Mexico | 18,701 | 5,700 | Maromokotro | Madagascar | 9,436 | 2,876 |
| Columbia, Mt. | Canada | 12,293 | 3,747 | Matterhorn | Italy- | | |
| Cook, Mt. | New Zealand | 12,349 | 3,764 | | Switzerland | 14,692 | 4,478 |
| Cristóbal Colón, | | | | Mauna Loa | U.S. | 13,679 | 4,169 |
| Pico | Colombia | 18,947 | 5,775 | McKinley, Mt. | U.S. (Alaska) | 20,320 | 6,194 |
| Dhaulāgiri | Nepal | 26,811 | 8,172 | Mitchell, Mt. | U.S. | 6,684 | 2,037 |
| Dimlang | Nigeria | 6,699 | 2,042 | Mogotón, Cerro | Nicaragua | 6,913 | 2,107 |
| Duarte, Pico | Dominican | | | Mulhacén | Spain | 11,411 | 3,478 |
| | Republic | 10,417 | 3,175 | Nanda Devi | India | 25,646 | 7,817 |
| Dufour Spitze | Italy- | | | Nānga Parbat | Pakistan | 26,660 | 8,126 |
| | Switzerland | 15,203 | 4,634 | Narodnaja, Gora | Russia | 6,214 | 1,894 |
| Elbert, Mt. | U.S. | 14,433 | 4,399 | Nevis, Ben | U.K. | 4,406 | 1,343 |
| El'brus, Gora | Russia | 18,510 | 5,642 | Ojos del Salado, | Argentina- | | |
| Etna, Monte | Italy | 10,902 | 3,323 | Nevado | Chile | 22,572 | 6,880 |
| Everest, Mt. | China-Nepal | 29,028 | 8,848 | Ólimbos (Mt. | | | |
| Fuji-san | Japan | 12,388 | 3,776 | Olympus) | Greece | 9,570 | 2,917 |
| Gannett Pk. | U.S. | 13,804 | 4,207 | Olympus, Mt. | U.S. | 7,965 | 2,428 |
| Glittertinden | Norway | 8,110 | 2,472 | Orohena, Mt. | French | | |
| Grand Teton | U.S. | 13,770 | 4,197 | | Polynesia | 7,333 | 2,235 |
| Grossglockner | Austria | 12,457 | 3,797 | Ossa, Mt. | Australia | 5,305 | 1,617 |
| Guadalupe Pk. | U.S. | 8,749 | 2,667 | Pelée, Montagne | Martinique | 4,583 | 1,397 |
| Hood, Mt. | U.S. | 11,234 | 3,424 | Pidurutalagala | Sri Lanka | 8,281 | 2,524 |
| Huascarán, Nevado | Peru | 22,205 | 6,768 | Pikes Pk. | U.S. | 14,110 | 4,301 |
| Humphreys Pk. | U.S. | 12,633 | 3,851 | Pobedy, pik | China-Russia | 24,406 | 7,439 |
| Hvannadalshnúkur | Iceland | 6,952 | 2,119 | Popocatépetl, | | | |
| Illimani, Nevado | Bolivia | 21,004 | 6,402 | Volcán | Mexico | 17,887 | 5,452 |
| Inthanon, Doi | Thailand | 8,513 | 2,595 | Rainier, Mt. | U.S. | 14,410 | 4,392 |
| Inyangani | Zimbabwe | 8,507 | 2,593 | Ras Dashen | Ethiopia | 15,157 | 4,620 |
| Jaya, Puncak | Indonesia | 16,503 | 5,030 | Sajama, Nevado | Bolivia | 21,463 | 6,540 |
| Jungfrau | Switzerland | 13,642 | 4,158 | Selle, Châine de la | Haiti | 8,773 | 2,674 |
| K2 (Qogir Feng) | China- | | | Shasta, Mt. | U.S. | 14,162 | 4,317 |
| | Pakistan | 28,251 | 8,611 | Tahat | Algeria | 9,852 | 3,003 |
| Kānchenjunga | Nepal-India | 28,209 | 8,598 | Tajumulco, Volcán | Guatemala | 13,845 | 4,220 |
| Kāmet | China-India | 25,446 | 7,756 | Toubkal, Jbel | Morocco | 13,665 | 4,165 |
| Katrīnah, Jabal | Egypt | 8,668 | 2,642 | Triglav | Yugoslavia | 9,393 | 2,863 |
| Kebnekaise | Sweden | 6,926 | 2,111 | Uncompahgre Pk. | U.S. | 14,309 | 4,361 |
| Kerinci, Gunung | Indonesia | 12,467 | 3,800 | Vesuvio | Italy | 4,190 | 1,277 |
| Kilimanjaro | Tanzania | 19,341 | 5,895 | | | | |

## Oceans, Seas, and Gulfs

| Name | Location | Sq. Mi. | Sq. Km. |
|---|---|---|---|
| Arabian Sea | Asia-Africa | 1,492,000 | 3,864,000 |
| Arctic Ocean | | 5,400,000 | 14,000,000 |
| Atlantic Ocean | | 31,800,000 | 82,400,000 |
| Baltic Sea | Eur. | 163,000 | 422,000 |
| Bengal, Bay of | Asia | 839,000 | 2,173,000 |
| Bering Sea | Asia-N.A. | 876,000 | 2,269,000 |
| Black Sea | Eur.-Asia | 178,000 | 461,000 |
| Caribbean Sea | N.A.-S.A. | 1,063,000 | 2,753,000 |
| Greenland Sea | Eur.-N.A. | 465,000 | 1,204,000 |
| Hudson Bay | Canada | 475,000 | 1,230,000 |
| Indian Ocean | | 28,900,000 | 74,900,000 |
| Mediterranean Sea | | 967,000 | 2,505,000 |
| Mexico, Gulf of | N.A. | 596,000 | 1,544,000 |
| North Sea | Eur. | 222,000 | 575,000 |
| Norwegian Sea | Eur.-N.A. | 597,000 | 1,546,000 |
| Pacific Ocean | | 63,800,000 | 165,200,000 |
| Red Sea | Africa-Asia | 169,000 | 438,000 |
| South China Sea | Asia | 1,331,000 | 3,447,000 |
| Yellow Sea | China-Korea | 480,000 | 1,200,000 |

## Principal Islands

| Name | Location | Sq. Mi. | Sq. Km. |
|---|---|---|---|
| Baffin I. | Canada | 195,928 | 507,451 |
| Banks I. | Canada | 27,038 | 70,028 |
| Borneo | Asia | 287,300 | 744,100 |
| Bougainville | Papua New Guinea | 3,600 | 9,300 |
| Cape Breton I. | Canada | 3,981 | 10,311 |
| Corse (Corsica) | France | 3,352 | 8,681 |
| Cuba | N.A. | 42,800 | 110,800 |
| Devon I. | Canada | 21,331 | 55,247 |
| Ellesmere I. | Canada | 75,767 | 196,236 |
| Great Britain | United Kingdom | 88,795 | 229,978 |
| Greenland | N.A. | 840,000 | 2,175,600 |
| Hainan Dao | China | 13,100 | 34,000 |
| Hawaii | U.S. | 4,034 | 10,448 |
| Hispaniola | N.A. | 29,300 | 76,000 |
| Hokkaidō | Japan | 32,245 | 83,515 |
| Honshū | Japan | 89,176 | 230,966 |
| Ireland | Europe | 32,600 | 84,400 |
| Ísland | Europe | 39,800 | 103,000 |
| Jamaica | N.A. | 4,200 | 11,000 |
| Jawa (Java) | Indonesia | 51,038 | 132,187 |
| Kípros / Kıbrıs | Asia | 3,572 | 9,251 |
| Kodiak I. | U.S. | 3,670 | 9,505 |
| Kríti (Crete) | Greece | 3,189 | 8,259 |
| Kyūshū | Japan | 17,129 | 44,363 |
| Long I. | U.S. | 1,377 | 3,566 |
| Luzon | Philippines | 40,420 | 104,688 |
| Madagascar | Africa | 227,000 | 587,000 |
| Melville I. | Canada | 16,274 | 42,149 |
| Mindanao | Philippines | 36,537 | 94,630 |
| Mindoro | Philippines | 3,759 | 9,735 |
| Negros | Philippines | 4,907 | 12,710 |
| New Britain | Papua New Guinea | 14,093 | 36,500 |
| New Caledonia | Oceania | 6,252 | 16,192 |
| Newfoundland | Canada | 42,031 | 108,860 |
| New Guinea | Oceania | 309,000 | 800,000 |
| North I. | New Zealand | 44,274 | 114,669 |
| Novaja Zeml'a | Russia | 31,900 | 82,600 |
| Palawan | Philippines | 4,550 | 11,785 |
| Prince of Wales I. | Canada | 12,872 | 33,339 |
| Puerto Rico | N.A. | 3,500 | 9,100 |
| Sachalin, Ostrov | Russia | 29,500 | 76,400 |
| Samar | Philippines | 5,100 | 13,080 |
| Sardegna (Sardinia) | Italy | 9,301 | 24,090 |
| Seram (Ceram) | Indonesia | 7,191 | 18,625 |
| Shikoku | Japan | 7,258 | 18,799 |
| Sicilia (Sicily) | Italy | 9,926 | 25,708 |
| Somerset I. | Canada | 9,570 | 24,786 |
| Southampton I. | Canada | 15,913 | 41,214 |
| South I. | New Zealand | 57,870 | 149,883 |
| Spitsbergen | Norway | 15,260 | 39,523 |
| Sri Lanka | Asia | 24,900 | 64,600 |
| Sulawesi (Celebes) | Indonesia | 73,057 | 189,216 |
| Sumatera (Sumatra) | Indonesia | 182,860 | 473,606 |
| T'aiwan | Asia | 13,900 | 36,000 |
| Tasmania | Austl. | 26,200 | 67,800 |

## Principal Lakes

| Name | Location | Sq. Mi. | Sq. Km. |
| --- | --- | --- | --- |
| Albert, L. | Uganda-Zaire | 2,160 | 5,594 |
| Aral Sea | Kazakhstan-Uzbekistan | 24,700 | 64,100 |
| Athabasca, L. | Canada | 3,064 | 7,935 |
| Bajkal, Ozero (L. Baikal) | Russia | 12,200 | 31,500 |
| Balqash kölï (L. Balkhash) | Kazakhstan | 7,100 | 18,300 |
| Caspian Sea | Asia-Europe | 143,240 | 370,990 |
| Chad, L. | Cameroon-Chad-Nigeria | 6,300 | 16,300 |
| Erie, L. | Canada-U.S. | 9,910 | 25,667 |
| Eyre, L. | Australia | 3,700 | 9,500 |
| Great Bear L. | Canada | 12,095 | 31,326 |
| Great Salt L. | U.S. | 1,680 | 4,351 |
| Great Slave L. | Canada | 11,030 | 28,568 |
| Huron, L. | Canada-U.S. | 23,000 | 60,000 |
| Mai-Ndombe, Lac | Zaire | 3,100 | 8,000 |
| Michigan, L. | U.S. | 22,300 | 57,800 |
| Nicaragua, Lago de | Nicaragua | 3,150 | 8,158 |
| Nyasa, L. | Malawi-Mozambique-Tanzania | 11,150 | 28,878 |
| Ontario, L. | Canada-U.S. | 7,540 | 19,529 |
| Rudolf, L. | Ethiopia-Kenya | 2,473 | 6,405 |
| Superior, L. | Canada-U.S. | 31,700 | 82,100 |
| Tanganyika. L. | Africa | 12,350 | 31,986 |
| Titicaca, Lago | Bolivia-Peru | 3,200 | 8,300 |
| Tônlé Sab | Cambodia | 2,500 | 6,500 |
| Vänern | Sweden | 2,156 | 5,584 |
| Victoria, L. | Kenya-Tanzania-Uganda | 26,820 | 69,463 |
| Winnipeg, L. | Canada | 9,416 | 24,387 |
| Woods, Lake of the | Canada-U.S. | 1,727 | 4,472 |

## Principal Rivers

| Name | Location | Mi. | Km. |
| --- | --- | --- | --- |
| Amazon-Ucayali | S.A. | 4,000 | 6,400 |
| Amur (Heilong) | Asia | 2,744 | 4,416 |
| Angara | Asia | 1,105 | 1,779 |
| Arkansas | N.A. | 1,459 | 2,348 |
| Ayeyarwady (Irrawaddy) | Asia | 1,300 | 2,100 |
| Brahmaputra | Asia | 1,770 | 2,849 |
| Changjiang (Yangtze) | Asia | 3,900 | 6,300 |
| Churchill | N.A. | 1,000 | 1,600 |
| Colorado | N.A. | 1,450 | 2,334 |
| Columbia | N.A. | 1,200 | 2,000 |
| Congo (Zaïre) | Africa | 2,900 | 4,700 |
| Danube | Europe | 1,776 | 2,858 |
| Darling | Australia | 864 | 1,390 |
| Dnestr | Europe | 840 | 1,352 |
| Dnieper | Europe | 1,400 | 2,200 |
| Don | Europe | 1,162 | 1,870 |
| Euphrates (Al-Furāt) | Asia | 1,510 | 2,430 |
| Ganges | Asia | 1,560 | 2,511 |
| Grande, Rio | N.A. | 1,885 | 3,034 |
| Huanghe (Yellow) | Asia | 3,395 | 5,464 |
| Indus | Asia | 1,800 | 2,900 |
| Jenisej (Yenisey) | Asia | 2,543 | 4,092 |
| Kasai | Africa | 1,338 | 2,153 |
| Lena | Asia | 2,700 | 4,400 |
| Limpopo | Africa | 1,100 | 1,800 |
| Mackenzie | N.A. | 2,635 | 4,241 |
| Madeira | S.A. | 2,013 | 3,240 |
| Mekong | Asia | 2,600 | 4,200 |
| Mississippi | N.A. | 2,348 | 3,779 |
| Mississippi-Missouri | N.A. | 3,740 | 6,019 |
| Murray | Australia | 1,566 | 2,520 |
| Negro | S.A. | 1,300 | 2,100 |
| Niger | Africa | 2,600 | 4,200 |
| Nile | Africa | 4,145 | 6,671 |
| Ob'-Irtyš | Asia | 3,362 | 5,410 |
| Ohio | N.A. | 981 | 1,579 |
| Orange | Africa | 1,300 | 2,100 |
| Orinoco | S.A. | 1,600 | 2,600 |
| Paraguay | S.A. | 1,610 | 2,591 |
| Peace | N.A. | 1,195 | 1,923 |
| Pečora | Europe | 1,124 | 1,809 |
| Purus | S.A. | 1,860 | 2,993 |
| Red | N.A. | 1,270 | 2,044 |
| Rhine (Rhein) | Europe | 820 | 1,320 |
| Rio de la Plata--Paraná | S.A. | 3,030 | 4,876 |
| St. Lawrence | N.A. | 800 | 1,300 |
| Salween (Nu) | Asia | 1,750 | 2,816 |
| São Francisco | S.A. | 1,988 | 3,199 |
| Saskatchewan--Bow | N.A. | 1,205 | 1,939 |
| Snake | N.A. | 1,038 | 1,670 |
| Tennessee | N.A. | 652 | 1,049 |
| Tigris | Asia | 1,180 | 1,899 |
| Ural | Asia | 1,509 | 2,428 |
| Uruguay | S.A. | 1,025 | 1,650 |
| Volga | Europe | 2,194 | 3,531 |
| Yukon | N.A. | 1,770 | 2,849 |
| Zambezi | Africa | 1,700 | 2,700 |

## Largest Countries: Area

| | Country | Area Sq. Mi. | Area Sq. Km. |
|---|---|---|---|
| 1 | Russia | 6,592,849 | 17,075,400 |
| 2 | Canada | 3,849,674 | 9,970,610 |
| 3 | United States | 3,787,425 | 9,809,431 |
| 4 | China | 3,689,631 | 9,556,100 |
| 5 | Brazil | 3,286,488 | 8,511,965 |
| 6 | Australia | 2,966,155 | 7,682,300 |
| 7 | India | 1,237,062 | 3,203,975 |
| 8 | Argentina | 1,073,400 | 2,780,092 |
| 9 | Kazakhstan | 1,049,156 | 2,717,300 |
| 10 | Sudan | 967,500 | 2,505,813 |
| 11 | Algeria | 919,595 | 2,381,741 |
| 12 | Zaire | 905,446 | 2,345,095 |
| 13 | Greenland | 840,004 | 2,175,600 |
| 14 | Saudi Arabia | 830,000 | 2,149,690 |
| 15 | Mexico | 756,066 | 1,958,201 |
| 16 | Indonesia | 752,410 | 1,948,732 |
| 17 | Libya | 679,362 | 1,759,540 |
| 18 | Iran | 632,457 | 1,638,057 |
| 19 | Mongolia | 604,829 | 1,566,500 |
| 20 | Peru | 496,225 | 1,285,216 |
| 21 | Chad | 495,755 | 1,284,000 |
| 22 | Niger | 489,191 | 1,267,000 |
| 23 | Angola | 481,354 | 1,246,700 |
| 24 | Mali | 478,767 | 1,240,000 |
| 25 | South Africa | 471,090 | 1,220,118 |
| 26 | Ethiopia | 446,953 | 1,157,603 |
| 27 | Colombia | 440,831 | 1,141,748 |
| 28 | Bolivia | 424,165 | 1,098,581 |
| 29 | Mauritania | 395,956 | 1,025,520 |
| 30 | Egypt | 386,662 | 1,001,449 |
| 31 | Tanzania | 364,900 | 945,087 |
| 32 | Nigeria | 356,669 | 923,768 |
| 33 | Venezuela | 352,145 | 912,050 |
| 34 | Pakistan | 339,732 | 879,902 |
| 35 | Namibia | 317,818 | 823,144 |
| 36 | Mozambique | 308,642 | 799,380 |
| 37 | Turkey | 300,948 | 779,452 |
| 38 | Chile | 292,135 | 756,626 |
| 39 | Zambia | 290,586 | 752,614 |
| 40 | Myanmar | 261,228 | 676,577 |
| 41 | Afghanistan | 251,826 | 652,225 |
| 42 | Somalia | 246,201 | 637,657 |
| 43 | Central African Republic | 240,535 | 622,984 |
| 44 | Ukraine | 233,090 | 603,700 |
| 45 | Madagascar | 226,658 | 587,041 |
| 46 | Kenya | 224,961 | 582,646 |
| 47 | Botswana | 224,711 | 582,000 |
| 48 | France | 211,208 | 547,026 |
| 49 | Yemen | 205,356 | 531,869 |
| 50 | Thailand | 198,115 | 513,115 |
| 51 | Spain | 194,885 | 504,750 |
| 52 | Turkmenistan | 188,456 | 488,100 |
| 53 | Cameroon | 183,569 | 475,442 |
| 54 | Papua New Guinea | 178,704 | 462,840 |

## Smallest Countries: Area

| | Country | Area Sq. Mi. | Area Sq. Km. |
|---|---|---|---|
| 1 | Vatican City | 0.2 | 0.4 |
| 2 | Monaco | 0.7 | 1.9 |
| 3 | Nauru | 8.1 | 21 |
| 4 | Tuvalu | 10 | 26 |
| 5 | San Marino | 24 | 61 |
| 6 | Anguilla | 35 | 91 |
| 7 | Liechtenstein | 62 | 160 |
| 8 | Marshall Islands | 70 | 181 |
| 9 | Aruba | 75 | 193 |
| 10 | Cook Islands | 91 | 236 |
| 11 | Niue | 100 | 258 |
| 12 | St. Kitts and Nevis | 104 | 269 |
| 13 | Maldives | 115 | 298 |
| 14 | Malta | 122 | 316 |
| 15 | Grenada | 133 | 344 |
| 16 | St. Vincent and the Grenadines | 150 | 388 |
| 17 | Barbados | 166 | 430 |
| 18 | Antigua and Barbuda | 171 | 443 |
| 19 | Andorra | 175 | 453 |
| | Seychelles | 175 | 453 |
| 20 | Northern Mariana Islands | 184 | 477 |
| 21 | Palau | 196 | 508 |
| 22 | Isle of Man | 221 | 572 |
| 23 | St. Lucia | 238 | 616 |
| 24 | Singapore | 246 | 636 |
| 25 | Bahrain | 267 | 691 |
| 26 | Micronesia, Federated States of | 271 | 702 |
| 27 | Tonga | 290 | 750 |
| 28 | Dominica | 305 | 790 |
| 29 | Netherlands Antilles | 309 | 800 |
| 30 | Kiribati | 313 | 811 |
| 31 | Sao Tome and Principe | 372 | 964 |
| 32 | Faeroe Islands | 540 | 1,399 |
| 33 | Mauritius | 788 | 2,040 |
| 34 | Comoros | 863 | 2,235 |
| 35 | Luxembourg | 998 | 2,586 |
| 36 | Western Samoa | 1,093 | 2,831 |
| 37 | Cyprus, North | 1,295 | 3,355 |
| 38 | Cape Verde | 1,557 | 4,033 |
| 39 | Trinidad and Tobago | 1,980 | 5,128 |
| 40 | Brunei | 2,226 | 5,765 |
| 41 | Cyprus | 2,276 | 5,896 |
| 42 | Puerto Rico | 3,515 | 9,104 |
| 43 | Lebanon | 4,015 | 10,400 |
| 44 | Gambia | 4,127 | 10,689 |
| 45 | Jamaica | 4,244 | 10,991 |
| 46 | Qatar | 4,416 | 11,437 |
| 47 | Vanuatu | 4,707 | 12,190 |
| 48 | Bahamas | 5,382 | 13,939 |
| 49 | Swaziland | 6,704 | 17,364 |
| 50 | Kuwait | 6,880 | 17,818 |
| 51 | Fiji | 7,078 | 18,333 |

## Largest Countries: Population

| | Country | Population |
|---|---|---|
| 1 | China | 1,181,580,000 |
| 2 | India | 874,150,000 |
| 3 | United States | 253,510,000 |
| 4 | Indonesia | 195,300,000 |
| 5 | Brazil | 156,750,000 |
| 6 | Russia | 150,505,000 |
| 7 | Nigeria | 124,300,000 |
| 8 | Japan | 124,270,000 |
| 9 | Pakistan | 119,000,000 |
| 10 | Bangladesh | 118,000,000 |
| 11 | Mexico | 91,000,000 |
| 12 | Germany | 79,710,000 |
| 13 | Vietnam | 68,310,000 |
| 14 | Philippines | 62,380,000 |
| 15 | Iran | 60,000,000 |
| 16 | Turkey | 58,850,000 |
| 17 | Italy | 57,830,000 |
| 18 | United Kingdom | 57,630,000 |
| 19 | Thailand | 57,200,000 |
| 20 | France | 57,010,000 |
| 21 | Egypt | 55,105,000 |
| 22 | Ukraine | 52,800,000 |
| 23 | Ethiopia | 51,715,000 |
| 24 | Korea, South | 43,305,000 |
| 25 | Myanmar | 42,615,000 |
| 26 | South Africa | 42,224,000 |
| 27 | Spain | 39,465,000 |
| 28 | Zaire | 38,475,000 |
| 29 | Poland | 37,840,000 |
| 30 | Colombia | 33,170,000 |
| 31 | Argentina | 32,860,000 |
| 32 | Sudan | 27,630,000 |
| 33 | Tanzania | 27,325,000 |
| 34 | Canada | 26,985,000 |
| 35 | Morocco | 26,470,000 |
| 36 | Algeria | 26,360,000 |
| 37 | Kenya | 25,695,000 |
| 38 | Romania | 23,465,000 |
| 39 | Peru | 22,585,000 |
| 40 | Korea, North | 22,250,000 |
| 41 | Taiwan | 20,785,000 |
| 42 | Venezuela | 20,430,000 |
| 43 | Uzbekistan | 20,325,000 |
| 44 | Iraq | 19,915,000 |
| 45 | Nepal | 19,845,000 |
| 46 | Uganda | 18,485,000 |
| 47 | Malaysia | 18,200,000 |
| 48 | Sri Lanka | 17,530,000 |
| 49 | Australia | 17,420,000 |
| 50 | Kazakhstan | 16,880,000 |
| | Afghanistan | 16,880,000 |
| 51 | Saudi Arabia | 16,690,000 |
| 52 | Ghana | 15,865,000 |
| 53 | Mozambique | 15,460,000 |

## Smallest Countries: Population

| | Country | Population |
|---|---|---|
| 1 | Vatican City | 800 |
| 2 | Niue | 1,800 |
| 3 | Anguilla | 7,000 |
| 4 | Tuvalu | 9,000 |
| | Nauru | 9,000 |
| 5 | Palau | 15,000 |
| 6 | Cook Islands | 18,000 |
| 7 | San Marino | 23,000 |
| 8 | Liechtenstein | 28,000 |
| 9 | Monaco | 30,000 |
| 10 | St. Kitts and Nevis | 42,000 |
| 11 | Northern Mariana Islands | 46,000 |
| 12 | Faeroe Islands | 48,000 |
| 13 | Marshall Islands | 49,000 |
| 14 | Andorra | 54,000 |
| 15 | Greenland | 57,000 |
| 16 | Isle of Man | 64,000 |
| | Aruba | 64,000 |
| | Antigua and Barbuda | 64,000 |
| 17 | Seychelles | 69,000 |
| 18 | Kiribati | 72,000 |
| 19 | Dominica | 87,000 |
| 20 | Grenada | 98,000 |
| 21 | Tonga | 103,000 |
| 22 | Micronesia, Fed. States of | 109,000 |
| 23 | St. Vincent and the Grenadines | 115,000 |
| 24 | Sao Tome and Principe | 130,000 |
| 25 | Vanuatu | 153,000 |
| 26 | St. Lucia | 155,000 |
| 27 | Netherlands Antilles | 190,000 |
| 28 | Cyprus, North | 192,000 |
| | Western Samoa | 192,000 |
| 29 | Maldives | 230,000 |
| 30 | Belize | 232,000 |
| 31 | Barbados | 257,000 |
| 32 | Bahamas | 260,000 |
| 33 | Iceland | 261,000 |
| 34 | Djibouti | 351,000 |
| 35 | Solomon Islands | 353,000 |
| 36 | Malta | 357,000 |
| 37 | Equatorial Guinea | 384,000 |
| 38 | Luxembourg | 390,000 |
| 39 | Cape Verde | 393,000 |
| 40 | Suriname | 405,000 |
| 41 | Brunei | 411,000 |
| 42 | Comoros | 484,000 |
| 43 | Qatar | 532,000 |
| 44 | Bahrain | 546,000 |
| 45 | Cyprus | 713,000 |
| 46 | Fiji | 747,000 |
| 47 | Guyana | 748,000 |
| 48 | Swaziland | 875,000 |
| 49 | Gambia | 889,000 |

## Highest Urban Population

| Country | Percent Urban |
|---|---|
| 1 Monaco | 100% |
| Singapore | 100% |
| Vatican City | 100% |
| 2 Belgium | 97% |
| 3 Kuwait | 96% |
| 4 United Kingdom | 93% |
| 5 Israel | 92% |
| 6 Iceland | 91% |
| Venezuela | 91% |
| 7 Qatar | 90% |
| 8 Netherlands | 89% |
| 9 Malta | 87% |
| 10 Argentina | 86% |
| Australia | 86% |
| Chile | 86% |
| Denmark | 86% |
| Uruguay | 86% |
| 11 Germany | 84% |
| Lebanon | 84% |
| Luxembourg | 84% |
| New Zealand | 84% |
| Sweden | 84% |

## Lowest Urban Population

| Country | Percent Urban |
|---|---|
| 1 Bhutan | 5% |
| 2 Burundi | 7% |
| 3 Rwanda | 8% |
| 4 Burkina Faso | 9% |
| 5 Nepal | 10% |
| Uganda | 10% |
| 6 Oman | 11% |
| Solomon Islands | 11% |
| 7 Cambodia | 12% |
| 8 Ethiopia | 13% |
| 9 Bangladesh | 14% |
| 10 Grenada | 15% |
| Malawi | 15% |
| 11 Northern Mariana Islands | 16% |
| Papua New Guinea | 16% |
| 12 Laos | 19% |
| Mali | 19% |
| Micronesia, Fed. States of | 19% |
| 13 Lesotho | 20% |
| Niger | 20% |
| 14 China | 21% |
| Sri Lanka | 21% |

## Highest Life Expectancy

| Country | Years M | F |
|---|---|---|
| 1 Japan | 76 | 82 |
| 2 Iceland | 75 | 81 |
| Sweden | 75 | 81 |
| Switzerland | 75 | 81 |
| 3 Andorra | 74 | 81 |
| Canada | 74 | 81 |
| Netherlands | 74 | 81 |
| Norway | 74 | 81 |
| 4 France | 73 | 81 |
| 5 Australia | 74 | 80 |
| Spain | 74 | 80 |
| 6 Cyprus | 74 | 79 |
| Greece | 74 | 79 |
| 7 Faeroe Islands | 73 | 80 |
| Italy | 73 | 80 |
| United States | 73 | 80 |
| 8 Denmark | 73 | 79 |
| New Zealand | 73 | 79 |
| Puerto Rico | 73 | 79 |
| United Kingdom | 73 | 79 |
| 9 Finland | 72 | 80 |
| Monaco | 72 | 80 |

## Lowest Life Expectancy

| Country | Years M | F |
|---|---|---|
| 1 Gambia | 34 | 47 |
| 2 Ethiopia | 41 | 45 |
| Sierra Leone | 41 | 45 |
| 3 Afghanistan | 43 | 44 |
| 4 Guinea | 43 | 46 |
| 5 Mali | 44 | 48 |
| 6 Angola | 45 | 48 |
| Niger | 45 | 48 |
| 7 Guinea-Bissau | 45 | 49 |
| Somalia | 45 | 49 |
| 8 Central African Republic | 46 | 49 |
| Chad | 46 | 49 |
| 9 Mauritania | 46 | 50 |
| Senegal | 46 | 50 |
| 10 Benin | 47 | 50 |
| Equatorial Guinea | 47 | 50 |
| Mozambique | 47 | 50 |
| 11 Djibouti | 47 | 51 |
| 12 Malawi | 48 | 50 |
| 13 Burkina Faso | 48 | 51 |
| 14 Bhutan | 49 | 47 |

## Highest Literacy

| Country | Percent Literate |
|---|---|
| 1 Australia | 100% |
| Finland | 100% |
| Iceland | 100% |
| Liechtenstein | 100% |
| Luxembourg | 100% |
| Tonga | 100% |
| Vatican City | 100% |
| 2 Armenia | 99% |
| Austria | 99% |
| Barbados | 99% |
| Belarus | 99% |
| Belgium | 99% |
| Canada | 99% |
| Denmark | 99% |
| France | 99% |
| Georgia | 99% |
| Germany | 99% |
| Hungary | 99% |
| Japan | 99% |
| Netherlands | 99% |
| New Zealand | 99% |
| Norway | 99% |
| Poland | 99% |
| Russia | 99% |
| Slovenia | 99% |
| Sweden | 99% |
| Switzerland | 99% |
| United Kingdom | 99% |

## Lowest Literacy

| Country | Percent Literate |
|---|---|
| 1 Burkina Faso | 18% |
| 2 Sierra Leone | 21% |
| 3 Malawi | 22% |
| 4 Benin | 23% |
| Botswana | 23% |
| 5 Guinea | 24% |
| Somalia | 24% |
| 6 Nepal | 26% |
| 7 Central African Republic | 27% |
| Gambia | 27% |
| Sudan | 27% |
| 8 Niger | 28% |
| 9 Afghanistan | 29% |
| 10 Chad | 30% |
| 11 Mali | 32% |
| 12 Mozambique | 33% |
| 13 Mauritania | 34% |
| 14 Bangladesh | 35% |
| Cambodia | 35% |
| Pakistan | 35% |
| 15 Guinea-Bissau | 36% |
| 16 Namibia | 38% |
| Senegal | 38% |
| Yemen | 38% |
| 17 Liberia | 40% |
| 18 Angola | 42% |
| 19 Tanzania | 46% |
| 20 Egypt | 48% |
| India | 48% |

## Highest GDP U.S. $ / Capita

| Country | GDP/ Capita |
|---|---|
| 1 Liechtenstein | $22,500 |
| 2 United States | *21,847* |
| 3 Qatar | 20,625 |
| 4 Canada | 19,561 |
| 5 Switzerland | 19,025 |
| 6 Luxembourg | 18,110 |
| 7 Norway | 17,658 |
| 8 Japan | *17,148* |
| 9 Iceland | 16,535 |
| 10 San Marino | 16,375 |
| 11 Sweden | 16,206 |
| 12 France | 15,540 |
| 13 Finland | 15,507 |
| 14 Denmark | 15,190 |
| 15 Australia | 15,009 |
| 16 United Kingdom | 14,970 |
| 17 Germany | 14,798 |
| 18 Netherlands | 14,705 |
| 19 Belgium | 14,660 |
| 20 Italy | 14,659 |

## Lowest GDP U.S. $ / Capita

| Country | GDP/ Capita |
|---|---|
| 1 Mozambique | $ 91 |
| 2 Cambodia | 132 |
| 3 Ethiopia | 136 |
| 4 Laos | 151 |
| 5 Nepal | 158 |
| 6 Guinea-Bissau | 160 |
| 7 Bhutan | 183 |
| 8 Zaire | 188 |
| 9 Bangladesh | 190 |
| 10 Malawi | 192 |
| 11 Burkina Faso | 204 |
| Burundi | 204 |
| 12 Afghanistan | 205 |
| 13 Madagascar | 207 |
| 14 Chad | 209 |
| 15 Somalia | 216 |
| 16 Mali | 221 |
| 17 Vietnam | *232* |
| 18 Lesotho | 237 |
| 19 Gambia | 242 |

**Figures in italics are GNP.**

# Index

## Introduction to the Index

This universal index includes in a single alphabetical list more than 7,000 names of features that appear on the world travel maps on pages 81 through 144. Each name is followed by latitude and longitude coordinates and a page reference.

**Names:** Local official names are used on the maps and in the index. The names are shown in full, including diacritical marks. Features that extend beyond the boundaries of one country and have no single official name are usually named in English. Many conventional English names and former names are cross-referenced to the official names. Names that appear in shortened versions on the maps due to space limitiations are spelled out in full in the index. The portions of these names omitted from the maps are enclosed in brackets—for example, Acapulco [de Juárez].

**Transliteration:** For names in languages not written in the Roman alphabet, the locally official transliteration system has been used where one exists. Thus, names in Russia and Bulgaria have been transliterated according to the systems adopted by the academies of science of these countries. Similarly, the transliteration for mainland Chinese names follows the Pinyin system, which has been officially adopted in mainland China. For languages with no one locally accepted system, notably Arabic, transliteration closely follows a system adopted by the United States Board on Geographic Names.

**Abbreviation and Capitalization:** Abbreviations of names on the maps have been standardized as much as possible. Names that are abbreviated on the maps are generally spelled out in full in the index. Periods are used after all abbreviations regardless of local practice. The abbreviation "St." is used only for "Saint". "Sankt" and other forms of this term are spelled out.

Most initial letters of names are capitalized, except for a few Dutch names, such as "'s-Gravenhage". Capitalization of noninitial words in a name generally follows local practice.

**Alphabetization:** Names are alphabetized in the order of the letters of the English alphabet. Spanish *ll* and *ch*, for example, are not treated as distinct letters. Furthermore, diacritical marks are disregarded in alphabetization—German or Scandinavian *ä* or *ö* are treated as *a* or *o*.

The names of physical features may appear inverted, since they are always alphabetized under the proper,

not the generic, part of the name, thus: "Gibraltar, Strait of ᵾ". Otherwise every entry, whether consisting of one word or more, is alphabetized as a single continuous entity. "La Habana," for example, appears after "Lagunillas" and before "Lahaina." Names beginning with articles (Le Havre, Den Helder, Al-Qāhirah, As-Suways) are not inverted. Names beginning "St.", "Ste." and "Sainte" are alphabetized as though spelled "Saint."

In the case of identical names, towns are listed first, then political divisions, then physical features. Entries that are completely identical (including symbols, discussed below) are distinguished by abbreviations of their country names. The country abbreviations used for places in the United States, Canada and United Kingdom indicate the state, province or political division in which the feature is located. (See List of Abbreviations on page 154).

**Symbols:** City names are not followed by symbols. The names of all other features are followed by symbols that graphically represent broad categories of features, for example, ᴧ for mountain (Everest, Mount ᴧ). Superior numbers indicate finer distinctions, for example, ᴧ¹ for volcano (Fuji-san ᴧ¹). A complete list of symbols, including those with superior numbers, follows the List of Abbreviations.

All cross-references are indicated by the symbol →.

**Page References and Geographical Coordinates:** The page references and geographical coordinates are found in the last three columns of each entry.

The page number generally refers to the map that shows the feature at the best scale. Countries, mountain ranges and other extensive features are usually indexed to maps that both show the features completely and also show them in their relationship to broad areas. Page references to two-page maps always refer to the left-hand page. If a page contains several maps or insets, a lowercase letter may identify the specific map or inset.

Latitude and longitude coordinates for point features, such as cities and mountain peaks, indicate the locations of the symbols. For extensive areal features, such as countries or mountain ranges, locations are given for the approximate center of the feature. Those for linear features, such as canals and rivers, are given to the mouth or terminal point.

## List of Abbreviations

| | English | Local Name |
|---|---|---|
| **Ab., Can.** | Alberta, Can. | Alberta |
| **Afg.** | Afghanistan | Afghānestān |
| **Afr.** | Africa | — |
| **Ak., U.S.** | Alaska, U.S. | Alaska |
| **Al., U.S.** | Alabama, U.S. | Alabama |
| **Alb.** | Albania | Shqipëri |
| **Alg.** | Algeria | Algérie (French) / Djazaïr (Arabic) |
| **Am. Sam.** | American Samoa | American Samoa (English) / Amerika Samoa (Samoan) |
| **And.** | Andorra | Andorra |
| **Ang.** | Angola | Angola |
| **Anguilla** | Anguilla | Anguilla |
| **Ant.** | Antarctica | — |
| **Antig.** | Antigua and Barbuda | Antigua and Barbuda |
| **Ar., U.S.** | Arkansas, U.S. | Arkansas |
| **Arg.** | Argentina | Argentina |
| **Arm.** | Armenia | Hayastan |
| **Aruba** | Aruba | Aruba |
| **Asia** | Asia | — |
| **Aus.** | Austria | Österreich |
| **Austl.** | Australia | Australia |
| **Az., U.S.** | Arizona, U.S. | Arizona |
| **Azer.** | Azerbaijan | Azerbaijan |
| **Bah.** | Bahamas | Bahamas |
| **Bahr.** | Bahrain | Al-Baḥrayn |
| **Barb.** | Barbados | Barbados |
| **B.C., Can.** | British Columbia, Can. | British Columbia (English) / Colombie-Britannique (French) |
| **Bdi.** | Burundi | Burundi |
| **Bel.** | Belgium | Belgique (French) / België (Flemish) |
| **Bela.** | Belarus | Belarus |
| **Belize** | Belize | Belize |
| **Benin** | Benin | Bénin |
| **Ber.** | Bermuda | Bermuda |
| **Bhu.** | Bhutan | Druk-Yul |
| **B.I.O.T.** | British Indian Ocean Territory | British Indian Ocean Territory |
| **Bngl.** | Bangladesh | Bangladesh |
| **Bol.** | Bolivia | Bolivia |
| **Bos.** | Bosnia and Herzegovina | Bosna i Hercegovina |
| **Bots.** | Botswana | Botswana |
| **Braz.** | Brazil | Brasil |
| **Br. Vir. Is.** | British Virgin Islands | British Virgin Islands |
| **Bru.** | Brunei | Brunei |
| **Bul.** | Bulgaria | Bâlgarija |
| **Burkina** | Burkina Faso | Burkina Faso |

| | English | Local Name |
|---|---|---|
| **Ca., U.S.** | California, U.S. | California |
| **Cam.** | Cameroon | Cameroun (French) / Cameroon (English) |
| **Camb.** | Cambodia | Kâmpŭchéa |
| **Can.** | Canada | Canada |
| **C.A.R.** | Central African Republic | République centrafricaine |
| **Cay. Is.** | Cayman Islands | Cayman Islands |
| **Chad** | Chad | Tchad |
| **Chile** | Chile | Chile |
| **China** | China | Zhongguo |
| **Christ. I.** | Christmas Island | Christmas Island |
| **C. Iv.** | Cote d'Ivoire | Côte d'Ivoire |
| **Co., U.S.** | Colorado, U.S. | Colorado |
| **Cocos Is.** | Cocos (Keeling) Islands | Cocos (Keeling) Islands |
| **Col.** | Colombia | Colombia |
| **Com.** | Comoros | Comores (French) / Al-Qumur (Arabic) |
| **Congo** | Congo | Congo |
| **Cook Is.** | Cook Islands | Cook Islands |
| **C.R.** | Costa Rica | Costa Rica |
| **Cro.** | Croatia | Hrvatska |
| **Ct., U.S.** | Connecticut, U.S. | Connecticut |
| **Cuba** | Cuba | Cuba |
| **C.V.** | Cape Verde | Cabo Verde |
| **Cyp.** | Cyprus | Kípros (Greek) / Kıbrıs (Turkish) |
| **Czech Rep.** | Czech Republic | Česká Republika |
| **D.C., U.S.** | District of Columbia, U.S. | District of Columbia |
| **De., U.S.** | Delaware, U.S. | Delaware |
| **Den.** | Denmark | Danmark |
| **Dji.** | Djibouti | Djibouti |
| **Dom.** | Dominica | Dominica |
| **Dom. Rep.** | Dominican Republic | República Dominicana |
| **Ger.** | Germany | Deutschland |
| **Ec.** | Ecuador | Ecuador |
| **Egypt** | Egypt | Mişr |
| **El Sal.** | El Salvador | El Salvador |
| **Eng., U.K.** | England, U.K. | England |
| **Eq. Gui.** | Equatorial Guinea | Guinea Ecuatorial |
| **Erit.** | Eritrea | Eritrea |
| **Est.** | Estonia | Eesti |
| **Eth.** | Ethiopia | Ityopiya |
| **Eur.** | Europe | — |
| **Faer. Is.** | Faeroe Islands | Føroyar |
| **Falk. Is.** | Falkland Islands | Falkland Islands |

| | English | Local Name | | English | Local Name |
|---|---|---|---|---|---|
| **Fiji** | Fiji | Fiji | **Kor., N.** | North Korea | Chosŏn- |
| **Fin.** | Finland | Suomi | | | minjujuŭi- |
| | | (Finnish) / | | | inmĭn- |
| | | Finland | | | konghwaguk |
| | | (Swedish) | **Kor., S.** | South Korea | Taehan- |
| **Fl., U.S.** | Florida, U.S. | Florida | | | min'guk |
| **Fr.** | France | France | **Ks., U.S.** | Kansas, U.S. | Kansas |
| **Fr. Gu.** | French Guiana | Guyane | **Kuw.** | Kuwait | Al-Kuwayt |
| | | française | **Ky., U.S.** | Kentucky, U.S. | Kentucky |
| **Fr. Poly.** | French | Polynésie | **Kyrg.** | Kyrgyzstan | Kyrgyzstan |
| | Polynesia | française | **La., U.S.** | Louisiana, | Louisiana |
| **Ga., U.S.** | Georgia, U.S. | Georgia | | U.S. | |
| **Gabon** | Gabon | Gabon | **Laos** | Laos | Lao |
| **Gam.** | Gambia | Gambia | **Lat.** | Latvia | Latvija |
| **Geor.** | Georgia | Sakartvelo | **Leb.** | Lebanon | Lubnān |
| **Ghana** | Ghana | Ghana | **Leso.** | Lesotho | Lesotho |
| **Gib.** | Gibraltar | Gibraltar | **Lib.** | Liberia | Liberia |
| **Grc.** | Greece | Ellás | **Libya** | Libya | Lībiyā |
| **Gren.** | Grenada | Grenada | **Liech.** | Liechtenstein | Liechtenstein |
| **Grnld.** | Greenland | Kalaallit | **Lith.** | Lithuania | Lietuva |
| | | Nunaat | **Lux.** | Luxembourg | Luxembourg |
| | | (Eskimo) / | **Ma., U.S.** | Massachusetts, | Massachusetts |
| | | Grønland | | U.S. | |
| | | (Danish) | **Macao** | Macao | Macau |
| **Guad.** | Guadeloupe | Guadeloupe | **Mac.** | Macedonia | Makedonija |
| **Guam** | Guam | Guam | **Madag.** | Madagascar | Madagasikara |
| **Guat.** | Guatemala | Guatemala | | | (Malagasy) / |
| **Guernsey** | Guernsey | Guernsey | | | Madagascar |
| **Gui.** | Guinea | Guinée | | | (French) |
| **Gui.-B.** | Guinea-Bissau | Guiné-Bissau | **Malay.** | Malaysia | Malaysia |
| **Guy.** | Guyana | Guyana | **Mald.** | Maldives | Maldives |
| **Haiti** | Haiti | Haïti | **Mali** | Mali | Mali |
| **Hi., U.S.** | Hawaii, U.S. | Hawaii | **Malta** | Malta | Malta |
| **H.K.** | Hong Kong | Hong Kong | **Marsh. Is.** | Marshall | Marshall |
| **Hond.** | Honduras | Honduras | | Islands | Islands |
| **Hung.** | Hungary | Magyarország | **Mart.** | Martinique | Martinique |
| **Ia., U.S.** | Iowa, U.S. | Iowa | **Maur.** | Mauritania | Mauritanie |
| **Ice.** | Iceland | Ísland | | | (French) / |
| **Id., U.S.** | Idaho, U.S. | Idaho | | | Mūrītāniyā |
| **Il., U.S.** | Illinois, U.S. | Illinois | | | (Arabic) |
| **In., U.S.** | Indiana, U.S. | Indiana | **May.** | Mayotte | Mayotte |
| **India** | India | India (English) | **Mb., Can.** | Manitoba, | Manitoba |
| | | / Bharat | | Can. | |
| | | (Hindi) | **Md., U.S.** | Maryland, | Maryland |
| **Indon.** | Indonesia | Indonesia | | U.S. | |
| **I. of Man** | Isle of Man | Isle of Man | **Me., U.S.** | Maine, U.S. | Maine |
| **Iran** | Iran | Īrān | **Mex.** | Mexico | México |
| **Iraq** | Iraq | Al-'Irāq | **Mi., U.S.** | Michigan, U.S. | Michigan |
| **Ire.** | Ireland | Ireland | **Micron.** | Federated | Federated |
| | | (English) / | | States of | States of |
| | | Éire (Gaelic) | | Micronesia | Micronesia |
| **Isr.** | Israel | Yisra'el | **Mid. Is.** | Midway | Midway |
| | | (Hebrew) / | | Islands | Islands |
| | | Isrā'īl | **Mn., U.S.** | Minnesota, | Minnesota |
| | | (Arabic) | | U.S. | |
| **Isr. Occ.** | Israeli | — | **Mo., U.S.** | Missouri, U.S. | Missouri |
| | Occupied | | **Mol.** | Moldova | Moldova |
| | Areas | | **Mon.** | Monaco | Monaco |
| **Italy** | Italy | Italia | **Mong.** | Mongolia | Mongol Ard |
| **Jam.** | Jamaica | Jamaica | | | Uls |
| **Japan** | Japan | Nihon | **Monts.** | Montserrat | Montserrat |
| **Jersey** | Jersey | Jersey | **Mor.** | Morocco | Al-Magreb |
| **Jord.** | Jordan | Al-Urdun | **Moz.** | Mozambique | Moçambique |
| **Kaz.** | Kazakhstan | Kazachstan | **Mrts.** | Mauritius | Mauritius |
| **Kenya** | Kenya | Kenya | **Ms., U.S.** | Mississippi, | Mississippi |
| **Kir.** | Kiribati | Kiribati | | U.S. | |
| | | | **Mt., U.S.** | Montana, U.S. | Montana |

| | English | Local Name | | English | Local Name |
|---|---|---|---|---|---|
| Sp. N. Afr. | Spanish North Africa | Plazas de Soberanía en el Norte de África | U.A.E. | United Arab Emirates | Al-Imārāt al-'Arabīyah al-Muttaḥidah |
| Sri L. | Sri Lanka | Sri Lanka | Ug. | Uganda | Uganda |
| St. Hel. | St. Helena | St. Helena | U.K. | United Kingdom | United Kingdom |
| St. K./N. | St. Kitts and Nevis | St. Kitts and Nevis | Ukr. | Ukraine | Ukraina |
| St. Luc. | St. Lucia | St. Lucia | Ur. | Uruguay | Uruguay |
| St. P./M. | St. Pierre and Miquelon | Saint-Pierre-et-Miquelon | U.S. | United States | United States |
| | | | Ut., U.S. | Utah, U.S. | Utah |
| S. Tom./P. | Sao Tome and Principe | São Tomé e Príncipe | Uzb. | Uzbekistan | Uzbekistan |
| | | | Va., U.S. | Virginia, U.S. | Virginia |
| St. Vin. | St. Vincent and the Grenadines | St. Vincent and the Grenadines | Vanuatu | Vanuatu | Vanuatu |
| | | | Vat. | Vatican City | Cittá del Vaticano |
| Sudan | Sudan | As-Sūdān | Ven. | Venezuela | Venezuela |
| Sur. | Suriname | Suriname | Viet | Vietnam | Viet Nam |
| Swaz. | Swaziland | Swaziland | V.I.U.S. | Virgin Islands (U.S.) | Virgin Islands (U.S.) |
| Swe. | Sweden | Sverige | Vt., U.S. | Vermont, U.S. | Vermont |
| Switz. | Switzerland | Schweiz (German) / Suisse (French) / Svizzera (Italian) | Wa., U.S. | Washington, U.S. | Washington |
| | | | Wake I. | Wake Island | Wake Island |
| | | | Wales, U.K. | Wales, U.K. | Wales |
| Syria | Syria | Sūrīyah | Wal./F. | Wallis and Futuna | Wallis et Futuna |
| Tai. | Taiwan | T'aiwan | Wi., U.S. | Wisconsin, U.S. | Wisconsin |
| Taj. | Tajikistan | Tajikistan | | | |
| Tan. | Tanzania | Tanzania | W. Sah. | Western Sahara | — |
| T./C. Is. | Turks and Caicos Islands | Turks and Caicos Islands | W. Sam. | Western Samoa | Western Samoa (English) / Samoa i Sisifo (Samoan) |
| Thai. | Thailand | Prathet Thai | | | |
| Tn., U.S. | Tennessee, U.S. | Tennessee | | | |
| Togo | Togo | Togo | W.V., U.S. | West Virginia, U.S. | West Virginia |
| Tok. | Tokelau | Tokelau | Wy., U.S. | Wyoming, U.S. | Wyoming |
| Tonga | Tonga | Tonga | | | |
| Trin. | Trinidad and Tobago | Trinidad and Tobago | Yemen | Yemen | Al-Yaman |
| Tun. | Tunisia | Tunisie (French) / Tunis (Arabic) | Yk., Can. | Yukon Territory, Can. | Yukon Territory |
| Tur. | Turkey | Türkiye | Yugo. | Yugoslavia | Jugoslavija |
| Turk. | Turkmenistan | Turkmenistan | Zaire | Zaire | Zaïre |
| Tuvalu | Tuvalu | Tuvalu | Zam. | Zambia | Zambia |
| Tx., U.S. | Texas, U.S. | Texas | Zimb. | Zimbabwe | Zimbabwe |

## Key to Symbols

| | | | | | | | | |
|---|---|---|---|---|---|---|---|---|
| ⋏ | **Mountain** | ‖ | **Islands** | c¹ | Estuary | □³ | State, Canton, |
| ⋏¹ | Volcano | | | c² | Fjord | | Republic |
| ⋏² | Hill | ⊥ | **Other Topographic** | c³ | Bight | □⁴ | Province, Region, |
| ⋄ | **Mountains** | | **Features** | | | | Oblast |
| ⋄¹ | Plateau | ⊥¹ | Continent | ⊜ | **Lake, Lakes** | □⁵ | Department, District, |
| ⋄² | Hills | ⊥² | Coast, Beach | ⊜¹ | Reservoir | | Prefecture |
| )( | **Pass** | ⊥³ | Isthmus | | | □⁸ | Miscellaneous |
| | | ⊥⁴ | Cliff | ⋮ | **Swamp** | □⁹ | Historical |
| Ⅴ | **Valley, Canyon** | ⊥⁶ | Crater | ⋈ | **Ice Features, Glacier** | | |
| ≃ | **Plain** | ⊥⁸ | Dunes | | | ✦ | **Recreational Site** |
| ≃¹ | Basin | ⊥⁹ | Lava Flow | ⊤ | **Other Hydrographic** | | |
| ≃² | Delta | ≃ | River | | **Features** | ➤ | **Miscellaneous** |
| ➤ | **Cape** | ≊ | Canal | ⊤¹ | Ocean | ➤¹ | Region |
| ➤¹ | Peninsula | | | ⊤² | Sea | ➤² | Desert |
| | | ʟ | **Waterfall, Rapids** | ⊤⁴ | Oasis, Well, Spring | ➤³ | Forest, Moor |
| ▮ | **Island** | ꙡ | **Strait** | □ | **Political Unit** | ➤⁴ | Reserve, Reservation |
| ▮¹ | Atoll | | | □¹ | Independent Nation | ➤⁶ | Dam |
| | | c | **Bay, Gulf** | □² | Dependency | ➤⁸ | Neighborhood |

## Index to the Maps

| Name | Page No. | Lat. | Long. |
|---|---|---|---|
| Alaska □³ | 144 | 65.00N | 153.00W |
| Alaska, Gulf of ⊂ | 144 | 58.00N | 146.00W |
| Alaska Peninsula ≻¹ | 144 | 57.00N | 158.00W |
| Alaska Range ⋌ | 144 | 62.30N | 150.00W |
| Albacete | 94 | 38.59N | 1.51W |
| Albanel, Lac ⊜ | 136 | 50.55N | 73.12W |
| Albania □¹ | 86 | 41.00N | 20.00 E |
| Albany, Austl. | 122 | 35.02S | 117.53 E |
| Albany, Ga., U.S. | 138 | 31.34N | 84.09W |
| Albany, N.Y., U.S. | 140 | 42.39N | 73.45W |
| Al-Baṣrah | 108 | 30.30N | 47.47 E |
| Albert, Lake ⊜ | 106 | 1.40N | 31.00 E |
| Alberta □⁴ | 136 | 54.00N | 113.00W |
| Albert Nile ≃ | 108 | 3.36N | 32.02 E |
| Ålborg | 89 | 57.03N | 9.56 E |
| Albuquerque | 138 | 35.05N | 106.39W |
| Albury | 122 | 36.05S | 146.55 E |
| Alcalá de Guadaira | 94 | 37.20N | 5.50W |
| Alcalá de Henares | 94 | 40.29N | 3.22W |
| Alcira | 94 | 39.09N | 0.26W |
| Alcoy | 94 | 38.42N | 0.28W |
| Aldabra Islands I¹ | 106 | 9.25S | 46.22 E |
| Aldama | 128 | 28.51N | 105.54W |
| Aldan | 102 | 58.37N | 125.24 E |
| Aleksandrovsk-Sachalinskij | 102 | 50.54N | 142.10 E |
| Alentejo □⁹ | 94 | 38.00N | 8.00W |
| Alenuihaha Channel ⋃ | 143 | 20.26N | 156.00W |
| Alessandria | 96 | 44.54N | 8.37 E |
| Aleutian Islands II | 144 | 52.00N | 176.00W |
| Alexander, Cape ≻ | 127a | 6.35S | 156.30 E |
| Alexander Archipelago II | 144 | 56.30N | 134.00W |
| Alexander Bay | 106 | 28.40S | 16.30 E |
| Alexandra | 126 | 45.15S | 169.24 E |
| Alexandria → Al-Iskandarīyah, Egypt | 104 | 31.12N | 29.54 E |
| Alexandria, Rom. | 98 | 43.58N | 25.20 E |
| Alexandria, La., U.S. | 128 | 31.18N | 92.26W |
| Alexandria, Va., U.S. | 140 | 38.48N | 77.02W |
| Alexandria Bay | 140 | 44.20N | 75.55W |
| Alexandroúpolis | 98 | 40.50N | 25.52 E |
| Al-Fāshir | 104 | 13.38N | 25.21 E |
| Al-Fayyūm | 104 | 29.19N | 30.50 E |
| Alfenas | 135 | 21.25S | 45.57W |
| Alfred | 140 | 45.34N | 74.53W |
| Algeciras | 94 | 36.08N | 5.30W |
| Algeria □¹ | 104 | 28.00N | 3.00 E |
| Alghero | 96 | 40.34N | 8.19 E |
| Algiers → El Djazaïr | 104 | 36.47N | 3.03 E |
| Al-Ḥarrah ⚲⁹ | 109 | 31.00N | 38.30 E |
| Al-Ḥijāz ◆¹ | 109 | 24.30N | 38.30 E |
| Al-Ḥudaydah | 108 | 14.48N | 42.57 E |
| Al-Hufūf | 108 | 25.22N | 49.34 E |
| Alicante | 94 | 38.21N | 0.29W |
| Alice | 128 | 27.45N | 98.04W |
| Alice Springs | 122 | 23.42S | 133.53 E |
| Alīgarh | 112 | 27.54N | 78.05 E |
| Al-Iskandarīyah (Alexandria) | 104 | 31.12N | 29.54 E |
| Al-Ismāʿīlīyah | 109 | 30.35N | 32.16 E |
| Al-Jawf | 108 | 29.50N | 39.52 E |
| Al-Jīzah | 104 | 30.01N | 31.13 E |
| Al-Khandaq | 104 | 18.36N | 30.34 E |
| Al-Kharṭūm (Khartoum) | 104 | 15.36N | 32.32 E |
| Alkmaar | 90 | 52.37N | 4.44 E |
| Al-Kuwayt | 108 | 29.20N | 47.59 E |
| Al-Lādhiqīyah (Latakia) | 109 | 35.31N | 35.47 E |
| Allāhābād | 112 | 25.27N | 81.51 E |
| Allegheny Mountains ⋌ | 140 | 38.30N | 80.00W |
| Allentown | 140 | 40.36N | 75.28W |
| Al-Madīnah (Medina) | 108 | 24.28N | 39.36 E |
| Al-Manāmah | 108 | 26.13N | 50.35 E |

| Name | Page No. | Lat. | Long. |
|---|---|---|---|
| Al-Manṣūrah | 109 | 31.03N | 31.23 E |
| Almaty (Alma-Ata) | 102 | 43.15N | 76.57 E |
| Al-Mawṣil | 108 | 36.20N | 43.08 E |
| Almendralejo | 94 | 38.41N | 6.24W |
| Almería | 94 | 36.50N | 2.27W |
| Al-Minyā | 104 | 28.06N | 30.45 E |
| Al-Mukallā | 108 | 14.32N | 49.08 E |
| Al-Mukhā | 108 | 13.19N | 43.15 E |
| Alor Setar | 120 | 6.07N | 100.22 E |
| Alpena | 140 | 45.03N | 83.25W |
| Alpine | 128 | 30.21N | 103.39W |
| Alps ⋌ | 92 | 46.25N | 10.00 E |
| Al-Qaḍārif | 104 | 14.02N | 35.24 E |
| Al-Qāhirah (Cairo) | 104 | 30.03N | 31.15 E |
| Al-Qāmishlī | 109 | 37.02N | 41.14 E |
| Al-Qaṭrūn | 104 | 24.56N | 14.38 E |
| Alsace □⁹ | 92 | 48.30N | 7.30 E |
| Alta | 89 | 69.55N | 23.12 E |
| Altagracia de Orituco | 130 | 9.52N | 66.23W |
| Altamura | 96 | 40.50N | 16.33 E |
| Altiplano ⋌¹ | 132 | 18.00S | 68.00W |
| Alton | 138 | 38.53N | 90.11W |
| Altoona | 140 | 40.31N | 78.23W |
| Al-Ubayyid | 104 | 13.11N | 30.13 E |
| Al-Uqṣur (Luxor) | 104 | 25.41N | 32.39 E |
| Alva | 138 | 36.48N | 98.39W |
| Alvarado | 128 | 18.46N | 95.46W |
| Amami-shotō II | 117b | 28.16N | 129.21 E |
| Amarillo | 138 | 35.13N | 101.49W |
| Amazon (Solimões) (Amazonas) ≃ | 132 | 0.05S | 50.00W |
| Amberg | 90 | 49.27N | 11.52 E |
| Ambon | 118 | 3.43S | 128.12 E |
| Ambositra | 106 | 20.31S | 47.15 E |
| Ambre, Cap d' ≻ | 106 | 11.57S | 49.17 E |
| Amecameca [de Juárez] | 128 | 19.07N | 98.46W |
| American Highland ⋌¹ | 85 | 72.30S | 78.00 E |
| American Samoa □² | 127e | 14.20S | 170.00W |
| Amherstburg | 140 | 42.06N | 83.06W |
| Amiens | 92 | 49.54N | 2.18 E |
| Amīndīvi Islands II | 111 | 11.23N | 72.23 E |
| Amirante Islands II | 106 | 6.00S | 53.10 E |
| ʿAmmān | 109 | 31.57N | 35.56 E |
| Ammókhostos (Famagusta) | 109 | 35.07N | 33.57 E |
| Åmot | 89 | 59.35N | 8.00 E |
| Amoy → Xiamen | 114 | 24.28N | 118.07 E |
| Amrāvati | 112 | 20.56N | 77.45 E |
| Amritsar | 112 | 31.35N | 74.53 E |
| Amsterdam, Neth. | 90 | 52.22N | 4.54 E |
| Amsterdam, N.Y., U.S. | 140 | 42.56N | 74.11W |
| Amu Darya (Amudarja) ≃ | 110 | 42.30N | 59.15 E |
| Amundsen Gulf ⊂ | 136 | 71.00N | 124.00W |
| Amundsen Sea ⊤² | 85 | 72.30S | 112.00W |
| Amur (Heilongjiang) ≃ | 102 | 52.56N | 141.10 E |
| Anaheim | 142 | 33.50N | 117.54W |
| Anakāpalle | 111 | 17.41N | 83.01 E |
| Anápolis | 135 | 16.20S | 48.58W |
| Añatuya | 134 | 28.28S | 62.50W |
| Anchorage | 144 | 61.13N | 149.54W |
| Ancona | 96 | 43.38N | 13.30 E |
| Ancud | 134 | 41.52S | 73.50W |
| Andalucía □⁹ | 94 | 37.36N | 4.30W |
| Andaman Islands II | 120 | 12.00N | 92.45 E |
| Andaman Sea ⊤² | 120 | 10.00N | 95.00 E |
| Andes ⋌ | 82 | 20.00S | 68.00W |
| Andfjorden ⋃ | 89 | 69.10N | 16.20 E |
| Andhra Pradesh □³ | 111 | 16.00N | 79.00 E |
| Andkhvoy | 112 | 36.56N | 65.08 E |
| Andoany | 106 | 13.25S | 48.16 E |
| Andorra | 94 | 42.30N | 1.31 E |
| Andorra □¹ | 86 | 42.30N | 1.30 E |
| Andradina | 135 | 20.54S | 51.23W |

| Name | Page No. | Lat. | Long. |
|---|---|---|---|
| Asenovgrad | 98 | 42.01 N | 24.52 E |
| Ashburton | 126 | 43.55 S | 171.45 E |
| Asheville | 138 | 35.36 N | 82.33 W |
| Ashikaga | 116 | 36.20 N | 139.27 E |
| Ashland, Ky., U.S. | 140 | 38.28 N | 82.38 W |
| Ashland, N.H., U.S. | 140 | 43.41 N | 71.37 W |
| Ashland, Or., U.S. | 142 | 42.11 N | 122.42 W |
| Ashland, Wi., U.S. | 138 | 46.35 N | 90.53 W |
| Ashtabula | 140 | 41.51 N | 80.47 W |
| Ashville | 140 | 39.42 N | 82.57 W |
| Asia ± 1 | 82 | 50.00 N | 100.00 E |
| Asia Minor ← 1 | 86 | 39.00 N | 32.00 E |
| Askham | 106 | 26.59 S | 20.47 E |
| Asmera | 108 | 15.20 N | 38.53 E |
| Aspiring, Mount ▲ | 126 | 44.23 S | 168.44 E |
| Assam □ 3 | 112 | 26.00 N | 92.00 E |
| Assen | 90 | 52.59 N | 6.34 E |
| Assiniboine, Mount ▲ | 136 | 50.52 N | 115.39 W |
| As-Sulaymānīyah | 86 | 35.33 N | 45.26 E |
| As-Suwaydā' | 109 | 32.42 N | 36.34 E |
| As-Suways (Suez) | 104 | 29.58 N | 32.33 E |
| Asti | 96 | 44.54 N | 8.12 E |
| Astrachan' | 86 | 46.21 N | 48.03 E |
| Astrolabe, Cape ➤ | 127a | 8.20 S | 160.34 E |
| Asunción | 134 | 25.16 S | 57.40 W |
| Aswān | 104 | 24.05 N | 32.53 E |
| Aswān High Dam ← 6 | 108 | 24.05 N | 32.53 E |
| Asyūţ | 104 | 27.11 N | 31.11 E |
| Atacama, Desierto de ← 2 | 132 | 20.00 S | 69.15 W |
| Atar | 104 | 20.31 N | 13.03 W |
| Atbarah | 104 | 17.42 N | 33.59 E |
| Atbasar | 102 | 51.48 N | 68.20 E |
| Athabasca | 136 | 54.43 N | 113.17 W |
| Athabasca, Lake ⊜ | 136 | 59.07 N | 110.00 W |
| Athens |  |  |  |
| → Athínai, Grc. | 98 | 37.58 N | 23.43 E |
| Athens, Ga., U.S. | 138 | 33.57 N | 83.22 W |
| Athens, Oh., U.S. | 140 | 39.19 N | 82.06 W |
| Athens, Pa., U.S. | 140 | 41.57 N | 76.31 W |
| Athínai (Athens) | 98 | 37.58 N | 23.43 E |
| Athlone | 88 | 53.25 N | 7.56 W |
| Atikokan | 136 | 48.45 N | 91.37 W |
| Atikonak Lake ⊜ | 136 | 52.40 N | 64.30 W |
| Atka Island I | 144 | 52.15 N | 174.30 W |
| Atlanta | 138 | 33.44 N | 84.23 W |
| Atlantic City | 140 | 39.21 N | 74.25 W |
| Atlantic Ocean ▼ 1 | 82 | 0.00 | 25.00 W |
| Atlas Mountains ✗ | 104 | 33.00 N | 2.00 W |
| Atlas Saharien ✗ | 104 | 33.25 N | 1.20 E |
| Atotonilco el Alto | 128 | 20.33 N | 102.31 W |
| Atrato ≃ | 130 | 8.17 N | 76.58 W |
| Attawapiskat | 136 | 52.55 N | 82.26 W |
| Attu Island I | 144 | 52.55 N | 173.00 E |
| Atyraū | 86 | 47.07 N | 51.56 E |
| Auburn | 140 | 42.55 N | 76.33 W |
| Auckland | 126 | 36.52 S | 174.46 E |
| Augsburg | 90 | 48.23 N | 10.53 E |
| Augusta, Austl. | 122 | 34.19 S | 115.10 E |
| Augusta, Italy | 96 | 37.13 N | 15.13 E |
| Augusta, Ga., U.S. | 138 | 33.28 N | 82.01 W |
| Augusta, Ky., U.S. | 140 | 38.46 N | 84.00 W |
| Augusta, Me., U.S. | 140 | 44.18 N | 69.46 W |
| Augustus, Mount ▲ | 122 | 24.20 S | 116.50 E |
| Aurillac | 92 | 44.56 N | 2.26 E |
| Aurora | 140 | 44.00 N | 79.28 W |
| Aus | 106 | 26.40 S | 16.15 E |
| Austin | 138 | 30.16 N | 97.44 W |
| Australia □ 1 | 122 | 25.00 S | 135.00 E |
| Australian Capital Territory □ 8 | 124 | 35.30 S | 149.00 E |
| Austria □ 1 | 86 | 47.20 N | 13.20 E |
| Autlán de Navarro | 128 | 19.46 N | 104.22 W |
| Auvergne □ 9 | 92 | 45.25 N | 2.30 E |
| Auxerre | 92 | 47.48 N | 3.34 E |
| Aveiro | 94 | 40.38 N | 8.39 W |
| Avellino | 96 | 40.54 N | 14.47 E |
| Avesta | 89 | 60.09 N | 16.12 E |
| Avezzano | 96 | 42.02 N | 13.25 E |
| Avignon | 92 | 43.57 N | 4.49 E |
| Ávila | 94 | 40.39 N | 4.42 W |
| Avilés | 94 | 43.33 N | 5.55 W |
| Avon | 140 | 42.54 N | 77.44 W |
| Axiós (Vardar) ≃ | 98 | 40.31 N | 22.43 E |
| Aydın | 98 | 37.51 N | 27.51 E |
| Ayeyarwady ≃ | 120 | 15.50 N | 95.06 E |
| Aylmer West | 140 | 42.46 N | 80.59 W |
| Ayr | 88 | 55.28 N | 4.38 W |
| Azerbaijan □ 1 | 86 | 40.30 N | 47.30 E |
| Azogues | 132 | 2.44 S | 78.50 W |
| Azores |  |  |  |
| → Açores II | 82 | 38.30 N | 28.00 W |
| Azov, Sea of ▼ 2 | 86 | 46.00 N | 36.00 E |
| Azraq, Al-Bahr al- (Blue Nile) ≃ | 104 | 15.38 N | 32.31 E |
| Azua | 130 | 18.27 N | 70.44 W |
| Azuaga | 94 | 38.16 N | 5.41 W |
| Azuero, Península de ➤ 1 | 130 | 7.40 N | 80.35 W |
| Azul | 134 | 36.47 S | 59.51 W |
| Az-Zaqāzīq | 104 | 30.35 N | 31.31 E |
| Az-Zarqā' | 109 | 32.05 N | 36.06 E |

**B**

| Name | Page No. | Lat. | Long. |
|---|---|---|---|
| Babaeski | 98 | 41.26 N | 27.06 E |
| Babelthuap I | 118 | 7.30 N | 134.36 E |
| Babuyan Islands II | 118 | 19.10 N | 121.40 E |
| Bacău | 98 | 46.34 N | 26.55 E |
| Bac Lieu | 120 | 9.17 N | 105.44 E |
| Bacolod | 118 | 10.40 N | 122.57 E |
| Badajoz | 94 | 38.53 N | 6.58 W |
| Badalona | 94 | 41.27 N | 2.15 E |
| Baden, Aus. | 90 | 48.00 N | 16.14 E |
| Baden, Switz. | 92 | 47.29 N | 8.18 E |
| Baden-Baden | 90 | 48.46 N | 8.14 E |
| Bad Ischl | 90 | 47.43 N | 13.37 E |
| Bad Kreuznach | 90 | 49.52 N | 7.51 E |
| Baffin Bay c | 136 | 73.00 N | 66.00 W |
| Baffin Island I | 136 | 68.00 N | 70.00 W |
| Bāgalkot | 111 | 16.11 N | 75.42 E |
| Bagdad |  |  |  |
| → Baghdād | 108 | 33.21 N | 44.25 E |
| Bagé | 134 | 31.20 S | 54.06 W |
| Baghdād | 108 | 33.21 N | 44.25 E |
| Bagheria | 96 | 38.05 N | 13.30 E |
| Baghlān | 112 | 36.13 N | 68.46 E |
| Bago | 120 | 17.20 N | 96.29 E |
| Baguio | 118 | 16.25 N | 120.36 E |
| Bahamas □ 1 | 130 | 24.15 N | 76.00 W |
| Bahāwalnagar | 112 | 29.59 N | 73.16 E |
| Bahāwalpur | 110 | 29.24 N | 71.41 E |
| Bahía, Islas de la II | 130 | 16.20 N | 86.30 W |
| Bahía Blanca | 134 | 38.43 S | 62.17 W |
| Bahrain □ 1 | 108 | 26.00 N | 50.30 E |
| Baia-Mare | 98 | 47.40 N | 23.35 E |
| Baie-Comeau | 136 | 49.13 N | 68.10 W |
| Baie-Saint-Paul | 136 | 47.27 N | 70.30 W |
| Băilești | 98 | 44.02 N | 23.21 E |
| Baja | 90 | 46.11 N | 18.57 E |
| Baja California ➤ 1 | 128 | 28.00 N | 113.30 W |
| Bajkal, Ozero (Lake Baikal) ⊜ | 102 | 53.00 N | 107.40 E |
| Baker, Mt., U.S. | 138 | 46.22 N | 104.17 W |
| Baker, Or., U.S. | 138 | 44.46 N | 117.49 W |
| Baker Lake | 136 | 64.15 N | 96.00 W |
| Bakersfield | 142 | 35.22 N | 119.01 W |
| Bakhtaran | 108 | 34.19 N | 47.04 E |
| Baku | 86 | 40.23 N | 49.51 E |
| Balakovo | 86 | 52.02 N | 47.47 E |
| Balaton ⊜ | 90 | 46.50 N | 17.45 E |

| Name | Page No. | Lat. | Long. |
|---|---|---|---|
| Bâle | | | |
| → Basel | 92 | 47.33N | 7.35 E |
| Baleares, Islas (Balearic Islands) ‖ | 94 | 39.30N | 3.00 E |
| Bali ‖ | 118 | 8.20S | 115.00 E |
| Balikesir | 98 | 39.39N | 27.53 E |
| Balikpapan | 118 | 1.17S | 116.50 E |
| Balkan Mountains | | | |
| → Stara Planina ⨍ | 98 | 43.15N | 25.00 E |
| Ballina | 88 | 54.07N | 9.09W |
| Ballinger | 128 | 31.44N | 99.56W |
| Balmoral Castle | 88 | 57.02N | 3.15W |
| Balqash | 102 | 46.49N | 74.59 E |
| Balqash kölï ⊜ | 102 | 46.00N | 74.00 E |
| Balsas ≃ | 128 | 17.55N | 102.10W |
| Baltic Sea ⊤² | 89 | 57.00N | 19.00 E |
| Baltimore | 140 | 39.17N | 76.36W |
| Baluchistan □⁹ | 110 | 28.00N | 63.00 E |
| Bamako | 104 | 12.39N | 8.00W |
| Bambari | 104 | 5.45N | 20.40 E |
| Bamenda | 104 | 5.56N | 10.10 E |
| Banbury | 88 | 52.04N | 1.20W |
| Banda, Laut (Banda Sea) ⊤² | 118 | 5.00S | 128.00 E |
| Banda Aceh | 118 | 5.34N | 95.20 E |
| Bandar-e 'Abbās | 108 | 27.11N | 56.17 E |
| Bandar Seri Begawan | 118 | 4.56N | 114.55 E |
| Bandırma | 98 | 40.20N | 27.58 E |
| Bandon | 142 | 43.07N | 124.24W |
| Bandundu | 106 | 3.18S | 17.20 E |
| Bandung | 118 | 6.54S | 107.36 E |
| Banes | 130 | 20.58N | 75.43W |
| Bangalore | 111 | 12.59N | 77.35 E |
| Bangassou | 104 | 4.50N | 23.07 E |
| Banggai, Kepulauan ‖ | 118 | 1.30S | 123.15 E |
| Banghāzī | 104 | 32.07N | 20.04 E |
| Bangkok | | | |
| → Krung Thep | 120 | 13.45N | 100.31 E |
| Bangladesh □¹ | 110 | 24.00N | 90.00 E |
| Bangor, N. Ire., U.K. | 88 | 54.40N | 5.40W |
| Bangor, Wales, U.K. | 88 | 53.13N | 4.08W |
| Bangor, Me., U.S. | 140 | 44.48N | 68.46W |
| Bangui | 104 | 4.22N | 18.35 E |
| Bani ≃ | 104 | 14.30N | 4.12W |
| Banī Mazār | 104 | 28.30N | 30.48 E |
| Banī Suwayf | 104 | 29.05N | 31.05 E |
| Banja Luka | 96 | 44.46N | 17.11 E |
| Banjarmasin | 118 | 3.20S | 114.35 E |
| Banjul | 104 | 13.28N | 16.39W |
| Banks Island ‖ | 136 | 73.15N | 121.30W |
| Banks Islands ‖ | 127b | 13.50S | 167.30 E |
| Banks Peninsula ➤¹ | 126 | 43.45S | 173.00 E |
| Bannu | 112 | 32.59N | 70.36 E |
| Ban Pak Phraek | 120 | 8.13N | 100.12 E |
| Banská Bystrica | 90 | 48.44N | 19.07 E |
| Baoding | 114 | 38.52N | 115.29 E |
| Baoji | 114 | 34.22N | 107.14 E |
| Baotou | 114 | 40.40N | 109.59 E |
| Baquedano | 134 | 23.20S | 69.51W |
| Baraawe | 108 | 1.05N | 44.02 E |
| Barbacena | 135 | 21.14S | 43.46W |
| Barbados □¹ | 130 | 13.10N | 59.32W |
| Barbaros | 98 | 40.54N | 27.27 E |
| Barbas, Cabo ➤ | 104 | 22.18N | 16.41W |
| Barbuda ‖ | 130 | 17.38N | 61.48W |
| Barcelona, Mex. | 128 | 26.12N | 103.25W |
| Barcelona, Spain | 94 | 41.23N | 2.11 E |
| Barcelona, Ven. | 130 | 10.08N | 64.42W |
| Bardufoss | 89 | 69.04N | 18.30 E |
| Bareilly | 112 | 28.21N | 79.25 E |
| Barents Sea ⊤² | 84 | 74.00N | 36.00 E |
| Bar Harbor | 140 | 44.23N | 68.12W |
| Bari | 96 | 41.07N | 16.52 E |
| Barinas | 130 | 8.38N | 70.12W |
| Barisāl | 112 | 22.42N | 90.22 E |
| Barlee, Lake ⊜ | 122 | 29.10S | 119.30 E |

| Name | Page No. | Lat. | Long. |
|---|---|---|---|
| Barletta | 96 | 41.19N | 16.17 E |
| Barmouth | 88 | 52.43N | 4.03W |
| Barnaul | 102 | 53.22N | 83.45 E |
| Barnegat | 140 | 39.45N | 74.13W |
| Baroda | 112 | 22.18N | 73.12 E |
| Barqah (Cyrenaica) ◆¹ | 104 | 31.00N | 22.30 E |
| Barquisimeto | 132 | 10.04N | 69.19W |
| Barra Falsa, Ponta da ➤ | 106 | 22.55S | 35.37 E |
| Barranquilla | 132 | 10.59N | 74.48W |
| Barre | 140 | 44.11N | 72.30W |
| Barreiro | 94 | 38.40N | 9.04W |
| Barretos | 132 | 20.33S | 48.33W |
| Barrie | 140 | 44.24N | 79.40W |
| Barrow, Point ➤ | 144 | 71.23N | 156.30W |
| Barrow Creek | 122 | 21.33S | 133.53 E |
| Barrow-in-Furness | 88 | 54.07N | 3.14W |
| Barstow | 142 | 34.53N | 117.01W |
| Barú, Volcán ⋀¹ | 130 | 8.48N | 82.33W |
| Basatongwula Shan ⋀ | 114 | 33.05N | 91.30 E |
| Basel (Bâle) | 92 | 47.33N | 7.35 E |
| Baskatong, Réservoir ⊜¹ | 136 | 46.48N | 75.50W |
| Basseterre | 130 | 17.18N | 62.43W |
| Basse-Terre ‖ | 130 | 16.10N | 61.40W |
| Bass Harbor | 140 | 44.14N | 68.20W |
| Bass Strait ⋃ | 124 | 39.20S | 145.30 E |
| Bastia | 92 | 42.42N | 9.27 E |
| Bastogne | 90 | 50.00N | 5.43 E |
| Bastrop | 128 | 32.46N | 91.54W |
| Batabanó, Golfo de ⊂ | 130 | 22.15N | 82.30W |
| Batamaj | 102 | 63.31N | 129.27 E |
| Batan Islands ‖ | 118 | 20.30N | 121.50 E |
| Batatais | 135 | 20.53S | 47.37W |
| Batavia | 140 | 42.59N | 78.11W |
| Bătdâmbâng | 120 | 13.06N | 103.12 E |
| Bath, Eng., U.K. | 88 | 51.23N | 2.22W |
| Bath, Me., U.S. | 140 | 43.54N | 69.49W |
| Bath, N.Y., U.S. | 140 | 42.20N | 77.19W |
| Bathurst | 136 | 47.36N | 65.39W |
| Bathurst Island ‖, Austl. | 122 | 11.37S | 130.27 E |
| Bathurst Island ‖, N.T., Can. | 136 | 76.00N | 100.30W |
| Batna | 104 | 35.34N | 6.11 E |
| Baton Rouge | 138 | 30.27N | 91.09W |
| Batouri | 104 | 4.26N | 14.22 E |
| Battle Creek | 140 | 42.19N | 85.10W |
| Battle Harbour | 136 | 52.16N | 55.35W |
| Battle Mountain | 142 | 40.38N | 116.56W |
| Batumi | 86 | 41.38N | 41.38 E |
| Bauru | 132 | 22.19S | 49.04W |
| Bautzen | 90 | 51.11N | 14.26 E |
| Bayamo | 130 | 20.23N | 76.39W |
| Bay City, Mi., U.S. | 140 | 43.35N | 83.53W |
| Bay City, Tx., U.S. | 138 | 28.58N | 95.58W |
| Baydhabo (Baidoa) | 108 | 3.04N | 43.48 E |
| Bayerische Alpen ⨍ | 90 | 47.30N | 11.00 E |
| Bayonne | 92 | 43.29N | 1.29W |
| Bayreuth | 90 | 49.57N | 11.35 E |
| Bayrūt (Beirut) | 109 | 33.53N | 35.30 E |
| Bay Shore | 140 | 40.43N | 73.14W |
| Be, Nosy ‖ | 106 | 13.20S | 48.15 E |
| Beatrice | 138 | 40.16N | 96.44W |
| Beatty | 142 | 36.54N | 116.45W |
| Beaufort Sea ⊤² | 84 | 73.00N | 140.00W |
| Beaufort West | 106 | 32.18S | 22.36 E |
| Beaumont, N.Z. | 126 | 45.49S | 169.32 E |
| Beaumont, Tx., U.S. | 138 | 30.05N | 94.06W |
| Beautemps-Beaupré, Île ‖ | 127b | 20.24S | 166.09 E |
| Beaver Falls | 140 | 40.45N | 80.19W |
| Bečej | 98 | 45.37N | 20.03 E |
| Béchar | 104 | 31.37N | 2.13W |
| Beckley | 140 | 37.46N | 81.11W |
| Be'er Sheva' | 109 | 31.14N | 34.47 E |
| Beeville | 128 | 28.24N | 97.44W |

| Name | Page No. | Lat. | Long. |
|------|----------|------|-------|
| Bridgeton | 140 | 39.25N | 75.14W |
| Bridgetown | 130 | 13.06N | 59.37W |
| Bridgeville | 140 | 38.44N | 75.36W |
| Brighton | 88 | 50.50N | 0.08W |
| Brindisi | 96 | 40.38N | 17.56 E |
| Brisbane | 122 | 27.28S | 153.02 E |
| Bristol, Eng., U.K. | 88 | 51.27N | 2.35W |
| Bristol, Ct., U.S. | 140 | 41.41N | 72.57W |
| Bristol Bay c | 144 | 58.00N | 159.00W |
| British Columbia □⁴ | 136 | 54.00N | 125.00W |
| Brno | 90 | 49.12N | 16.37 E |
| Brochet | 136 | 57.53N | 101.40W |
| Brockton | 140 | 42.05N | 71.01W |
| Brockville | 140 | 44.35N | 75.41W |
| Broken Hill, Austl. | 122 | 31.57S | 141.27 E |
| Broken Hill | | | |
| ⟶ Kabwe, Zam. | 106 | 14.27S | 28.27 E |
| Brokopondo | 132 | 5.04N | 54.58W |
| Bronlund Peak ʌ | 136 | 57.26N | 126.38W |
| Brookings, Or., U.S. | 142 | 42.03N | 124.16W |
| Brookings, S.D., U.S. | 138 | 44.18N | 96.47W |
| Brooks Range ⋌ | 144 | 68.00N | 154.00W |
| Broome | 122 | 17.58S | 122.14 E |
| Brown City | 140 | 43.12N | 82.59W |
| Brownsville | 138 | 25.54N | 97.29W |
| Brownville Junction | 140 | 45.21N | 69.03W |
| Brownwood | 128 | 31.42N | 98.59W |
| Bruce, Mount ʌ | 122 | 22.36S | 118.08 E |
| Bruce Peninsula ⋗¹ | 140 | 44.50N | 81.20W |
| Brugge | 90 | 51.13N | 3.14 E |
| Bruneau | 142 | 42.52N | 115.47W |
| Bruneau ≃ | 142 | 42.57N | 115.58W |
| Brunei □¹ | 118 | 4.30N | 114.40 E |
| Brus Laguna | 130 | 15.47N | 84.35W |
| Brussels | | | |
| ⟶ Bruxelles | 90 | 50.50N | 4.20 E |
| Bruxelles (Brussel) | 90 | 50.50N | 4.20 E |
| Bryan | 140 | 41.28N | 84.33W |
| Brzeg | 90 | 50.52N | 17.27 E |
| Bucaramanga | 132 | 7.08N | 73.09W |
| Buchanan | 104 | 5.57N | 10.02W |
| Bucharest | | | |
| ⟶ București | 98 | 44.26N | 26.06 E |
| Buckhannon | 140 | 38.59N | 80.13W |
| Buckingham | 140 | 45.35N | 75.25W |
| București (Bucharest) | 98 | 44.26N | 26.06 E |
| Budapest | 90 | 47.30N | 19.05 E |
| Buenaventura | 132 | 3.53N | 77.04W |
| Buena Vista | 132 | 17.27S | 63.40W |
| Buenos Aires | 134 | 34.36S | 58.27W |
| Buffalo | 140 | 42.53N | 78.52W |
| Bug ≃ | 86 | 52.31N | 21.05 E |
| Buhuși | 98 | 46.43N | 26.41 E |
| Bujumbura | 106 | 3.23S | 29.22 E |
| Buka Island I | 127a | 5.15S | 154.35 E |
| Bukavu | 106 | 2.30S | 28.52 E |
| Bukovina □⁹ | 98 | 48.00N | 25.30 E |
| Bulawayo | 106 | 20.09S | 28.36 E |
| Bulgan | 114 | 48.45N | 103.34 E |
| Bulgaria □¹ | 86 | 43.00N | 25.00 E |
| Bunbury | 122 | 33.19S | 115.38 E |
| Bundaberg | 122 | 24.52S | 152.21 E |
| Bunguran Utara, | | | |
| Kepulauan II | 118 | 4.40N | 108.00 E |
| Bunia | 106 | 1.34N | 30.15 E |
| Buon Me Thuot | 120 | 12.40N | 108.03 E |
| Burgas | 98 | 42.30N | 27.28 E |
| Burgos | 94 | 42.21N | 3.42W |
| Buriram | 120 | 15.00N | 103.07 E |
| Burkina Faso □¹ | 104 | 13.00N | 2.00W |
| Burlington, Ia., U.S. | 138 | 40.48N | 91.06W |
| Burlington, Vt., U.S. | 140 | 44.28N | 73.12W |
| Burma | | | |
| ⟶ Myanmar □¹ | 118 | 22.00N | 98.00 E |
| Burnie | 122 | 41.04S | 145.54 E |
| Burns | 142 | 43.35N | 119.03W |
| Burns Lake | 136 | 54.14N | 125.46W |
| Bursa | 98 | 40.11N | 29.04 E |
| Būr Saʿīd (Port Said) | 104 | 31.16N | 32.18 E |
| Būr Sūdān (Port | | | |
| Sudan) | 104 | 19.37N | 37.14 E |
| Burton | 140 | 43.02N | 83.36W |
| Buru I | 118 | 3.24S | 126.40 E |
| Burundi □¹ | 106 | 3.15S | 30.00 E |
| Burwick | 88 | 58.44N | 2.57W |
| Buta | 104 | 2.48N | 24.44 E |
| Butler, Oh., U.S. | 140 | 40.35N | 82.25W |
| Butler, Pa., U.S. | 140 | 40.51N | 79.53W |
| Butte | 138 | 46.00N | 112.32W |
| Butterworth | 120 | 5.25N | 100.24 E |
| Butung, Pulau I | 118 | 5.00S | 122.55 E |
| Büyükmenderes ≃ | 98 | 37.27N | 27.11 E |
| Buzău | 98 | 45.09N | 26.49 E |
| Buzuluk | 86 | 52.47N | 52.15 E |
| Bydgoszcz | 90 | 53.08N | 18.00 E |
| Bytom (Beuthen) | 90 | 50.22N | 18.54 E |

## C

| Name | Page No. | Lat. | Long. |
|------|----------|------|-------|
| Cabimas | 132 | 10.23N | 71.28W |
| Cabinda □⁵ | 106 | 5.00S | 12.30 E |
| Cáceres, Col. | 130 | 7.35N | 75.20W |
| Cáceres, Spain | 94 | 39.29N | 6.22W |
| Cache Peak ʌ | 142 | 42.11N | 113.40W |
| Cachoeira | 135 | 12.36S | 38.58W |
| Cachoeiro de | | | |
| Itapemirim | 132 | 20.51S | 41.06W |
| Cadillac | 140 | 44.15N | 85.24W |
| Cádiz | 94 | 36.32N | 6.18W |
| Cádiz, Golfo de c | 94 | 36.50N | 7.10W |
| Caen | 92 | 49.11N | 0.21W |
| Caernarvon | 88 | 53.08N | 4.16W |
| Cagliari | 96 | 39.20N | 9.00 E |
| Caguas | 130 | 18.14N | 66.02W |
| Caiapó, Serra ⋌ | 135 | 17.00S | 52.00W |
| Caicos Islands II | 130 | 21.56N | 71.58W |
| Cairns | 122 | 16.55S | 145.46 E |
| Cairo | | | |
| ⟶ Al-Qāhirah, Egypt | 104 | 30.03N | 31.15 E |
| Cairo, Il., U.S. | 138 | 37.00N | 89.10W |
| Cajamarca | 132 | 7.10S | 78.31W |
| Calabozo | 132 | 8.56N | 67.26W |
| Calais, Fr. | 92 | 50.57N | 1.50 E |
| Calais, Me., U.S. | 140 | 45.11N | 67.16W |
| Calais, Pas de (Strait | | | |
| of Dover) u | 92 | 51.00N | 1.30 E |
| Calamian Group II | 118 | 12.00N | 120.00 E |
| Călărași | 98 | 44.11N | 27.20 E |
| Calcutta | 112 | 22.32N | 88.22 E |
| Caldas da Rainha | 94 | 39.24N | 9.08W |
| Calexico | 142 | 32.40N | 115.29W |
| Calgary | 136 | 51.03N | 114.05W |
| Cali | 132 | 3.27N | 76.31W |
| Calicut | 111 | 11.15N | 75.46 E |
| Caliente | 142 | 37.36N | 114.30W |
| California □³ | 138 | 37.30N | 119.30W |
| California, Golfo de c | 128 | 28.00N | 112.00W |
| Callao | 132 | 12.04S | 77.09W |
| Caltagirone | 96 | 37.14N | 14.31 E |
| Caltanissetta | 96 | 37.29N | 14.04 E |
| Camacho | 128 | 24.25N | 102.18W |
| Camagüey | 130 | 21.23N | 77.55W |
| Ca Mau, Mui ⋗ | 120 | 8.38N | 104.44 E |
| Cambodia □¹ | 118 | 13.00N | 105.00 E |
| Cambrian Mountains ⋌ | 88 | 52.35N | 3.35W |
| Cambridge, On., Can. | 140 | 43.22N | 80.19W |
| Cambridge, Eng., U.K. | 88 | 52.13N | 0.08 E |
| Cambridge, Md., U.S. | 140 | 38.33N | 76.04W |
| Cambridge, Oh., U.S. | 140 | 40.02N | 81.35W |
| Cambridge Bay | 136 | 69.03N | 105.05W |
| Camden, Me., U.S. | 140 | 44.12N | 69.03W |

| Name | Page No. | Lat. | Long. |
|------|----------|------|-------|
| Camden, N.J., U.S. | 140 | 39.55N | 75.07W |
| Cameroon □¹ | 104 | 6.00N | 12.00 E |
| Cameroun, Mont ▲ | 104 | 4.12N | 9.11 E |
| Campbell Island I | 85 | 52.30S | 169.05 E |
| Campbell River | 136 | 50.01N | 125.15W |
| Campbells Bay | 140 | 45.44N | 76.36W |
| Campbelltown | 88 | 55.26N | 5.36W |
| Campeche | 128 | 19.51N | 90.32W |
| Campeche, Bahía de c | 128 | 20.00N | 94.00W |
| Campina Grande | 132 | 7.13S | 35.53W |
| Campinas | 132 | 22.54S | 47.05W |
| Campobasso | 96 | 41.34N | 14.39 E |
| Campo Grande | 132 | 20.27S | 54.37W |
| Campos | 132 | 21.45S | 41.18W |
| Cam Ranh | 120 | 11.54N | 109.09 E |
| Cam Ranh, Vinh c | 120 | 11.53N | 109.10 E |
| Canada □¹ | 136 | 60.00N | 95.00W |
| Çanakkale | 98 | 40.09N | 26.24 E |
| Çanakkale Boğazı (Dardanelles) ʊ | 98 | 40.15N | 26.25 E |
| Cananea | 128 | 30.57N | 110.18W |
| Canarias, Islas (Canary Islands) II | 104 | 28.00N | 15.30W |
| Canaveral, Cape ≻ | 138 | 28.27N | 80.32W |
| Canavieiras | 135 | 15.39S | 38.57W |
| Canberra | 122 | 35.17S | 149.08 E |
| Caniapiscau ≃ | 136 | 57.40N | 69.30W |
| Caniapiscau, Lac ⊛ | 136 | 54.10N | 69.55W |
| Cannes | 92 | 43.33N | 7.01 E |
| Cantábrica, Cordillera ⋇ | 94 | 43.00N | 5.00W |
| Cantaura | 130 | 9.19N | 64.21W |
| Canterbury | 88 | 51.17N | 1.05 E |
| Canterbury Bight c³ | 126 | 44.15S | 171.38 E |
| Canton → Guangzhou, China | 114 | 23.06N | 113.16 E |
| Canton, Oh., U.S. | 140 | 40.47N | 81.22W |
| Canyonville | 142 | 42.55N | 123.16W |
| Cape Breton Island I | 136 | 46.00N | 60.30W |
| Cape Cod National Seashore ◆ | 140 | 41.56N | 70.06W |
| Cape Girardeau | 138 | 37.18N | 89.31W |
| Cape May | 140 | 38.56N | 74.54W |
| Cape Town (Kaapstad) | 106 | 33.55S | 18.22 E |
| Cape York Peninsula ≻¹ | 122 | 14.00S | 142.30 E |
| Cap-Haïtien | 130 | 19.45N | 72.12W |
| Caprivi Strip □⁹ | 106 | 17.59S | 23.00 E |
| Caracal | 98 | 44.07N | 24.21 E |
| Caracas | 132 | 10.30N | 66.56W |
| Carangola | 135 | 20.44S | 42.02W |
| Caratinga | 135 | 19.47S | 42.08W |
| Carbó | 128 | 29.42N | 110.58W |
| Carbondale | 140 | 41.34N | 75.30W |
| Carcans, Étang de c | 92 | 45.08N | 1.08W |
| Carcassonne | 92 | 43.13N | 2.21 E |
| Cárdenas | 130 | 23.02N | 81.12W |
| Cardiff | 88 | 51.29N | 3.13W |
| Cardigan | 88 | 52.06N | 4.40W |
| Caribbean Sea ₸² | 130 | 15.00N | 73.00W |
| Caripito | 130 | 10.08N | 63.06W |
| Carleton Place | 140 | 45.08N | 76.09W |
| Carlisle, Eng., U.K. | 88 | 54.54N | 2.55W |
| Carlisle, Pa., U.S. | 140 | 40.12N | 77.11W |
| Carlsbad | 128 | 32.25N | 104.13W |
| Carlsbad Caverns National Park ◆ | 128 | 32.08N | 104.35W |
| Carmacks | 136 | 62.05N | 136.18W |
| Carmarthen | 88 | 51.52N | 4.19W |
| Carmona | 94 | 37.28N | 5.38W |
| Caroline Islands II | 118 | 8.00N | 140.00 E |
| Caroní ≃ | 130 | 8.21N | 62.43W |
| Carpathian Mountains ⋇ | 86 | 48.00N | 24.00 E |
| Carpaţii Meridionali ⋇ | 98 | 45.30N | 24.15 E |
| Carpentaria, Gulf of c | 122 | 14.00S | 139.00 E |
| Carrara | 96 | 44.05N | 10.06 E |
| Carrauntoohill ▲ | 88 | 52.00N | 9.45W |
| Carrizo Springs | 128 | 28.31N | 99.51W |
| Carson City | 142 | 39.10N | 119.46W |
| Cartagena, Col. | 132 | 10.25N | 75.32W |
| Cartagena, Spain | 94 | 37.36N | 0.59W |
| Cartago | 130 | 9.52N | 83.55W |
| Caruaru | 132 | 8.17S | 35.58W |
| Carúpano | 130 | 10.40N | 63.14W |
| Casablanca (Dar-el-Beida) | 104 | 33.39N | 7.35W |
| Casa Grande | 128 | 32.52N | 111.45W |
| Casale Monferrato | 96 | 45.08N | 8.27 E |
| Cascade Point ≻ | 126 | 44.00S | 168.22 E |
| Cascade Range ⋇ | 138 | 49.00N | 120.00W |
| Cascais | 94 | 38.42N | 9.25W |
| Casper | 138 | 42.52N | 106.18W |
| Caspian Sea ₸² | 86 | 42.00N | 50.30 E |
| Cassai (Kasai) ≃ | 106 | 3.06S | 16.57 E |
| Castelo Branco | 94 | 39.49N | 7.30W |
| Castile | 140 | 42.37N | 78.03W |
| Castletown | 88 | 54.04N | 4.40W |
| Castres | 92 | 43.36N | 2.15 E |
| Castries | 130 | 14.01N | 61.00W |
| Catalão | 135 | 18.10S | 47.57W |
| Cataluña □⁹ | 94 | 42.00N | 2.00 E |
| Catamarca | 134 | 28.28S | 65.47W |
| Catanduanes Island I | 118 | 13.45N | 124.15 E |
| Catanduva | 135 | 21.08S | 48.58W |
| Catania | 96 | 37.30N | 15.06 E |
| Catanzaro | 96 | 38.54N | 16.36 E |
| Cat Island I | 130 | 24.27N | 75.30W |
| Catoche, Cabo ≻ | 128 | 21.35N | 87.05W |
| Catskill Mountains ⋇ | 140 | 42.10N | 74.30W |
| Caucasus ⋇ | 86 | 42.30N | 45.00 E |
| Caxambu | 135 | 21.59S | 44.56W |
| Caxias do Sul | 134 | 29.10S | 51.11W |
| Cayenne | 132 | 4.56N | 52.20W |
| Cayman Islands □² | 130 | 19.30N | 80.40W |
| Cayuga Lake ⊛ | 140 | 42.45N | 76.45W |
| Cazaux, Étang de c | 92 | 44.30N | 1.10W |
| Čeboksary | 86 | 56.09N | 47.15 E |
| Cebu | 118 | 10.18N | 123.54 E |
| Čechy □⁹ | 90 | 49.50N | 14.00 E |
| Cedar City | 138 | 37.40N | 113.03W |
| Cedar Rapids | 138 | 42.00N | 91.38W |
| Cegléd | 90 | 47.10N | 19.48 E |
| Čeľabinsk | 86 | 55.10N | 61.24 E |
| Celaya | 128 | 20.31N | 100.49W |
| Celebes → Sulawesi I | 118 | 2.00S | 121.00 E |
| Celebes Sea ₸² | 118 | 3.00N | 122.00 E |
| Celestún | 128 | 20.52N | 90.24W |
| Celle | 90 | 52.37N | 10.05 E |
| Čeľuskin, Mys ≻ | 102 | 77.45N | 104.20 E |
| Cenderawasih, Teluk c | 118 | 2.30S | 135.20 E |
| Central, Cordillera ⋇ | 132 | 8.00S | 77.00W |
| Central, Massif ⋇ | 92 | 45.00N | 3.10 E |
| Central, Planalto ⋇¹ | 132 | 18.00S | 47.00W |
| Central, Sistema ⋇ | 94 | 40.30N | 5.00W |
| Central African Republic □¹ | 104 | 7.00N | 21.00 E |
| Čeremchovo | 102 | 53.09N | 103.05 E |
| Čerepovec | 100 | 59.08N | 37.54 E |
| Čereté | 130 | 8.53N | 75.48W |
| Černogorsk | 102 | 53.49N | 91.18 E |
| Cerritos | 128 | 22.26N | 100.17W |
| Cerro de Pasco | 132 | 10.41S | 76.16W |
| Čerskogo, Chrebet ⋇ | 102 | 65.00N | 144.00 E |
| Cesena | 96 | 44.08N | 12.15 E |
| České Budějovice | 90 | 48.59N | 14.28 E |
| Ceuta | 104 | 35.53N | 5.19W |
| Chabarovsk | 102 | 48.27N | 135.06 E |
| Chad □¹ | 104 | 15.00N | 19.00 E |

| Name | Page No. | Lat. | Long. |
|------|----------|------|-------|
| Chad, Lake (Lac | | | |
| Tchad) ⊖ | 104 | 13.20N | 14.00 E |
| Chadron | 138 | 42.49N | 103.00W |
| Chalbi Desert ◆² | 108 | 3.00N | 37.20 E |
| Chalmette | 128 | 29.56N | 89.57W |
| Châlons-sur-Marne | 92 | 48.57N | 4.22 E |
| Chalon-sur-Saône | 92 | 46.47N | 4.51 E |
| Chaltel, Cerro (Monte | | | |
| Fitzroy) ⋀ | 134 | 49.17S | 73.05W |
| Chambal ≃ | 110 | 26.30N | 79.15 E |
| Chamberlain | 138 | 43.48N | 99.19W |
| Chambéry | 92 | 45.34N | 5.56 E |
| Champagne □⁹ | 92 | 49.00N | 4.30 E |
| Champaign | 138 | 40.06N | 88.14W |
| Champasak | 120 | 14.53N | 105.52 E |
| Champlain | 140 | 44.42N | 73.24W |
| Champlain, Lake ⊖ | 140 | 44.45N | 73.15W |
| Chañaral | 134 | 26.21S | 70.37W |
| Chandeleur Islands II | 128 | 29.48N | 88.51W |
| Chang (Yangtze) ≃ | 114 | 31.48N | 121.10 E |
| Changchun | 114 | 43.53N | 125.19 E |
| Changsha | 114 | 28.11N | 113.01 E |
| Changzhi | 114 | 36.11N | 113.08 E |
| Chanka, Ozero | | | |
| (Xingkathu) ⊖ | 114 | 45.00N | 132.24 E |
| Channel Islands II, Eur. | 92 | 49.20N | 2.20W |
| Channel Islands II, Ca., | | | |
| U.S. | 142 | 34.00N | 120.00W |
| Channel-Port-aux-Basques | 136 | 47.34N | 59.09W |
| Chanthaburi | 120 | 12.36N | 102.09 E |
| Chao Phraya ≃ | 120 | 13.32N | 100.36 E |
| Chapala, Lago de ⊖ | 128 | 20.15N | 103.00W |
| Chapmanville | 140 | 37.58N | 82.01W |
| Charcas | 128 | 23.08N | 101.07W |
| Charente ≃ | 92 | 45.57N | 1.05W |
| Chari ≃ | 104 | 12.58N | 14.31 E |
| Charity | 132 | 7.24N | 58.36W |
| Char'kov | | | |
| → Kharkiv | 86 | 50.00N | 36.15 E |
| Charleroi | 90 | 50.25N | 4.26 E |
| Charleston, S.C., U.S. | 138 | 32.46N | 79.55W |
| Charleston, W.V., U.S. | 140 | 38.20N | 81.37W |
| Charleston Peak ⋀ | 142 | 36.16N | 115.42W |
| Charleville | 122 | 26.24S | 146.15 E |
| Charlotte | 138 | 35.13N | 80.50W |
| Charlotte Amalie | 130 | 18.21N | 64.56W |
| Charlottesville | 140 | 38.01N | 78.28W |
| Charlottetown | 136 | 46.14N | 63.08W |
| Chärsadda | 112 | 34.09N | 71.44 E |
| Chartres | 92 | 48.27N | 1.30 E |
| Chatanga | 102 | 71.58N | 102.30 E |
| Châtellerault | 92 | 46.49N | 0.33 E |
| Chatham | 140 | 42.24N | 82.11W |
| Chattahoochee ≃ | 138 | 30.52N | 84.57W |
| Chattanooga | 138 | 35.02N | 85.18W |
| Chau Doc | 120 | 10.42N | 105.07 E |
| Chauk | 120 | 20.54N | 94.50 E |
| Chaves | 94 | 41.44N | 7.28W |
| Cheb | 90 | 50.01N | 12.25 E |
| Cheboygan | 140 | 45.38N | 84.28W |
| Chech, Erg ◆² | 104 | 25.00N | 2.15W |
| Cheju-do I | 114 | 33.20N | 126.30 E |
| Chełm | 90 | 51.10N | 23.28 E |
| Chelmsford | 88 | 51.44N | 0.28 E |
| Chelyabinsk | | | |
| → Čel'abinsk | 86 | 55.10N | 61.24 E |
| Chemnitz | 90 | 50.50N | 12.55 E |
| Chénéville | 140 | 45.53N | 75.03W |
| Chengde | 114 | 40.58N | 117.53 E |
| Chengdu | 114 | 30.39N | 104.04 E |
| Chepo | 130 | 9.10N | 79.06W |
| Cher ≃ | 92 | 47.21N | 0.29 E |
| Cherbourg | 92 | 49.39N | 1.39W |
| Cherkasy | 86 | 49.26N | 32.04 E |
| Chernihov | 86 | 51.30N | 31.18 E |
| Chernivtsy | 86 | 48.18N | 25.56 E |

| Name | Page No. | Lat. | Long. |
|------|----------|------|-------|
| Chesapeake Bay C | 140 | 38.40N | 76.25W |
| Chesapeake Beach | 140 | 38.41N | 76.32W |
| Chester | 140 | 39.50N | 75.21W |
| Chesterfield, Îles II | 122 | 19.30S | 158.00 E |
| Chesterfield Inlet | 136 | 63.21N | 90.42W |
| Chesuncook Lake ⊖ | 140 | 46.00N | 69.20W |
| Cheyenne | 138 | 41.08N | 104.49W |
| Chiang Mai | 120 | 18.47N | 98.59 E |
| Chiang Rai | 120 | 19.54N | 99.50 E |
| Chiautla de Tapia | 128 | 18.17N | 98.36W |
| Chiba | 116 | 35.36N | 140.07 E |
| Chibougamau | 136 | 49.55N | 74.22W |
| Chicago | 138 | 41.51N | 87.39W |
| Chichagof Island I | 144 | 57.30N | 135.30W |
| Chichén Itzá | 128 | 20.40N | 88.34W |
| Chiclayo | 132 | 6.46S | 79.51W |
| Chico | 142 | 39.43N | 121.50W |
| Chicoutimi | 136 | 48.26N | 71.04W |
| Chidley, Cape ⋗ | 136 | 60.23N | 64.26W |
| Chieti | 96 | 42.21N | 14.10 E |
| Chigasaki | 116 | 35.19N | 139.24 E |
| Chihuahua | 128 | 28.38N | 106.05W |
| Chile □¹ | 134 | 30.00S | 71.00W |
| Chillicothe | 140 | 39.19N | 82.58W |
| Chiloé, Isla de I | 134 | 42.30S | 73.55W |
| Chilpancingo [de los | | | |
| Bravos] | 128 | 17.33N | 99.30W |
| Chimborazo ⋀¹ | 132 | 1.28S | 78.48W |
| Chimbote | 132 | 9.05S | 78.36W |
| China □¹ | 114 | 35.00N | 105.00 E |
| Chinandega | 130 | 12.37N | 87.09W |
| Chindwinn ≃ | 120 | 21.26N | 95.15 E |
| Chinhoyi | 106 | 17.22S | 30.12 E |
| Chinko ≃ | 104 | 4.50N | 23.53 E |
| Chioggia | 96 | 45.13N | 12.17 E |
| Chīrāla | 111 | 15.49N | 80.21 E |
| Chiricahua National | | | |
| Monument ◆ | 128 | 32.02N | 109.19W |
| Chiriquí, Golfo C | 130 | 8.00N | 82.20W |
| Chirripó, Cerro ⋀ | 130 | 9.29N | 83.30W |
| Chisasibi | 136 | 53.50N | 79.00W |
| Chişinău | 98 | 47.00N | 28.50 E |
| Chittagong | 112 | 22.20N | 91.50 E |
| Choapan | 128 | 17.20N | 95.57W |
| Choele-Choel | 134 | 39.16S | 65.41W |
| Choiseul I | 127a | 7.05S | 157.00 E |
| Chomutov | 90 | 50.28N | 13.26 E |
| Chon Buri | 120 | 13.22N | 100.59 E |
| Ch'öngjin | 114 | 41.47N | 129.50 E |
| Chongqing | 114 | 29.39N | 106.34 E |
| Chŏnju | 114 | 35.49N | 127.08 E |
| Chonos, Archipiélago | | | |
| de los II | 134 | 45.00S | 74.00W |
| Chōshi | 116 | 35.44N | 140.50 E |
| Chos Malal | 134 | 37.23S | 70.16W |
| Chovd | 114 | 48.01N | 91.38 E |
| Christchurch | 126 | 43.32S | 172.38 E |
| Christmas Island □² | 118 | 10.30S | 105.40 E |
| Chukchi Sea ⊤² | 84 | 69.00N | 171.00W |
| Chula Vista | 142 | 32.38N | 117.05W |
| Chum Saeng | 120 | 15.54N | 100.19 E |
| Chungking | | | |
| → Chongqing | 114 | 29.39N | 106.34 E |
| Chur | 92 | 46.51N | 9.32 E |
| Churchill | 136 | 58.46N | 94.10W |
| Churchill ≃ | 136 | 58.47N | 94.12W |
| Churchill Lake ⊖ | 136 | 55.55N | 108.20W |
| Ciego de Avila | 130 | 21.51N | 78.46W |
| Ciénaga | 130 | 11.01N | 74.15W |
| Cienfuegos | 130 | 22.09N | 80.27W |
| Cieza | 94 | 38.14N | 1.25W |
| Čimkent | 110 | 42.18N | 69.36 E |
| Cincinnati | 140 | 39.09N | 84.27W |
| Cirebon | 118 | 6.44S | 108.34 E |
| Čita | 102 | 52.03N | 113.30 E |
| Citrus Heights | 142 | 38.42N | 121.16W |

| Name | Page No. | Lat. | Long. |
|---|---|---|---|
| Ciudad Acuña | 128 | 29.18N | 100.55W |
| Ciudad Anáhuac | 128 | 27.14N | 100.09W |
| Ciudad Bolívar | 132 | 8.08N | 63.33W |
| Ciudad Camargo | 128 | 26.19N | 98.50W |
| Ciudad Chetumal | 128 | 18.30N | 88.18W |
| Ciudad del Carmen | 128 | 18.38N | 91.50W |
| Ciudad de México (Mexico City) | 128 | 19.24N | 99.09W |
| Ciudad de Valles | 128 | 21.59N | 99.01W |
| Ciudad de Villaldama | 128 | 26.30N | 100.26W |
| Ciudad Guayana | 132 | 8.22N | 62.40W |
| Ciudad Guerrero | 128 | 28.33N | 107.30W |
| Ciudad Ixtepec | 128 | 16.34N | 95.06W |
| Ciudad Jiménez | 128 | 27.08N | 104.55W |
| Ciudad Juárez | 128 | 31.44N | 106.29W |
| Ciudad Madero | 128 | 22.16N | 97.50W |
| Ciudad Mante | 128 | 22.44N | 98.57W |
| Ciudad Melchor Múzquiz | 128 | 27.53N | 101.31W |
| Ciudad Obregón | 128 | 27.29N | 109.56W |
| Ciudad Ojeda | 130 | 10.12N | 71.19W |
| Ciudad Real | 94 | 38.59N | 3.56W |
| Ciudad Victoria | 128 | 23.44N | 99.08W |
| Clanwilliam | 106 | 32.11S | 18.54E |
| Claremont | 140 | 43.22N | 72.20W |
| Clarksburg | 140 | 39.16N | 80.20W |
| Clearfield | 140 | 41.01N | 78.26W |
| Clear Lake ☉¹ | 142 | 39.02N | 122.50W |
| Clermont-Ferrand | 92 | 45.47N | 3.05E |
| Cleveland, Oh., U.S. | 140 | 41.29N | 81.41W |
| Cleveland, Tx., U.S. | 128 | 30.20N | 95.05W |
| Clifton Forge | 140 | 37.48N | 79.49W |
| Clinton, Mi., U.S. | 140 | 42.04N | 83.58W |
| Clinton, Ok., U.S. | 138 | 35.30N | 98.58W |
| Clio | 138 | 31.42N | 85.36W |
| Cloncurry | 122 | 20.42S | 140.30E |
| Clonmel | 88 | 52.21N | 7.42W |
| Clovis | 138 | 34.24N | 103.12W |
| Cluj-Napoca | 98 | 46.47N | 23.36E |
| Clyde | 136 | 70.25N | 68.30W |
| Clyde, Firth of ᴄ¹ | 88 | 55.42N | 5.00W |
| Coalinga | 142 | 36.08N | 120.21W |
| Coast Mountains ⋗ | 136 | 55.00N | 129.00W |
| Coast Ranges ⋗ | 138 | 41.00N | 123.30W |
| Coaticook | 140 | 45.08N | 71.48W |
| Coatzacoalcos | 128 | 18.09N | 94.25W |
| Cobija | 132 | 11.02S | 68.44W |
| Cobourg | 140 | 43.58N | 78.10W |
| Coburg | 90 | 50.15N | 10.58E |
| Cochabamba | 132 | 17.24S | 66.09W |
| Cochin | 110 | 9.58N | 76.15E |
| Coco ≃ | 130 | 15.00N | 83.10W |
| Coco Channel ᴜ | 120 | 13.45N | 93.00E |
| Cod, Cape ⋗ | 140 | 41.42N | 70.15W |
| Cognac | 92 | 45.42N | 0.20W |
| Coiba, Isla de I | 130 | 7.27N | 81.45W |
| Coimbatore | 111 | 11.00N | 76.58E |
| Coimbra | 94 | 40.12N | 8.25W |
| Čojbalsan | 114 | 48.34N | 114.50E |
| Colatina | 132 | 19.32S | 40.37W |
| Coldwater | 140 | 40.28N | 84.37W |
| Coleman | 140 | 43.45N | 84.35W |
| Coleraine | 88 | 55.08N | 6.40W |
| Colima | 128 | 19.14N | 103.43W |
| Cologne → Köln | 90 | 50.56N | 6.59E |
| Colombia □¹ | 132 | 4.00N | 72.00W |
| Colombo | 111 | 6.56N | 79.51E |
| Colón | 130 | 9.22N | 79.54W |
| Colón, Archipiélago de (Galapagos Islands) II | 82 | 0.30S | 90.30W |
| Colonia Dora | 134 | 28.36S | 62.57W |
| Colonia Las Heras | 134 | 46.33S | 68.57W |
| Colorado □³ | 138 | 39.30N | 105.30W |
| Colorado ≃, Arg. | 134 | 39.50S | 62.08W |
| Colorado ≃, N.A. | 138 | 31.54N | 114.57W |
| Colorado ≃, Tx., U.S. | 128 | 28.36N | 95.58W |
| Colorado Springs | 138 | 38.50N | 104.49W |
| Columbia, Md., U.S. | 140 | 39.14N | 76.50W |
| Columbia, S.C., U.S. | 138 | 34.00N | 81.02W |
| Columbia ≃ | 136 | 46.15N | 124.05W |
| Columbia, Mount ⋀ | 136 | 52.09N | 117.25W |
| Columbia Plateau ⋌¹ | 142 | 44.00N | 117.30W |
| Columbus, Ga., U.S. | 138 | 32.29N | 84.59W |
| Columbus, Ne., U.S. | 138 | 41.25N | 97.22W |
| Columbus, Oh., U.S. | 140 | 39.57N | 82.59W |
| Colville ≃ | 144 | 70.25N | 150.30W |
| Comitán [de Domínguez] | 128 | 16.15N | 92.08W |
| Communism Peak → Kommunizma, Pik ⋀ | 110 | 38.57N | 72.01E |
| Como | 96 | 45.47N | 9.05E |
| Como, Lago di ☉ | 96 | 46.00N | 9.20E |
| Comodoro Rivadavia | 134 | 45.52S | 67.30W |
| Comorin, Cape ⋗ | 111 | 8.04N | 77.34E |
| Comoros □¹ | 106 | 12.10S | 44.10E |
| Compiègne | 92 | 49.25N | 2.50E |
| Conakry | 104 | 9.31N | 13.43W |
| Concepción, Bol. | 132 | 16.15S | 62.04W |
| Concepción, Chile | 134 | 36.50S | 73.03W |
| Concepción, Para. | 134 | 23.25S | 57.17W |
| Concepción de la Vega | 130 | 19.13N | 70.31W |
| Concepción del Uruguay | 134 | 32.29S | 58.14W |
| Conchos ≃ | 128 | 29.35N | 104.25W |
| Concord | 140 | 43.12N | 71.32W |
| Congo □¹ | 106 | 1.00S | 15.00E |
| Congo (Zaïre) ≃ | 106 | 6.04S | 12.24E |
| Connaught ⋌⁹ | 88 | 53.45N | 9.00W |
| Connecticut □³ | 138 | 41.45N | 72.45W |
| Connemara ◆¹ | 88 | 53.25N | 9.45W |
| Connersville | 140 | 39.38N | 85.15W |
| Constanţa | 98 | 44.11N | 28.39E |
| Contas, Rio de ≃ | 135 | 14.17S | 39.01W |
| Conway, N.H., U.S. | 140 | 43.58N | 71.07W |
| Conway, S.C., U.S. | 138 | 33.50N | 79.02W |
| Cook, Mount ⋀ | 126 | 43.36S | 170.10E |
| Cook Inlet ᴄ | 144 | 60.30N | 152.00W |
| Cook Islands □² | 82 | 20.00S | 158.00W |
| Cook Strait ᴜ | 126 | 41.15S | 174.30E |
| Cooktown | 122 | 15.28S | 145.15E |
| Cooperstown | 140 | 42.42N | 74.55W |
| Coos Bay | 142 | 43.22N | 124.12W |
| Copenhagen → København | 89 | 55.40N | 12.35E |
| Copiapó | 134 | 27.22S | 70.20W |
| Copper ≃ | 144 | 60.30N | 144.50W |
| Coral Sea ⲧ² | 82 | 20.00S | 158.00E |
| Córdoba, Arg. | 134 | 31.24S | 64.11W |
| Córdoba, Mex. | 128 | 18.53N | 96.56W |
| Córdoba, Spain | 94 | 37.53N | 4.46W |
| Cordova | 144 | 60.33N | 145.46W |
| Corfu → Kérkira I | 98 | 39.40N | 19.42E |
| Corinth, Gulf of → Korinthiakós Kólpos ᴄ | 98 | 38.19N | 22.04E |
| Cork | 88 | 51.54N | 8.28W |
| Çorlu | 98 | 41.09N | 27.48E |
| Corner Brook | 136 | 48.57N | 57.57W |
| Corning | 140 | 42.08N | 77.03W |
| Cornwall | 140 | 45.02N | 74.44W |
| Coro | 132 | 11.25N | 69.41W |
| Coromandel Coast ⋐² | 111 | 14.00N | 80.10E |
| Coromandel Peninsula ⋗¹ | 126 | 36.50S | 175.35E |
| Coronel Pringles | 134 | 37.58S | 61.22W |
| Corpus Christi | 138 | 27.48N | 97.23W |
| Corrientes | 134 | 27.28S | 58.50W |
| Corrientes, Cabo ⋗, Col. | 132 | 5.30N | 77.34W |

| Name | Page No. | Lat. | Long. |
|---|---|---|---|
| Corrientes, Cabo ⌐, Cuba | 130 | 21.45N | 84.31W |
| Corrientes, Cabo ⌐, Mex. | 128 | 20.25N | 105.42W |
| Corry | 140 | 41.55N | 79.38W |
| Corse (Corsica) I | 96 | 42.00N | 9.00 E |
| Corse, Cap ⌐ | 96 | 43.00N | 9.25 E |
| Corsica → Corse I | 96 | 42.00N | 9.00 E |
| Corsicana | 128 | 32.05N | 96.28W |
| Cortland | 140 | 42.36N | 76.10W |
| Corumbá | 132 | 19.01S | 57.39W |
| Cosenza | 96 | 39.17N | 16.15 E |
| Coshocton | 140 | 40.16N | 81.51W |
| Costa Rica □¹ | 130 | 10.00N | 84.00W |
| Cote d'Ivoire □¹ | 104 | 8.00N | 5.00W |
| Cotonou | 104 | 6.21N | 2.26 E |
| Cottbus | 90 | 51.45N | 14.19 E |
| Coubre, Pointe de la ⌐ | 92 | 45.41N | 1.13W |
| Council Bluffs | 138 | 41.15N | 95.51W |
| Coventry | 88 | 52.25N | 1.30W |
| Covilhã | 94 | 40.17N | 7.30W |
| Covington | 140 | 39.05N | 84.30W |
| Cowansville | 140 | 45.12N | 72.45W |
| Cozumel, Isla de I | 128 | 20.25N | 86.55W |
| Craiova | 98 | 44.19N | 23.48 E |
| Crane Mountain ⋀ | 142 | 42.04N | 120.13W |
| Crasna (Kraszna) ≃ | 90 | 48.09N | 22.20 E |
| Crater Lake ◎ | 142 | 42.56N | 122.06W |
| Crater Lake National Park ♦ | 142 | 42.49N | 122.08W |
| Craters of the Moon National Monument ♦ | 142 | 43.20N | 113.35W |
| Crawley | 92 | 51.07N | 0.12W |
| Cremona | 96 | 45.07N | 10.02 E |
| Cres, Otok I | 96 | 44.50N | 14.25 E |
| Crescent | 142 | 43.27N | 121.41W |
| Crete → Kríti I | 98 | 35.29N | 24.42 E |
| Crete, Sea of → Kritikón Pélagos ₹² | 98 | 35.46N | 23.54 E |
| Cristóbal Colón, Pico ⋀ | 132 | 10.50N | 73.41W |
| Croatia □¹ | 96 | 45.10N | 15.30 E |
| Crooked Island I | 130 | 22.45N | 74.13W |
| Crooked Island Passage ʯ | 130 | 22.55N | 74.35W |
| Crystal City | 128 | 28.40N | 99.49W |
| Cuango | 106 | 6.17S | 16.41 E |
| Cuango (Kwango) ≃ | 106 | 3.14S | 17.23 E |
| Cuba □¹ | 130 | 21.30N | 80.00W |
| Cubango (Okavango) ≃ | 106 | 18.50S | 22.25 E |
| Cúcuta | 132 | 7.54N | 72.31W |
| Čudskoje Ozero (Peipsi Järv) ◎ | 100 | 58.45N | 27.30 E |
| Cuenca, Ec. | 132 | 2.53S | 78.59W |
| Cuenca, Spain | 94 | 40.04N | 2.08W |
| Cuernavaca | 128 | 18.55N | 99.15W |
| Cuiabá | 132 | 15.35S | 56.05W |
| Culiacán | 128 | 24.48N | 107.24W |
| Cumaná | 132 | 10.28N | 64.10W |
| Cumberland | 140 | 39.39N | 78.45W |
| Cunene ≃ | 106 | 17.20S | 11.50 E |
| Cuneo | 96 | 44.23N | 7.32 E |
| Curaçao I | 130 | 12.11N | 69.00W |
| Curitiba | 134 | 25.25S | 49.15W |
| Curvelo | 135 | 18.45S | 44.25W |
| Čusovoj | 86 | 58.17N | 57.49 E |
| Cuttack | 112 | 20.30N | 85.50 E |
| Cuxhaven | 90 | 53.52N | 8.42 E |
| Cuzco | 132 | 13.31S | 71.59W |
| Cyclades → Kikládhes II | 98 | 37.30N | 25.00 E |
| Cynthiana | 140 | 38.23N | 84.17W |

| Name | Page No. | Lat. | Long. |
|---|---|---|---|
| Cyprus □¹ | 109 | 35.00N | 33.00 E |
| Cyprus, North □¹ | 109 | 35.15N | 33.40 E |
| Czech Republic □¹ | 86 | 49.30N | 17.00 E |
| Częstochowa | 90 | 50.49N | 19.06 E |
| **D** | | | |
| Da → Black ≃ | 120 | 21.15N | 105.20 E |
| Dacca → Dhaka | 112 | 23.43N | 90.25 E |
| Dachau | 90 | 48.15N | 11.27 E |
| Dādra and Nagar Haveli □⁸ | 111 | 20.05N | 73.00 E |
| Dahlak Archipelago II | 108 | 15.45N | 40.30 E |
| Daimiel | 94 | 39.04N | 3.37W |
| Dakar | 104 | 14.40N | 17.26W |
| Dakhla | 104 | 23.43N | 15.57W |
| Dalälven ≃ | 89 | 60.38N | 17.27 E |
| Da Lat | 120 | 11.56N | 108.25 E |
| Dalhart | 138 | 36.03N | 102.30W |
| Dalian | 114 | 38.53N | 121.35 E |
| Dallas | 138 | 32.46N | 96.47W |
| Dalmacija □⁹ | 96 | 43.00N | 17.00 E |
| Dalwallinu | 122 | 30.17S | 116.40 E |
| Damān □⁸ | 111 | 20.10N | 73.00 E |
| Damascus → Dimashq | 109 | 33.30N | 36.18 E |
| Dāmāvand, Qolleh-ye ⋀ | 86 | 35.56N | 52.08 E |
| Dampier Archipelago II | 122 | 20.35S | 116.35 E |
| Da Nang | 120 | 16.04N | 108.13 E |
| Danbury | 140 | 41.23N | 73.27W |
| Dandong | 114 | 40.08N | 124.20 E |
| Danforth | 140 | 45.39N | 67.52W |
| Dansville | 140 | 42.33N | 77.41W |
| Danube (Donau) (Dunaj) (Duna) ≃ | 90 | 45.20N | 29.40 E |
| Danville, Ky., U.S. | 140 | 37.42N | 84.46W |
| Danville, Pa., U.S. | 140 | 40.57N | 76.36W |
| Danzig, Gulf of c | 90 | 54.40N | 19.15 E |
| Darchan | 114 | 49.29N | 105.55 E |
| Dardanelles → Çanakkale Boğazı ʯ | 98 | 40.15N | 26.25 E |
| Dar es Salaam | 106 | 6.48S | 39.17 E |
| Dargaville | 126 | 35.56S | 173.53 E |
| Darling ≃ | 124 | 34.07S | 141.55 E |
| Darling Range ⋋ | 122 | 32.00S | 116.30 E |
| Darmstadt | 90 | 49.53N | 8.40 E |
| Dartmouth | 136 | 44.40N | 63.34W |
| Daru | 118 | 9.04S | 143.21 E |
| Darwin | 122 | 12.28S | 130.50 E |
| Datong | 114 | 40.08N | 113.13 E |
| Daugava (Zapadnaja Dvina) ≃ | 100 | 57.04N | 24.03 E |
| Daugavpils | 100 | 55.53N | 26.32 E |
| Dauphin | 136 | 51.09N | 100.03W |
| Davao | 118 | 7.04N | 125.36 E |
| Davenport | 138 | 41.31N | 90.34W |
| David | 130 | 8.26N | 82.26W |
| Davis Strait ʯ | 136 | 67.00N | 57.00W |
| Dawa (Daua) ≃ | 108 | 4.11N | 42.06 E |
| Dawei | 120 | 14.05N | 98.12 E |
| Dawson | 136 | 64.04N | 139.25W |
| Dayr az-Zawr | 109 | 35.20N | 40.09 E |
| Dayton | 140 | 39.45N | 84.11W |
| Daytona Beach | 138 | 29.12N | 81.01W |
| De Aar | 106 | 30.39S | 24.00 E |
| Dead Sea ◎ | 109 | 31.30N | 35.30 E |
| Deán Funes | 134 | 30.26S | 64.21W |
| Dearborn | 140 | 42.18N | 83.10W |
| Death Valley ⋁ | 142 | 36.30N | 117.00W |
| Death Valley National Monument ♦ | 142 | 36.30N | 117.00W |

| Name | Page No. | Lat. | Long. |
|---|---|---|---|
| Dubrovnik | 98 | 42.38N | 18.07 E |
| Duero (Douro) ☱ | 94 | 41.08N | 8.40W |
| Dufourspitze ʌ | 92 | 45.55N | 7.52 E |
| Dugi Otok I | 96 | 44.00N | 15.04 E |
| Duisburg | 90 | 51.25N | 6.46 E |
| Duluth | 138 | 46.45N | 92.07W |
| Dumfries | 88 | 55.04N | 3.37W |
| Dumyāṭ | 109 | 31.25N | 31.48 E |
| Duna |  |  |  |
| → Danube ☱ | 90 | 45.20N | 29.40 E |
| Dunaj |  |  |  |
| → Danube ☱ | 90 | 45.20N | 29.40 E |
| Dunaújváros | 90 | 46.58N | 18.57 E |
| Dundalk | 88 | 54.01N | 6.25W |
| Dundee | 88 | 56.28N | 3.00W |
| Dunedin | 126 | 45.52S | 170.30 E |
| Dungarvan | 88 | 52.05N | 7.37W |
| Dunkirk, In., U.S. | 140 | 40.22N | 85.12W |
| Dunkirk, N.Y., U.S. | 140 | 42.28N | 79.20W |
| Dunkirk, Oh., U.S. | 140 | 40.47N | 83.38W |
| Dun Laoghaire | 88 | 53.17N | 6.08W |
| Dunnville | 140 | 42.54N | 79.36W |
| Durance ☱ | 94 | 43.55N | 4.44 E |
| Durango | 128 | 24.02N | 104.40W |
| Durban | 106 | 29.55S | 30.56 E |
| Durham | 140 | 44.10N | 80.49W |
| Durmitor ʌ | 98 | 43.08N | 19.01 E |
| Durness | 88 | 58.33N | 4.45W |
| Durrësi | 98 | 41.19N | 19.26 E |
| D'Urville Island I | 126 | 40.50S | 173.52 E |
| Dušanbe | 110 | 38.35N | 68.48 E |
| Düsseldorf | 90 | 51.12N | 6.47 E |
| Dzaoudzi | 106 | 12.47S | 45.17 E |
| Dzierżoniów |  |  |  |
| (Reichenbach) | 90 | 50.44N | 16.39 E |
|  |  |  |  |
| **E** |  |  |  |
|  |  |  |  |
| Eagle Pass | 138 | 28.42N | 100.29W |
| East Aurora | 140 | 42.46N | 78.36W |
| East Cape ⟩ | 126 | 37.41S | 178.33 E |
| East China Sea ⲧ² | 114 | 30.00N | 126.00 E |
| Eastern Ghāts ⤧ | 111 | 14.00N | 78.50 E |
| East Falkland I | 134 | 51.55S | 59.00W |
| East Lansing | 140 | 42.44N | 84.29W |
| East Liverpool | 140 | 40.37N | 80.34W |
| East London |  |  |  |
| (Oos-Londen) | 106 | 33.00S | 27.55 E |
| Eastmain | 136 | 52.15N | 78.30W |
| Easton | 140 | 40.41N | 75.13W |
| East Stroudsburg | 140 | 40.59N | 75.10W |
| East Tawas | 140 | 44.16N | 83.29W |
| Eau Claire | 138 | 44.48N | 91.29W |
| Eberswalde | 90 | 52.50N | 13.49 E |
| Ebro ☱ | 94 | 40.43N | 0.54 E |
| Ebro, Delta del ☱² | 94 | 40.43N | 0.54 E |
| Écija | 94 | 37.32N | 5.05W |
| Ecuador □¹ | 132 | 2.00S | 77.30W |
| Edinburg, Tx., U.S. | 128 | 26.18N | 98.09W |
| Edinburg, Va., U.S. | 140 | 38.49N | 78.33W |
| Edinburgh | 88 | 55.57N | 3.13W |
| Edirne | 98 | 41.40N | 26.34 E |
| Edmonton | 136 | 53.33N | 113.28W |
| Edremit | 98 | 39.35N | 27.01 E |
| Edson | 136 | 53.35N | 116.26W |
| Eel ☱ | 142 | 40.40N | 124.20W |
| Efate I | 127b | 17.40S | 168.25 E |
| Eganville | 140 | 45.32N | 77.06W |
| Eger | 90 | 47.54N | 20.23 E |
| Egypt □¹ | 104 | 27.00N | 30.00 E |
| Eindhoven | 90 | 51.26N | 5.28 E |
| Eisenach | 90 | 50.59N | 10.19 E |
| Eisenhüttenstadt | 90 | 52.10N | 14.39 E |
| Eisenstadt | 90 | 47.51N | 16.32 E |
| Eisleben | 90 | 51.31N | 11.32 E |
| Ekwan ☱ | 136 | 53.14N | 82.13W |
| El Aaiún | 104 | 27.09N | 13.12W |
| Elat | 109 | 29.33N | 34.57 E |
| Elba, Isola d' I | 96 | 42.46N | 10.17 E |
| El Banco | 130 | 9.00N | 73.58W |
| Elbasani | 98 | 41.06N | 20.05 E |
| Elbe (Labe) ☱ | 90 | 53.50N | 9.00 E |
| Elblag (Elbing) | 90 | 54.10N | 19.25 E |
| El'brus, Gora ʌ | 86 | 43.21N | 42.26 E |
| El Cajon | 142 | 32.47N | 116.57W |
| El Campo | 128 | 29.11N | 96.16W |
| El Capitan ʌ | 138 | 46.01N | 114.23W |
| Elche | 94 | 38.15N | 0.42W |
| Elda | 94 | 38.29N | 0.47W |
| El Djazaïr (Algiers) | 104 | 36.47N | 3.03 E |
| El Djouf ↞² | 104 | 20.30N | 8.00W |
| El Dorado | 138 | 33.12N | 92.39W |
| Eldoret | 106 | 0.31N | 35.17 E |
| El Encanto | 132 | 1.37S | 73.14W |
| Elephant Mountain ʌ | 140 | 44.46N | 70.46W |
| El Estor | 130 | 15.32N | 89.21W |
| Eleuthera I | 130 | 25.10N | 76.14W |
| Elgin | 88 | 57.39N | 3.20W |
| Elizabeth City | 138 | 36.18N | 76.13W |
| Ełk | 90 | 53.50N | 22.22 E |
| El Kef | 96 | 36.11N | 8.43 E |
| Elkins | 140 | 38.55N | 79.50W |
| Elko | 142 | 40.49N | 115.45W |
| Elk Rapids | 140 | 44.53N | 85.24W |
| Elkton | 140 | 39.36N | 75.50W |
| Ellesmere Island I | 84 | 81.00N | 80.00W |
| Ellsworth | 140 | 44.32N | 68.25W |
| Elmer | 140 | 39.35N | 75.10W |
| Elmira | 140 | 42.05N | 76.48W |
| Elmore | 124 | 36.30S | 144.37 E |
| Elmshorn | 90 | 53.45N | 9.39 E |
| El Nevado, Cerro ʌ | 134 | 35.35S | 68.30W |
| El Palmar | 130 | 7.58N | 61.53W |
| El Paso | 138 | 31.45N | 106.29W |
| El Progreso | 130 | 15.21N | 87.49W |
| El Salvador □¹ | 130 | 13.50N | 88.55W |
| El Sauce | 130 | 12.53N | 86.32W |
| El Tigre | 132 | 8.55N | 64.15W |
| El Turbio | 134 | 51.41S | 72.05W |
| Elvas | 94 | 38.53N | 7.10W |
| Ely | 142 | 39.14N | 114.53W |
| Embarcación | 134 | 23.13S | 64.06W |
| Emden | 90 | 53.22N | 7.12 E |
| Emerald | 122 | 23.32S | 148.10 E |
| Empoli | 96 | 43.43N | 10.57 E |
| Emporia | 138 | 38.24N | 96.10W |
| Emporium | 140 | 41.30N | 78.14W |
| Encarnación | 134 | 27.20S | 55.54W |
| Encontrados | 130 | 9.03N | 72.14W |
| Enderby Land ↞¹ | 85 | 67.30S | 53.00 E |
| Endicott | 140 | 42.05N | 76.02W |
| Engel's | 86 | 51.30N | 46.07 E |
| England □⁸ | 88 | 52.30N | 1.30W |
| English Channel (La |  |  |  |
| Manche) ⴑ | 92 | 50.20N | 1.00W |
| Enns ☱ | 96 | 48.14N | 14.32 E |
| Enschede | 90 | 52.12N | 6.53 E |
| Ensenada | 128 | 31.52N | 116.37W |
| Entebbe | 106 | 0.04N | 32.28 E |
| Enugu | 104 | 6.27N | 7.27 E |
| Eolie, Isole II | 96 | 38.30N | 15.00 E |
| Épinal | 92 | 48.11N | 6.27 E |
| Equatorial Guinea □¹ | 104 | 2.00N | 9.00 E |
| Erechim | 134 | 27.38S | 52.17W |
| Erfurt | 90 | 50.58N | 11.01 E |
| Erie | 140 | 42.07N | 80.05W |
| Erie, Lake ⊜ | 138 | 42.15N | 81.00W |
| Eritrea □¹, Afr. | 108 | 15.20N | 39.00 E |
| Erlangen | 90 | 49.36N | 11.01 E |
| Eromanga I | 127b | 18.45S | 169.05 E |
| Erzurum | 86 | 39.55N | 41.17 E |

| Name | Page No. | Lat. | Long. |
|---|---|---|---|
| Esbjerg | 89 | 55.28 N | 8.27 E |
| Esch-sur-Alzette | 90 | 49.30 N | 5.59 E |
| Escondido | 142 | 33.07 N | 117.05 W |
| Escuintla | 130 | 14.18 N | 90.47 W |
| Eṣfahān | 108 | 32.40 N | 51.38 E |
| Eskilstuna | 89 | 59.22 N | 16.30 E |
| Eskimo Point | 136 | 61.07 N | 94.03 W |
| Eskişehir | 86 | 39.46 N | 30.32 E |
| Esmeraldas | 132 | 0.59 N | 79.42 W |
| Esperance | 122 | 33.51 S | 121.53 E |
| Espinhaço, Serra do ⋏ | 132 | 17.30 S | 43.30 W |
| Espíritu Santo I | 127b | 15.50 S | 166.50 E |
| Espoo (Esbo) | 89 | 60.13 N | 24.40 E |
| Esquel | 134 | 42.54 S | 71.19 W |
| Essen | 90 | 51.28 N | 7.01 E |
| Estados, Isla de los I | 134 | 54.47 S | 64.15 W |
| Estelí | 130 | 13.05 N | 86.23 W |
| Estonia □¹ | 86 | 59.00 N | 26.00 E |
| Estrela ⋀ | 94 | 40.19 N | 7.37 W |
| Ethiopia □¹ | 108 | 9.00 N | 39.00 E |
| Etna, Monte ⋀¹ | 96 | 37.46 N | 15.00 E |
| Ettelbruck | 90 | 49.52 N | 6.05 E |
| Eucla | 122 | 31.43 S | 128.52 E |
| Eugene | 138 | 44.03 N | 123.05 W |
| Eugenia, Punta ≻ | 138 | 27.50 N | 115.05 W |
| Euphrates (Al-Furāt) ≃ | 108 | 31.00 N | 47.25 E |
| Eureka, Ca., U.S. | 142 | 40.48 N | 124.09 W |
| Eureka, Nv., U.S. | 142 | 39.30 N | 115.57 W |
| Europa, Île I | 106 | 22.20 S | 40.22 E |
| Europe ⋅≛¹ | 82 | 50.00 N | 20.00 E |
| Evansville | 138 | 37.58 N | 87.33 W |
| Everest, Mount ⋀ | 112 | 27.59 N | 86.56 E |
| Everglades National Park ✦ | 130 | 25.27 N | 80.53 W |
| Évora | 94 | 38.34 N | 7.54 W |
| Évreux | 92 | 49.01 N | 1.09 E |
| Evrótas ≃ | 98 | 36.48 N | 22.40 E |
| Évvoia I | 98 | 38.34 N | 23.50 E |
| Exeter | 88 | 50.43 N | 3.31 W |
| Exuma Sound ⨆ | 130 | 24.15 N | 76.00 W |
| Eyre North, Lake ⊜ | 124 | 28.40 S | 137.10 E |
| Eyre Peninsula ≻¹ | 124 | 34.00 S | 135.45 E |
| Eyre South, Lake ⊜ | 124 | 29.30 S | 137.20 E |

**F**

| | | | |
|---|---|---|---|
| Fada | 104 | 17.14 N | 21.33 E |
| Faenza | 96 | 44.17 N | 11.53 E |
| Faeroe Islands □² | 86 | 62.00 N | 7.00 W |
| Fairbanks | 144 | 64.51 N | 147.43 W |
| Fairfield, Ca., U.S. | 142 | 38.14 N | 122.02 W |
| Fairfield, Oh., U.S. | 140 | 39.20 N | 84.33 W |
| Fairlie | 126 | 44.06 S | 170.50 E |
| Fairmont | 140 | 39.29 N | 80.08 W |
| Fairview | 140 | 44.43 N | 84.03 W |
| Fairweather, Mount ⋀ | 136 | 58.54 N | 137.32 W |
| Fais I | 118 | 9.46 N | 140.31 E |
| Faisalabad | 110 | 31.25 N | 73.05 E |
| Falevai | 127e | 13.55 S | 171.59 W |
| Falfurrias | 128 | 27.13 N | 98.08 W |
| Falkland Islands □² | 134 | 51.45 S | 59.00 W |
| Falköping | 89 | 58.10 N | 13.31 E |
| Fallon | 142 | 39.28 N | 118.46 W |
| Fall River | 140 | 41.42 N | 71.09 W |
| Falun | 89 | 60.36 N | 15.38 E |
| Faradofay | 106 | 25.02 S | 47.00 E |
| Farāh | 110 | 32.22 N | 62.07 E |
| Farewell, Cape ≻ | 126 | 40.30 S | 172.41 E |
| Fargo | 138 | 46.52 N | 96.47 W |
| Farmington | 138 | 36.43 N | 108.13 W |
| Faro | 94 | 37.01 N | 7.56 W |
| Farquhar Group II | 106 | 10.10 S | 51.10 E |
| Farvel, Kap ≻ | 136 | 59.45 N | 44.00 W |
| Farwell | 140 | 43.50 N | 84.52 W |
| Fayetteville | 138 | 35.03 N | 78.52 W |

| Name | Page No. | Lat. | Long. |
|---|---|---|---|
| Fazzān (Fezzan) ◂¹ | 104 | 26.00 N | 14.00 E |
| Feira de Santana | 132 | 12.15 S | 38.57 W |
| Fenton | 140 | 42.47 N | 83.42 W |
| Fernando de Noronha, Ilha I | 132 | 3.51 S | 32.25 W |
| Fernandópolis | 135 | 20.16 S | 50.14 W |
| Fernando Póo → Bioko I | 104 | 3.30 N | 8.40 E |
| Ferrara | 96 | 44.50 N | 11.35 E |
| Fès | 104 | 34.05 N | 4.57 W |
| Feuilles, Rivière aux ≃ | 136 | 58.47 N | 70.04 W |
| Feyzābād | 110 | 35.01 N | 58.46 E |
| Fianarantsoa | 106 | 21.26 S | 47.05 E |
| Fichtelberg ⋀ | 90 | 50.26 N | 12.57 E |
| Figueira da Foz | 94 | 40.09 N | 8.52 W |
| Figueras | 94 | 42.16 N | 2.58 E |
| Fiji □¹ | 82 | 18.00 S | 175.00 W |
| Filchner Ice Shelf ⧖ | 85 | 79.00 S | 40.00 W |
| Findlay | 140 | 41.02 N | 83.39 W |
| Finland □¹ | 86 | 64.00 N | 26.00 E |
| Finland, Gulf of ⊂ | 89 | 60.00 N | 27.00 E |
| Firenze (Florence) | 96 | 43.46 N | 11.15 E |
| Fitchburg | 140 | 42.35 N | 71.48 W |
| Fitzroy, Monte (Cerro Chaltel) ⋀ | 134 | 49.17 S | 73.05 W |
| Flagstaff | 138 | 35.11 N | 111.39 W |
| Flemingsburg | 140 | 38.25 N | 83.44 W |
| Flensburg | 90 | 54.47 N | 9.26 E |
| Flinders Island I | 124 | 40.00 S | 148.00 E |
| Flinders Range ⋏ | 122 | 31.00 S | 139.00 E |
| Flin Flon | 136 | 54.46 N | 101.53 W |
| Flint | 140 | 42.59 N | 83.45 W |
| Florence → Firenze | 96 | 43.46 N | 11.15 E |
| Florencia | 132 | 1.36 N | 75.36 W |
| Flores I | 118 | 8.30 S | 121.00 E |
| Flores, Laut (Flores Sea) ⫯² | 118 | 8.00 S | 120.00 E |
| Florianópolis | 134 | 27.35 S | 48.34 W |
| Florida | 130 | 21.32 N | 78.14 W |
| Florida □³ | 138 | 28.00 N | 82.00 W |
| Florida, Straits of ⨆ | 130 | 25.00 N | 79.45 W |
| Florida Keys II | 138 | 24.45 N | 81.00 W |
| Fly ≃ | 118 | 8.30 S | 143.41 E |
| Focşani | 98 | 45.41 N | 27.11 E |
| Foggia | 96 | 41.27 N | 15.34 E |
| Folkestone | 88 | 51.05 N | 1.11 E |
| Fond du Lac | 136 | 59.19 N | 107.10 W |
| Fontainebleau | 92 | 48.24 N | 2.42 E |
| Fontur ≻ | 86 | 66.23 N | 14.30 W |
| Formiga | 135 | 20.27 S | 45.25 W |
| Formosa | 134 | 26.11 S | 58.11 W |
| Forrest | 122 | 30.51 S | 128.06 E |
| Forst | 90 | 51.44 N | 14.39 E |
| Fortaleza | 132 | 3.43 S | 38.30 W |
| Fort Chipewyan | 136 | 58.42 N | 111.08 W |
| Fort-de-France | 130 | 14.36 N | 61.05 W |
| Fort Fitzgerald | 136 | 59.53 N | 111.37 W |
| Fort Franklin | 136 | 65.11 N | 123.46 W |
| Fort Good Hope | 136 | 66.15 N | 128.38 W |
| Forth, Firth of ⊂¹ | 88 | 56.05 N | 2.55 W |
| Fort-Lamy → N'Djamena | 104 | 12.07 N | 15.03 E |
| Fort Lauderdale | 138 | 26.07 N | 80.08 W |
| Fort Macleod | 136 | 49.43 N | 113.25 W |
| Fort McMurray | 136 | 56.44 N | 111.23 W |
| Fort Myers | 130 | 26.38 N | 81.52 W |
| Fort Nelson | 136 | 58.49 N | 122.39 W |
| Fort Norman | 136 | 64.54 N | 125.34 W |
| Fort Peck Lake ⊜¹ | 136 | 47.45 N | 106.50 W |
| Fort Reliance | 136 | 62.42 N | 109.08 W |
| Fort Resolution | 136 | 61.10 N | 113.40 W |
| Fort Saint John | 136 | 56.15 N | 120.51 W |
| Fort Simpson | 136 | 61.52 N | 121.23 W |
| Fort Smith | 138 | 35.23 N | 94.23 W |
| Fort Stockton | 138 | 30.53 N | 102.52 W |

| Name | Page No. | Lat. | Long. |
|------|----------|------|-------|
| Fort Wayne | 138 | 41.07 N | 85.07 W |
| Fort Worth | 138 | 32.43 N | 97.19 W |
| Fort Yukon | 144 | 66.34 N | 145.17 W |
| Foshan | 114 | 23.03 N | 113.09 E |
| Fostoria | 140 | 41.09 N | 83.25 W |
| Foveaux Strait ≒ | 126 | 46.35 S | 168.00 E |
| Foxe Basin ⊂ | 136 | 68.25 N | 77.00 W |
| Fox Islands II | 144 | 54.00 N | 168.00 W |
| Framingham | 140 | 42.16 N | 71.25 W |
| France □¹ | 86 | 46.00 N | 2.00 E |
| Franceville | 106 | 1.38 S | 13.35 E |
| Francistown | 106 | 21.11 S | 27.32 E |
| Frankfort | 138 | 38.12 N | 84.52 W |
| Frankfurt am Main | 90 | 50.07 N | 8.40 E |
| Frankfurt an der Oder | 90 | 52.20 N | 14.33 E |
| Fraser ≃ | 136 | 49.09 N | 123.12 W |
| Fraserburgh | 88 | 57.42 N | 2.00 W |
| Fraser Island I | 124 | 25.15 S | 153.10 E |
| Fredericia | 89 | 55.35 N | 9.46 E |
| Frederick | 140 | 39.24 N | 77.24 W |
| Fredericksburg, Tx., U.S. | 128 | 30.16 N | 98.52 W |
| Fredericksburg, Va., U.S. | 140 | 38.18 N | 77.27 W |
| Fredericton | 136 | 45.58 N | 66.39 W |
| Frederikshåb | 136 | 62.00 N | 49.43 W |
| Frederikshavn | 89 | 57.26 N | 10.32 E |
| Fredrikstad | 89 | 59.13 N | 10.57 E |
| Freels, Cape ➤ | 136 | 49.15 N | 53.28 W |
| Freeport, N.Y., U.S. | 140 | 40.39 N | 73.35 W |
| Freeport, Tx., U.S. | 128 | 28.57 N | 95.21 W |
| Freer | 128 | 27.52 N | 98.37 W |
| Freetown | 104 | 8.30 N | 13.15 W |
| Freiberg | 90 | 50.54 N | 13.20 E |
| Freiburg → Fribourg | 92 | 46.48 N | 7.09 E |
| Freiburg [im Breisgau] | 90 | 47.59 N | 7.51 E |
| Freising | 90 | 48.23 N | 11.44 E |
| Fréjus | 92 | 43.26 N | 6.44 E |
| French Guiana □² | 132 | 4.00 N | 53.00 W |
| French Polynesia □² | 82 | 15.00 S | 140.00 W |
| Fresnillo | 128 | 23.10 N | 102.53 W |
| Fresno | 142 | 36.44 N | 119.46 W |
| Fria, Cape ➤ | 106 | 18.30 S | 12.01 E |
| Fribourg (Freiburg) | 92 | 46.48 N | 7.09 E |
| Friedrichshafen | 90 | 47.39 N | 9.28 E |
| Friesland □⁹ | 90 | 53.00 N | 5.40 E |
| Frome, Lake ⊜ | 124 | 30.48 S | 139.48 E |
| Frostburg | 140 | 39.39 N | 78.55 W |
| Fuji-san ⋀¹ | 116 | 35.22 N | 138.44 E |
| Fukui | 116 | 36.04 N | 136.13 E |
| Fukuoka | 116 | 33.35 N | 130.24 E |
| Fukushima | 116 | 37.45 N | 140.28 E |
| Fukuyama | 116 | 34.29 N | 133.22 E |
| Fulda | 90 | 50.33 N | 9.41 E |
| Fulton | 140 | 43.19 N | 76.25 W |
| Funchal | 104 | 32.38 N | 16.54 W |
| Furneaux Group II | 124 | 40.10 S | 148.05 E |
| Fürstenwalde | 90 | 52.21 N | 14.04 E |
| Fürth | 90 | 49.28 N | 10.59 E |
| Fushun | 114 | 41.52 N | 123.53 E |
| Fuzhou | 114 | 26.06 N | 119.17 E |
| Fyn I | 89 | 55.20 N | 10.30 E |
| **G** | | | |
| Gaalkacyo | 108 | 6.49 N | 47.23 E |
| Gabbs | 142 | 38.52 N | 117.55 W |
| Gabon □¹ | 106 | 1.00 S | 11.45 E |
| Gaborone | 106 | 24.45 S | 25.55 E |
| Gabrovo | 98 | 42.52 N | 25.19 E |
| Gadsden | 138 | 34.00 N | 86.00 W |
| Gaferut I | 118 | 9.14 N | 145.23 E |
| Gagnon | 136 | 51.53 N | 68.10 W |
| Gainesville | 138 | 29.39 N | 82.19 W |

| Name | Page No. | Lat. | Long. |
|------|----------|------|-------|
| Gairdner, Lake ⊜ | 122 | 31.35 S | 136.00 E |
| Galán, Cerro ⋀ | 134 | 25.55 S | 66.52 W |
| Galapagos Islands → Colón, Archipiélago de II | 82 | 0.30 S | 90.30 W |
| Galashiels | 88 | 55.37 N | 2.49 W |
| Galați | 98 | 45.26 N | 28.03 E |
| Galicia □⁹ | 90 | 49.50 N | 21.00 E |
| Gallarate | 96 | 45.40 N | 8.47 E |
| Galle | 111 | 6.02 N | 80.13 E |
| Gallipoli | 140 | 38.48 N | 82.12 W |
| Gällivare | 89 | 67.07 N | 20.45 E |
| Galloo Island I | 140 | 43.54 N | 76.25 W |
| Gallup | 138 | 35.31 N | 108.44 W |
| Galveston | 138 | 29.17 N | 94.47 W |
| Galveston Island I | 128 | 29.13 N | 94.55 W |
| Galway | 88 | 53.16 N | 9.03 W |
| Gamarra | 130 | 8.20 N | 73.45 W |
| Gambia □¹ | 104 | 13.30 N | 15.30 W |
| Gand → Gent | 90 | 51.03 N | 3.43 E |
| Gandía | 94 | 38.58 N | 0.11 W |
| Ganges (Ganga) (Padma) ≃ | 112 | 23.22 N | 90.32 E |
| Gangtok | 112 | 27.20 N | 88.37 E |
| Ganzhou | 114 | 25.54 N | 114.55 E |
| Gao | 104 | 16.16 N | 0.03 W |
| Garda, Lago di ⊜ | 96 | 45.40 N | 10.41 E |
| Garden City | 138 | 37.58 N | 100.52 W |
| Gardēz | 112 | 33.37 N | 69.07 E |
| Gardner | 140 | 42.34 N | 71.59 W |
| Gardnerville | 142 | 38.56 N | 119.44 W |
| Garies | 106 | 30.30 S | 18.00 E |
| Garonne ≃ | 92 | 45.02 N | 0.36 W |
| Garrett | 140 | 41.20 N | 85.08 W |
| Gary | 138 | 41.35 N | 87.20 W |
| Gata, Cabo de ➤ | 94 | 36.43 N | 2.12 W |
| Gátas, Akrotírion ➤ | 109 | 34.34 N | 33.02 E |
| Gatere, Mount ⋀ | 127a | 7.49 S | 158.54 E |
| Gatineau, Parc ♦ | 140 | 45.30 N | 76.05 W |
| Gävle | 89 | 60.40 N | 17.10 E |
| Gaziantep | 109 | 37.05 N | 37.22 E |
| Gdańsk (Danzig) | 90 | 54.23 N | 18.40 E |
| Gdynia | 90 | 54.32 N | 18.33 E |
| Gearhart Mountain ⋀ | 142 | 42.30 N | 120.53 W |
| Geelong | 122 | 38.08 S | 144.21 E |
| Gejiu | 114 | 23.22 N | 103.06 E |
| Gelibolu | 98 | 40.24 N | 26.40 E |
| Gelibolu Yarımadası (Gallipoli Peninsula) ➤¹ | 98 | 40.20 N | 26.30 E |
| General Eugenio A. Garay | 132 | 20.31 S | 62.08 W |
| General Pinedo | 134 | 27.19 S | 61.17 W |
| General Roca | 134 | 39.02 S | 67.35 W |
| Geneva, In., U.S. | 140 | 40.35 N | 84.57 W |
| Geneva, N.Y., U.S. | 140 | 42.52 N | 77.00 W |
| Geneva, Lake ⊜ | 92 | 46.25 N | 6.30 E |
| Genève (Geneva) | 92 | 46.12 N | 6.09 E |
| Genk | 90 | 50.58 N | 5.30 E |
| Genova (Genoa) | 96 | 44.25 N | 8.57 E |
| Genova, Golfo di ⊂ | 92 | 44.10 N | 8.55 E |
| Gent (Gand) | 90 | 51.03 N | 3.43 E |
| George ≃ | 136 | 58.49 N | 66.10 W |
| Georgetown, On., Can. | 140 | 43.39 N | 79.55 W |
| Georgetown, Cay. Is. | 130 | 19.18 N | 81.23 W |
| Georgetown, Guy. | 132 | 6.48 N | 58.10 W |
| George Town (Pinang), Malay. | 120 | 5.25 N | 100.20 E |
| Georgetown, Oh., U.S. | 140 | 38.51 N | 83.54 W |
| Georgetown, Tx., U.S. | 128 | 30.37 N | 97.40 W |
| Georgia □¹ | 86 | 42.00 N | 43.30 E |
| Georgia □³ | 138 | 32.50 N | 83.15 W |
| Georgian Bay ⊂ | 140 | 45.15 N | 80.50 W |
| Gera | 90 | 50.52 N | 12.04 E |
| Geraldton, Austl. | 122 | 28.46 S | 114.36 E |

| Name | Page No. | Lat. | Long. |
|---|---|---|---|
| Great Sandy Desert | | | |
| ◆², Or., U.S. | 142 | 43.35N | 120.15W |
| Great Slave Lake ⊝ | 136 | 61.30N | 114.00W |
| Great Victoria Desert | | | |
| ◆² | 122 | 28.30S | 127.45 E |
| Great Yarmouth | 88 | 52.37N | 1.44 E |
| Gréboun, Mont ⋀ | 104 | 20.00N | 8.35 E |
| Greece □¹ | 86 | 39.00N | 22.00 E |
| Green Bay | 138 | 44.31N | 88.01W |
| Greenfield | 140 | 42.35N | 72.36W |
| Greenland □² | 82 | 70.00N | 40.00W |
| Greenland Sea ▼² | 84 | 77.00N | 1.00W |
| Green Mountains ⋌ | 140 | 43.45N | 72.45W |
| Greenock | 88 | 55.57N | 4.45W |
| Greensboro | 138 | 36.04N | 79.47W |
| Greensburg | 140 | 40.18N | 79.32W |
| Greenville, Mi., U.S. | 140 | 43.10N | 85.15W |
| Greenville, S.C., U.S. | 138 | 34.51N | 82.23W |
| Greenville, Tx., U.S. | 138 | 33.08N | 96.06W |
| Greenwood | 138 | 33.30N | 90.10W |
| Greifswald | 90 | 54.05N | 13.23 E |
| Grenada □¹ | 130 | 12.07N | 61.40W |
| Grenoble | 92 | 45.10N | 5.43 E |
| Greymouth | 126 | 42.28S | 171.12 E |
| Grey Range ⋌ | 124 | 27.00S | 143.35 E |
| Grimsby | 88 | 53.35N | 0.05W |
| Grodno | 100 | 53.41N | 23.50 E |
| Groningen | 90 | 53.13N | 6.33 E |
| Groote Eylandt I | 122 | 14.00S | 136.40 E |
| Grosseto | 96 | 42.46N | 11.08 E |
| Grossglockner ⋀ | 90 | 47.04N | 12.42 E |
| Grove City | 140 | 41.09N | 80.05W |
| Groznyj | 86 | 43.20N | 45.42 E |
| Grudziądz | 90 | 53.29N | 18.45 E |
| Guadalajara, Mex. | 128 | 20.40N | 103.20W |
| Guadalajara, Spain | 94 | 40.38N | 3.10W |
| Guadalcanal I | 127a | 9.32S | 160.12 E |
| Guadalquivir ≃ | 94 | 36.47N | 6.22W |
| Guadalupe | 128 | 25.41N | 100.15W |
| Guadalupe Peak ⋀ | 128 | 31.50N | 104.52W |
| Guadeloupe □² | 130 | 16.15N | 61.35W |
| Guadiana ≃ | 94 | 37.14N | 7.22W |
| Guam □² | 118 | 13.28N | 144.47 E |
| Guanajuato | 128 | 21.01N | 101.15W |
| Guangzhou (Canton) | 114 | 23.06N | 113.16 E |
| Guantánamo | 130 | 20.08N | 75.12W |
| Guaratinguetá | 135 | 22.49S | 45.13W |
| Guardafui, Cape ➤ | 108 | 11.48N | 51.22 E |
| Guatemala | 130 | 14.38N | 90.31W |
| Guatemala □¹ | 130 | 15.30N | 90.15W |
| Guayaquil | 132 | 2.10S | 79.50W |
| Guayaquil, Golfo de ⊂ | 132 | 3.00S | 80.30W |
| Guaymas | 128 | 27.56N | 110.54W |
| Gubkin | 86 | 51.18N | 37.32 E |
| Guelma | 96 | 36.28N | 7.26 E |
| Guernsey □² | 92 | 49.28N | 2.35W |
| Guildford | 88 | 51.14N | 0.35W |
| Guilin | 114 | 25.11N | 110.09 E |
| Guinea □¹ | 104 | 11.00N | 10.00W |
| Guinea, Gulf of ⊂ | 104 | 2.00N | 2.30 E |
| Guinea-Bissau □¹ | 104 | 12.00N | 15.00W |
| Güines | 130 | 22.50N | 82.02W |
| Güiria | 130 | 10.34N | 62.18W |
| Guiyang | 114 | 26.35N | 106.43 E |
| Gujarat □³ | 112 | 22.00N | 72.00 E |
| Gujrānwāla | 110 | 32.26N | 74.33 E |
| Gujrāt | 110 | 32.34N | 74.05 E |
| Gulfport | 128 | 30.22N | 89.05W |
| Guntūr | 111 | 16.18N | 80.27 E |
| Guyana □¹ | 132 | 5.00N | 59.00W |
| Gwalior | 112 | 26.13N | 78.10 E |
| Gwanda | 106 | 20.57S | 29.01 E |
| Gweru | 106 | 19.27S | 29.49 E |
| Gydanskaja Guba ⊂ | 102 | 71.20N | 76.30 E |
| Gyöngyös | 90 | 47.47N | 19.56 E |
| Györ | 90 | 47.42N | 17.38 E |

**H**

| Name | Page No. | Lat. | Long. |
|---|---|---|---|
| Haarlem | 90 | 52.23N | 4.38 E |
| Haast | 126 | 43.53S | 169.03 E |
| Hachinohe | 116 | 40.30N | 141.29 E |
| Hachiōji | 116 | 35.39N | 139.20 E |
| Hadera | 109 | 32.26N | 34.55 E |
| Ha Dong | 120 | 20.58N | 105.46 E |
| Ḩaḑūr Shu'ayb ⋀ | 108 | 15.18N | 43.59 E |
| Hagerstown | 140 | 39.37N | 77.45W |
| Ha Giang | 120 | 22.50N | 104.59 E |
| Haikou | 114 | 20.06N | 110.21 E |
| Hainan □⁴ | 114 | 19.00N | 109.30 E |
| Hainan Dao I | 120 | 19.00N | 109.30 E |
| Hai Phong | 120 | 20.52N | 106.41 E |
| Haiti □¹ | 130 | 19.00N | 72.25W |
| Hakodate | 116a | 41.45N | 140.43 E |
| Halab (Aleppo) | 109 | 36.12N | 37.10 E |
| Haleakala Crater ⋆⁶ | 143 | 20.43N | 156.13W |
| Halifax | 136 | 44.39N | 63.36W |
| Halle | 90 | 51.29N | 11.58 E |
| Hallowell | 140 | 44.17N | 69.47W |
| Halls Creek | 122 | 18.16S | 127.46 E |
| Halmahera I | 118 | 1.00N | 128.00 E |
| Halmstad | 89 | 56.39N | 12.50 E |
| Haltiatunturi ⋀ | 89 | 69.18N | 21.16 E |
| Hamadān | 108 | 34.48N | 48.30 E |
| Ḩamāh | 109 | 35.08N | 36.45 E |
| Hamamatsu | 116 | 34.42N | 137.44 E |
| Hamar | 89 | 60.48N | 11.06 E |
| Hamburg | 90 | 53.33N | 9.59 E |
| Hämeenlinna | 89 | 61.00N | 24.27 E |
| Hameln | 90 | 52.06N | 9.21 E |
| Hamhŭng | 114 | 39.54N | 127.32 E |
| Hamilton, Ber. | 138 | 32.17N | 64.46W |
| Hamilton, On., Can. | 136 | 43.15N | 79.51W |
| Hamilton, N.Z. | 126 | 37.47S | 175.17 E |
| Hamilton, Oh., U.S. | 140 | 39.23N | 84.33W |
| Hammamet, Golfe de | | | |
| ⊂ | 96 | 36.05N | 10.40 E |
| Hammam Lif | 96 | 36.44N | 10.20 E |
| Hammerfest | 89 | 70.40N | 23.42 E |
| Hammond | 128 | 30.30N | 90.27W |
| Handan | 114 | 36.37N | 114.29 E |
| Hangzhou | 114 | 30.15N | 120.10 E |
| Hannover | 90 | 52.24N | 9.44 E |
| Ha Noi | 120 | 21.02N | 105.51 E |
| Hanover | 140 | 39.48N | 76.59W |
| Hanzhong | 114 | 32.59N | 107.11 E |
| Happy Valley-Goose | | | |
| Bay | 136 | 53.20N | 60.25W |
| Harare | 106 | 17.50S | 31.03 E |
| Harbin | 114 | 45.45N | 126.41 E |
| Hardangerfjorden ⊂² | 89 | 60.10N | 6.00 E |
| Harer | 108 | 9.18N | 42.08 E |
| Hargeysa | 108 | 9.30N | 44.03 E |
| Harlingen | 128 | 26.11N | 97.41W |
| Harney Basin ⥿¹ | 142 | 43.15N | 120.40W |
| Härnösand | 89 | 62.38N | 17.56 E |
| Harrisburg | 140 | 40.16N | 76.53W |
| Harrison, Cape ➤ | 136 | 54.55N | 57.55W |
| Harrisonburg | 140 | 38.26N | 78.52W |
| Harrisville, Mi., U.S. | 140 | 44.39N | 83.17W |
| Harrisville, N.Y., U.S. | 140 | 43.35N | 75.31W |
| Harstad | 89 | 68.46N | 16.30 E |
| Hartford | 140 | 41.46N | 72.41W |
| Harts ≃ | 106 | 28.24S | 24.17 E |
| Haryana □³ | 112 | 29.20N | 76.20 E |
| Haskovo | 98 | 41.56N | 25.33 E |
| Hastings, N.Z. | 126 | 39.38S | 176.51 E |
| Hastings, Eng., U.K. | 88 | 50.51N | 0.36 E |
| Hattiesburg | 138 | 31.19N | 89.17W |
| Hat Yai | 120 | 7.01N | 100.28 E |
| Haugesund | 89 | 59.25N | 5.18 E |
| Havana | | | |
| → La Habana | 130 | 23.08N | 82.22W |

| Name | Page No. | Lat. | Long. |
|---|---|---|---|
| Hutchinson | 138 | 38.03N | 97.55W |
| Hvannadalshnúkur ʌ | 86 | 64.01N | 16.41W |
| Hwange | 106 | 18.22S | 26.29 E |
| Hwang Ho | | | |
| → Huang ≈ | 114 | 37.32N | 118.19 E |
| Hyannis | 140 | 41.39N | 70.17W |
| Hyde Park | 140 | 41.47N | 73.56W |
| Hyderābād, India | 111 | 17.23N | 78.29 E |
| Hyderābād, Pak. | 110 | 25.22N | 68.22 E |
| Hyères | 92 | 43.07N | 6.07 E |
| Hyvinkää | 89 | 60.38N | 24.52 E |

## I

| Name | Page No. | Lat. | Long. |
|---|---|---|---|
| Ialomiţa ≈ | 98 | 44.42N | 27.51 E |
| Iaşi | 98 | 47.10N | 27.35 E |
| Ibadan | 104 | 7.17N | 3.30 E |
| Ibagué | 132 | 4.27N | 75.14W |
| Ibapah Peak ʌ | 142 | 39.50N | 113.55W |
| Ibérico, Sistema ⋏ | 94 | 41.00N | 2.30W |
| Ibiza I | 94 | 39.00N | 1.25 E |
| Ica | 132 | 14.04S | 75.42W |
| Içá (Putumayo) ≈ | 132 | 3.07S | 67.58W |
| Iceland □¹ | 86 | 65.00N | 18.00W |
| Ich Bogd Uul ⋏ | 114 | 44.55N | 100.20 E |
| Idaho □³ | 138 | 45.00N | 115.00W |
| Idaho Falls | 138 | 43.28N | 112.02W |
| Ídhi Óros ʌ | 98 | 35.18N | 24.43 E |
| Iforas, Adrar des ⋏ | 104 | 20.00N | 2.00 E |
| Iglesias | 96 | 39.19N | 8.32 E |
| Igloolik | 136 | 69.24N | 81.49W |
| Iguala | 128 | 18.21N | 99.32W |
| Iguéla | 106 | 1.55S | 9.19 E |
| Iguídi, 'Erg ⋆⁸ | 104 | 26.35N | 5.40W |
| Ijill, Kediet ʌ | 104 | 22.38N | 12.33W |
| IJsselmeer (Zuiderzee) | | | |
| ⊤² | 90 | 52.45N | 5.25 E |
| Ikaría I | 98 | 37.41N | 26.20 E |
| Ilhéus | 132 | 14.49S | 39.02W |
| Iliamna Lake ⊜ | 144 | 59.30N | 155.00W |
| Ilion | 140 | 43.00N | 75.02W |
| Illimani, Nevado ʌ | 132 | 16.39S | 67.48W |
| Illinois □³ | 138 | 40.00N | 89.00W |
| Ilo | 132 | 17.38S | 71.20W |
| Iloilo | 118 | 10.42N | 122.34 E |
| Imabari | 116 | 34.03N | 133.00 E |
| Imperia | 96 | 43.53N | 8.03 E |
| Imperial Valley V | 142 | 32.50N | 115.30W |
| Inari | 89 | 68.54N | 27.01 E |
| Inari ⊜ | 89 | 69.00N | 28.00 E |
| Inch'ŏn | 114 | 37.28N | 126.38 E |
| India □¹ | 110 | 20.00N | 77.00 E |
| Indiana | 140 | 40.37N | 79.09W |
| Indiana □³ | 138 | 40.00N | 86.15W |
| Indianapolis | 138 | 39.46N | 86.09W |
| Indian Ocean ⊤¹ | 82 | 10.00S | 70.00 E |
| Indian Peak ʌ | 142 | 38.16N | 113.53W |
| Indian Springs | 142 | 36.34N | 115.40W |
| Indigirka ≈ | 102 | 70.48N | 148.54 E |
| Indio | 142 | 33.43N | 116.12W |
| Indispensable Strait ⋃ | 127a | 9.00S | 160.30 E |
| Indonesia □¹ | 118 | 5.00S | 120.00 E |
| Indore | 112 | 22.43N | 75.50 E |
| Indus ≈ | 112 | 24.20N | 67.47 E |
| İnegöl | 98 | 40.05N | 29.31 E |
| Inez | 140 | 37.51N | 82.32W |
| Infiernillo, Presa del | | | |
| ⊜¹ | 128 | 18.35N | 101.45W |
| In Guezzam | 104 | 19.32N | 5.42 E |
| Inhambane | 106 | 23.51S | 35.29 E |
| Inharrime | 106 | 24.29S | 35.01 E |
| Injasuti ʌ | 106 | 29.09S | 29.23 E |
| Inn (En) ≈ | 92 | 48.35N | 13.28 E |

| Name | Page No. | Lat. | Long. |
|---|---|---|---|
| Inner Mongolia | | | |
| → Nei Monggol | | | |
| Zizhiqu □⁴ | 114 | 43.00N | 115.00 E |
| Innsbruck | 90 | 47.16N | 11.24 E |
| Inowrocław | 90 | 52.48N | 18.15 E |
| In Salah | 104 | 27.12N | 2.28 E |
| Interlaken | 92 | 46.41N | 7.51 E |
| International Falls | 138 | 48.36N | 93.24W |
| Inthanon, Doi ʌ | 120 | 18.35N | 98.29 E |
| Inukjuak | 136 | 58.27N | 78.06W |
| Inuvik | 136 | 68.25N | 133.30W |
| Invercargill | 126 | 46.24S | 168.21 E |
| Inverness | 88 | 57.27N | 4.15W |
| Inyangani ʌ | 106 | 18.20S | 32.50 E |
| Ioánnina | 98 | 39.40N | 20.50 E |
| Ionia | 140 | 42.59N | 85.04W |
| Ionian Islands | | | |
| → Iónioi Nísoi II | 98 | 38.30N | 20.30 E |
| Ionian Sea ⊤² | 86 | 39.00N | 19.00 E |
| Iónioi Nísoi II | 98 | 38.30N | 20.30 E |
| Iowa □³ | 138 | 42.15N | 93.15W |
| Ípeiros □¹ | 98 | 39.40N | 20.50 E |
| Ipiaú | 135 | 14.08S | 39.44W |
| Ipoh | 120 | 4.35N | 101.05 E |
| Ipswich, Austl. | 122 | 27.36S | 152.46 E |
| Ipswich, Eng., U.K. | 88 | 52.04N | 1.10 E |
| Iqaluit | 136 | 63.44N | 68.28W |
| Iquique | 132 | 20.13S | 70.10W |
| Iquitos | 132 | 3.46S | 73.15W |
| Iráklion | 98 | 35.20N | 25.09 E |
| Iran □¹ | 82 | 32.00N | 53.00 E |
| Irapuato | 128 | 20.41N | 101.21W |
| Iraq □¹ | 108 | 33.00N | 44.00 E |
| Irbil | 86 | 36.11N | 44.01 E |
| Ireland □¹ | 86 | 53.00N | 8.00W |
| Iringa | 106 | 7.46S | 35.42 E |
| Irish Sea ⊤² | 88 | 53.30N | 5.20W |
| Irkutsk | 102 | 52.16N | 104.20 E |
| Iron Gate Reservoir ⊜¹ | 98 | 44.30N | 22.00 E |
| Iroquois | 140 | 44.51N | 75.19W |
| Irtyš ≈ | 102 | 61.04N | 68.52 E |
| Irún | 94 | 43.21N | 1.47W |
| Isabelia, Cordillera ⋏ | 130 | 13.45N | 85.15W |
| Isar ≈ | 92 | 48.49N | 12.58 E |
| Ise | 116 | 34.29N | 136.42 E |
| Išim ≈ | 102 | 56.09N | 69.27 E |
| İskenderun | 109 | 36.37N | 36.07 E |
| Islāmābād | 110 | 33.42N | 73.10 E |
| Island Pond | 140 | 44.48N | 71.52W |
| Islas Malvinas | | | |
| → Falkland Islands | | | |
| □² | 134 | 51.45S | 59.00W |
| Isle of Man □² | 86 | 54.15N | 4.30W |
| Israel □¹ | 109 | 31.30N | 35.00 E |
| İstanbul | 98 | 41.01N | 28.58 E |
| İstanbul Boğazı | | | |
| (Bosporus) ⋃ | 98 | 41.06N | 29.04 E |
| Itabira | 135 | 19.37S | 43.13W |
| Itabuna | 132 | 14.48S | 39.16W |
| Itajaí | 134 | 26.53S | 48.39W |
| Itajubá | 135 | 22.26S | 45.27W |
| Italy □¹ | 86 | 42.50N | 12.50 E |
| Itapetinga | 135 | 15.15S | 40.15W |
| Itapetininga | 135 | 23.36S | 48.03W |
| Itararé | 135 | 24.07S | 49.20W |
| Ithaca | 140 | 42.26N | 76.29W |
| Ituiutaba | 132 | 18.58S | 49.28W |
| Itumbiara | 135 | 18.25S | 49.13W |
| Itzehoe | 90 | 53.55N | 9.31 E |
| Ivano-Frankivs'k | 86 | 48.55N | 24.43 E |
| Ivanovo | 100 | 57.00N | 40.59 E |
| Ivory Coast | | | |
| → Cote d'Ivoire □¹ | 104 | 8.00N | 5.00W |
| Iwaki (Taira) | 116 | 37.03N | 140.55 E |
| Iwakuni | 116 | 34.09N | 132.11 E |
| Iwo | 104 | 7.38N | 4.11 E |

| Name | Page No. | Lat. | Long. |
|------|----------|------|-------|
| Kalispell | 138 | 48.11 N | 114.18 W |
| Kalixälven ≃ | 89 | 65.50 N | 23.11 E |
| Kalmar | 89 | 56.40 N | 16.22 E |
| Kaluga | 100 | 54.31 N | 36.16 E |
| Kamälia | 112 | 30.44 N | 72.39 E |
| Kamčatka, Poluostrov |  |  |  |
| ⋗ ¹ | 102 | 56.00 N | 160.00 E |
| Kamen'-na-Obi | 102 | 53.47 N | 81.20 E |
| Kamensk-Ural'skij | 102 | 56.28 N | 61.54 E |
| Kamina | 106 | 8.44 S | 25.00 E |
| Kamloops | 136 | 50.40 N | 120.20 W |
| Kampala | 106 | 0.19 N | 32.25 E |
| Kampen | 90 | 52.33 N | 5.54 E |
| Kâmpóng Cham | 120 | 12.00 N | 105.27 E |
| Kâmpóng Chhnăng | 120 | 12.15 N | 104.40 E |
| Kâmpóng Thum | 120 | 12.42 N | 104.54 E |
| Kâmpôt | 120 | 10.37 N | 104.11 E |
| Kananga (Luluabourg) | 106 | 5.54 S | 22.25 E |
| Kanazawa | 116 | 36.34 N | 136.39 E |
| Kanchanaburi | 120 | 14.01 N | 99.32 E |
| Kandavu I | 127c | 19.03 S | 178.13 E |
| Kandavu Passage ⋃ | 127c | 18.45 S | 178.00 E |
| Kandy | 111 | 7.18 N | 80.38 E |
| Kane | 140 | 41.39 N | 78.48 W |
| Kangaroo Island I | 124 | 35.50 S | 137.06 E |
| Kangiqsualujjuaq | 136 | 58.32 N | 65.54 W |
| Kangiqsujuaq | 136 | 61.36 N | 71.58 W |
| Kangirsuk | 136 | 60.01 N | 70.01 W |
| Kankakee | 138 | 41.07 N | 87.51 W |
| Kankan | 104 | 10.23 N | 9.18 W |
| Kano | 104 | 12.00 N | 8.30 E |
| Kānpur | 112 | 26.28 N | 80.21 E |
| Kansas □ ³ | 138 | 38.45 N | 98.15 W |
| Kansas City, Ks., U.S. | 138 | 39.06 N | 94.37 W |
| Kansas City, Mo., U.S. | 138 | 39.05 N | 94.34 W |
| Kansk | 102 | 56.13 N | 95.41 E |
| Kanye | 106 | 24.59 S | 25.19 E |
| Kaohsiung | 114 | 22.38 N | 120.17 E |
| Kaolack | 104 | 14.09 N | 16.04 W |
| Kapfenberg | 90 | 47.26 N | 15.18 E |
| Kaposvár | 90 | 46.22 N | 17.47 E |
| Kapuas ≃ | 118 | 0.25 S | 109.40 E |
| Kapuskasing | 136 | 49.25 N | 82.26 W |
| Karacaköy | 98 | 41.24 N | 28.22 E |
| Karāchi | 110 | 24.52 N | 67.03 E |
| Karakoram Range ⋌ | 112 | 35.30 N | 77.00 E |
| Karamea Bight C ³ | 126 | 41.30 S | 171.40 E |
| Karasburg | 106 | 28.00 S | 18.43 E |
| Karawanken ⋌ | 96 | 46.30 N | 14.25 E |
| Karcag | 90 | 47.19 N | 20.56 E |
| Kardhítsa | 98 | 39.21 N | 21.55 E |
| Kǎrdžali | 98 | 41.39 N | 25.22 E |
| Kariba, Lake ⊜ ¹ | 106 | 17.00 S | 28.00 E |
| Karigasniemi | 89 | 69.24 N | 25.50 E |
| Karlovac | 96 | 45.29 N | 15.34 E |
| Karlovy Vary | 90 | 50.11 N | 12.52 E |
| Karlskoga | 89 | 59.20 N | 14.31 E |
| Karlskrona | 89 | 56.10 N | 15.35 E |
| Karlsruhe | 90 | 49.03 N | 8.24 E |
| Karlstad | 89 | 59.22 N | 13.30 E |
| Kárpathos I | 98 | 35.40 N | 27.10 E |
| Karskoje More (Kara |  |  |  |
| Sea) ▼ ² | 102 | 76.00 N | 80.00 E |
| Karviná | 90 | 49.50 N | 18.30 E |
| Kasai (Cassai) ≃ | 106 | 3.06 S | 16.57 E |
| Kasanga | 106 | 8.28 S | 31.09 E |
| Kashi (Kashgar) | 114 | 39.29 N | 75.59 E |
| Kasr, Ra's ⋗ | 104 | 18.02 N | 38.35 E |
| Kassalā | 104 | 15.28 N | 36.24 E |
| Kassel | 90 | 51.19 N | 9.29 E |
| Kasugai | 116 | 35.14 N | 136.58 E |
| Kasūr | 112 | 31.07 N | 74.27 E |
| Katahdin, Mount ⋀ | 140 | 45.55 N | 68.55 W |
| Kateríni | 98 | 40.16 N | 22.30 E |
| Katherine | 122 | 14.28 S | 132.16 E |
| Kāthiāwār ⋗ ¹ | 112 | 22.00 N | 71.00 E |
| Kāṭhmāṇḍaū | 112 | 27.43 N | 85.19 E |
| Katmandu |  |  |  |
| → Kāṭhmāṇḍaū | 112 | 27.43 N | 85.19 E |
| Katowice | 90 | 50.16 N | 19.00 E |
| Kātrīnā, Jabal ⋀ | 109 | 28.31 N | 33.57 E |
| Katrineholm | 89 | 59.00 N | 16.12 E |
| Katsina | 104 | 13.00 N | 7.32 E |
| Kattegat ⋃ | 89 | 57.00 N | 11.00 E |
| Kauai I | 143 | 22.00 N | 159.30 W |
| Kauai Channel ⋃ | 143 | 21.45 N | 158.50 W |
| Kaulakah Channel ⋃ | 143 | 22.00 N | 159.53 W |
| Kaunas | 100 | 54.54 N | 23.54 E |
| Kavála | 98 | 40.56 N | 24.25 E |
| Kawasaki | 116 | 35.32 N | 139.43 E |
| Kayes | 104 | 14.27 N | 11.26 W |
| Kayseri | 86 | 38.43 N | 35.30 E |
| Kazakhstan □ ¹ | 86 | 48.00 N | 68.00 E |
| Kazan' | 86 | 55.49 N | 49.08 E |
| Kazanlǎk | 98 | 42.38 N | 25.21 E |
| Kebnekaise ⋀ | 89 | 67.53 N | 18.33 E |
| Kecskemét | 90 | 46.54 N | 19.42 E |
| Keele Peak ⋀ | 136 | 63.26 N | 130.19 W |
| Keene | 140 | 42.56 N | 72.16 W |
| Keetmanshoop | 106 | 26.36 S | 18.08 E |
| Kefallinía I | 98 | 38.15 N | 20.35 E |
| Keg River | 136 | 57.48 N | 117.52 W |
| Kékes ⋀ | 90 | 47.55 N | 20.02 E |
| Kelibia | 96 | 36.51 N | 11.06 E |
| Kelowna | 136 | 49.53 N | 119.29 W |
| Keluang | 120 | 2.02 N | 103.19 E |
| Kemerovo | 102 | 55.20 N | 86.05 E |
| Kemi | 89 | 65.49 N | 24.32 E |
| Kemijoki ≃ | 89 | 65.47 N | 24.30 E |
| Kempten [Allgäu] | 90 | 47.43 N | 10.19 E |
| Kemptville | 140 | 45.01 N | 75.38 W |
| Kenai | 144 | 60.33 N | 151.15 W |
| Kenai Peninsula ⋗ ¹ | 144 | 60.10 N | 150.00 W |
| Kenhardt | 106 | 29.19 S | 21.12 E |
| Kenora | 136 | 49.47 N | 94.29 W |
| Kent | 140 | 41.09 N | 81.21 W |
| Kentucky □ ³ | 138 | 37.30 N | 85.15 W |
| Kentucky ≃ | 140 | 38.40 N | 85.09 W |
| Kenya □ ¹ | 106 | 1.00 N | 38.00 E |
| Kenya, Mount |  |  |  |
| → Kirinyaga ⋀ | 106 | 2.43 N | 36.51 E |
| Kerala □ ³ | 111 | 10.00 N | 76.30 E |
| Kerinci, Gunung ⋀ | 118 | 1.42 S | 101.16 E |
| Kérkira (Corfu) | 98 | 39.36 N | 19.56 E |
| Kérkira (Corfu) I | 98 | 39.40 N | 19.42 E |
| Kermān | 108 | 30.17 N | 57.05 E |
| Kermit | 128 | 31.51 N | 103.05 W |
| Ket' ≃ | 102 | 58.55 N | 81.32 E |
| Ketchikan | 144 | 55.21 N | 131.35 W |
| Kettering | 140 | 39.41 N | 84.10 W |
| Key West | 138 | 24.33 N | 81.46 W |
| Khadaungnge ⋀ | 120 | 18.57 N | 94.37 E |
| Khalkidhikí □ ⁹ | 98 | 40.25 N | 23.27 E |
| Khalkís | 98 | 38.28 N | 23.36 E |
| Khambhāt, Gulf of C | 112 | 21.00 N | 72.30 E |
| Khānābād | 112 | 36.41 N | 69.07 E |
| Khānewāl | 112 | 30.18 N | 71.56 E |
| Khaniá | 98 | 35.31 N | 24.02 E |
| Kharkiv | 86 | 50.00 N | 36.15 E |
| Kharkov |  |  |  |
| → Kharkiv | 86 | 50.00 N | 36.15 E |
| Khartoum |  |  |  |
| → Al-Kharṭūm | 104 | 15.36 N | 32.32 E |
| Kherson | 86 | 46.38 N | 32.35 E |
| Khíos | 98 | 38.22 N | 26.08 E |
| Khíos I | 98 | 38.22 N | 26.00 E |
| Kholm | 112 | 36.42 N | 67.41 E |
| Khon Kaen | 120 | 16.26 N | 102.50 E |
| Khulna | 112 | 22.48 N | 89.33 E |
| Khunjerab Pass )( | 112 | 36.52 N | 75.27 E |
| Khyber Pass )( | 112 | 34.05 N | 71.10 E |
| Kiel | 90 | 54.20 N | 10.08 E |

| Name | Page No. | Lat. | Long. |
|---|---|---|---|
| Kielce | 90 | 50.52 N | 20.37 E |
| Kieler Bucht c | 90 | 54.35 N | 10.35 E |
| Kiev |  |  |  |
| → Kyyiv | 86 | 50.26 N | 30.31 E |
| Kigali | 106 | 1.57 S | 30.04 E |
| Kijev |  |  |  |
| → Kyyiv | 86 | 50.26 N | 30.31 E |
| Kikinda | 98 | 45.50 N | 20.28 E |
| Kikládhes II | 98 | 37.30 N | 25.00 E |
| Kikwit | 106 | 5.02 S | 18.49 E |
| Kilauea Crater ± 6 | 143 | 19.25 N | 155.17 W |
| Kilimanjaro ʌ | 106 | 3.04 S | 37.22 E |
| Kilkenny | 88 | 52.39 N | 7.15 W |
| Killarney | 140 | 45.58 N | 81.31 W |
| Killeen | 138 | 31.07 N | 97.43 W |
| Kilmarnock | 88 | 55.36 N | 4.30 W |
| Kimberley | 106 | 28.43 S | 24.46 E |
| Kimberley Plateau ⋌ 1 | 122 | 17.00 S | 127.00 E |
| Kimch'aek | 114 | 40.41 N | 129.12 E |
| Kinabalu, Gunong ʌ | 118 | 6.05 N | 116.33 E |
| Kindersley | 136 | 51.27 N | 109.10 W |
| Kindu | 106 | 2.57 S | 25.56 E |
| King Island I | 124 | 39.50 S | 144.00 E |
| Kingman | 142 | 35.11 N | 114.03 W |
| Kings Canyon National |  |  |  |
| Park ✦ | 142 | 36.48 N | 118.30 W |
| King's Lynn | 88 | 52.45 N | 0.24 E |
| Kingston, On., Can. | 136 | 44.14 N | 76.30 W |
| Kingston, Jam. | 130 | 18.00 N | 76.48 W |
| Kingston, N.Z. | 126 | 45.20 S | 168.42 E |
| Kingston, N.Y., U.S. | 140 | 41.55 N | 73.59 W |
| Kingston upon Hull | 88 | 53.45 N | 0.20 W |
| Kingstown | 130 | 13.09 N | 61.14 W |
| Kingsville | 128 | 27.30 N | 97.51 W |
| Kinshasa |  |  |  |
| (Léopoldville) | 106 | 4.18 S | 15.18 E |
| Kinyeti ʌ | 108 | 3.57 N | 32.54 E |
| Kiparissiakós Kólpos c | 98 | 37.37 N | 21.24 E |
| Kira Kira | 127a | 10.27 S | 161.55 E |
| Kirensk | 102 | 57.46 N | 108.08 E |
| Kiribati □ 1 | 82 | 4.00 S | 175.00 E |
| Kirínia | 109 | 35.20 N | 33.19 E |
| Kirinyaga ʌ | 106 | 2.43 N | 36.51 E |
| Kirkcaldy | 88 | 56.07 N | 3.10 W |
| Kırklareli | 98 | 41.44 N | 27.12 E |
| Kirksville | 138 | 40.11 N | 92.34 W |
| Kirkük | 108 | 35.28 N | 44.28 E |
| Kirkwall | 88 | 58.59 N | 2.58 W |
| Kirov | 100 | 54.05 N | 34.20 E |
| Kirovohrad | 86 | 48.30 N | 32.18 E |
| Kirthar Range ⋌ | 112 | 27.00 N | 67.10 E |
| Kiruna | 89 | 67.51 N | 20.16 E |
| Kiryū | 116 | 36.24 N | 139.20 E |
| Kisangani |  |  |  |
| (Stanleyville) | 106 | 0.30 N | 25.12 E |
| Kishinev |  |  |  |
| → Chişinău | 98 | 47.00 N | 28.50 E |
| Kishiwada | 116 | 34.28 N | 135.22 E |
| Kišin'ov |  |  |  |
| → Chişinău | 98 | 47.00 N | 28.50 E |
| Kiskörei-víztároló ⌷ 1 | 90 | 47.35 N | 20.40 E |
| Kiskunfélegyháza | 90 | 46.43 N | 19.52 E |
| Kiskunhalas | 90 | 46.26 N | 19.30 E |
| Kismaayo | 106 | 0.23 S | 42.30 E |
| Kissidougou | 104 | 9.11 N | 10.06 W |
| Kita | 104 | 13.03 N | 9.29 W |
| Kitakyūshū | 116 | 33.53 N | 130.50 E |
| Kitami | 116a | 43.48 N | 143.54 E |
| Kitchener | 136 | 43.27 N | 80.29 W |
| Kíthira I | 98 | 36.20 N | 22.58 E |
| Kitwe | 106 | 12.49 S | 28.13 E |
| Kjustendil | 98 | 42.17 N | 22.41 E |
| Kladno | 90 | 50.08 N | 14.05 E |
| Klagenfurt | 90 | 46.38 N | 14.18 E |
| Klamath ≃ | 142 | 41.33 N | 124.04 W |
| Klamath Falls | 138 | 42.13 N | 121.46 W |

| Name | Page No. | Lat. | Long. |
|---|---|---|---|
| Klamath Mountains ⋌ | 142 | 41.40 N | 123.20 W |
| Klarälven ≃ | 89 | 59.23 N | 13.32 E |
| Klerksdorp | 106 | 26.58 S | 26.39 E |
| Klincy | 100 | 52.47 N | 32.14 E |
| Kłodzko | 90 | 50.27 N | 16.39 E |
| Klondike □ 9 | 144 | 63.30 N | 139.00 W |
| Kl'učevskaja Sopka, |  |  |  |
| Vulkan ʌ 1 | 102 | 56.04 N | 160.38 E |
| Kneža | 98 | 43.30 N | 24.05 E |
| Knoxville | 138 | 35.57 N | 83.55 W |
| Kōbe | 116 | 34.41 N | 135.10 E |
| København |  |  |  |
| (Copenhagen) | 89 | 55.40 N | 12.35 E |
| Koblenz | 90 | 50.21 N | 7.35 E |
| Kōchi | 116 | 33.33 N | 133.33 E |
| Kodiak | 144 | 57.48 N | 152.23 W |
| Kodiak Island I | 144 | 57.30 N | 153.30 W |
| Koes | 106 | 25.59 S | 19.08 E |
| Kōfu | 116 | 35.39 N | 138.35 E |
| Kokkola |  |  |  |
| (Gamlakarleby) | 89 | 63.50 N | 23.07 E |
| Koksoak ≃ | 136 | 58.32 N | 68.10 W |
| Kola Peninsula |  |  |  |
| → Kol'skij |  |  |  |
| Poluostrov ⋋ 1 | 102 | 67.30 N | 37.00 E |
| Kolhāpur | 111 | 16.42 N | 74.13 E |
| Koliganek | 144 | 59.48 N | 157.25 W |
| Köln (Cologne) | 90 | 50.56 N | 6.59 E |
| Kolovrat, Mount ʌ | 127a | 9.10 S | 161.05 E |
| Kolpaševo | 102 | 58.20 N | 82.50 E |
| Kol'skij Poluostrov |  |  |  |
| (Kola Peninsula) ⋋ 1 | 102 | 67.30 N | 37.00 E |
| Kolwezi | 106 | 10.43 S | 25.28 E |
| Kolyma ≃ | 102 | 69.30 N | 161.00 E |
| Komárno | 90 | 47.45 N | 18.09 E |
| Komatsu | 116 | 36.24 N | 136.27 E |
| Komló | 90 | 46.12 N | 18.16 E |
| Kommunizma, Pik |  |  |  |
| (Communism Peak) |  |  |  |
| ʌ | 110 | 38.57 N | 72.01 E |
| Komotiní | 98 | 41.08 N | 25.25 E |
| Komsomolec, Ostrov I | 102 | 80.30 N | 95.00 E |
| Komsomol'sk-na-Amure | 102 | 50.35 N | 137.02 E |
| Kona Coast ± 2 | 143 | 19.25 N | 155.55 W |
| Koné | 127b | 21.04 S | 164.52 E |
| Kŏng, Kaôh I | 120 | 11.20 N | 103.00 E |
| Königsberg |  |  |  |
| → Kaliningrad | 100 | 54.43 N | 20.30 E |
| Konin | 90 | 52.13 N | 18.16 E |
| Könkämäälven ≃ | 89 | 68.29 N | 22.17 E |
| Konstanz | 90 | 47.40 N | 9.10 E |
| Kontagora | 104 | 10.24 N | 5.28 E |
| Konya | 86 | 37.52 N | 32.31 E |
| Kor'akskoje Nagorje ⋌ | 102 | 62.30 N | 172.00 E |
| Korça | 98 | 40.37 N | 20.46 E |
| Korea, North □ 1 | 114 | 40.00 N | 127.00 E |
| Korea, South □ 1 | 114 | 36.30 N | 128.00 E |
| Korinthiakós Kólpos c | 98 | 38.19 N | 22.04 E |
| Kórinthos (Corinth) | 98 | 37.56 N | 22.56 E |
| Korolevu | 127c | 18.13 S | 177.44 E |
| Koro Sea ⊤ 2 | 127c | 18.00 S | 179.50 E |
| Korsør | 89 | 55.20 N | 11.09 E |
| Kortrijk (Courtrai) | 90 | 50.50 N | 3.16 E |
| Kos I | 98 | 36.50 N | 27.10 E |
| Kosciusko, Mount ʌ | 124 | 36.27 S | 148.16 E |
| Košice | 90 | 48.43 N | 21.15 E |
| Kosovska Mitrovica | 98 | 42.53 N | 20.52 E |
| Kostroma | 100 | 57.46 N | 40.55 E |
| Koszalin (Köslin) | 90 | 54.12 N | 16.09 E |
| Kota Baharu | 120 | 6.08 N | 102.15 E |
| Kota Kinabalu | 118 | 5.59 N | 116.04 E |
| Kotel'nyj, Ostrov I | 102 | 75.45 N | 138.44 E |
| Kotka | 89 | 60.28 N | 26.55 E |
| Kotuj ≃ | 102 | 71.55 N | 102.05 E |
| Kotzebue Sound ⋃ | 144 | 66.20 N | 163.00 W |
| Koussi, Emi ʌ | 104 | 19.50 N | 18.30 E |

| Name | Page No. | Lat. | Long. |
|------|----------|------|-------|
| Lingga, Kepulauan **II** | 118 | 0.05S | 104.35 E |
| Linköping | 89 | 58.25N | 15.37 E |
| Lins | 135 | 21.40S | 49.45W |
| Linton | 138 | 46.16N | 100.13W |
| Linz | 90 | 48.18N | 14.18 E |
| Lion, Golfe du **c** | 92 | 43.00N | 4.00 E |
| Lipeck | 100 | 52.37N | 39.35 E |
| Lippstadt | 90 | 51.40N | 8.19 E |
| Lisboa (Lisbon) | 94 | 38.43N | 9.08W |
| Lismore | 122 | 28.48S | 153.17 E |
| Lithuania □¹ | 86 | 56.00N | 24.00 E |
| Little Current | 140 | 45.58N | 81.56W |
| Little Inagua **I** | 130 | 21.30N | 73.00W |
| Little Minch **U** | 88 | 57.35N | 6.45W |
| Little Rock | 138 | 34.44N | 92.17W |
| Liuzhou | 114 | 24.22N | 109.32 E |
| Livermore Falls | 140 | 44.28N | 70.11W |
| Liverpool | 88 | 53.25N | 2.55W |
| Livingston | 138 | 45.39N | 110.33W |
| Livingstone | 106 | 17.50S | 25.53 E |
| Livny | 100 | 52.25N | 37.37 E |
| Livonia | 140 | 42.22N | 83.21W |
| Livorno (Leghorn) | 96 | 43.33N | 10.19 E |
| Ljubljana | 96 | 46.03N | 14.31 E |
| Ljusnan **≃** | 89 | 61.12N | 17.08 E |
| Llanos **≊** | 132 | 5.00N | 70.00W |
| Lloydminster | 136 | 53.17N | 110.00W |
| Lobito | 106 | 12.20S | 13.34 E |
| Lochgilphead | 88 | 56.03N | 5.26W |
| Lochinver | 88 | 58.09N | 5.15W |
| Lock Haven | 140 | 41.08N | 77.26W |
| Lockport | 140 | 43.10N | 78.41W |
| Lodi | 142 | 38.07N | 121.16W |
| Łódź | 90 | 51.46N | 19.30 E |
| Lofoten **II** | 89 | 68.30N | 15.00 E |
| Logan, Mount **^** | 136 | 60.34N | 140.24W |
| Logroño | 94 | 42.28N | 2.27W |
| Loire **≃** | 92 | 47.16N | 2.11W |
| Loja | 132 | 4.00S | 79.13W |
| Lom | 98 | 43.49N | 23.14 E |
| Loma Mansa **^** | 104 | 9.13N | 11.07W |
| Lombok **I** | 118 | 8.45S | 116.30 E |
| Lomé | 104 | 6.08N | 1.13 E |
| Lompoc | 142 | 34.38N | 120.27W |
| Łomża | 90 | 53.11N | 22.05 E |
| London, On., Can. | 140 | 42.59N | 81.14W |
| London, Eng., U.K. | 88 | 51.30N | 0.10W |
| Londonderry | 88 | 55.00N | 7.19W |
| Londrina | 135 | 23.18S | 51.09W |
| Long Beach | 142 | 33.46N | 118.11W |
| Long Branch | 140 | 40.18N | 73.59W |
| Long Island **I**, Bah. | 130 | 23.15N | 75.07W |
| Long Island **I**, N.Y., U.S. | 140 | 40.50N | 73.00W |
| Long Point **>¹** | 140 | 42.34N | 80.15W |
| Longview | 128 | 32.30N | 94.44W |
| Longwy | 92 | 49.31N | 5.46 E |
| Long Xuyen | 120 | 10.23N | 105.25 E |
| Lop Buri | 120 | 14.48N | 100.37 E |
| Lorain | 140 | 41.27N | 82.10W |
| Lorca | 94 | 37.40N | 1.42W |
| Lord Howe Island **I** | 122 | 31.33S | 159.05 E |
| Lordsburg | 128 | 32.21N | 108.42W |
| Lorica | 130 | 9.14N | 75.49W |
| Lorient | 92 | 47.45N | 3.22W |
| Lorraine □⁹ | 92 | 49.00N | 6.00 E |
| Los Alamos | 138 | 35.53N | 106.19W |
| Los Ángeles, Chile | 134 | 37.28S | 72.21W |
| Los Angeles, Ca., U.S. | 142 | 34.03N | 118.14W |
| Los Banos | 142 | 37.03N | 120.50W |
| Los Blancos | 134 | 23.36S | 62.36W |
| Los Mochis | 128 | 25.45N | 108.57W |
| Los Roques, Islas **II** | 130 | 11.50N | 66.45W |
| Los Vilos | 134 | 31.55S | 71.31W |
| Louang Namtha | 120 | 20.57N | 101.25 E |
| Louangphrabang | 120 | 19.52N | 102.08 E |

| Name | Page No. | Lat. | Long. |
|------|----------|------|-------|
| Louisiade Archipelago **II** | 122 | 11.00S | 153.00 E |
| Louisiana □³ | 138 | 31.15N | 92.15W |
| Louis Trichardt | 106 | 23.01S | 29.43 E |
| Louisville | 138 | 38.15N | 85.45W |
| Lourdes | 92 | 43.06N | 0.03W |
| Lourenço Marques → Maputo | 106 | 25.58S | 32.35 E |
| Loveč | 98 | 43.08N | 24.43 E |
| Lovelock | 142 | 40.10N | 118.28W |
| Lowell | 140 | 42.38N | 71.19W |
| Lower Hutt | 126 | 41.13S | 174.55 E |
| Loyauté, Îles (Loyalty Islands) **II** | 127b | 21.00S | 167.00 E |
| Lualaba **≃** | 106 | 0.26N | 25.20 E |
| Luanda | 106 | 8.48S | 13.14 E |
| Luanguinga **≃** | 106 | 15.11S | 22.56 E |
| Luanshya | 106 | 13.08S | 28.24 E |
| Luao | 106 | 12.12S | 15.52 E |
| Lubango | 106 | 14.55S | 13.30 E |
| Lubbock | 138 | 33.34N | 101.51W |
| Lübeck | 90 | 53.52N | 10.40 E |
| Lublin | 90 | 51.15N | 22.35 E |
| Lubudi | 106 | 6.51S | 21.18 E |
| Lubumbashi (Élisabethville) | 106 | 11.40S | 27.28 E |
| Lucasville | 140 | 38.52N | 82.59W |
| Lucena | 94 | 37.24N | 4.29W |
| Luckenwalde | 90 | 52.05N | 13.10 E |
| Lucknow | 112 | 26.51N | 80.55 E |
| Ludlow | 140 | 43.23N | 72.42W |
| Ludwigsburg | 90 | 48.53N | 9.11 E |
| Ludwigshafen | 90 | 49.29N | 8.26 E |
| Lufkin | 128 | 31.20N | 94.43W |
| Lugano | 92 | 46.01N | 8.58 E |
| Luganville | 127b | 15.32S | 167.08 E |
| Lugo | 94 | 43.00N | 7.34W |
| Lugoj | 98 | 45.41N | 21.54 E |
| Luhans'k | 86 | 48.34N | 39.20 E |
| Lukeville | 128 | 31.52N | 112.48W |
| Luleå | 89 | 65.34N | 22.10 E |
| Luleälven **≃** | 89 | 65.35N | 22.03 E |
| Lüleburgaz | 98 | 41.24N | 27.21 E |
| Lund | 89 | 55.42N | 13.11 E |
| Lüneburg | 90 | 53.15N | 10.23 E |
| Luoyang | 114 | 34.41N | 112.28 E |
| Lupeni | 98 | 45.22N | 23.13 E |
| Luray | 140 | 38.39N | 78.27W |
| Lusaka | 106 | 15.25S | 28.17 E |
| Lushnja | 98 | 40.56N | 19.42 E |
| Lūt, Dasht-e **≈²** | 108 | 33.00N | 57.00 E |
| Luton | 88 | 51.53N | 0.25W |
| Luts'k | 86 | 50.44N | 25.20 E |
| Luwegu **≃** | 106 | 8.31S | 37.23 E |
| Luxembourg | 90 | 49.36N | 6.09 E |
| Luxembourg □¹ | 86 | 49.45N | 6.05 E |
| Luzern | 92 | 47.03N | 8.18 E |
| Luzhou | 114 | 28.54N | 105.27 E |
| Luzon **I** | 118 | 16.00N | 121.00 E |
| Luzon Strait **U** | 118 | 20.30N | 121.00 E |
| L'viv | 86 | 49.50N | 24.00 E |
| L'vov → L'viv | 86 | 49.50N | 24.00 E |
| Lynch, Lac **⊜** | 140 | 46.25N | 77.05W |
| Lynn | 140 | 42.28N | 70.57W |
| Lynn Lake | 136 | 56.51N | 101.03W |
| Lyon | 92 | 45.45N | 4.51 E |

**M**

| | | | |
|------|----------|------|-------|
| Ma'ān | 109 | 30.12N | 35.44 E |
| Maastricht | 90 | 50.52N | 5.43 E |
| Macaé | 135 | 22.23S | 41.47W |
| Macapá | 132 | 0.02N | 51.03W |
| Macau | 114 | 22.14N | 113.35 E |

| Name | Page No. | Lat. | Long. | Name | Page No. | Lat. | Long. |
|---|---|---|---|---|---|---|---|
| Manton | 140 | 44.24N | 85.23W | Massena | 140 | 44.55N | 74.53W |
| Mantova | 96 | 45.09N | 10.48 E | Massillon | 140 | 40.48N | 81.32W |
| Manzanares | 94 | 39.00N | 3.22W | Masterton | 126 | 40.57S | 175.40 E |
| Manzanillo, Cuba | 130 | 20.21N | 77.07W | Matadi | 106 | 5.49S | 13.27 E |
| Manzanillo, Mex. | 128 | 19.03N | 104.20W | Matagalpa | 130 | 12.55N | 85.55W |
| Maoke, Pegunungan ⋏ | 118 | 4.00S | 138.00 E | Matagorda Island I | 128 | 28.15N | 96.30W |
| Mapire | 130 | 7.45N | 64.42W | Matamoros | 128 | 25.53N | 97.30W |
| Maputo (Lourenço | | | | Matanzas | 130 | 23.03N | 81.35W |
| Marques) | 106 | 25.58S | 32.35 E | Matías Romero | 128 | 16.53N | 95.02W |
| Maqat | 86 | 47.39N | 53.19 E | Mato Grosso, Planalto | | | |
| Maracaibo | 132 | 10.40N | 71.37W | do ⋏ [1] | 132 | 15.30S | 56.00W |
| Maracaibo, Lago de ⊜ | 130 | 9.50N | 71.30W | Matsue | 116 | 35.28N | 133.04 E |
| Maracay | 132 | 10.15N | 67.36W | Matsumoto | 116 | 36.14N | 137.58 E |
| Maragogipe | 135 | 12.46S | 38.55W | Matsuyama | 116 | 33.50N | 132.45 E |
| Marañón ≃ | 132 | 4.30S | 73.27W | Mattagami ≃ | 136 | 50.43N | 81.29W |
| Marathon | 136 | 48.40N | 86.25W | Mattawamkeag | 140 | 45.30N | 68.21W |
| Maravovo | 127a | 9.17S | 159.38 E | Matterhorn ▲ | 92 | 45.59N | 7.43 E |
| Marcy, Mount ▲ | 140 | 44.07N | 73.56W | Matthew Town | 130 | 20.57N | 73.40W |
| Mardān | 112 | 34.12N | 72.02 E | Maturín | 132 | 9.45N | 63.11W |
| Mar del Plata | 134 | 38.00S | 57.33W | Maubeuge | 92 | 50.17N | 3.58 E |
| Maré, Île I | 127b | 21.30S | 168.00 E | Maug Islands II | 118 | 20.01N | 145.13 E |
| Margarita, Isla de I | 130 | 11.00N | 64.00W | Maui I | 143 | 20.45N | 156.15W |
| Margherita Peak ▲ | 106 | 0.22N | 29.51 E | Maumee | 140 | 41.33N | 83.39W |
| Mariana Islands II | 118 | 16.00N | 145.30 E | Mauna Loa ▲ [1] | 143 | 19.29N | 155.36W |
| Marianao | 130 | 23.05N | 82.26W | Maunath Bhanjan | 112 | 25.57N | 83.33 E |
| Marías, Islas II | 128 | 21.25N | 106.28W | Mauritania □ [1] | 104 | 20.00N | 12.00W |
| Maribor | 96 | 46.33N | 15.39 E | Mauritius □ [1] | 106 | 20.17S | 57.33 E |
| Mariental | 106 | 24.36S | 17.59 E | Mawlamyine | 120 | 16.30N | 97.38 E |
| Marietta | 140 | 39.24N | 81.27W | Mayaguana I | 130 | 22.23N | 72.57W |
| Marília | 135 | 22.13S | 49.56W | Mayagüez | 130 | 18.12N | 67.09W |
| Marinette | 138 | 45.06N | 87.37W | Maymyo | 120 | 22.02N | 96.28 E |
| Maringá | 134 | 23.25S | 51.55W | Mayotte □ [2] | 106 | 12.50S | 45.10 E |
| Marion, Mi., U.S. | 140 | 44.06N | 85.08W | Mayotte I | 106 | 12.50S | 45.10 E |
| Marion, Oh., U.S. | 140 | 40.35N | 83.07W | Maysville | 140 | 38.38N | 83.44W |
| Maripa | 130 | 7.26N | 65.09W | Mazara del Vallo | 96 | 37.39N | 12.36 E |
| Mariscal Estigarribia | 134 | 22.02S | 60.38W | Mazār-e-Sharīf | 112 | 36.42N | 67.06 E |
| Maritime Alps ⋏ | 92 | 44.15N | 7.10 E | Mazatlán | 128 | 23.13N | 106.25W |
| Mariupol' | 86 | 47.06N | 37.33 E | Mazury ◆ [1] | 90 | 53.45N | 21.00 E |
| Markham, Mount ▲ | 85 | 82.51S | 161.21 E | Mbabane | 106 | 26.18S | 31.06 E |
| Marlborough | 140 | 42.20N | 71.33W | Mbala | 106 | 8.50S | 31.22 E |
| Marmara Denizi (Sea | | | | Mbale | 106 | 1.05N | 34.10 E |
| of Marmara) ⊤ [2] | 98 | 40.40N | 28.15 E | Mbandaka | | | |
| Marmara Gölü ⊜ | 98 | 38.37N | 28.02 E | (Coquilhatville) | 106 | 0.04N | 18.16 E |
| Marmet | 140 | 38.14N | 81.34W | Mbomou (Bomu) ≃ | 104 | 4.08N | 22.26 E |
| Marne ≃ | 92 | 48.49N | 2.24 E | Mbuji-Mayi | | | |
| Maroa | 132 | 2.43N | 67.33W | (Bakwanga) | 106 | 6.09S | 23.38 E |
| Maromokotro ▲ | 106 | 14.01S | 48.59 E | McAdam | 140 | 45.36N | 67.20W |
| Maroua | 104 | 10.36N | 14.20 E | McAlester | 138 | 34.56N | 95.46W |
| Marovoay | 106 | 16.06S | 46.39 E | McAllen | 128 | 26.12N | 98.13W |
| Marquette | 138 | 46.32N | 87.23W | McComb | 128 | 31.14N | 90.27W |
| Marrah, Jabal ▲ | 104 | 14.04N | 24.21 E | McConnellsburg | 140 | 39.55N | 77.59W |
| Marrakech | 104 | 31.38N | 8.00W | McCook | 138 | 40.12N | 100.37W |
| Marsabit | 108 | 2.20N | 37.59 E | McGill | 142 | 39.24N | 114.46W |
| Marsala | 96 | 37.48N | 12.26 E | Mcgrath | 144 | 62.58N | 155.38W |
| Marseille | 92 | 43.18N | 5.24 E | McKinley, Mount ▲ | 144 | 63.30N | 151.00W |
| Marshall | 138 | 32.32N | 94.22W | M'Clintock Channel ⋃ | 136 | 71.00N | 101.00W |
| Marsh Island I | 128 | 29.35N | 91.53W | McLoughlin, Mount ▲ | 142 | 42.27N | 122.19W |
| Marsing | 142 | 43.32N | 116.48W | Mead, Lake ⊜ [1] | 142 | 36.05N | 114.25W |
| Martaban, Gulf of C | 120 | 16.30N | 97.00 E | Meadville | 140 | 41.38N | 80.09W |
| Martha's Vineyard I | 140 | 41.25N | 70.40W | Meander River | 136 | 59.02N | 117.42W |
| Martigny | 92 | 46.06N | 7.04 E | Meath □ [9] | 88 | 53.36N | 6.54W |
| Martigues | 92 | 43.24N | 5.03 E | Mecca | | | |
| Martin | 90 | 49.05N | 18.55 E | → Makkah | 108 | 21.27N | 39.49 E |
| Martinique □ [2] | 130 | 14.40N | 61.00W | Mechelen | 90 | 51.02N | 4.28 E |
| Martinsburg | 140 | 39.27N | 77.57W | Mecklenburg □ [9] | 90 | 53.30N | 13.00 E |
| Maryborough | 122 | 25.32S | 152.42 E | Medan | 118 | 3.35N | 98.40 E |
| Maryland □ [3] | 138 | 39.00N | 76.45W | Medellín | 132 | 6.15N | 75.35W |
| Marysville | 142 | 39.08N | 121.35W | Médenine | 104 | 32.21N | 10.30 E |
| Masai Steppe ⋏ [1] | 106 | 4.45S | 37.00 E | Medford | 142 | 42.19N | 122.52W |
| Mascarene Islands II | 106 | 21.00S | 57.00 E | Medgidia | 98 | 44.15N | 28.16 E |
| Masherbrum ▲ | 112 | 35.38N | 76.18 E | Medicine Hat | 136 | 50.03N | 110.40W |
| Mason City | 138 | 43.09N | 93.12W | Mediterranean Sea ⊤ [2] | 82 | 35.00N | 20.00 E |
| Masqaţ (Muscat) | 108 | 23.37N | 58.35 E | Medjerda, Monts de la | | | |
| Massa | 96 | 44.01N | 10.09 E | ⋏ | 96 | 36.35N | 8.15 E |
| Massachusetts □ [3] | 138 | 42.15N | 71.50W | Meekatharra | 122 | 26.36S | 118.29 E |
| Massachusetts Bay C | 140 | 42.20N | 70.50W | Meerut | 112 | 28.59N | 77.42 E |

| Name | Page No. | Lat. | Long. |
|------|----------|------|-------|
| Meiktila | 120 | 20.52N | 95.52 E |
| Meiningen | 90 | 50.34N | 10.25 E |
| Meissen | 90 | 51.10N | 13.28 E |
| Mekambo | 106 | 1.01N | 13.56 E |
| Mekong ≃ | 120 | 10.33N | 105.24 E |
| Melaka | 120 | 2.12N | 102.15 E |
| Melanesia II | 82 | 13.00S | 164.00 E |
| Melbourne, Austl. | 122 | 37.49S | 144.58 E |
| Melbourne, Fl., U.S. | 138 | 28.04N | 80.36 W |
| Melby House | 88 | 60.18N | 1.39 W |
| Melilla | 104 | 35.19N | 2.58 W |
| Melita | 136 | 49.16N | 101.00 W |
| Melitopol' | 86 | 46.50N | 35.22 E |
| Melville Island I, Austl. | 122 | 11.40S | 131.00 E |
| Melville Island I, N.T., Can. | 136 | 75.15N | 110.00 W |
| Melville Peninsula ➤¹ | 136 | 68.00N | 84.00 W |
| Memmingen | 90 | 47.59N | 10.11 E |
| Memphis | 138 | 35.08N | 90.02 W |
| Mendocino, Cape ➤ | 142 | 40.25N | 124.25 W |
| Mendoza | 134 | 32.53S | 68.49 W |
| Menorca I | 94 | 40.00N | 4.00 E |
| Mentawai, Kepulauan II | 118 | 2.00S | 99.30 E |
| Menzel Bourguiba | 96 | 37.10N | 9.48 E |
| Merano (Meran) | 96 | 46.40N | 11.09 E |
| Merced | 142 | 37.18N | 120.28 W |
| Mercedes | 134 | 33.40S | 65.28 W |
| Mergui (Myeik) | 120 | 12.26N | 98.36 E |
| Mergui Archipelago II | 120 | 12.00N | 98.00 E |
| Mérida, Mex. | 128 | 20.58N | 89.37 W |
| Mérida, Spain | 94 | 38.55N | 6.20 W |
| Mérida, Ven. | 130 | 8.30N | 71.10 W |
| Meriden | 140 | 41.32N | 72.48 W |
| Meridian | 138 | 32.21N | 88.42 W |
| Merseburg | 90 | 51.21N | 11.59 E |
| Mersin | 109 | 36.48N | 34.38 E |
| Merthyr Tydfil | 88 | 51.46N | 3.23 W |
| Mesa | 138 | 33.25N | 111.49 W |
| Mesopotamia ◆¹ | 108 | 34.00N | 44.00 E |
| Mesquite | 142 | 36.48N | 114.03 W |
| Messina, Italy | 96 | 38.11N | 15.33 E |
| Messina, S. Afr. | 106 | 22.23S | 30.00 E |
| Metán | 134 | 25.29S | 64.57 W |
| Metz | 92 | 49.08N | 6.10 E |
| Meuse (Maas) ≃ | 90 | 51.49N | 5.01 E |
| Mexicali | 128 | 32.40N | 115.29 W |
| Mexico | 138 | 39.10N | 91.52 W |
| Mexico □¹ | 128 | 23.00N | 102.00 W |
| Mexico, Gulf of c | 128 | 24.00N | 93.00 W |
| Mexico City → Ciudad de México | 128 | 19.24N | 99.09 W |
| Meymaneh | 112 | 35.55N | 64.47 E |
| Miami | 138 | 25.46N | 80.11 W |
| Miānwāli | 112 | 32.35N | 71.33 E |
| Miass | 86 | 54.59N | 60.06 E |
| Michigan □³ | 138 | 44.00N | 85.00 W |
| Michigan, Lake ❷ | 138 | 44.00N | 87.00 W |
| Micronesia II | 82 | 11.00N | 159.00 E |
| Micronesia, Federated States of □¹ | 118 | 5.00N | 152.00 E |
| Mičurinsk | 100 | 52.54N | 40.30 E |
| Middelburg | 106 | 31.30S | 25.00 E |
| Middlebury | 140 | 44.00N | 73.10 W |
| Middlesbrough | 88 | 54.35N | 1.14 W |
| Middletown, N.Y., U.S. | 140 | 41.26N | 74.25 W |
| Middletown, Oh., U.S. | 140 | 39.30N | 84.23 W |
| Midland, On., Can. | 140 | 44.45N | 79.53 W |
| Midland, Mi., U.S. | 140 | 43.36N | 84.14 W |
| Midland, Tx., U.S. | 138 | 31.59N | 102.04 W |
| Mielec | 90 | 50.18N | 21.25 E |
| Miguel Alemán, Presa ❷¹ | 128 | 18.13N | 96.32 W |
| Mihajlovgrad | 98 | 43.25N | 23.13 E |
| Mikkeli | 89 | 61.41N | 27.15 E |
| Milan → Milano, Italy | 96 | 45.28N | 9.12 E |
| Milan, Mi., U.S. | 140 | 42.05N | 83.40 W |
| Milano (Milan) | 96 | 45.28N | 9.12 E |
| Mildura | 122 | 34.12S | 142.09 E |
| Miles City | 138 | 46.24N | 105.50 W |
| Milford | 140 | 38.54N | 75.25 W |
| Milford Haven | 88 | 51.40N | 5.02 W |
| Millau | 92 | 44.06N | 3.05 E |
| Millinocket | 140 | 45.39N | 68.42 W |
| Milltown Malbay | 88 | 52.52N | 9.23 W |
| Mílos I | 98 | 36.41N | 24.15 E |
| Milparinka | 122 | 29.44S | 141.53 E |
| Milwaukee | 138 | 43.02N | 87.54 W |
| Minas | 134 | 34.23S | 55.14 W |
| Minas, Sierra de las ⚹ | 130 | 15.10N | 89.40 W |
| Minatitlán | 128 | 17.59N | 94.31 W |
| Mindanao I | 118 | 8.00N | 125.00 E |
| Minden | 128 | 32.36N | 93.17 W |
| Mindoro I | 118 | 12.50N | 121.05 E |
| Mineral Wells | 138 | 32.48N | 98.06 W |
| Minho (Miño) ≃ | 94 | 41.52N | 8.51 W |
| Minneapolis | 138 | 44.58N | 93.15 W |
| Minnesota □³ | 138 | 46.00N | 94.15 W |
| Miño (Minho) ≃ | 94 | 41.52N | 8.51 W |
| Minorca → Menorca I | 94 | 40.00N | 4.00 E |
| Minot | 138 | 48.13N | 101.17 W |
| Minsk | 100 | 53.54N | 27.34 E |
| Minto, Lac ❻ | 136 | 51.00N | 73.37 W |
| Minūf | 109 | 30.28N | 30.56 E |
| Mirtóōn Pélagos ▼² | 98 | 36.51N | 23.18 E |
| Miskolc | 90 | 48.06N | 20.47 E |
| Mississippi □³ | 138 | 32.50N | 89.30 W |
| Mississippi ≃ | 138 | 29.00N | 89.15 W |
| Mississippi Delta ≃² | 138 | 29.10N | 89.15 W |
| Missoula | 138 | 46.52N | 113.59 W |
| Missouri □³ | 138 | 38.30N | 93.30 W |
| Missouri ≃ | 138 | 38.50N | 90.08 W |
| Mistassini, Lac ❻ | 136 | 51.00N | 73.37 W |
| Mitilíni | 98 | 39.06N | 26.32 E |
| Mito | 116 | 36.22N | 140.28 E |
| Mitsiwa | 108 | 15.38N | 39.28 E |
| Mitú | 132 | 1.08N | 70.03 W |
| Mitumba, Monts ⚹ | 106 | 6.00S | 29.00 E |
| Miyakonojō | 116 | 31.44N | 131.04 E |
| Miyazaki | 116 | 31.54N | 131.26 E |
| Mizoram □⁸ | 112 | 23.30N | 93.00 E |
| Mladá Boleslav | 90 | 50.23N | 14.59 E |
| Mobile | 138 | 30.41N | 88.02 W |
| Moçambique | 106 | 15.03S | 40.42 E |
| Mochudi | 106 | 24.28S | 26.05 E |
| Mococa | 135 | 21.28S | 47.01 W |
| Modena | 96 | 44.40N | 10.55 E |
| Modesto | 142 | 37.38N | 120.59 W |
| Moffat | 88 | 55.20N | 3.27 W |
| Moga | 112 | 30.48N | 75.10 E |
| Mogaung | 120 | 25.18N | 96.56 E |
| Mogil'ov | 100 | 53.54N | 30.21 E |
| Mohave, Lake ❻¹ | 142 | 35.25N | 114.38 W |
| Mohawk ≃ | 140 | 42.47N | 73.42 W |
| Moisie ≃ | 136 | 50.12N | 66.04 W |
| Mojave Desert ◆² | 142 | 35.00N | 117.00 W |
| Mokp'o | 114 | 34.48N | 126.22 E |
| Moldavia □⁹ | 98 | 46.30N | 27.00 E |
| Molde | 89 | 62.44N | 7.11 E |
| Moldova □¹ | 86 | 47.00N | 29.00 E |
| Moldoveanu ⋀ | 98 | 45.36N | 24.44 E |
| Molfetta | 96 | 41.12N | 16.36 E |
| Mollendo | 132 | 17.02S | 72.01 W |
| Mölndal | 89 | 57.39N | 12.01 E |
| Molokai I | 143 | 21.07N | 157.00 W |
| Molopo ≃ | 106 | 28.30S | 20.13 E |
| Moluccas → Maluku II | 118 | 2.00S | 128.00 E |
| Mombasa | 106 | 4.03S | 39.40 E |

| Name | Page No. | Lat. | Long. |
|------|----------|------|-------|
| Momi | 127c | 17.55S | 177.17 E |
| Monaco □¹ | 86 | 43.45N | 7.25 E |
| Mončegorsk | 86 | 67.54N | 32.58 E |
| Mönchengladbach | 90 | 51.12N | 6.28 E |
| Monclova | 128 | 26.54N | 101.25W |
| Moncton | 136 | 46.06N | 64.47W |
| Monessen | 140 | 40.08N | 79.53W |
| Monfalcone | 96 | 45.49N | 13.32 E |
| Mongolia □¹ | 114 | 46.00N | 105.00 E |
| Mono Lake ◎ | 142 | 38.00N | 119.00W |
| Monroe, La., U.S. | 138 | 32.30N | 92.07W |
| Monroe, Mi., U.S. | 140 | 41.54N | 83.23W |
| Monrovia | 104 | 6.18N | 10.47W |
| Montana □³ | 138 | 47.00N | 110.00W |
| Montargis | 92 | 48.00N | 2.45 E |
| Montauban | 92 | 44.01N | 1.21 E |
| Montauk | 140 | 41.02N | 71.57W |
| Montbéliard | 92 | 47.31N | 6.48 E |
| Montceau [-les-Mines] | 92 | 46.40N | 4.22 E |
| Mont-de-Marsan | 92 | 43.53N | 0.30W |
| Monte Caseros | 134 | 30.15S | 57.39W |
| Monte Comán | 134 | 34.36S | 67.54W |
| Montego Bay | 130 | 18.28N | 77.55W |
| Montenegro □³ | 98 | 42.30N | 19.20 E |
| Monterey | 142 | 36.36N | 121.53W |
| Monterey Bay c | 142 | 36.45N | 121.55W |
| Montería | 132 | 8.46N | 75.53W |
| Monterrey | 128 | 25.40N | 100.19W |
| Montes Claros | 132 | 16.43S | 43.52W |
| Montevideo | 134 | 34.53S | 56.11W |
| Montgomery | 138 | 32.23N | 86.18W |
| Montluçon | 92 | 46.21N | 2.36 E |
| Montpelier | 140 | 44.15N | 72.34W |
| Montpellier | 92 | 43.36N | 3.53 E |
| Montréal | 140 | 45.31N | 73.34W |
| Montrose | 140 | 41.50N | 75.52W |
| Montserrat □² | 130 | 16.45N | 62.12W |
| Monywa | 120 | 22.05N | 95.08 E |
| Monza | 96 | 45.35N | 9.16 E |
| Moorea I | 127d | 17.32S | 149.50W |
| Moosehead Lake ◎ | 140 | 45.40N | 69.40W |
| Moose Jaw | 136 | 50.23N | 105.32W |
| Mooselookmeguntic Lake ◎ | 140 | 44.53N | 70.48W |
| Moosonee | 136 | 51.17N | 80.39W |
| Mopti | 104 | 14.30N | 4.12W |
| Morādābād | 112 | 28.50N | 78.47 E |
| Morava □⁹ | 90 | 49.20N | 17.00 E |
| Morawhanna | 132 | 8.16N | 59.45W |
| Morden | 136 | 49.11N | 98.05W |
| More, Ben ▲ | 88 | 56.23N | 4.31W |
| More Assynt, Ben ▲ | 88 | 58.07N | 4.51W |
| Morehead | 140 | 38.11N | 83.25W |
| Morelia | 128 | 19.42N | 101.07W |
| Morena, Sierra ⚲ | 94 | 38.00N | 5.00W |
| Morgantown | 140 | 39.37N | 79.57W |
| Moriah, Mount ▲ | 142 | 39.17N | 114.12W |
| Morioka | 116 | 39.42N | 141.09 E |
| Morocco □¹ | 104 | 32.00N | 5.00W |
| Morogoro | 106 | 6.49S | 37.40 E |
| Moro Gulf c | 118 | 6.51N | 123.00 E |
| Morondava | 106 | 20.17S | 44.17 E |
| Morón de la Frontera | 94 | 37.08N | 5.27W |
| Moroni | 106 | 11.41S | 43.16 E |
| Morrinsville | 126 | 37.39S | 175.32 E |
| Moscos Islands II | 120 | 14.00N | 97.45 E |
| Moscow → Moskva | 100 | 55.45N | 37.35 E |
| Mosel (Moselle) ≃ | 92 | 50.22N | 7.36 E |
| Moselle (Mosel) ≃ | 92 | 50.22N | 7.36 E |
| Moskva (Moscow) | 100 | 55.45N | 37.35 E |
| Moskva ≃ | 100 | 55.05N | 38.50 E |
| Mosquitos, Golfo de los c | 130 | 9.00N | 81.15W |
| Mossburn | 126 | 45.40S | 168.15 E |
| Mosselbaai | 106 | 34.11S | 22.08 E |
| Mossoró | 132 | 5.11S | 37.20W |
| Most | 90 | 50.32N | 13.39 E |
| Mostar | 96 | 43.20N | 17.49 E |
| Motala | 89 | 58.33N | 15.03 E |
| Motherwell | 88 | 55.48N | 4.00W |
| Moulins | 92 | 46.34N | 3.20 E |
| Moundou | 104 | 8.34N | 16.05 E |
| Moundsville | 140 | 39.55N | 80.44W |
| Mountain Home | 142 | 43.07N | 115.41W |
| Mountain Nile (Baḥr al-Jabal) ≃ | 108 | 9.30N | 30.30 E |
| Mount Forest | 140 | 43.59N | 80.44W |
| Mount Gambier | 122 | 37.50S | 140.46 E |
| Mount Isa | 122 | 20.44S | 139.30 E |
| Mount Magnet | 122 | 28.04S | 117.49 E |
| Mount Morris | 140 | 42.43N | 77.52W |
| Mount Olivet | 140 | 38.31N | 84.02W |
| Mount Pleasant | 140 | 43.35N | 84.46W |
| Mount Union | 140 | 40.23N | 77.52W |
| Mozambique □¹ | 106 | 18.15S | 35.00 E |
| Mozambique Channel ᵁ | 106 | 19.00S | 41.00 E |
| Mozyr' | 86 | 52.03N | 29.14 E |
| Mrhila, Djebel ▲ | 96 | 35.25N | 9.14 E |
| Mtwara | 106 | 10.16S | 40.11 E |
| Muang Không | 120 | 14.07N | 105.51 E |
| Muang Khôngxédôn | 120 | 15.34N | 105.49 E |
| Muang Xaignabouri | 120 | 19.15N | 101.45 E |
| Muar (Bandar Maharani) | 120 | 2.02N | 102.34 E |
| Muchinga Mountains ⚲ | 106 | 12.00S | 31.45 E |
| Mudanjiang | 114 | 44.35N | 129.36 E |
| Mufulira | 106 | 12.33S | 28.14 E |
| Muhammad, Ra's ⟩ | 109 | 27.44N | 34.15 E |
| Mühlviertel ◆¹ | 90 | 48.25N | 14.10 E |
| Mukden → Shenyang | 114 | 41.48N | 123.27 E |
| Mulatupo | 130 | 8.57N | 77.45W |
| Mulhacén ▲ | 94 | 37.03N | 3.19W |
| Mulhouse | 92 | 47.45N | 7.20 E |
| Mull, Island of I | 88 | 56.27N | 6.00W |
| Multān | 110 | 30.11N | 71.29 E |
| München (Munich) | 90 | 48.08N | 11.34 E |
| Munhango | 106 | 12.12S | 18.42 E |
| Munich → München | 90 | 48.08N | 11.34 E |
| Münster | 90 | 51.57N | 7.37 E |
| Munster □⁹ | 88 | 52.25N | 8.20W |
| Muqdisho (Mogadishu) | 108 | 2.01N | 45.20 E |
| Mura (Mur) ≃ | 90 | 46.18N | 16.53 E |
| Murcia | 94 | 37.59N | 1.07W |
| Murcia □⁹ | 94 | 38.30N | 1.45W |
| Mureş (Maros) ≃ | 90 | 46.15N | 20.13 E |
| Murfreesboro | 138 | 35.50N | 86.23W |
| Murmansk | 86 | 68.58N | 33.05 E |
| Murom | 100 | 55.34N | 42.02 E |
| Muroran | 116a | 42.18N | 140.59 E |
| Murray ≃ | 124 | 35.22S | 139.22 E |
| Murraysburg | 106 | 31.58S | 23.47 E |
| Murrumbidgee ≃ | 124 | 34.43S | 143.12 E |
| Murupara | 126 | 38.28S | 176.42 E |
| Mürzzuschlag | 90 | 47.36N | 15.41 E |
| Mūsā, Jabal (Mount Sinai) ▲ | 109 | 28.32N | 33.59 E |
| Musala ▲ | 98 | 42.11N | 23.34 E |
| Muscat → Masqaṭ | 108 | 23.37N | 58.35 E |
| Mustafakemalpaşa | 98 | 40.02N | 28.24 E |
| Mutá, Ponta do ⟩ | 135 | 13.52S | 38.56W |
| Mutare | 106 | 18.58S | 32.40 E |
| Mwanza | 106 | 2.31S | 32.54 E |
| Myanaung | 120 | 18.17N | 95.19 E |
| Myanmar (Burma) □¹ | 118 | 22.00N | 98.00 E |
| Myingyan | 120 | 21.28N | 95.23 E |
| Myitkyinā | 120 | 25.23N | 97.24 E |
| Mykolayiv | 86 | 46.58N | 32.00 E |

| Name | Page No. | Lat. | Long. |
|------|----------|------|-------|
| Mymensingh | 112 | 24.45N | 90.24 E |
| Myrtle Point | 142 | 43.03N | 124.08W |
| Mysore | 111 | 12.18N | 76.39 E |
| **N** | | | |
| Naalehu | 143 | 19.03N | 155.35W |
| Naas | 88 | 53.13N | 6.39W |
| Nabeul | 96 | 36.27N | 10.44 E |
| Nābulus | 109 | 32.13N | 35.16 E |
| Nacogdoches | 138 | 31.36N | 94.39W |
| Næstved | 89 | 55.14N | 11.46 E |
| Naga | 118 | 13.37N | 123.11 E |
| Nāgāland □³ | 112 | 26.00N | 95.00 E |
| Nagano | 116 | 36.39N | 138.11 E |
| Nagaoka | 116 | 37.27N | 138.51 E |
| Nagasaki | 116 | 32.48N | 129.55 E |
| Nagoya | 116 | 35.10N | 136.55 E |
| Nāgpur | 112 | 21.09N | 79.06 E |
| Nagykanizsa | 90 | 46.27N | 17.00 E |
| Naha | 117b | 26.13N | 127.40 E |
| Nain | 136 | 56.32N | 61.41W |
| Nairobi | 106 | 1.17S | 36.49 E |
| Najin | 114 | 42.15N | 130.18 E |
| Nakhon Pathom | 120 | 13.49N | 100.03 E |
| Nakhon Ratchasima | 120 | 14.58N | 102.07 E |
| Nakhon Sawan | 120 | 15.41N | 100.07 E |
| Nakhon Si Thammarat | 120 | 8.26N | 99.58 E |
| Nakuru | 106 | 0.17S | 36.04 E |
| Nal'čik | 86 | 43.29N | 43.37 E |
| Namangan | 110 | 41.00N | 71.40 E |
| Nam Dinh | 120 | 20.25N | 106.10 E |
| Namib Desert ➡² | 106 | 23.00S | 15.00 E |
| Namibe | 106 | 15.10S | 12.09 E |
| Namibia □¹ | 106 | 22.00S | 17.00 E |
| Nampa | 138 | 43.32N | 116.33W |
| Namp'o | 114 | 38.45N | 125.23 E |
| Nampula | 106 | 15.07S | 39.15 E |
| Namsos | 89 | 64.29N | 11.30 E |
| Nanchang | 114 | 28.41N | 115.53 E |
| Nanchong | 114 | 30.48N | 106.04 E |
| Nancy | 92 | 48.41N | 6.12 E |
| Nanda Devi ⋀ | 112 | 30.23N | 79.59 E |
| Nānga Parbat ⋀ | 112 | 35.15N | 74.36 E |
| Nanjing (Nanking) | 114 | 32.03N | 118.47 E |
| Nanling ⋇ | 114 | 25.00N | 112.00 E |
| Nanning | 114 | 22.48N | 108.20 E |
| Nansei-shotō (Ryukyu Islands) ⅠⅠ | 114 | 26.30N | 128.00 E |
| Nantes | 92 | 47.13N | 1.33W |
| Nantong | 114 | 32.02N | 120.53 E |
| Nantucket Island Ⅰ | 140 | 41.16N | 70.03W |
| Nanuque | 132 | 17.50S | 40.21W |
| Napanee | 140 | 44.15N | 76.57W |
| Napier | 126 | 39.29S | 176.55 E |
| Naples → Napoli | 96 | 40.51N | 14.17 E |
| Napo ≃ | 132 | 3.20S | 72.40W |
| Napoleon | 140 | 41.23N | 84.07W |
| Napoli (Naples) | 96 | 40.51N | 14.17 E |
| Nara | 116 | 34.41N | 135.50 E |
| Narathiwat | 120 | 6.26N | 101.50 E |
| Nārāyanganj | 112 | 23.37N | 90.30 E |
| Narbonne | 92 | 43.11N | 3.00 E |
| Narew ≃ | 90 | 52.26N | 20.42 E |
| Narmada ≃ | 112 | 21.38N | 72.36 E |
| Narodnaja, Gora ⋀ | 102 | 65.04N | 60.09 E |
| Narva | 100 | 59.23N | 28.12 E |
| Narvik | 89 | 68.26N | 17.25 E |
| Nashua | 140 | 42.45N | 71.28W |
| Nashville | 138 | 36.09N | 86.47W |
| Nāsik | 111 | 19.59N | 73.48 E |
| Nassau | 130 | 25.05N | 77.21W |
| Nasser, Lake ⊜¹ | 108 | 22.40N | 32.00 E |
| Natal | 132 | 5.47S | 35.13W |
| Natchez | 138 | 31.33N | 91.24W |
| Natchitoches | 128 | 31.45N | 93.05W |
| Natuna Besar Ⅰ | 120 | 4.00N | 108.15 E |
| Naumburg | 90 | 51.09N | 11.48 E |
| Nausori | 127c | 18.02S | 175.32 E |
| Navojoa | 128 | 27.06N | 109.26W |
| Nawābganj | 112 | 24.36N | 88.17 E |
| Nawābshāh | 112 | 26.15N | 68.25 E |
| Náxos Ⅰ | 98 | 37.02N | 25.35 E |
| Nazaré | 135 | 13.02S | 39.00W |
| Nazca | 132 | 14.50S | 74.57W |
| Naze | 117b | 28.23N | 129.30 E |
| Nazilli | 98 | 37.55N | 28.21 E |
| N'Djamena (Fort-Lamy) | 104 | 12.07N | 15.03 E |
| Ndola | 106 | 12.58S | 28.38 E |
| Néa Páfos (Paphos) | 109 | 34.45N | 32.25 E |
| Near Islands ⅠⅠ | 144 | 52.40N | 173.30 E |
| Nebraska □³ | 138 | 41.30N | 100.00W |
| Nechí | 130 | 8.07N | 74.46W |
| Neepawa | 136 | 50.13N | 99.29W |
| Negele | 108 | 5.20N | 39.36 E |
| Negombo | 111 | 7.13N | 79.50 E |
| Negra, Punta ➤ | 132 | 6.06S | 81.09W |
| Negro ≃, Arg. | 134 | 41.02S | 62.47W |
| Negro ≃, S.A. | 132 | 3.08S | 59.55W |
| Negros Ⅰ | 118 | 10.00N | 123.00 E |
| Nei Monggol Zizhiqu (Inner Mongolia) □⁴ | 114 | 43.00N | 115.00 E |
| Neisse ≃ | 90 | 52.04N | 14.46 E |
| Neiva | 132 | 2.56N | 75.18W |
| Nelson, B.C., Can. | 136 | 49.29N | 117.17W |
| Nelson, N.Z. | 126 | 41.17S | 173.17 E |
| Neman (Nemunas) ≃ | 100 | 55.18N | 21.23 E |
| Nemunas (Neman) ≃ | 100 | 55.18N | 21.23 E |
| Nemuro | 116a | 43.20N | 145.35 E |
| Nemuro Strait ⋃ | 116a | 44.00N | 145.20 E |
| Nenana | 144 | 64.34N | 149.07W |
| Nepal □¹ | 110 | 28.00N | 84.00 E |
| Nerastro, Sarīr ➡² | 104 | 24.20N | 20.37 E |
| Ness, Loch ⊜ | 88 | 57.15N | 4.30W |
| Netherlands □¹ | 86 | 52.15N | 5.30 E |
| Netherlands Antilles □² | 130 | 12.15N | 69.00W |
| Neubrandenburg | 90 | 53.33N | 13.15 E |
| Neuchâtel, Lac de ⊜ | 92 | 46.52N | 6.50 E |
| Neumünster | 90 | 54.04N | 9.59 E |
| Neunkirchen | 90 | 49.20N | 7.10 E |
| Neusiedler See ⊜ | 96 | 47.50N | 16.46 E |
| Neustrelitz | 90 | 53.21N | 13.04 E |
| Nevada □³ | 138 | 39.00N | 117.00W |
| Nevada, Sierra ⋇ | 142 | 38.00N | 119.15W |
| Nevers | 92 | 47.00N | 3.09 E |
| Nevinnomyssk | 86 | 44.38N | 41.56 E |
| Nevis, Ben ⋀ | 88 | 56.48N | 5.01W |
| New Amsterdam | 132 | 6.15N | 57.31W |
| Newark, N.J., U.S. | 140 | 40.44N | 74.10W |
| Newark, Oh., U.S. | 140 | 40.04N | 82.24W |
| New Bedford | 140 | 41.38N | 70.56W |
| New Braunfels | 128 | 29.42N | 98.07W |
| New Brunswick | 140 | 40.29N | 74.27W |
| New Brunswick □⁴ | 136 | 46.30N | 66.15W |
| Newburgh | 140 | 41.30N | 74.00W |
| New Caledonia □² | 127b | 21.30S | 165.30 E |
| Newcastle, Austl. | 122 | 32.56S | 151.46 E |
| Newcastle, N.B., Can. | 136 | 47.00N | 65.34W |
| New Castle, Pa., U.S. | 140 | 41.00N | 80.20W |
| Newcastle upon Tyne | 88 | 54.59N | 1.35W |
| Newcastle Waters | 122 | 17.24S | 133.24 E |
| New Delhi | 112 | 28.36N | 77.12 E |
| Newfoundland □⁴ | 136 | 52.00N | 56.00W |
| Newfoundland Ⅰ | 136 | 48.30N | 56.00W |
| New Georgia Ⅰ | 127a | 8.15S | 157.30 E |
| New Georgia Group ⅠⅠ | 127a | 8.30S | 157.20 E |
| New Glasgow | 136 | 45.35N | 62.39W |
| New Guinea Ⅰ | 118 | 5.00S | 140.00 E |
| New Hampshire □³ | 138 | 43.35N | 71.40W |

| Name | Page No. | Lat. | Long. |
|---|---|---|---|
| Plata, Río de la ⊂[1] | 134 | 35.00S | 57.00W |
| Platte ≃ | 138 | 39.16N | 94.50W |
| Plattsburgh | 140 | 44.41N | 73.27W |
| Plauen | 90 | 50.30N | 12.08 E |
| Plenty, Bay of ⊂ | 126 | 37.40S | 177.00 E |
| Plétipi, Lac ⊜ | 136 | 51.44N | 70.06W |
| Pleven | 98 | 43.25N | 24.37 E |
| Płock | 90 | 52.33N | 19.43 E |
| Ploiești | 98 | 44.56N | 26.02 E |
| Plovdiv | 98 | 42.09N | 24.45 E |
| Plymouth, Eng., U.K. | 88 | 50.23N | 4.10W |
| Plymouth, Ma., U.S. | 140 | 41.57N | 70.40W |
| Plzeň | 90 | 49.45N | 13.23 E |
| Po ≃ | 96 | 44.57N | 12.04 E |
| Pobeda, Gora ∧ | 102 | 65.12N | 146.12 E |
| Pocatello | 138 | 42.52N | 112.26W |
| Poços de Caldas | 135 | 21.48S | 46.34W |
| Podgorica | 98 | 42.26N | 19.14 E |
| Podlasie ◆[1] | 90 | 52.30N | 23.00 E |
| Podol'sk | 100 | 55.26N | 37.33 E |
| Podor | 104 | 16.40N | 14.57W |
| Pofadder | 106 | 29.10S | 19.22 E |
| Poiana Ruscăi, Munții ⋀ | 98 | 45.41N | 22.30 E |
| Pointe-à-Pitre | 130 | 16.14N | 61.32W |
| Pointe-Noire | 106 | 4.48S | 11.51 E |
| Point Pleasant | 140 | 40.04N | 74.04W |
| Point Reyes National Seashore ♦ | 142 | 38.00N | 122.58W |
| Poitiers | 92 | 46.35N | 0.20 E |
| Poland □[1] | 86 | 52.00N | 19.00 E |
| Polevskoj | 86 | 56.26N | 60.11 E |
| Poltava | 86 | 49.35N | 34.34 E |
| Poltimore | 140 | 45.47N | 75.43W |
| Polynesia II | 82 | 4.00S | 156.00W |
| Pomerania □[9] | 90 | 54.00N | 16.00 E |
| Pomeranian Bay ⊂ | 90 | 54.00N | 14.15 E |
| Ponca City | 138 | 36.42N | 97.05W |
| Ponce | 130 | 18.01N | 66.37W |
| Pondicherry □[8] | 111 | 11.56N | 79.50 E |
| Ponta Grossa | 134 | 25.05S | 50.09W |
| Pontchartrain, Lake ⊜ | 128 | 30.10N | 90.10W |
| Ponte Nova | 135 | 20.24S | 42.54W |
| Pontevedra | 94 | 42.26N | 8.38W |
| Pontiac | 140 | 42.38N | 83.17W |
| Pontianak | 118 | 0.02S | 109.20 E |
| Poopó, Lago ⊜ | 132 | 18.45S | 67.07W |
| Popayán | 132 | 2.27N | 76.36W |
| Poplar Bluff | 138 | 36.45N | 90.23W |
| Popocatépetl, Volcán ∧[1] | 128 | 19.02N | 98.38W |
| Popomanaseu, Mount ∧ | 122 | 9.42S | 160.04 E |
| Poprad | 90 | 49.03N | 20.18 E |
| Pordenone | 96 | 45.57N | 12.39 E |
| Pori | 89 | 61.29N | 21.47 E |
| Porlamar | 130 | 10.57N | 63.51W |
| Poronajsk | 102 | 49.14N | 143.04 E |
| Portadown | 88 | 54.26N | 6.27W |
| Portage | 140 | 42.12N | 85.34W |
| Port Allegany | 140 | 41.48N | 78.16W |
| Port Arthur | 138 | 29.53N | 93.55W |
| Port Augusta | 122 | 32.30S | 137.46 E |
| Port-au-Prince | 130 | 18.32N | 72.20W |
| Port Austin | 140 | 44.02N | 82.59W |
| Port Blair | 120 | 11.40N | 92.45 E |
| Port Clyde | 140 | 43.55N | 69.15W |
| Port Elgin | 140 | 44.26N | 81.24W |
| Port Elizabeth | 106 | 33.58S | 25.40 E |
| Port Ellen | 88 | 55.39N | 6.12W |
| Porterville | 142 | 36.03N | 119.00W |
| Port-Gentil | 106 | 0.43S | 8.47 E |
| Port Harcourt | 104 | 4.43N | 7.05 E |
| Port Hedland | 122 | 20.19S | 118.34 E |
| Port Henry | 140 | 44.02N | 73.27W |
| Port Huron | 140 | 42.58N | 82.25W |
| Portland, Austl. | 122 | 38.21S | 141.36 E |
| Portland, Me., U.S. | 140 | 43.39N | 70.15W |
| Portland, Or., U.S. | 138 | 45.31N | 122.40W |
| Port Lavaca | 128 | 28.36N | 96.37W |
| Port Lincoln | 122 | 34.44S | 135.52 E |
| Port Louis | 106 | 20.10S | 57.30 E |
| Port Macquarie | 122 | 31.26S | 152.55 E |
| Port Moresby | 122 | 9.30S | 147.10 E |
| Port Nolloth | 106 | 29.17S | 16.51 E |
| Porto | 94 | 41.11N | 8.36W |
| Pôrto Alegre | 134 | 30.04S | 51.11W |
| Porto Amboim | 106 | 10.44S | 13.44 E |
| Portobelo | 130 | 9.33N | 79.39W |
| Port of Spain | 130 | 10.39N | 61.31W |
| Porto-Novo | 104 | 6.29N | 2.37 E |
| Port Orford | 142 | 42.44N | 124.29W |
| Porto-Vecchio | 96 | 41.35N | 9.16 E |
| Pôrto Velho | 132 | 8.46S | 63.54W |
| Port Pirie | 122 | 33.11S | 138.01 E |
| Port Said → Būr Sa'īd | 104 | 31.16N | 32.18 E |
| Port Shepstone | 106 | 30.46S | 30.22 E |
| Portsmouth, Eng., U.K. | 88 | 50.48N | 1.05W |
| Portsmouth, N.H., U.S. | 140 | 43.04N | 70.45W |
| Portsmouth, Oh., U.S. | 140 | 38.43N | 82.59W |
| Porttipahdan tekojärvi ⊜[1] | 89 | 68.08N | 26.40 E |
| Portugal □[1] | 86 | 39.30N | 8.00W |
| Portugalete | 94 | 43.19N | 3.01W |
| Posadas | 134 | 27.23S | 55.53W |
| Potenza | 96 | 40.38N | 15.49 E |
| Potgietersrus | 106 | 24.15S | 28.55 E |
| Potomac ≃ | 140 | 38.00N | 76.18W |
| Potosí | 132 | 19.35S | 65.45W |
| Potsdam | 90 | 52.24N | 13.04 E |
| Poughkeepsie | 140 | 41.42N | 73.55W |
| Poume | 127b | 20.14S | 164.02 E |
| Pouso Alegre | 135 | 22.13S | 45.56W |
| Poŭthĭsăt | 120 | 12.32N | 103.55 E |
| Povungnituk | 136 | 60.02N | 77.10W |
| Powassan | 140 | 46.05N | 79.22W |
| Powell, Lake ⊜[1] | 138 | 37.25N | 110.45W |
| Poza Rica de Hidalgo | 128 | 20.33N | 97.27W |
| Poznań | 90 | 52.25N | 16.55 E |
| Prague → Praha | 90 | 50.05N | 14.26 E |
| Praha (Prague) | 90 | 50.05N | 14.26 E |
| Preparis North Channel ⋓ | 120 | 15.27N | 94.05 E |
| Preparis South Channel ⋓ | 120 | 14.40N | 94.00 E |
| Presidente Epitácio | 135 | 21.46S | 52.06W |
| Presidente Prudente | 132 | 22.07S | 51.22W |
| Presidio | 128 | 29.33N | 104.22W |
| Prešov | 90 | 49.00N | 21.15 E |
| Prespa, Lake ⊜ | 98 | 40.55N | 21.00 E |
| Presque Isle | 138 | 46.40N | 68.00W |
| Preston, Eng., U.K. | 88 | 53.46N | 2.42W |
| Preston, Id., U.S. | 138 | 42.05N | 111.52W |
| Pretoria | 106 | 25.45S | 28.10 E |
| Prey Vêng | 120 | 11.29N | 105.19 E |
| Příbram | 90 | 49.42N | 14.01 E |
| Prievidza | 90 | 48.47N | 18.37 E |
| Prilep | 98 | 41.20N | 21.33 E |
| Prince Albert | 136 | 53.12N | 105.46W |
| Prince Edward Island □[4] | 136 | 46.20N | 63.20W |
| Prince George | 136 | 53.55N | 122.45W |
| Prince of Wales Island I, N.T., Can. | 136 | 72.40N | 99.00W |
| Prince of Wales Island I, Ak., U.S. | 144 | 55.47N | 132.50W |
| Prince Rupert | 136 | 54.19N | 130.19W |
| Princeton | 140 | 40.20N | 74.39W |

| Name | Page No. | Lat. | Long. |
|---|---|---|---|
| Prinzapolca | 130 | 13.24N | 83.34W |
| Priština | 98 | 42.39N | 21.10 E |
| Prizren | 98 | 42.12N | 20.44 E |
| Proctor | 140 | 43.39N | 73.02W |
| Prokopjevsk | 102 | 53.53N | 86.45 E |
| Prome (Pyè) | 120 | 18.49N | 95.13 E |
| Prostějov | 90 | 49.29N | 17.07 E |
| Provence □[9] | 92 | 44.00N | 6.00 E |
| Providence | 140 | 41.49N | 71.24W |
| Providence, Cape ≻ | 126 | 46.01S | 166.28 E |
| Provincetown | 140 | 42.03N | 70.10W |
| Provo | 138 | 40.14N | 111.39W |
| Prudhoe Bay c | 144 | 70.20N | 148.20W |
| Pruszków | 90 | 52.11N | 20.48 E |
| Prut ≃ | 98 | 45.30N | 28.12 E |
| Przemyśl | 90 | 49.47N | 22.47 E |
| Pskov | 100 | 57.50N | 28.20 E |
| Puapua | 127e | 13.34S | 172.09W |
| Pucallpa | 132 | 8.23S | 74.32W |
| Pudukkottai | 111 | 10.23N | 78.49 E |
| Puebla [de Zaragoza] | 128 | 19.03N | 98.12W |
| Pueblo | 138 | 38.15N | 104.36W |
| Puerto Aisén | 134 | 45.24S | 72.42W |
| Puerto Armuelles | 130 | 8.17N | 82.52W |
| Puerto Asís | 132 | 0.30N | 76.31W |
| Puerto Barrios | 130 | 15.43N | 88.36W |
| Puerto Berrío | 132 | 6.29N | 74.24W |
| Puerto Cabello | 130 | 10.28N | 68.01W |
| Puerto Cabezas | 130 | 14.02N | 83.23W |
| Puerto Carreño | 132 | 6.12N | 67.22W |
| Puerto Casado | 134 | 22.20S | 57.55W |
| Puerto Cortés, C.R. | 130 | 8.58N | 83.32W |
| Puerto Cortés, Hond. | 130 | 15.48N | 87.56W |
| Puerto Cumarebo | 130 | 11.29N | 69.21W |
| Puerto de Nutrias | 132 | 8.05N | 69.18W |
| Puerto Deseado | 134 | 47.45S | 65.54W |
| Puerto la Cruz | 132 | 10.13N | 64.38W |
| Puerto Leguízamo | 132 | 0.12S | 74.46W |
| Puertollano | 94 | 38.41N | 4.07W |
| Puerto Lobos | 134 | 42.00S | 65.06W |
| Puerto Madryn | 134 | 42.46S | 65.03W |
| Puerto Maldonado | 132 | 12.36S | 69.11W |
| Puerto Montt | 134 | 41.28S | 72.57W |
| Puerto Natales | 134 | 51.44S | 72.31W |
| Puerto Rico □[2] | 130 | 18.15N | 66.30W |
| Puerto Vallarta | 128 | 20.37N | 105.15W |
| Pula | 96 | 44.52N | 13.50 E |
| Pulaski | 140 | 43.34N | 76.07W |
| Puławy | 90 | 51.25N | 21.57 E |
| Pune (Poona) | 111 | 18.32N | 73.52 E |
| Punjab □[3] | 112 | 31.00N | 75.30 E |
| Puno | 132 | 15.50S | 70.02W |
| Punta Arenas | 134 | 53.09S | 70.55W |
| Puntarenas | 130 | 9.58N | 84.50W |
| Punto Fijo | 132 | 11.42N | 70.13W |
| Puri | 112 | 19.48N | 85.51 E |
| Purnea | 112 | 25.47N | 87.31 E |
| Purus (Purús) ≃ | 132 | 3.42S | 61.28W |
| Pusan | 114 | 35.06N | 129.03 E |
| Puto | 127a | 5.41S | 154.43 E |
| Putumayo (Içá) ≃ | 132 | 3.07S | 67.58W |
| Puy de Sancy ∧ | 92 | 45.32N | 2.49 E |
| Pyinmana | 120 | 19.44N | 96.13 E |
| P'yŏngyang | 114 | 39.01N | 125.45 E |
| Pyramid Lake ⊜ | 142 | 40.00N | 119.35W |
| Pyrenees ⋀ | 94 | 42.40N | 1.00 E |
| Pyu | 120 | 18.29N | 96.26 E |

**Q**

| Name | Page No. | Lat. | Long. |
|---|---|---|---|
| Qacentina | 104 | 36.22N | 6.37 E |
| Qaidam Pendi ≚[1] | 114 | 37.00N | 95.00 E |
| Qalāt | 112 | 32.07N | 66.54 E |
| Qamar, Ghubbat al- c | 108 | 16.00N | 52.30 E |
| Qandahār | 112 | 31.32N | 65.30 E |
| Qaraghandy | 102 | 49.50N | 73.10 E |
| Qatar □[1] | 108 | 25.00N | 51.10 E |
| Qinā | 109 | 26.10N | 32.43 E |
| Qingdao (Tsingtao) | 114 | 36.06N | 120.19 E |
| Qinhuangdao | 114 | 39.56N | 119.36 E |
| Qiqihar | 114 | 47.19N | 123.55 E |
| Qom | 108 | 34.39N | 50.54 E |
| Qostanay | 86 | 53.10N | 63.35 E |
| Quanzhou | 114 | 24.54N | 118.35 E |
| Quartzsite | 142 | 33.39N | 114.13W |
| Québec | 136 | 46.49N | 71.14W |
| Quebec (Québec) □[4] | 136 | 52.00N | 72.00W |
| Quedlinburg | 90 | 51.48N | 11.09 E |
| Queen Charlotte Islands II | 136 | 53.00N | 132.00W |
| Queen Charlotte Sound ʉ | 136 | 51.30N | 129.30W |
| Queen Maud Land •[1] | 85 | 72.30S | 12.00 E |
| Queen Maud Mountains ⋀ | 85 | 86.00S | 160.00W |
| Queensland □[3] | 122 | 22.00S | 145.00 E |
| Queenstown, N.Z. | 126 | 45.02S | 168.40 E |
| Queenstown, S. Afr. | 106 | 31.52S | 26.52 E |
| Quelimane | 106 | 17.53S | 36.51 E |
| Querétaro | 128 | 20.36N | 100.23W |
| Quetta | 112 | 30.12N | 67.00 E |
| Quezon City | 118 | 14.38N | 121.00 E |
| Quibdó | 132 | 5.42N | 76.40W |
| Quilpie | 122 | 26.37S | 144.15 E |
| Quimper | 92 | 48.00N | 4.06W |
| Quincemil | 132 | 13.16S | 70.38W |
| Qui Nhon | 120 | 13.46N | 109.14 E |
| Quiros, Cape ≻ | 127b | 14.55S | 167.01 E |
| Quito | 132 | 0.13S | 78.30W |
| Qūṣ | 109 | 25.55N | 32.45 E |

**R**

| Name | Page No. | Lat. | Long. |
|---|---|---|---|
| Rabat (Victoria), Malta | 96 | 36.02N | 14.14 E |
| Rabat, Mor. | 104 | 34.02N | 6.51W |
| Rach Gia | 120 | 10.01N | 105.05 E |
| Racibórz (Ratibor) | 90 | 50.06N | 18.13 E |
| Radom | 90 | 51.25N | 21.10 E |
| Radomsko | 90 | 51.05N | 19.25 E |
| Raetihi | 126 | 39.26S | 175.17 E |
| Rafaela | 134 | 31.16S | 61.29W |
| Rafaḥ | 109 | 31.18N | 34.15 E |
| Ragusa | 96 | 36.55N | 14.44 E |
| Rahīmyār Khān | 112 | 28.25N | 70.18 E |
| Raiatea ⊜ | 127d | 16.50S | 151.25W |
| Rāichūr | 111 | 16.12N | 77.22 E |
| Raipur | 112 | 21.14N | 81.38 E |
| Rājahmundry | 111 | 16.59N | 81.47 E |
| Rajang ≃ | 118 | 2.04N | 111.12 E |
| Rājapālaiyam | 111 | 9.27N | 77.34 E |
| Rājasthān □[4] | 112 | 27.00N | 74.00 E |
| Rajčichinsk | 102 | 49.46N | 129.25 E |
| Rājkot | 112 | 22.18N | 70.47 E |
| Raleigh | 138 | 35.46N | 78.38W |
| Rama | 130 | 12.09N | 84.15W |
| Ramm, Jabal ∧ | 109 | 29.35N | 35.24 E |
| Rāmpur | 112 | 28.49N | 79.02 E |
| Ramree Island I | 120 | 19.06N | 93.48 E |
| Ramu ≃ | 118 | 5.00S | 144.40 E |
| Rancagua | 134 | 34.10S | 70.45W |
| Rānchī | 112 | 23.21N | 85.20 E |
| Randers | 89 | 56.28N | 10.03 E |
| Randolph | 140 | 43.55N | 72.39W |
| Rangeley | 140 | 44.57N | 70.38W |
| Rangitikei ≃ | 126 | 40.18S | 175.14 E |
| Rangoon (Yangon) | 120 | 16.47N | 96.10 E |
| Rangpur | 112 | 25.45N | 89.15 E |
| Rankin Inlet | 136 | 62.45N | 92.10W |
| Rann of Kutch ≚ | 112 | 24.00N | 70.00 E |
| Rantauprapat | 120 | 2.06N | 99.50 E |

| Name | Page No. | Lat. | Long. |
|------|----------|------|-------|
| Rapid City | 138 | 44.04N | 103.13W |
| Ras Dashen Terara ▲ | 108 | 13.10N | 38.26 E |
| Rasht | 86 | 37.16N | 49.36 E |
| Rat Islands **II** | 144 | 52.00N | 178.00 E |
| Ratlām | 112 | 23.19N | 75.04 E |
| Rauma | 89 | 61.08N | 21.30 E |
| Ravena | 140 | 42.28N | 73.49W |
| Ravenna | 96 | 44.25N | 12.12 E |
| Ravensburg | 90 | 47.47N | 9.37 E |
| Ravenshoe | 122 | 17.37S | 145.29 E |
| Ravensthorpe | 122 | 33.35S | 120.02 E |
| Rāwalpindi | 112 | 33.36N | 73.04 E |
| Rawson | 134 | 43.18S | 65.06W |
| Raz, Pointe du ➤ | 92 | 48.02N | 4.44W |
| R'azan' | 100 | 54.38N | 39.44 E |
| Razgrad | 98 | 43.32N | 26.31 E |
| Ré, Île de **I** | 92 | 46.12N | 1.25W |
| Reading, Eng., U.K. | 88 | 51.28N | 0.59W |
| Reading, Pa., U.S. | 140 | 40.20N | 75.55W |
| Real, Cordillera ↗ | 132 | 19.00S | 66.30W |
| Realicó | 134 | 35.02S | 64.15W |
| Recherche, Cape ➤ | 127a | 10.11S | 161.19 E |
| Recife | 132 | 8.03S | 34.54W |
| Recklinghausen | 90 | 51.36N | 7.13 E |
| Red (Hong) (Yuan) ≃, Asia | 120 | 20.17N | 106.34 E |
| Red ≃, U.S. | 138 | 31.00N | 91.40W |
| Red Deer | 136 | 52.16N | 113.48W |
| Redding | 142 | 40.35N | 122.23W |
| Red Lake | 136 | 51.03N | 93.49W |
| Red Sea ⊤² | 108 | 20.00N | 38.00 E |
| Reed City | 140 | 43.52N | 85.30W |
| Reefton | 126 | 42.07S | 171.52 E |
| Regensburg | 90 | 49.01N | 12.06 E |
| Reggio di Calabria | 96 | 38.07N | 15.39 E |
| Reggio nell'Emilia | 96 | 44.43N | 10.36 E |
| Regina | 136 | 50.25N | 104.39W |
| Rehoboth Beach | 140 | 38.43N | 75.04W |
| Reḥovot | 109 | 31.54N | 34.49 E |
| Reims | 92 | 49.15N | 4.02 E |
| Remada | 104 | 32.19N | 10.24 E |
| Rendsburg | 90 | 54.18N | 9.40 E |
| Renfrew | 140 | 45.28N | 76.41W |
| Rennes | 92 | 48.05N | 1.41W |
| Reno | 142 | 39.31N | 119.48W |
| Reschenpass )( | 92 | 46.50N | 10.30 E |
| Resistencia | 134 | 27.27S | 58.59W |
| Reşiţa | 98 | 45.17N | 21.53 E |
| Réthimnon | 98 | 35.22N | 24.29 E |
| Reunion □² | 106 | 21.06S | 55.36 E |
| Reus | 94 | 41.09N | 1.07 E |
| Reutlingen | 90 | 48.29N | 9.11 E |
| Revelstoke | 136 | 50.59N | 118.12W |
| Revillagigedo, Islas **II** | 128 | 19.00N | 111.30W |
| Rewa | 112 | 24.32N | 81.18 E |
| Rewāri | 112 | 28.11N | 76.37 E |
| Rey, Isla del **I** | 130 | 8.22N | 78.55W |
| Reyes | 132 | 14.19S | 67.23W |
| Reykjavík | 86 | 64.09N | 21.51W |
| Reynosa | 128 | 26.07N | 98.18W |
| Rhaetian Alps ↗ | 92 | 46.30N | 10.00 E |
| Rhein → Rhine ≃ | 90 | 51.52N | 6.02 E |
| Rheine | 90 | 52.17N | 7.26 E |
| Rhine (Rhein) (Rhin) ≃ | 90 | 51.52N | 6.02 E |
| Rhinelander | 138 | 45.38N | 89.24W |
| Rhode Island □³ | 138 | 41.40N | 71.30W |
| Rhodes → Ródhos **I** | 98 | 36.10N | 28.00 E |
| Rhodope Mountains ↗ | 98 | 41.30N | 24.30 E |
| Rhône ≃ | 92 | 43.20N | 4.50 E |
| Riau, Kepulauan **II** | 120 | 1.00N | 104.30 E |
| Ribeirão Prêto | 132 | 21.10S | 47.48W |
| Riberalta | 132 | 10.59S | 66.06W |
| Richfield, Id., U.S. | 142 | 43.02N | 114.09W |
| Richfield, Ut., U.S. | 138 | 38.46N | 112.05W |
| Richmond, In., U.S. | 140 | 39.49N | 84.53W |
| Richmond, Ky., U.S. | 140 | 37.44N | 84.17W |
| Richmond, Va., U.S. | 138 | 37.33N | 77.27W |
| Richwood | 140 | 38.13N | 80.32W |
| Riesa | 90 | 51.18N | 13.17 E |
| Rieti | 96 | 42.24N | 12.51 E |
| Rif ↗ | 94 | 35.00N | 4.00W |
| Rift Valley ⋁ | 106 | 3.00S | 29.00 E |
| Rīga | 100 | 56.57N | 24.06 E |
| Riga, Gulf of c | 100 | 57.30N | 23.35 E |
| Rīgestān ➤¹ | 110 | 31.00N | 65.00 E |
| Rijeka | 96 | 45.20N | 14.27 E |
| Rimini | 96 | 44.04N | 12.34 E |
| Ringgold Isles **II** | 127c | 16.15S | 179.25W |
| Ringvassøya **I** | 89 | 69.55N | 19.15 E |
| Riobamba | 132 | 1.40S | 78.38W |
| Rio Branco | 132 | 9.58S | 67.48W |
| Río Cuarto | 134 | 33.08S | 64.21W |
| Rio de Janeiro | 132 | 22.54S | 43.14W |
| Río Gallegos | 134 | 51.38S | 69.13W |
| Río Grande, Arg. | 134 | 53.47S | 67.42W |
| Rio Grande, Braz. | 134 | 32.02S | 52.05W |
| Ríohacha | 132 | 11.33N | 72.55W |
| Río Hato | 130 | 8.23N | 80.10W |
| Río Mayo | 134 | 45.41S | 70.16W |
| Rio Verde | 135 | 17.43S | 50.56W |
| Ripley | 140 | 38.49N | 81.42W |
| Ritter, Mount ▲ | 142 | 37.42N | 119.12W |
| Rivas | 130 | 11.26N | 85.50W |
| Rivera | 134 | 30.54S | 55.31W |
| Riverhead | 140 | 40.55N | 72.39W |
| Riverina ➤¹ | 124 | 35.30S | 145.30 E |
| Riverside | 142 | 33.57N | 117.23W |
| Rivne | 86 | 50.37N | 26.15 E |
| Riyadh → Ar-Riyāḍ | 108 | 24.38N | 46.43 E |
| Rizzuto, Capo ➤ | 96 | 38.54N | 17.06 E |
| Roanne | 92 | 46.02N | 4.04 E |
| Roanoke | 138 | 37.16N | 79.56W |
| Roberts Peak ▲ | 136 | 52.57N | 120.32W |
| Roberval | 136 | 48.31N | 72.13W |
| Roboré | 132 | 18.20S | 59.45W |
| Rocha | 134 | 34.29S | 54.20W |
| Rochefort | 92 | 45.57N | 0.58W |
| Rochester, Mn., U.S. | 138 | 44.01N | 92.28W |
| Rochester, N.H., U.S. | 140 | 43.18N | 70.58W |
| Rochester, N.Y., U.S. | 140 | 43.09N | 77.36W |
| Rockefeller Plateau ↗¹ | 85 | 80.00S | 135.00W |
| Rockford, Il., U.S. | 138 | 42.16N | 89.05W |
| Rockford, Mi., U.S. | 140 | 43.07N | 85.33W |
| Rockhampton | 122 | 23.23S | 150.31 E |
| Rock Island | 138 | 41.30N | 90.34W |
| Rockland | 140 | 44.06N | 69.06W |
| Rock Springs | 138 | 41.35N | 109.12W |
| Rockville | 140 | 39.05N | 77.09W |
| Rocky Mountains ↗ | 82 | 48.00N | 116.00W |
| Rodez | 92 | 44.21N | 2.35 E |
| Ródhos (Rhodes) | 98 | 36.26N | 28.13 E |
| Ródhos **I** | 98 | 36.10N | 28.00 E |
| Roebourne | 122 | 20.47S | 117.09 E |
| Roeselare | 90 | 50.57N | 3.08 E |
| Rogue ≃ | 142 | 42.26N | 124.25W |
| Rohtak | 112 | 28.54N | 76.34 E |
| Roma (Rome) | 96 | 41.54N | 12.29 E |
| Roman | 98 | 46.55N | 26.56 E |
| Romania □¹ | 86 | 46.00N | 25.30 E |
| Romans [-sur-Isère] | 92 | 45.03N | 5.03 E |
| Rome → Roma, Italy | 96 | 41.54N | 12.29 E |
| Rome, Ga., U.S. | 138 | 34.15N | 85.09W |
| Rome, N.Y., U.S. | 140 | 43.12N | 75.27W |
| Romeo | 140 | 42.48N | 83.00W |
| Ron, Mui ➤ | 120 | 18.07N | 106.22 E |
| Roncador, Serra do ↗¹ | 132 | 12.00S | 52.00W |
| Ronne Ice Shelf ⋈ | 85 | 78.30S | 61.00W |

| Name | Page No. | Lat. | Long. |
|---|---|---|---|
| Roosevelt Island I | 85 | 79.30S | 162.00W |
| Roraima, Mount ▲ | 132 | 5.12N | 60.44W |
| Rosario | 134 | 32.57S | 60.40W |
| Roscommon | 88 | 53.38N | 8.11W |
| Roseau | 130 | 15.18N | 61.24W |
| Roseburg | 142 | 43.13N | 123.20W |
| Rosenheim | 90 | 47.51N | 12.07 E |
| Ross Ice Shelf ⊠ | 85 | 81.30S | 175.00W |
| Rosslare | 88 | 52.17N | 6.23W |
| Ross Sea ⊽² | 85 | 76.00S | 175.00W |
| Rostock | 90 | 54.05N | 12.07 E |
| Rostov-na-Donu | 86 | 47.14N | 39.42 E |
| Roswell | 138 | 33.23N | 104.31W |
| Rotorua | 126 | 38.09S | 176.15 E |
| Rotterdam | 90 | 51.55N | 4.28 E |
| Roubaix | 92 | 50.42N | 3.10 E |
| Rouen | 92 | 49.26N | 1.05 E |
| Rouyn-Noranda | 136 | 48.15N | 79.01W |
| Rovaniemi | 89 | 66.34N | 25.48 E |
| Royan | 92 | 45.37N | 1.01W |
| Ruapehu ▲ | 126 | 39.17S | 175.34 E |
| Rubcovsk | 102 | 51.33N | 81.10 E |
| Ruby | 144 | 64.44N | 155.30W |
| Ruby Lake ≋ | 142 | 40.10N | 115.30W |
| Rudolf, Lake ⊜ | 108 | 3.30N | 36.00 E |
| Rügen I | 90 | 54.25N | 13.24 E |
| Rukwa, Lake ⊜ | 106 | 8.00S | 32.25 E |
| Rump Mountain ▲ | 140 | 45.12N | 71.04W |
| Rupert | 142 | 42.37N | 113.40W |
| Ruse | 98 | 43.50N | 25.57 E |
| Rüsselsheim | 90 | 50.00N | 8.25 E |
| Russia ◻¹ | 86 | 60.00N | 100.00 E |
| Rutland | 140 | 43.36N | 72.58W |
| Ruvuma (Rovuma) ≏ | 106 | 10.29S | 40.28 E |
| Rwanda ◻¹ | 106 | 2.30S | 30.00 E |
| Rybinsk | 100 | 58.03N | 38.52 E |
| Rybinskoje Vodochranilišče ⊜¹ | 100 | 58.30N | 38.25 E |
| Rysy ▲ | 90 | 49.12N | 20.04 E |
| Ryukyu Islands → Nansei-shotō II | 114 | 26.30N | 128.00 E |
| Rzeszów | 90 | 50.03N | 22.00 E |

### S

| | | | |
|---|---|---|---|
| Saarbrücken | 90 | 49.14N | 6.59 E |
| Saaremaa I | 100 | 58.25N | 22.30 E |
| Sab, Tônlé ⊜ | 120 | 13.00N | 104.00 E |
| Sabinas Hidalgo | 128 | 26.30N | 100.10W |
| Sabine ≏ | 128 | 30.00N | 93.45W |
| Sable, Île de I | 122 | 19.15S | 159.56 E |
| Sachalin, Ostrov (Sakhalin) I | 102 | 51.00N | 143.00 E |
| Šachty | 86 | 47.42N | 40.13 E |
| Sacramento | 142 | 38.34N | 121.29W |
| Sacramento ≏ | 142 | 38.03N | 121.56W |
| Sacramento Valley V | 142 | 39.15N | 122.00W |
| Sado I | 116 | 38.00N | 138.25 E |
| Saga | 116 | 33.15N | 130.18 E |
| Sagami-nada c | 116 | 35.00N | 139.30 E |
| Sägar | 112 | 23.50N | 78.45 E |
| Saginaw | 140 | 43.25N | 83.56W |
| Saginaw Bay c | 140 | 43.50N | 83.40W |
| Sagua de Tánamo | 130 | 20.35N | 75.14W |
| Sagua la Grande | 130 | 22.49N | 80.05W |
| Saguaro National Monument ♦ | 128 | 32.12N | 110.38W |
| Sagunto | 94 | 39.41N | 0.16W |
| Sahara ←² | 104 | 26.00N | 13.00 E |
| Sahāranpur | 112 | 29.58N | 77.33 E |
| Saidpur | 112 | 25.47N | 88.54 E |
| Saigon → Thanh Pho Ho Chi Minh | 120 | 10.45N | 106.40 E |
| Saint Anthony | 136 | 51.22N | 55.35W |

| Name | Page No. | Lat. | Long. |
|---|---|---|---|
| Saint Augustine | 138 | 29.53N | 81.18W |
| Saint-Augustin-Saguenay | 136 | 51.14N | 58.39W |
| Saint-Brieuc | 92 | 48.31N | 2.47W |
| Saint Catharines | 140 | 43.10N | 79.15W |
| Saint-Chamond | 92 | 45.28N | 4.30 E |
| Saint Christopher (Saint Kitts) I | 130 | 17.20N | 62.45W |
| Saint Clair | 140 | 42.48N | 82.29W |
| Saint Croix I | 130 | 17.45N | 64.45W |
| Saint-Denis, Fr. | 92 | 48.56N | 2.22 E |
| Saint-Denis, Reu. | 106 | 20.52S | 55.28 E |
| Saint-Dizier | 92 | 48.38N | 4.57 E |
| Saint Elias, Mount ▲ | 144 | 60.18N | 140.55W |
| Saint-Étienne | 92 | 45.26N | 4.24 E |
| Saint George | 122 | 28.02S | 148.35 E |
| Saint George's | 130 | 12.03N | 61.45W |
| Saint George's Bay c | 136 | 48.20N | 59.00W |
| Saint George's Channel ʮ | 88 | 52.00N | 6.00W |
| Saint Helier | 92 | 49.12N | 2.37W |
| Saint-Hyacinthe | 140 | 45.38N | 72.57W |
| Saint James | 140 | 45.45N | 85.30W |
| Saint James, Cape ➢ | 136 | 51.56N | 131.01W |
| Saint-Jean | 140 | 45.19N | 73.16W |
| Saint-Jérôme | 140 | 45.46N | 74.00W |
| Saint John | 136 | 45.16N | 66.03W |
| Saint John, Cape ➢ | 136 | 50.00N | 55.32W |
| Saint John's | 136 | 47.34N | 52.43W |
| Saint Johnsbury | 140 | 44.25N | 72.00W |
| Saint Joseph | 138 | 39.46N | 94.50W |
| Saint Joseph, Lake ⊜ | 136 | 51.05N | 90.35W |
| Saint-Jovite | 140 | 46.07N | 74.36W |
| Saint Kilda I | 88 | 57.49N | 8.36W |
| Saint Kitts → Saint Christopher I | 130 | 17.20N | 62.45W |
| Saint Kitts and Nevis ◻¹ | 130 | 17.20N | 62.45W |
| Saint Lawrence ≏ | 136 | 49.30N | 67.00W |
| Saint Lawrence, Gulf of c | 136 | 48.00N | 62.00W |
| Saint Lawrence Island I | 144 | 63.30N | 170.30W |
| Saint-Lô | 92 | 49.07N | 1.05W |
| Saint-Louis, Sen. | 104 | 16.02N | 16.30W |
| Saint Louis, Mo., U.S. | 138 | 38.37N | 90.11W |
| Saint Lucia ◻¹ | 130 | 13.53N | 60.58W |
| Saint-Malo | 92 | 48.39N | 2.01W |
| Saint-Malo, Golfe de c | 92 | 48.45N | 2.00W |
| Sainte-Marie, Cap ➢ | 106 | 25.36S | 45.08 E |
| Saint Marys | 140 | 41.25N | 78.33W |
| Saint-Nazaire | 92 | 47.17N | 2.12W |
| Saint Paul | 138 | 44.57N | 93.05W |
| Saint Peter Port | 92 | 49.27N | 2.32W |
| Saint Petersburg → Sankt-Peterburg, Russia | 100 | 59.55N | 30.15 E |
| Saint Petersburg, Fl., U.S. | 138 | 27.46N | 82.40W |
| Saint Pierre and Miquelon ◻² | 136 | 46.55N | 56.10W |
| Saint-Quentin | 92 | 49.51N | 3.17 E |
| Saintes | 92 | 45.45N | 0.52W |
| Saint Thomas | 140 | 42.47N | 81.12W |
| Saint Vincent, Gulf c | 124 | 35.00S | 138.05 E |
| Saint Vincent and the Grenadines ◻¹ | 130 | 13.15N | 61.12W |
| Saipan I | 118 | 15.12N | 145.45 E |
| Sairecábur, Cerro ▲ | 132 | 22.43S | 67.54W |
| Saito | 116 | 32.06N | 131.24 E |
| Sajama, Nevado ▲ | 132 | 18.06S | 68.54W |
| Sakai | 116 | 34.35N | 135.28 E |
| Sakata | 116 | 38.55N | 139.50 E |
| Sakau | 127b | 16.49S | 168.24 E |
| Sakhalin → Sachalin, Ostrov I | 102 | 51.00N | 143.00 E |
| Saku | 116 | 36.09N | 138.26 E |

| Name | Page No. | Lat. | Long. |
|---|---|---|---|
| Santa Catalina, Gulf of c̄ | 142 | 33.20 N | 117.45 W |
| Santa Clara, Cuba | 130 | 22.24 N | 79.58 W |
| Santa Clara, Ca., U.S. | 142 | 37.20 N | 121.56 W |
| Santa Cruz, Bol. | 132 | 17.48 S | 63.10 W |
| Santa Cruz, Ca., U.S. | 142 | 36.58 N | 122.01 W |
| Santa Cruz de Tenerife | 104 | 28.27 N | 16.14 W |
| Santa Cruz Island I | 142 | 34.01 N | 119.45 W |
| Santa Fe, Arg. | 134 | 31.38 S | 60.42 W |
| Santa Fe, N.M., U.S. | 138 | 35.41 N | 105.56 W |
| Santa Fe de Bogotá | 132 | 4.36 N | 74.05 W |
| Santa Isabel I | 127a | 8.00 S | 159.00 E |
| Santa Lucia Range ⋏ | 142 | 36.00 N | 121.20 W |
| Santa Maria, Braz. | 134 | 29.41 S | 53.48 W |
| Santa Maria, Ca., U.S. | 142 | 34.57 N | 120.26 W |
| Santa Maria, Cabo de ⋎ | 106 | 13.25 S | 12.32 E |
| Santa María Island I | 127b | 14.15 S | 167.30 E |
| Santa Marta | 132 | 11.15 N | 74.13 W |
| Santana do Livramento | 134 | 30.53 S | 55.31 W |
| Santander | 94 | 43.28 N | 3.48 W |
| Santarém | 132 | 2.26 S | 54.42 W |
| Santa Rosa, Arg. | 134 | 36.37 S | 64.17 W |
| Santa Rosa, Arg. | 134 | 32.20 S | 65.12 W |
| Santa Rosa, Ca., U.S. | 142 | 38.26 N | 122.42 W |
| Santa Rosa Island I | 142 | 33.58 N | 120.06 W |
| Santiago | 134 | 33.27 S | 70.40 W |
| Santiago de Compostela | 94 | 42.53 N | 8.33 W |
| Santiago de Cuba | 130 | 20.01 N | 75.49 W |
| Santiago del Estero | 134 | 27.47 S | 64.16 W |
| Santiago [de los Caballeros] | 130 | 19.27 N | 70.42 W |
| Santo André | 135 | 23.40 S | 46.31 W |
| Santo Ângelo | 134 | 28.18 S | 54.16 W |
| Santo Antônio de Jesus | 135 | 12.58 S | 39.16 W |
| Santo Domingo | 130 | 18.28 N | 69.54 W |
| Santos | 132 | 23.57 S | 46.20 W |
| San Valentín, Cerro ⋏ | 134 | 46.36 S | 73.20 W |
| San Vicente | 130 | 13.38 N | 88.48 W |
| San Vicente de Baracaldo | 94 | 43.18 N | 2.59 W |
| San Vito, Capo ⋎ | 96 | 38.11 N | 12.43 E |
| São Carlos | 135 | 22.01 S | 47.54 W |
| São Francisco ≃ | 132 | 10.30 S | 36.24 W |
| São José do Rio Prêto | 132 | 20.48 S | 49.23 W |
| São José dos Campos | 135 | 23.11 S | 45.53 W |
| São Leopoldo | 134 | 29.46 S | 51.09 W |
| São Luís | 132 | 2.31 S | 44.16 W |
| São Mateus | 132 | 18.44 S | 39.51 W |
| Saône ≃ | 90 | 46.05 N | 4.45 E |
| São Paulo | 132 | 23.32 S | 46.20 W |
| São Roque, Cabo de ⋎ | 132 | 5.29 S | 35.16 W |
| São Sebastião, Ilha de I | 135 | 23.50 S | 45.18 W |
| São Sebastião, Ponta ⋎ | 106 | 22.07 S | 35.30 E |
| São Tomé | 106 | 0.20 N | 6.44 E |
| São Tomé, Cabo de ⋎ | 135 | 21.59 S | 40.59 W |
| Sao Tome and Principe □¹ | 106 | 1.00 N | 7.00 E |
| São Vicente, Cabo de ⋎ | 94 | 37.01 N | 9.00 W |
| Sapitwa ⋏ | 106 | 15.57 S | 35.36 E |
| Sapporo | 116a | 43.03 N | 141.21 E |
| Sarajevo | 98 | 43.52 N | 18.25 E |
| Saransk | 86 | 54.11 N | 45.11 E |
| Sarapul | 86 | 56.28 N | 53.48 E |
| Sarasota | 138 | 27.20 N | 82.31 W |
| Saratoga Springs | 140 | 43.04 N | 73.47 W |
| Saratov | 86 | 51.34 N | 46.02 E |
| Sardegna (Sardinia) I | 96 | 40.00 N | 9.00 E |
| Sargodha | 112 | 32.05 N | 72.40 E |
| Sarh | 104 | 9.09 N | 18.23 E |
| Sarmiento | 134 | 45.36 S | 69.05 W |
| Sarnia | 136 | 42.58 N | 82.23 W |
| Saronikós Kólpos c̄ | 98 | 37.54 N | 23.12 E |
| Sarthe ≃ | 92 | 47.30 N | 0.32 W |
| Sasamungga | 127a | 7.02 S | 156.47 E |

| Name | Page No. | Lat. | Long. |
|---|---|---|---|
| Sasebo | 116 | 33.10 N | 129.43 E |
| Saskatchewan □⁴ | 136 | 54.00 N | 105.00 W |
| Saskatoon | 136 | 52.07 N | 106.38 W |
| Sassandra ≃ | 104 | 4.58 N | 6.05 W |
| Sassari | 96 | 40.44 N | 8.33 E |
| Sätära | 111 | 17.41 N | 73.59 E |
| Sataua | 127e | 13.28 S | 172.40 W |
| Satna | 112 | 24.35 N | 80.50 E |
| Satsunan-shotō II | 117b | 29.00 N | 130.00 E |
| Satu Mare | 98 | 47.48 N | 22.53 E |
| Saudi Arabia □¹ | 108 | 25.00 N | 45.00 E |
| Sauerland ✦¹ | 90 | 51.10 N | 8.00 E |
| Saugerties | 140 | 42.04 N | 73.57 W |
| Sault Sainte Marie, On., Can. | 136 | 46.31 N | 84.20 W |
| Sault Sainte Marie, Mi., U.S. | 138 | 46.30 N | 84.21 W |
| Saumur | 92 | 47.16 N | 0.05 W |
| Saurimo | 106 | 9.39 S | 20.24 E |
| Sava ≃ | 98 | 44.50 N | 20.26 E |
| Savai'i I | 127e | 13.35 S | 172.25 W |
| Savannah | 138 | 32.05 N | 81.06 W |
| Savannakhét | 120 | 16.33 N | 104.45 E |
| Savona | 96 | 44.17 N | 8.30 E |
| Savusavu | 127c | 16.15 S | 179.21 E |
| Sawdā', Qurnat as- ⋏ | 109 | 34.18 N | 36.07 E |
| Sawhāj | 104 | 26.33 N | 31.42 E |
| Sawu, Laut (Savu Sea) ⫱² | 122 | 9.40 S | 122.00 E |
| Sayan Mountains (Sajany) ⋏ | 102 | 52.45 N | 96.00 E |
| Sayaxché | 130 | 16.31 N | 90.10 W |
| Schaffhausen | 92 | 47.42 N | 8.38 E |
| Schefferville | 136 | 54.48 N | 66.50 W |
| Schenectady | 140 | 42.48 N | 73.56 W |
| Schleswig | 90 | 54.31 N | 9.33 E |
| Schwaben □⁹ | 90 | 48.20 N | 10.30 E |
| Schwäbisch Gmünd | 90 | 48.48 N | 9.47 E |
| Schwarzwald ⋏ | 90 | 48.00 N | 8.15 E |
| Schwedt | 90 | 53.03 N | 14.17 E |
| Schweinfurt | 90 | 50.03 N | 10.14 E |
| Schwerin | 90 | 53.38 N | 11.25 E |
| Sciacca | 96 | 37.30 N | 13.06 E |
| Scotland □⁸ | 88 | 57.00 N | 4.00 W |
| Scott Islands II | 136 | 50.48 N | 128.40 W |
| Scottsbluff | 138 | 41.52 N | 103.40 W |
| Scranton | 140 | 41.24 N | 75.39 W |
| Scutari, Lake ⊜ | 98 | 42.12 N | 19.18 E |
| Searsport | 140 | 44.27 N | 68.55 W |
| Seattle | 138 | 47.36 N | 122.19 W |
| Sebastian, Cape ⋎ | 142 | 42.19 N | 124.26 W |
| Sebastián Vizcaíno, Bahía c̄ | 128 | 28.00 N | 114.30 W |
| Ségou | 104 | 13.27 N | 6.16 W |
| Segovia | 94 | 40.57 N | 4.07 W |
| Seguin | 128 | 29.34 N | 97.57 W |
| Seine ≃ | 92 | 49.26 N | 0.26 E |
| Seine, Baie de la c̄ | 92 | 49.30 N | 0.30 W |
| Sekondi-Takoradi | 104 | 4.59 N | 1.43 W |
| Selawik | 144 | 66.37 N | 160.03 W |
| Seldovia | 144 | 59.27 N | 151.43 W |
| Šelichova, Zaliv c̄ | 102 | 60.00 N | 158.00 E |
| Selma | 138 | 32.24 N | 87.01 W |
| Selva | 134 | 29.46 S | 62.03 W |
| Selvas ✦³ | 132 | 5.00 S | 68.00 W |
| Selwyn Mountains ⋏ | 136 | 63.10 N | 130.20 W |
| Semara | 104 | 26.44 N | 14.41 W |
| Semarang | 118 | 6.58 S | 110.25 E |
| Semey | 102 | 50.28 N | 80.13 E |
| Sendai | 116 | 38.15 N | 140.53 E |
| Seneca Lake ⊜ | 140 | 42.40 N | 76.57 W |
| Senegal □¹ | 104 | 14.00 N | 14.00 W |
| Sénégal ≃ | 104 | 15.48 N | 16.32 W |
| Senigallia | 96 | 43.43 N | 13.13 E |
| Senja I | 89 | 69.20 N | 17.30 E |
| Senmonorom | 120 | 12.27 N | 107.12 E |

| Name | Page No. | Lat. | Long. |
|---|---|---|---|
| Skagway | 144 | 59.28N | 135.19W |
| Skarżysko-Kamienna | 90 | 51.08N | 20.53 E |
| Skeldon | 132 | 5.53N | 57.08W |
| Skelleftea | 89 | 64.46N | 20.57 E |
| Skellefteälven ⇌ | 89 | 64.42N | 21.06 E |
| Skien | 89 | 59.12N | 9.36 E |
| Skíros | 98 | 38.53N | 24.33 E |
| Skíros I | 98 | 38.53N | 24.32 E |
| Skopje | 98 | 41.59N | 21.26 E |
| Skye, Island of I | 88 | 57.15N | 6.10W |
| Slanské Vrchy ⋏ | 90 | 48.50N | 21.30 E |
| Slavgorod | 102 | 53.00N | 78.40 E |
| Slavonija ⬩¹ | 96 | 45.00N | 18.00 E |
| Slavonski Brod | 98 | 45.10N | 18.01 E |
| Sligo | 88 | 54.17N | 8.28W |
| Sliven | 98 | 42.40N | 26.19 E |
| Slovakia ▫¹ | 90 | 49.00N | 19.30 E |
| Slovenia ▫¹ | 96 | 46.15N | 15.10 E |
| Słupsk (Stolp) | 90 | 54.28N | 17.01 E |
| Smederevo | 98 | 44.40N | 20.56 E |
| Smiths Falls | 140 | 44.54N | 76.01W |
| Smithton | 122 | 40.51S | 145.07 E |
| Smokey Dome ⋏ | 142 | 43.29N | 114.56W |
| Smolensk | 100 | 54.47N | 32.03 E |
| Smoljan | 98 | 41.35N | 24.41 E |
| Smythe, Mount ⋏ | 136 | 57.54N | 124.53W |
| Snake ⇌ | 138 | 46.12N | 119.02W |
| Snake River Plain ⇌ | 142 | 43.00N | 113.00W |
| Snina | 90 | 48.59N | 22.07 E |
| Snøtinden ⋏ | 89 | 66.38N | 14.00 E |
| Snow Hill | 140 | 38.10N | 75.23W |
| Snyder | 128 | 32.43N | 100.55W |
| Sobat ⇌ | 108 | 9.22N | 31.33 E |
| Sobral | 132 | 3.42S | 40.21W |
| Soči | 86 | 43.35N | 39.45 E |
| Société, Îles de la (Society Islands) II | 127d | 17.00S | 150.00W |
| Soc Trang | 120 | 9.36N | 105.58 E |
| Söderhamn | 89 | 61.18N | 17.03 E |
| Sofija (Sofia) | 98 | 42.41N | 23.19 E |
| Sognafjorden c² | 89 | 61.06N | 5.10 E |
| Soissons | 92 | 49.22N | 3.20 E |
| Söke | 98 | 37.45N | 27.24 E |
| Sokoto | 104 | 13.04N | 5.16 E |
| Solbad Hall in Tirol | 90 | 47.17N | 11.31 E |
| Soligorsk | 100 | 52.48N | 27.32 E |
| Solikamsk | 86 | 59.39N | 56.47 E |
| Solimões → Amazon ⇌ | 132 | 0.05S | 50.00W |
| Solomon Islands ▫¹ | 82 | 8.00S | 159.00 E |
| Solomon Sea ╤² | 122 | 8.00S | 155.00 E |
| Solothurn | 92 | 47.13N | 7.32 E |
| Somalia ▫¹ | 108 | 10.00N | 49.00 E |
| Sombor | 98 | 45.46N | 19.07 E |
| Somerset | 138 | 37.05N | 84.36W |
| Somerset Island I | 136 | 73.15N | 93.30W |
| Someşu Mic ⇌ | 98 | 47.09N | 23.55 E |
| Somosomo | 127c | 16.46S | 179.58W |
| Songkhla | 120 | 7.12N | 100.36 E |
| Sonneberg | 90 | 50.22N | 11.10 E |
| Sopron | 90 | 47.41N | 16.36 E |
| Sorel | 140 | 46.02N | 73.07W |
| Sorocaba | 135 | 23.29S | 47.27W |
| Sorol I¹ | 118 | 8.08N | 140.23 E |
| Sørøya I | 89 | 70.36N | 22.46 E |
| Sorsatunturi ⋏ | 89 | 67.24N | 29.38 E |
| Souk Ahras | 96 | 36.23N | 8.00 E |
| Sŏul (Seoul) | 114 | 37.33N | 126.58 E |
| Sousse | 96 | 35.49N | 10.38 E |
| South Africa ▫¹ | 106 | 30.00S | 26.00 E |
| South America ⬝¹ | 82 | 15.00S | 60.00W |
| Southampton | 88 | 50.55N | 1.25W |
| Southampton Island I | 136 | 64.20N | 84.40W |
| South Australia ▫³ | 122 | 30.00S | 135.00 E |
| Southbridge | 126 | 43.49S | 172.15 E |
| South Cape ≻ | 127c | 17.01S | 179.55 E |
| South Carolina ▫³ | 138 | 34.00N | 81.00W |
| South China Sea ╤² | 114 | 19.00N | 115.00 E |
| South Dakota ▫³ | 138 | 44.15N | 100.00W |
| Southend-on-Sea | 88 | 51.33N | 0.43 E |
| Southern Alps ⋏ | 126 | 43.30S | 170.30 E |
| Southern Cross | 122 | 31.13S | 119.19 E |
| South Georgia I | 134 | 54.15S | 36.45W |
| South Indian Lake | 136 | 56.46N | 98.57W |
| South Island I | 126 | 43.00S | 171.00 E |
| South Orkney Islands II | 85 | 60.35S | 45.30W |
| South Platte ⇌ | 138 | 41.07N | 100.42W |
| South Point ≻ | 124 | 39.00S | 146.20 E |
| South Pole ⬥ | 85 | 90.00S | 0.00 |
| Southport, Austl. | 124 | 27.58S | 153.25 E |
| Southport, Eng., U.K. | 88 | 53.39N | 3.01W |
| South Sandwich Islands II | 85 | 57.45S | 26.30W |
| South Shetland Islands II | 85 | 62.00S | 58.00W |
| South West Cape ≻ | 124 | 43.34S | 146.02 E |
| Sovetskaja Gavan' | 102 | 48.58N | 140.18 E |
| Spain ▫¹ | 86 | 40.00N | 4.00W |
| Spanish North Africa ▫² | 94 | 35.53N | 5.19W |
| Spanish Town | 130 | 17.59N | 76.57W |
| Sparks | 142 | 39.32N | 119.45W |
| Spárti (Sparta) | 98 | 37.05N | 22.27 E |
| Spassk-Dal'nij | 102 | 44.37N | 132.48 E |
| Spencer Gulf c | 124 | 34.00S | 137.00 E |
| Speyer | 90 | 49.19N | 8.26 E |
| Split | 96 | 43.31N | 16.27 E |
| Spokane | 138 | 47.39N | 117.25W |
| Spoleto | 96 | 42.44N | 12.44 E |
| Springbok | 106 | 29.43S | 17.55 E |
| Springdale | 136 | 49.30N | 56.04W |
| Springfield, Il., U.S. | 138 | 39.48N | 89.38W |
| Springfield, Ma., U.S. | 140 | 42.06N | 72.35W |
| Springfield, Mo., U.S. | 138 | 37.12N | 93.17W |
| Springfield, Oh., U.S. | 140 | 39.55N | 83.48W |
| Springfontein | 106 | 30.19S | 25.36 E |
| Springhill | 136 | 45.39N | 64.03W |
| Springs | 106 | 26.13S | 28.25 E |
| Spruce Knob ⋏ | 140 | 38.42N | 79.32W |
| Squillace, Golfo di c | 96 | 38.50N | 16.50 E |
| Srednesibirskoje Ploskogorje ⋏¹ | 102 | 65.00N | 105.00 E |
| Sri Lanka ▫¹ | 110 | 7.00N | 81.00 E |
| Sri Lanka I | 111 | 7.00N | 81.00 E |
| Srinagar | 112 | 34.05N | 74.49 E |
| Stade | 90 | 53.36N | 9.28 E |
| Stafford | 88 | 52.48N | 2.07W |
| Stalingrad → Volgograd | 86 | 48.44N | 44.25 E |
| Stamford | 140 | 41.03N | 73.32W |
| Standish | 140 | 43.58N | 83.57W |
| Stanke Dimitrov | 98 | 42.16N | 23.07 E |
| Stanley Falls → Boyoma Falls ↳ | 106 | 0.15N | 25.30 E |
| Stanovoje Nagorje (Stanovoy Mountains) ⋏ | 102 | 56.00N | 114.00 E |
| Stanton | 140 | 37.50N | 83.51W |
| Starachowice | 90 | 51.03N | 21.04 E |
| Staraja Russa | 100 | 58.00N | 31.23 E |
| Stara Planina (Balkan Mountains) ⋏ | 98 | 43.15N | 25.00 E |
| Stara Zagora | 98 | 42.25N | 25.38 E |
| Starogard Gdański | 90 | 53.59N | 18.33 E |
| State College | 140 | 40.47N | 77.51W |
| Staunton | 140 | 38.08N | 79.04W |
| Stavanger | 89 | 58.58N | 5.45 E |
| Stavropol' | 86 | 45.02N | 41.59 E |
| Steinkjer | 89 | 64.01N | 11.30 E |
| Stelvio, Passo dello ⋎ | 92 | 46.32N | 10.27 E |
| Stendal | 90 | 52.36N | 11.51 E |
| Sterling | 138 | 40.37N | 103.12W |

| Name | Page No. | Lat. | Long. |
|------|----------|------|-------|
| Sterlitamak | 86 | 53.37N | 55.58 E |
| Steubenville | 140 | 40.22N | 80.38W |
| Stewart | 136 | 55.56N | 129.59W |
| Stewart Island **I** | 126 | 47.00S | 167.50 E |
| Steyr | 90 | 48.03N | 14.25 E |
| Stockerau | 90 | 48.23N | 16.13 E |
| Stockholm | 89 | 59.20N | 18.03 E |
| Stockton | 142 | 37.57N | 121.17W |
| Stoke-on-Trent | 88 | 53.00N | 2.10W |
| Stowe | 140 | 44.27N | 72.41W |
| Stralsund | 90 | 54.19N | 13.05 E |
| Strasbourg | 92 | 48.35N | 7.45 E |
| Strasburg | 140 | 38.59N | 78.21W |
| Stratford | 140 | 43.22N | 80.57W |
| Stratford-upon-Avon | 88 | 52.12N | 1.41W |
| Stratton | 140 | 45.08N | 70.26W |
| Straubing | 90 | 48.53N | 12.34 E |
| Struma (Strimón) ≃ | 98 | 40.47N | 23.51 E |
| Sturgis | 140 | 41.47N | 85.25W |
| Stuttgart | 90 | 48.46N | 9.11 E |
| Subotica | 98 | 46.06N | 19.39 E |
| Suceava | 98 | 47.39N | 26.19 E |
| Suchumi | 86 | 43.01N | 41.02 E |
| Sucre | 132 | 19.02S | 65.17W |
| Sudan □ ¹ | 104 | 15.00N | 30.00 E |
| Sudan ◆ ¹ | 104 | 10.00N | 20.00 E |
| Sudbury | 136 | 46.30N | 81.00W |
| Sukkur | 112 | 27.42N | 68.52 E |
| Sula, Kepulauan **II** | 118 | 1.52S | 125.22 E |
| Sulaimān Range ⋏ | 112 | 30.30N | 70.10 E |
| Sulawesi (Celebes) **I** | 118 | 2.00S | 121.00 E |
| Sullana | 132 | 4.53S | 80.41W |
| Sulmona | 96 | 42.03N | 13.55 E |
| Sulu Archipelago **II** | 118 | 6.00N | 121.00 E |
| Sulu Sea ≂ ² | 118 | 8.00N | 120.00 E |
| Sumatera (Sumatra) **I** | 118 | 0.05S | 102.00 E |
| Sumba **I** | 118 | 10.00S | 120.00 E |
| Sumbawa **I** | 118 | 8.40S | 118.00 E |
| Šumen | 98 | 43.16N | 26.55 E |
| Summit Lake | 136 | 54.17N | 122.38W |
| Sumoto | 116 | 34.21N | 134.54 E |
| Sumy | 86 | 50.55N | 34.45 E |
| Sunbury | 140 | 40.51N | 76.47W |
| Sunderland | 88 | 54.55N | 1.23W |
| Sundsvall | 89 | 62.23N | 17.18 E |
| Sunnyvale | 142 | 37.22N | 122.02W |
| Superior, Lake ❷ | 138 | 48.00N | 88.00W |
| Suquṭrā (Socotra) **I** | 108 | 12.30N | 54.00 E |
| Şūr (Tyre) | 109 | 33.16N | 35.11 E |
| Surabaya | 118 | 7.15S | 112.45 E |
| Surakarta | 118 | 7.35S | 110.50 E |
| Surat | 112 | 21.10N | 72.50 E |
| Surat Thani (Ban Don) | 120 | 9.08N | 99.19 E |
| Surendranagar | 112 | 22.42N | 71.41 E |
| Suretamati, Mount ⋀ | 127b | 13.47S | 167.29 E |
| Surgut | 102 | 61.14N | 73.20 E |
| Suriname □ ¹ | 132 | 4.00N | 56.00W |
| Surt | 104 | 31.12N | 16.35 E |
| Surt, Khalīj ᴄ | 104 | 31.30N | 18.00 E |
| Surud Ad ⋀ | 108 | 10.41N | 47.18 E |
| Susquehanna ≃ | 140 | 39.33N | 76.05W |
| Sutlej (Satluj) (Langchuhe) ≃ | 112 | 29.23N | 71.02 E |
| Suva | 127c | 18.08S | 178.25 E |
| Suwa | 116 | 36.02N | 138.08 E |
| Suways, Khalīj as- (Gulf of Suez) ᴄ | 109 | 29.00N | 32.50 E |
| Suways, Qanāt as- (Suez Canal) ⌇ | 109 | 29.55N | 32.33 E |
| Suzhou | 114 | 31.18N | 120.37 E |
| Svartenhuk ⋋ ¹ | 136 | 71.55N | 55.00W |
| Svinecea ⋀ | 98 | 44.48N | 22.09 E |
| Svobodnyj | 102 | 51.24N | 128.08 E |
| Swan River | 136 | 52.06N | 101.16W |
| Swansea | 88 | 51.38N | 3.57W |
| Swaziland □ ¹ | 106 | 26.30S | 31.30 E |

| Name | Page No. | Lat. | Long. |
|------|----------|------|-------|
| Sweden □ ¹ | 86 | 62.00N | 15.00 E |
| Sweetwater | 138 | 32.28N | 100.24W |
| Swellendam | 106 | 34.02S | 20.26 E |
| Świdnica (Schweidnitz) | 90 | 50.51N | 16.29 E |
| Świnoujście (Swinemünde) | 90 | 53.53N | 14.14 E |
| Switzerland □ ¹ | 86 | 47.00N | 8.00 E |
| Sydney | 122 | 33.52S | 151.13 E |
| Syktyvkar | 86 | 61.40N | 50.46 E |
| Sylhet | 112 | 24.54N | 91.52 E |
| Syracuse | 140 | 43.02N | 76.08W |
| Syria □ ¹ | 109 | 35.00N | 38.00 E |
| Syzran' | 86 | 53.09N | 48.27 E |
| Szczecin (Stettin) | 90 | 53.24N | 14.32 E |
| Szczecinek (Neustettin) | 90 | 53.43N | 16.42 E |
| Szeged | 90 | 46.15N | 20.09 E |
| Székesfehérvár | 90 | 47.12N | 18.25 E |
| Szolnok | 90 | 47.10N | 20.12 E |
| Szombathely | 90 | 47.14N | 16.38 E |

**T**

| Name | Page No. | Lat. | Long. |
|------|----------|------|-------|
| Tábor, Czech. Rep. | 90 | 49.25N | 14.41 E |
| Tabor, Russia | 102 | 71.16N | 150.12 E |
| Tabora | 106 | 5.01S | 32.48 E |
| Tabou | 104 | 4.25N | 7.21W |
| Tabrīz | 86 | 38.05N | 46.18 E |
| Tacna | 132 | 18.01S | 70.15W |
| Tacoma | 138 | 47.15N | 122.26W |
| Tadinou | 127b | 21.33S | 167.52 E |
| Tadoule Lake ❷ | 136 | 58.36N | 98.20W |
| Taegu | 114 | 35.52N | 128.35 E |
| Taga | 127e | 13.46S | 172.28W |
| Tagus (Tejo) (Tajo) ≃ | 94 | 38.40N | 9.24W |
| Tahaa **I** | 127d | 16.48S | 151.30W |
| Tahat ⋀ | 104 | 23.18N | 5.47 E |
| Tahoe, Lake ❷ | 142 | 38.58N | 120.00W |
| Tahoua | 104 | 14.54N | 5.16 E |
| Taiarapu, Presqu'île de ⋋ ¹ | 127d | 17.47S | 149.14W |
| T'aichung | 114 | 24.09N | 120.41 E |
| Taihape | 126 | 39.40S | 175.48 E |
| T'ainan | 114 | 23.00N | 120.12 E |
| T'aipei | 114 | 25.03N | 121.30 E |
| Taiping | 120 | 4.51N | 100.44 E |
| Taiwan □ ¹ | 114 | 23.30N | 121.00 E |
| Taiwan Strait ⥹ | 114 | 24.00N | 119.00 E |
| Taiyuan | 114 | 37.55N | 112.30 E |
| Taizhou | 114 | 32.30N | 119.58 E |
| Tajikistan □ ¹ | 102 | 39.00N | 71.00 E |
| Tajmyr, Poluostrov ⋋ ¹ | 102 | 76.00N | 104.00 E |
| Tajšet | 102 | 55.57N | 98.00 E |
| Tajumulco, Volcán ⋀ ¹ | 130 | 15.02N | 91.55W |
| Takada | 116 | 37.06N | 138.15 E |
| Takaka | 126 | 40.51S | 172.48 E |
| Takamatsu | 116 | 34.20N | 134.03 E |
| Takaoka | 116 | 36.45N | 137.01 E |
| Takapuna | 126 | 36.47S | 174.47 E |
| Takasaki | 116 | 36.20N | 139.01 E |
| Takatsuki | 116 | 34.51N | 135.37 E |
| Takefu | 116 | 35.54N | 136.10 E |
| Takêv | 120 | 10.59N | 104.47 E |
| Takla Makan → Taklimakan Shamo ◆ ² | 114 | 39.00N | 83.00 E |
| Taklimakan Shamo ◆ ² | 114 | 39.00N | 83.00 E |
| Takuam, Mount ⋀ | 127a | 6.27S | 155.36 E |
| Talara | 132 | 4.34S | 81.17W |
| Talaud, Kepulauan **II** | 118 | 4.20N | 126.50 E |
| Talavera de la Reina | 94 | 39.57N | 4.50W |
| Talca | 134 | 35.26S | 71.40W |
| Talcahuano | 134 | 36.43S | 73.07W |
| Tallahassee | 138 | 30.26N | 84.16W |
| Tallinn | 100 | 59.25N | 24.45 E |
| Tamale | 104 | 9.25N | 0.50W |

| Name | Page No. | Lat. | Long. |
|------|----------|------|-------|
| Tambov | 100 | 52.43N | 41.25 E |
| Tamel Aike | 134 | 48.19S | 70.58W |
| Tamenghest | 104 | 22.56N | 5.30 E |
| Tamil Nadu □ ³ | 111 | 11.00N | 78.15 E |
| Tampa | 138 | 27.56N | 82.27W |
| Tampere | 89 | 61.30N | 23.45 E |
| Tampico | 128 | 22.13N | 97.51W |
| Tamworth | 122 | 31.05S | 150.55 E |
| Tana, Lake ⊜ | 108 | 12.00N | 37.20 E |
| Tananarive | | | |
| → Antananarivo | 106 | 18.55S | 47.31 E |
| Tandil | 134 | 37.19S | 59.09W |
| Tando Ādam | 112 | 25.46N | 68.40 E |
| Tanega-shima I | 117b | 30.40N | 131.00 E |
| Tanga | 106 | 5.04S | 39.06 E |
| Tanganyika, Lake ⊜ | 106 | 6.00S | 29.30 E |
| Tanger (Tangier) | 104 | 35.48N | 5.45W |
| Tangshan | 114 | 39.38N | 118.11 E |
| Tanimbar, Kepulauan | | | |
| II | 118 | 7.30S | 131.30 E |
| Tanjungbalai | 120 | 2.58N | 99.48 E |
| Tanjungpinang | 120 | 0.55N | 104.27 E |
| Tanoriki | 127b | 14.59S | 168.09 E |
| Tanṭā | 104 | 30.47N | 31.00 E |
| Tanzania □ ¹ | 106 | 6.00S | 35.00 E |
| Tapachula | 128 | 14.54N | 92.17W |
| Tapajós ≃ | 132 | 2.24S | 54.41W |
| Tāpi ≃ | 111 | 21.06N | 72.41 E |
| Tapuaenuku ʌ | 126 | 42.00S | 173.40 E |
| Tara | 102 | 56.54N | 74.22 E |
| Ṭarābulus (Tripoli), Leb. | 109 | 34.26N | 35.51 E |
| Ṭarābulus (Tripoli), Libya | 104 | 32.54N | 13.11 E |
| Ṭarābulus (Tripolitania) ◆¹ | 104 | 31.00N | 15.00 E |
| Taranto | 96 | 40.28N | 17.15 E |
| Taranto, Golfo di c | 96 | 40.10N | 17.20 E |
| Tărgovište, Bul. | 98 | 43.15N | 26.34 E |
| Tarija | 132 | 21.31S | 64.45W |
| Tarim Pendi ≌¹ | 114 | 39.00N | 83.00 E |
| Tarnów | 90 | 50.01N | 21.00 E |
| Tarragona | 94 | 41.07N | 1.15 E |
| Tarrasa | 94 | 41.34N | 2.01 E |
| Tartu | 100 | 58.23N | 26.43 E |
| Tarutung | 120 | 2.01N | 98.58 E |
| Tashi Gang Dzong | 112 | 27.19N | 91.34 E |
| Tasikmalaya | 118 | 7.20S | 108.12 E |
| Taškent | 110 | 41.20N | 69.18 E |
| Tasman Bay c | 126 | 41.00S | 173.20 E |
| Tasmania □ ³ | 122 | 43.00S | 147.00 E |
| Tasman Sea ▼ ² | 122 | 37.00S | 157.00 E |
| Taštagol | 102 | 52.47N | 87.53 E |
| Tatabánya | 90 | 47.34N | 18.26 E |
| Tatarsk | 102 | 55.13N | 75.58 E |
| Taumarunui | 126 | 38.52S | 175.17 E |
| Taunggyi | 120 | 20.47N | 97.02 E |
| Taupo | 126 | 38.41S | 176.05 E |
| Taupo, Lake ⊜ | 126 | 38.49S | 175.55 E |
| Tauranga | 126 | 37.42S | 176.10 E |
| Tauroa Point ≻ | 126 | 35.10S | 173.04 E |
| Tautira | 127d | 17.44S | 149.09W |
| Tavda | 102 | 58.03N | 65.15 E |
| Tawkar | 104 | 18.26N | 37.44 E |
| Tbilisi | 86 | 41.43N | 44.49 E |
| Tchibanga | 106 | 2.51S | 11.02 E |
| Te Anau | 126 | 45.25S | 167.43 E |
| Te Anau, Lake ⊜ | 126 | 45.12S | 167.48 E |
| Tebessa | 96 | 35.28N | 8.09 E |
| Tecuci | 98 | 45.50N | 27.26 E |
| Tegucigalpa | 130 | 14.06N | 87.13W |
| Tehrān | 86 | 35.40N | 51.26 E |
| Tehuacán | 128 | 18.27N | 97.23W |
| Tehuantepec | 128 | 16.20N | 95.14W |
| Tehuantepec, Golfo de c | 128 | 16.00N | 94.50W |

| Name | Page No. | Lat. | Long. |
|------|----------|------|-------|
| Tehuantepec, Istmo de ≛ ³ | 128 | 17.00N | 95.00W |
| Tejo | | | |
| → Tagus ≃ | 94 | 38.40N | 9.24W |
| Tekirdağ | 98 | 40.59N | 27.31 E |
| Te Kuiti | 126 | 38.20S | 175.10 E |
| Tel Aviv-Yafo | 109 | 32.04N | 34.46 E |
| Telén | 134 | 36.16S | 65.30W |
| Teleño ʌ | 94 | 42.21N | 6.23W |
| Telescope Peak ʌ | 142 | 36.10N | 117.05W |
| Telok Anson | 120 | 4.02N | 101.01 E |
| Tembeling ≃ | 120 | 4.04N | 102.20 E |
| Temirtau | 102 | 50.05N | 72.56 E |
| Temple | 128 | 31.05N | 97.20W |
| Temuco | 134 | 38.44S | 72.36W |
| Tenāli | 111 | 16.15N | 80.35 E |
| Tende, Col de ╳ | 92 | 44.09N | 7.34 E |
| Ténéré ◆² | 104 | 19.00N | 10.30 E |
| Tenerife I | 104 | 28.19N | 16.34W |
| Tennant Creek | 122 | 19.40S | 134.10 E |
| Tennessee □ ³ | 138 | 35.50N | 85.30W |
| Tenterfield | 122 | 29.03S | 152.01 E |
| Teófilo Otoni | 135 | 17.51S | 41.30W |
| Tepelena | 98 | 40.18N | 20.01 E |
| Tepic | 128 | 21.30N | 104.54W |
| Teramo | 96 | 42.39N | 13.42 E |
| Teresina | 132 | 5.05S | 42.49W |
| Terre Haute | 138 | 39.28N | 87.24W |
| Tete | 106 | 16.13S | 33.35 E |
| Tetiaroa I¹ | 127d | 17.05S | 149.32W |
| Tétouan | 94 | 35.34N | 5.23W |
| Tetovo | 98 | 42.01N | 20.58 E |
| Tevere (Tiber) ≃ | 92 | 41.44N | 12.14 E |
| Texarkana | 138 | 33.25N | 94.02W |
| Texas □ ³ | 138 | 31.30N | 99.00W |
| Texas City | 128 | 29.23N | 94.54W |
| Thabazimbi | 106 | 24.41S | 27.21 E |
| Thailand □ ¹ | 118 | 15.00N | 100.00 E |
| Thailand, Gulf of c | 120 | 10.00N | 101.00 E |
| Thai Nguyen | 120 | 21.36N | 105.50 E |
| Thames ≃ | 126 | 37.08S | 175.33 E |
| Thames ≃ | 88 | 51.28N | 0.43 E |
| Thamesville | 140 | 42.33N | 81.59W |
| Thāna | 111 | 19.12N | 72.58 E |
| Thanh Hoa | 120 | 19.48N | 105.46 E |
| Thanh Pho Ho Chi Minh (Saigon) | 120 | 10.45N | 106.40 E |
| Thar Desert (Great Indian Desert) ◆² | 110 | 27.00N | 71.00 E |
| Thásos I | 98 | 40.41N | 24.47 E |
| Thaton | 120 | 16.55N | 97.22 E |
| Thayetmyo | 120 | 19.19N | 95.11 E |
| The Everglades ⧫ | 130 | 26.00N | 81.00W |
| The Hague | | | |
| → 's-Gravenhage | 90 | 52.06N | 4.18 E |
| Theodore | 122 | 24.57S | 150.05 E |
| Thermaïkós Kólpos c | 98 | 40.23N | 22.47 E |
| The Slot ⋃ | 127a | 8.00S | 158.10 E |
| Thessalía ◆¹ | 98 | 39.30N | 22.00 E |
| Thessalon | 140 | 46.15N | 83.34W |
| Thessaloníki (Salonika) | 98 | 40.38N | 22.56 E |
| Thetford Mines | 140 | 46.05N | 71.18W |
| Thiel Mountains ⯒ | 85 | 85.15S | 91.00W |
| Thielsen, Mount ʌ | 142 | 43.09N | 122.04W |
| Thimphu | 114 | 27.28N | 89.39 E |
| Thionville | 92 | 49.22N | 6.10 E |
| Thíra I | 98 | 36.24N | 25.29 E |
| Thisted | 89 | 56.57N | 8.42 E |
| Thívai (Thebes) | 98 | 38.21N | 23.19 E |
| Thongwa | 120 | 16.46N | 96.32 E |
| Thonze | 120 | 17.38N | 95.47 E |
| Thrakikón Pélagos ▼² | 98 | 40.15N | 24.28 E |
| Thunder Bay | 136 | 48.23N | 89.15W |
| Thüringer Wald ⯒ | 92 | 50.30N | 10.30 E |
| Tianjin | 114 | 39.08N | 117.12 E |
| Tibasti, Sarīr ◆² | 104 | 24.15N | 17.15 E |

| Name | Page No. | Lat. | Long. |
|---|---|---|---|
| Tromelin **I** | 106 | 15.52S | 54.25 E |
| Tromsø | 89 | 69.40N | 18.58 E |
| Trondheim | 89 | 63.25N | 10.25 E |
| Trondheimsfjorden **c²** | 89 | 63.39N | 10.49 E |
| Troy, N.Y., U.S. | 140 | 42.43N | 73.41W |
| Troy, Oh., U.S. | 140 | 40.02N | 84.12W |
| Troyes | 92 | 48.18N | 4.05 E |
| Truckee **≃** | 142 | 39.51N | 119.24W |
| Trujillo, Peru | 132 | 8.07S | 79.02W |
| Trujillo, Ven. | 130 | 9.22N | 70.26W |
| Trutnov | 90 | 50.34N | 15.55 E |
| Tsingtao |  |  |  |
| → Qingdao | 114 | 36.06N | 120.19 E |
| Tsu | 116 | 34.43N | 136.31 E |
| Tsuchiura | 116 | 36.05N | 140.12 E |
| Tsugaru-kaikyō **ᴜ** | 116 | 41.35N | 141.00 E |
| Tsumeb | 106 | 19.13S | 17.42 E |
| Tsuruga | 116 | 35.39N | 136.04 E |
| Tsuruoka | 116 | 38.44N | 139.50 E |
| Tsuyama | 116 | 35.03N | 134.00 E |
| Tual | 118 | 5.40S | 132.45 E |
| Tubarão | 134 | 28.30S | 49.01W |
| Tübingen | 90 | 48.31N | 9.02 E |
| Tucson | 138 | 32.13N | 110.55W |
| Tucumcari | 138 | 35.10N | 103.43W |
| Tucupita | 130 | 9.04N | 62.03W |
| Tudmur (Palmyra) | 109 | 34.33N | 38.17 E |
| Tuktoyaktuk | 136 | 69.27N | 133.02W |
| Tula | 100 | 54.12N | 37.37 E |
| Tulancingo | 128 | 20.05N | 98.22W |
| Tulare | 142 | 36.12N | 119.20W |
| Tulcán | 132 | 0.48N | 77.43W |
| Tulcea | 98 | 45.11N | 28.48 E |
| Tulsa | 138 | 36.09N | 95.59W |
| Tulun | 102 | 54.35N | 100.33 E |
| Tumaco | 132 | 1.49N | 78.46W |
| Tumbes | 132 | 3.34S | 80.28W |
| T'umen' | 102 | 57.09N | 65.32 E |
| Tumeremo | 132 | 7.18N | 61.30W |
| Tumuc-Humac |  |  |  |
| Mountains **⋌** | 132 | 2.20N | 55.00W |
| Tundža (Tunca) **≃** | 98 | 41.40N | 26.34 E |
| Tunis | 104 | 36.48N | 10.11 E |
| Tunisia **□¹** | 104 | 34.00N | 9.00 E |
| Tunja | 132 | 5.31N | 73.22W |
| Tuolumne **≃** | 142 | 37.36N | 121.10W |
| Tupã | 135 | 21.56S | 50.30W |
| Tupaciguara | 135 | 18.35S | 48.42W |
| Tupelo | 138 | 34.15N | 88.42W |
| Tupper Lake | 140 | 44.13N | 74.29W |
| Turbo | 132 | 8.06N | 76.43W |
| Turda | 98 | 46.34N | 23.47 E |
| Turgutlu | 98 | 38.30N | 27.43 E |
| Turin |  |  |  |
| → Torino | 96 | 45.03N | 7.40 E |
| Turkey **□¹** | 86 | 39.00N | 35.00 E |
| Turkmenistan **□¹** | 86 | 40.00N | 60.00 E |
| Turks and Caicos |  |  |  |
| Islands **□²** | 130 | 21.45N | 71.35W |
| Turks Islands **II** | 130 | 21.24N | 71.07W |
| Turku (Åbo) | 89 | 60.27N | 22.17 E |
| Turquino, Pico **⋀** | 130 | 19.59N | 76.50W |
| Turuchansk | 102 | 65.49N | 87.59 E |
| Tuscaloosa | 138 | 33.12N | 87.34W |
| Tuticorin | 111 | 8.47N | 78.08 E |
| Tutuila **I** | 127e | 14.18S | 170.42W |
| Tuxpan de Rodríguez |  |  |  |
| Cano | 128 | 20.57N | 97.24W |
| Tuxtla Gutiérrez | 128 | 16.45N | 93.07W |
| Tuzla | 96 | 44.32N | 18.41 E |
| Tver' | 100 | 56.52N | 35.55 E |
| Twin Falls | 138 | 42.33N | 114.27W |
| Tyler | 138 | 32.21N | 95.18W |
| Tyrrhenian Sea (Mare |  |  |  |
| Tirreno) **⊤²** | 96 | 40.00N | 12.00 E |

| Name | Page No. | Lat. | Long. |
|---|---|---|---|
| **U** |  |  |  |
| Ubá | 135 | 21.07S | 42.56W |
| Ubangi (Oubangui) **≃** | 104 | 1.15N | 17.50 E |
| Ube | 116 | 33.56N | 131.15 E |
| Úbeda | 94 | 38.01N | 3.22W |
| Uberaba | 132 | 19.45S | 47.55W |
| Uberlândia | 132 | 18.56S | 48.18W |
| Ubon Ratchathani | 120 | 15.14N | 104.54 E |
| Ucayali **≃** | 132 | 4.30S | 73.27W |
| Uchta | 102 | 63.33N | 53.38 E |
| Udaipur | 112 | 24.35N | 73.41 E |
| Uddevalla | 89 | 58.21N | 11.55 E |
| Udine | 96 | 46.03N | 13.14 E |
| Udon Thani | 120 | 17.26N | 102.46 E |
| Ueda | 116 | 36.24N | 138.16 E |
| Ufa | 86 | 54.44N | 55.56 E |
| Uganda **□¹** | 106 | 1.00N | 32.00 E |
| Uitenhage | 106 | 33.40S | 25.28 E |
| Ujiji | 106 | 4.55S | 29.41 E |
| Ujungpandang | 118 | 5.07S | 119.24 E |
| Ukiah | 142 | 39.09N | 123.12W |
| Ukraine **□¹** | 86 | 49.00N | 32.00 E |
| Ulaanbaatar | 114 | 47.55N | 106.53 E |
| Ulan Bator |  |  |  |
| → Ulaanbaatar | 114 | 47.55N | 106.53 E |
| Ulan-Ude | 102 | 51.50N | 107.37 E |
| Uleza | 98 | 41.41N | 19.54 E |
| Uljanovsk | 86 | 54.20N | 48.24 E |
| Ullŭng-do **I** | 116 | 37.29N | 130.52 E |
| Ulm | 90 | 48.24N | 10.00 E |
| Umeå | 89 | 63.50N | 20.15 E |
| Umm Durmān |  |  |  |
| (Omdurman) | 104 | 15.38N | 32.30 E |
| Umnak Island **I** | 144 | 53.25N | 168.10W |
| Umpqua **≃** | 142 | 43.42N | 124.03W |
| Unalakleet | 144 | 63.53N | 160.47W |
| Unalaska Island **I** | 144 | 53.45N | 166.45W |
| 'Unayzah | 108 | 26.06N | 43.56 E |
| Uncompahgre Peak **⋀** | 138 | 38.04N | 107.28W |
| Undu Cape **⋗** | 127c | 16.08S | 179.57W |
| Ungava, Péninsule d' |  |  |  |
| **⋗¹** | 136 | 60.00N | 74.00W |
| Ungava Bay **c** | 136 | 59.30N | 67.30W |
| Unimak Island **I** | 144 | 54.50N | 164.00W |
| Uniontown | 140 | 39.54N | 79.44W |
| United Arab Emirates |  |  |  |
| **□¹** | 108 | 24.00N | 54.00 E |
| United Kingdom **□¹** | 86 | 54.00N | 2.00W |
| United States **□¹** | 138 | 38.00N | 97.00W |
| Uozu | 116 | 36.48N | 137.24 E |
| Upata | 130 | 8.01N | 62.24W |
| Upington | 106 | 28.25S | 21.15 E |
| Upolu **I** | 127e | 13.55S | 171.45W |
| Upper Arlington | 140 | 40.00N | 83.03W |
| Upper Klamath Lake **⊘** | 142 | 42.23N | 122.55W |
| Upper Volta |  |  |  |
| → Burkina Faso **□¹** | 104 | 13.00N | 2.00W |
| Uppsala | 89 | 59.52N | 17.38 E |
| Ural **≃** | 86 | 47.00N | 51.48 E |
| Ural'skije Gory **⋌** | 102 | 66.00N | 63.00 E |
| Urbana | 140 | 40.06N | 83.45W |
| Uruapan [del Progreso] | 128 | 19.25N | 102.04W |
| Uruguaiana | 134 | 29.45S | 57.05W |
| Uruguay **□¹** | 134 | 33.00S | 56.00W |
| Uruguay (Uruguai) **≃** | 134 | 34.12S | 58.18W |
| Ürümqi | 114 | 43.48N | 87.35 E |
| Usa | 116 | 33.31N | 131.22 E |
| Uşak | 98 | 38.41N | 29.25 E |
| Ushibuka | 116 | 32.11N | 130.01 E |
| Ushuaia | 134 | 54.48S | 68.18W |
| Ussuri (Wusulijiang) **≃** | 102 | 48.27N | 135.04 E |
| Ussurijsk | 102 | 43.48N | 131.59 E |
| Ust'-Čaun | 102 | 68.47N | 170.30 E |
| Ústí nad Labem | 90 | 50.40N | 14.02 E |
| Ust'-Kut | 102 | 56.46N | 105.40 E |

| Name | Page No. | Lat. | Long. |
|------|----------|------|-------|
| West Bengal □³ | 112 | 24.00N | 88.00 E |
| Westerly | 140 | 41.22N | 71.49W |
| Western Australia □³ | 122 | 25.00S | 122.00 E |
| Western Ghāts ⟡ | 111 | 14.00N | 75.00 E |
| Western Sahara □² | 104 | 24.30N | 13.00W |
| Western Samoa □¹ | 127e | 13.55S | 172.00W |
| Westerville | 140 | 40.07N | 82.55W |
| West Falkland I | 134 | 51.50S | 60.00W |
| Westfield | 140 | 42.19N | 79.34W |
| West Indies II | 130 | 19.00N | 70.00W |
| West Liberty | 140 | 37.55N | 83.15W |
| Westminster | 140 | 39.34N | 76.59W |
| West Palm Beach | 138 | 26.42N | 80.03W |
| Westport | 126 | 41.45S | 171.36 E |
| West Virginia □³ | 138 | 38.45N | 80.30W |
| Wetaskiwin | 136 | 52.58N | 113.22W |
| Wexford | 88 | 52.20N | 6.27W |
| Weymouth | 88 | 50.36N | 2.28W |
| Whangarei | 126 | 35.43S | 174.19 E |
| Whataroa | 126 | 43.17S | 170.25 E |
| Wheeler Peak ⋀, Nv., U.S. | 142 | 38.59N | 114.19W |
| Wheeler Peak ⋀, N.M., U.S. | 138 | 36.34N | 105.25W |
| Wheeling | 140 | 40.03N | 80.43W |
| Whitehaven | 88 | 54.33N | 3.35W |
| Whitehorse | 136 | 60.43N | 135.03W |
| White Mountains ⟡ | 140 | 44.10N | 71.35W |
| White Nile (Al-Baḥr al-Abyaḍ) ≃ | 108 | 15.38N | 32.31 E |
| White Plains | 140 | 41.02N | 73.45W |
| White Sands National Monument ⁕ | 128 | 32.48N | 106.20W |
| White Volta (Volta Blanche) ≃ | 104 | 9.10N | 1.15W |
| Whitney, Mount ⋀ | 142 | 36.35N | 118.18W |
| Whyalla | 124 | 33.02S | 137.35 E |
| Wichita | 138 | 37.41N | 97.20W |
| Wichita Falls | 138 | 33.54N | 98.29W |
| Wielkopolska ⬥¹ | 90 | 51.50N | 17.20 E |
| Wien (Vienna) | 90 | 48.13N | 16.20 E |
| Wiener Neustadt | 90 | 47.49N | 16.15 E |
| Wieprz ≃ | 90 | 51.34N | 21.49 E |
| Wieprz-Krzna, Kanał ≋ | 90 | 51.56N | 22.56 E |
| Wiesbaden | 90 | 50.05N | 8.14 E |
| Wilhelm, Mount ⋀ | 118 | 5.45S | 145.05 E |
| Wilhelmshaven | 90 | 53.31N | 8.08 E |
| Wilkes-Barre | 140 | 41.14N | 75.52W |
| Wilkes Land ⬥¹ | 85 | 69.00S | 120.00 E |
| Willard | 140 | 41.03N | 82.44W |
| Willemstad | 130 | 12.06N | 68.56W |
| Williams Lake | 136 | 52.08N | 122.09W |
| Williamsport | 140 | 41.14N | 76.59W |
| Williston | 138 | 48.08N | 103.38W |
| Wilmington, De., U.S. | 140 | 39.44N | 75.32W |
| Wilmington, N.C., U.S. | 138 | 34.13N | 77.56W |
| Wiluna | 122 | 26.36S | 120.13 E |
| Winchester, In., U.S. | 140 | 40.10N | 84.58W |
| Winchester, Va., U.S. | 140 | 39.11N | 78.10W |
| Windhoek | 106 | 22.34S | 17.06 E |
| Windsor, N.S., Can. | 136 | 44.59N | 64.08W |
| Windsor, On., Can. | 136 | 42.18N | 83.01W |
| Windsor, P.Q., Can. | 140 | 45.34N | 72.00W |
| Windsor, Eng., U.K. | 88 | 51.29N | 0.38W |
| Windward Islands II | 130 | 13.00N | 61.00W |
| Windward Passage ⋃ | 138 | 20.00N | 73.50W |
| Winisk | 136 | 55.15N | 85.12W |
| Winisk Lake ⊜ | 136 | 52.55N | 87.22W |
| Winnemucca | 142 | 40.58N | 117.44W |
| Winnfield | 128 | 31.55N | 92.38W |
| Winnipeg | 136 | 49.53N | 97.09W |
| Winnipeg, Lake ⊜ | 136 | 52.00N | 97.00W |
| Winnipesaukee, Lake ⊜ | 140 | 43.35N | 71.20W |
| Winslow | 140 | 44.32N | 69.37W |
| Winston-Salem | 138 | 36.05N | 80.14W |

| Name | Page No. | Lat. | Long. |
|------|----------|------|-------|
| Winterport | 140 | 44.38N | 68.51W |
| Winton, Austl. | 122 | 22.23S | 143.02 E |
| Winton, N.Z. | 126 | 46.09S | 168.20 E |
| Wisconsin □³ | 138 | 44.45N | 89.30W |
| Wisła ≃ | 90 | 5.42N | 18.55 E |
| Wismar, Ger. | 90 | 53.53N | 11.28 E |
| Wismar, Guy. | 132 | 6.00N | 58.18W |
| Wittenberg | 90 | 51.52N | 12.39 E |
| Wittenberge | 90 | 53.00N | 11.44 E |
| Woleai I¹ | 118 | 7.21N | 143.52 E |
| Wolfsberg | 90 | 46.51N | 14.51 E |
| Wolfsburg | 90 | 52.25N | 10.47 E |
| Wollongong | 124 | 34.25S | 150.54 E |
| Wŏnsan | 114 | 39.09N | 127.25 E |
| Woodbridge | 140 | 38.39N | 77.15W |
| Woodland | 142 | 38.40N | 121.46W |
| Woodlark Island I | 122 | 9.05S | 152.50 E |
| Woods, Lake of the ⊜ | 138 | 49.15N | 94.45W |
| Woodstock | 140 | 43.08N | 80.45W |
| Woodsville | 140 | 44.09N | 72.02W |
| Woodville | 126 | 40.20S | 175.52 E |
| Woomera | 122 | 31.31S | 137.10 E |
| Woonsocket | 140 | 42.00N | 71.30W |
| Worcester, Eng., U.K. | 88 | 52.11N | 2.13W |
| Worcester, Ma., U.S. | 140 | 42.15N | 71.48W |
| Wrangell | 144 | 56.28N | 132.23W |
| Wrangell Mountains ⟡ | 144 | 62.00N | 143.00W |
| Wrexham | 88 | 53.03N | 3.00W |
| Wrocław (Breslau) | 90 | 51.06N | 17.00 E |
| Wuhan | 114 | 30.36N | 114.17 E |
| Wuhu | 114 | 31.21N | 118.22 E |
| Wuppertal | 90 | 51.16N | 7.11 E |
| Würzburg | 90 | 49.48N | 9.56 E |
| Wusulijiang (Ussuri) ≃ | 102 | 48.27N | 135.04 E |
| Wutongqiao | 114 | 29.26N | 103.51 E |
| Wyndham | 122 | 15.28S | 128.06 E |
| Wyoming □³ | 138 | 43.00N | 107.30W |

**X**

| Name | Page No. | Lat. | Long. |
|------|----------|------|-------|
| Xai-Xai | 106 | 25.02S | 33.34 E |
| Xam Nua | 120 | 20.25N | 104.02 E |
| Xánthi | 98 | 41.08N | 24.53 E |
| Xenia | 140 | 39.41N | 83.55W |
| Xi ≃ | 114 | 22.25N | 113.23 E |
| Xiamen | 114 | 24.28N | 118.07 E |
| Xi'an (Sian) | 114 | 34.15N | 108.52 E |
| Xiangtan | 114 | 27.51N | 112.54 E |
| Xingu ≃ | 132 | 1.30S | 51.53W |
| Xining | 114 | 36.38N | 101.55 E |
| Xinjiang Uygur Zizhiqu (Sinkiang) □⁴ | 114 | 40.00N | 85.00 E |
| Xinxiang | 114 | 35.20N | 113.51 E |
| Xinyang | 114 | 32.19N | 114.01 E |
| Xizang Zizhiqu □⁴ | 114 | 32.00N | 88.00 E |
| Xuzhou | 114 | 34.16N | 117.11 E |

**Y**

| Name | Page No. | Lat. | Long. |
|------|----------|------|-------|
| Yaizu | 116 | 34.52N | 138.20 E |
| Yakima | 138 | 46.36N | 120.30W |
| Yakumo | 116a | 42.15N | 140.16 E |
| Yakutat | 144 | 59.33N | 139.44W |
| Yakutsk — Jakutsk | 102 | 62.13N | 129.49 E |
| Yala | 120 | 6.33N | 101.18 E |
| Yamagata | 116 | 38.15N | 140.20 E |
| Yamaguchi | 116 | 34.10N | 131.29 E |
| Yamoussoukro | 104 | 6.49N | 5.17W |
| Yamsay Mountain ⋀ | 142 | 42.56N | 121.22W |
| Yanbuʿ | 108 | 24.05N | 38.03 E |
| Yandoon | 120 | 17.02N | 95.39 E |
| Yangquan | 114 | 37.52N | 113.36 E |

| Name | Page No. | Lat. | Long. |
|------|----------|------|-------|
| Yangtze | | | |
| → Chang ≃ | 114 | 31.48N | 121.10 E |
| Yantai (Chefoo) | 114 | 37.33N | 121.20 E |
| Yaoundé | 104 | 3.52N | 11.31 E |
| Yap I | 118 | 9.31N | 138.06 E |
| Yasawa Group II | 127c | 17.00S | 177.23 E |
| Yaté | 127b | 22.09S | 166.57 E |
| Yatsushiro | 116 | 32.30N | 130.36 E |
| Yatta Plateau ⚐¹ | 106 | 2.00S | 38.00 E |
| Yaviza | 130 | 8.11N | 77.41W |
| Yawatahama | 116 | 33.27N | 132.24 E |
| Yazd | 108 | 31.53N | 54.25 E |
| Yazoo City | 128 | 32.51N | 90.24W |
| Ye | 120 | 15.15N | 97.51 E |
| Yekïbastüz | 102 | 51.42N | 75.22 E |
| Yellow | | | |
| → Huang ≃ | 114 | 37.32N | 118.19 E |
| Yellowknife | 136 | 62.27N | 114.21W |
| Yellow Sea ▽² | 114 | 36.00N | 123.00 E |
| Yellowstone ≃ | 138 | 47.58N | 103.59W |
| Yellowstone Lake ☺ | 138 | 44.25N | 110.22W |
| Yemen □¹ | 108 | 15.00N | 47.00 E |
| Yenangyaung | 120 | 20.28N | 94.52 E |
| Yendéré | 104 | 10.12N | 4.58W |
| Yenisey | | | |
| → Jenisej ≃ | 102 | 71.50N | 82.40 E |
| Yerevan | | | |
| → Jerevan | 86 | 40.11N | 44.30 E |
| Yerushalayim | | | |
| (Jerusalem) | 109 | 31.46N | 35.14 E |
| Yiannitsá | 98 | 40.48N | 22.25 E |
| Yibin | 114 | 28.47N | 104.38 E |
| Yinchuan | 114 | 38.30N | 106.18 E |
| Yingkou | 114 | 40.40N | 122.14 E |
| Yining (Kuldja) | 114 | 43.55N | 81.14 E |
| Yogyakarta | 118 | 7.48S | 110.22 E |
| Yokkaichi | 116 | 34.58N | 136.37 E |
| Yokohama | 116 | 35.27N | 139.39 E |
| Yokosuka | 116 | 35.18N | 139.40 E |
| Yonago | 116 | 35.26N | 133.20 E |
| Yonezawa | 116 | 37.55N | 140.07 E |
| Yonkers | 140 | 40.55N | 73.53W |
| York, Eng., U.K. | 88 | 53.58N | 1.05W |
| York, Pa., U.S. | 140 | 39.57N | 76.43W |
| York, Cape ➤ | 122 | 10.42S | 142.31 E |
| York Factory | 136 | 57.00N | 92.18W |
| Yorkton | 136 | 51.13N | 102.28W |
| Yoro | 130 | 15.09N | 87.07W |
| Yosemite National | | | |
| Park ◆ | 142 | 37.51N | 119.33W |
| Yos Sudarsa, Pulau I | 118 | 7.50S | 138.30 E |
| Youngstown | 140 | 41.05N | 80.38W |
| Yuba City | 142 | 39.08N | 121.36W |
| Yucatan Channel ⋃ | 130 | 21.45N | 85.45W |
| Yucatan Peninsula ➤¹ | 128 | 19.30N | 89.00W |
| Yucca | 142 | 34.52N | 114.08W |
| Yugoslavia □¹ | 86 | 44.00N | 20.00 E |
| Yukon □⁴ | 144 | 64.00N | 135.00W |
| Yukon ≃ | 144 | 62.33N | 163.59W |
| Yukuhashi | 116 | 33.44N | 130.59 E |
| Yuma | 138 | 32.43N | 114.37W |
| Yumen | 114 | 39.56N | 97.51 E |
| Yurimaguas | 132 | 5.54S | 76.05W |

| Name | Page No. | Lat. | Long. |
|------|----------|------|-------|
| **Z** | | | |
| Zaandam | 90 | 52.26N | 4.49 E |
| Zacapa | 128 | 14.58N | 89.32W |
| Zacatecas | 128 | 22.47N | 102.35W |
| Zagreb | 96 | 45.48N | 15.58 E |
| Zāgros, Kühhä-ye ⚲ | 108 | 33.40N | 47.00 E |
| Zaḥlah | 109 | 33.51N | 35.53 E |
| Zaire □¹ | 106 | 4.00S | 25.00 E |
| Zákinthos I | 98 | 37.52N | 20.44 E |
| Zalaegerszeg | 90 | 46.51N | 16.51 E |
| Zambezi (Zambeze) ≃ | 106 | 18.55S | 36.04 E |
| Zambia □¹ | 106 | 15.00S | 30.00 E |
| Zamboanga | 118 | 6.54N | 122.04 E |
| Zamora | 94 | 41.30N | 5.45W |
| Zamora de Hidalgo | 128 | 19.59N | 102.16W |
| Zamość | 90 | 50.44N | 23.15 E |
| Zanesville | 140 | 39.56N | 82.00W |
| Zanzibar | 106 | 6.10S | 39.11 E |
| Zanzibar Island I | 106 | 6.10S | 39.20 E |
| Zapadnaja Dvina | | | |
| (Daugava) ≃ | 100 | 57.04N | 24.03 E |
| Zapadno-Sibirskaja | | | |
| Nizmennost' ≅ | 102 | 60.00N | 75.00 E |
| Zapala | 134 | 38.54S | 70.04W |
| Zaporizhzhya | 86 | 47.50N | 35.10 E |
| Zaragoza | 94 | 41.38N | 0.53W |
| Zárate | 134 | 34.06S | 59.02W |
| Zaraza | 130 | 9.21N | 65.19W |
| Zaria | 104 | 11.07N | 7.44 E |
| Żary (Sorau) | 90 | 51.38N | 15.09 E |
| Zawiercie | 90 | 50.30N | 19.25 E |
| Zāwiyat al-Bayḍā' | 104 | 32.46N | 21.43 E |
| Zaysan kölï ☺ | 102 | 48.00N | 84.00 E |
| Zduńska Wola | 90 | 51.36N | 18.57 E |
| Zeerust | 106 | 25.33S | 26.06 E |
| Zeja | 102 | 53.45N | 127.15 E |
| Zelee, Cape ➤ | 127a | 9.45S | 161.34 E |
| Zgierz | 90 | 51.52N | 19.25 E |
| Zhambyl | 114 | 42.54N | 71.22 E |
| Zhangjiakou | 114 | 40.50N | 114.53 E |
| Zhangzhou | 114 | 24.33N | 117.39 E |
| Zhanjiang | 114 | 21.16N | 110.28 E |
| Zhengzhou | 114 | 34.48N | 113.39 E |
| Zhuzhou | 114 | 27.50N | 113.09 E |
| Zhytomyr | 86 | 50.16N | 28.40 E |
| Zigong | 114 | 29.24N | 104.47 E |
| Ziguinchor | 104 | 12.35N | 16.16W |
| Žilina | 90 | 49.14N | 18.46 E |
| Zimbabwe □¹ | 106 | 20.00S | 30.00 E |
| Zlín | 90 | 49.13N | 17.41 E |
| Złobin | 100 | 52.54N | 30.03 E |
| Znojmo | 90 | 48.52N | 16.02 E |
| Zomba | 106 | 15.23S | 35.18 E |
| Zudañez | 132 | 19.06S | 64.44W |
| Zugspitze ⋀ | 90 | 47.25N | 10.59 E |
| Zuiderzee | | | |
| → IJsselmeer ▽² | 90 | 52.45N | 5.25 E |
| Zululand □⁹ | 106 | 28.10S | 32.00 E |
| Zunyi | 114 | 27.39N | 106.57 E |
| Zürich | 92 | 47.23N | 8.32 E |
| Zvolen | 90 | 48.35N | 19.08 E |
| Zwettl | 90 | 48.37N | 15.10 E |
| Zwickau | 90 | 50.44N | 12.29 E |
| Zwolle | 90 | 52.30N | 6.05 E |

# World Flags

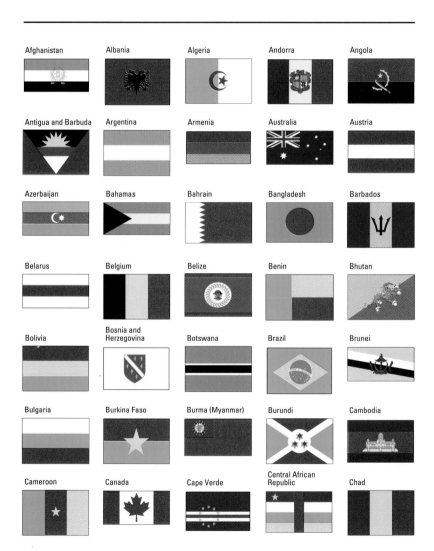

Afghanistan

Albania

Algeria

Andorra

Angola

Antigua and Barbuda

Argentina

Armenia

Australia

Austria

Azerbaijan

Bahamas

Bahrain

Bangladesh

Barbados

Belarus

Belgium

Belize

Benin

Bhutan

Bolivia

Bosnia and Herzegovina

Botswana

Brazil

Brunei

Bulgaria

Burkina Faso

Burma (Myanmar)

Burundi

Cambodia

Cameroon

Canada

Cape Verde

Central African Republic

Chad

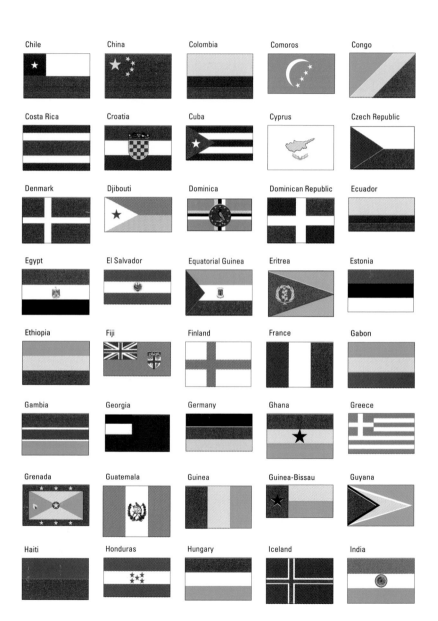

Chile

China

Colombia

Comoros

Congo

Costa Rica

Croatia

Cuba

Cyprus

Czech Republic

Denmark

Djibouti

Dominica

Dominican Republic

Ecuador

Egypt

El Salvador

Equatorial Guinea

Eritrea

Estonia

Ethiopia

Fiji

Finland

France

Gabon

Gambia

Georgia

Germany

Ghana

Greece

Grenada

Guatemala

Guinea

Guinea-Bissau

Guyana

Haiti

Honduras

Hungary

Iceland

India

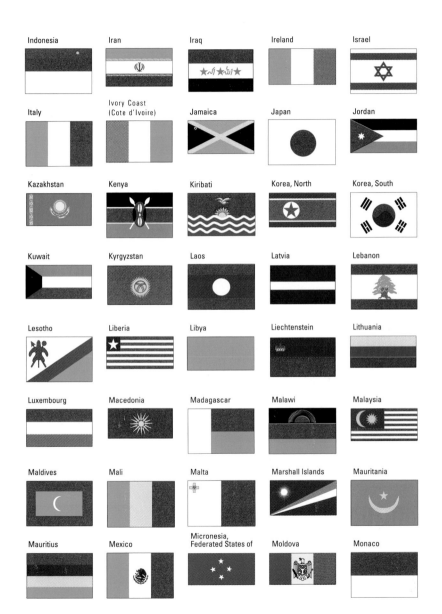

Indonesia

Iran

Iraq

Ireland

Israel

Italy

Ivory Coast
(Cote d'Ivoire)

Jamaica

Japan

Jordan

Kazakhstan

Kenya

Kiribati

Korea, North

Korea, South

Kuwait

Kyrgyzstan

Laos

Latvia

Lebanon

Lesotho

Liberia

Libya

Liechtenstein

Lithuania

Luxembourg

Macedonia

Madagascar

Malawi

Malaysia

Maldives

Mali

Malta

Marshall Islands

Mauritania

Mauritius

Mexico

Micronesia,
Federated States of

Moldova

Monaco

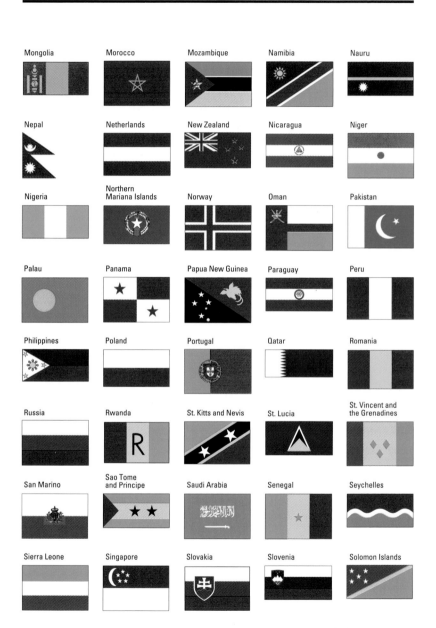

| Mongolia | Morocco | Mozambique | Namibia | Nauru |
| Nepal | Netherlands | New Zealand | Nicaragua | Niger |
| Nigeria | Northern Mariana Islands | Norway | Oman | Pakistan |
| Palau | Panama | Papua New Guinea | Paraguay | Peru |
| Philippines | Poland | Portugal | Qatar | Romania |
| Russia | Rwanda | St. Kitts and Nevis | St. Lucia | St. Vincent and the Grenadines |
| San Marino | Sao Tome and Principe | Saudi Arabia | Senegal | Seychelles |
| Sierra Leone | Singapore | Slovakia | Slovenia | Solomon Islands |

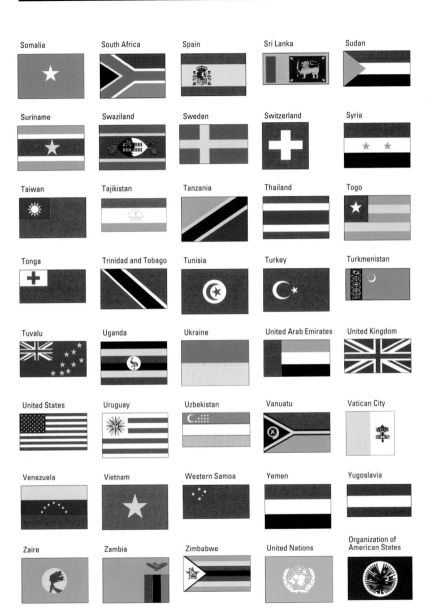

Somalia

South Africa

Spain

Sri Lanka

Sudan

Suriname

Swaziland

Sweden

Switzerland

Syria

Taiwan

Tajikistan

Tanzania

Thailand

Togo

Tonga

Trinidad and Tobago

Tunisia

Turkey

Turkmenistan

Tuvalu

Uganda

Ukraine

United Arab Emirates

United Kingdom

United States

Uruguay

Uzbekistan

Vanuatu

Vatican City

Venezuela

Vietnam

Western Samoa

Yemen

Yugoslavia

Zaire

Zambia

Zimbabwe

United Nations

Organization of
American States

# Country Profiles

## Afghanistan (Afghānestān)
**Location:** Southern Asia, landlocked
**Area:** 251,826 mi² (652,225 km²)
**Population:** 16,880,000 (Urban: 22%)
**Literacy:** 29%
**Capital:** Kabōl, 1,424,400
**Government:** Republic
**Languages:** Dari, Pashto, Uzbek, Turkmen
**Ethnic Groups:** Pathan 50%, Tajik 25%,
Uzbek 9%, Hazara 9%
**Religions:** Sunni Muslim 74%, Shiite
Muslim 15%
**Currency:** Afghani

## Albania (Shqipëria)
**Location:** Southeastern Europe
**Area:** 11,100 mi² (28,748 km²)
**Population:** 3,352,000 (Urban: 35%)
**Literacy:** 72%
**Capital:** Tiranë, 238,100
**Government:** Republic
**Languages:** Albanian, Greek
**Ethnic Groups:** Albanian (Illyrian) 96%
**Religions:** Muslim 20%, Christian 5%
**Currency:** Lek
**Tel. Area Code:** 355

## Algeria (El Djazaïr)
**Location:** Northern Africa
**Area:** 919,595 mi² (2,381,741 km²)
**Population:** 26,360,000 (Urban: 45%)
**Literacy:** 50%
**Capital:** El Djazaïr (Algiers), 1,507,241
**Government:** Provisional military
government
**Languages:** Arabic, Berber dialects, French
**Ethnic Groups:** Arab-Berber 99%
**Religions:** Sunni Muslim 99%, Christian and
Jewish
**Currency:** Dinar
**Tel. Area Code:** 213

## Angola
**Location:** Southern Africa
**Area:** 481,354 mi² (1,246,700 km²)
**Population:** 10,425,000 (Urban: 28%)
**Literacy:** 42%
**Capital:** Luanda, 1,459,900
**Government:** Republic
**Languages:** Portuguese, indigenous
**Ethnic Groups:** Ovimbundu 37%,
Mbundu 25%, Kongo 13%, mulatto 2%,
European 1%
**Religions:** Animist 47%, Roman
Catholic 38%, other Christian 15%
**Currency:** Kwanza
**Tel. Area Code:** 244

## Antigua and Barbuda
**Location:** Caribbean islands
**Area:** 171 mi² (443 km²)
**Population:** 64,000 (Urban: 32%)
**Literacy:** 89%
**Capital:** St. John's, 24,359
**Government:** Parliamentary state
**Languages:** English, local dialects
**Ethnic Groups:** Black
**Religions:** Anglican, Protestant, Roman
Catholic
**Currency:** East Caribbean dollar
**Tel. Area Code:** 809

## Argentina
**Location:** Southern South America
**Area:** 1,073,400 mi² (2,780,092 km²)
**Population:** 32,860,000 (Urban: 86%)
**Literacy:** 95%
**Capital:** Buenos Aires, 2,922,829
**Government:** Republic
**Languages:** Spanish, English, Italian,
German, French
**Ethnic Groups:** White 85%, mestizo,
Amerindian, and others 15%
**Religions:** Roman Catholic 90%, Jewish 2%,
Protestant
**Currency:** Peso
**Tel. Area Code:** 54

## Armenia (Hayastan)
**Location:** Southwestern Asia, landlocked
**Area:** 11,506 mi² (29,800 km²)
**Population:** 3,360,000 (Urban: 68%)
**Literacy:** 99%

Capital: Jerevan, 1,199,000
Government: Republic
Languages: Armenian, Azerbaijani, Russian
Ethnic Groups: Armenian 93%, Azeri 3%,
  Russian 2%
Religions: Armenian orthodox
Currency: Ruble
Tel. Area Code: 7

## Australia

Location: Continent between South Pacific
  and Indian oceans
Area: 2,966,155 mi$^2$ (7,682,300 km$^2$)
Population: 17,420,000 (Urban: 86%)
Literacy: 100%
Capital: Canberra, 247,194
Government: Parliamentary state
Languages: English, indigenous
Ethnic Groups: European 95%, Asian 4%,
  Aboriginal and other 1%
Religions: Anglican 24%, Roman
  Catholic 26%, other Christian 23%
Currency: Dollar
Tel. Area Code: 61

## Austria (Österreich)

Location: Central Europe, landlocked
Area: 32,377 mi$^2$ (83,855 km$^2$)
Population: 7,681,000 (Urban: 58%)
Literacy: 99%
Capital: Wien (Vienna), 1,482,800
Government: Republic
Languages: German
Ethnic Groups: German 99%
Religions: Roman Catholic 85%,
  Protestant 6%
Currency: Schilling
Tel. Area Code: 43

## Azerbaijan (Azerbajdžan)

Location: Southwestern Asia, landlocked
Area: 33,436 mi$^2$ (86,600 km$^2$)
Population: 7,170,000 (Urban: 54%)
Literacy: 98%
Capital: Bakı (Baku), 1,080,500
Government: Republic
Languages: Azerbaijani, Russian, Armenian
Ethnic Groups: Azeri 83%, Armenian 6%,
  Russian 6%
Religions: Muslim, Christian
Currency: Ruble
Tel. Area Code: 7

## Bahamas

Location: Caribbean islands
Area: 5,382 mi$^2$ (13,939 km$^2$)
Population: 260,000 (Urban: 59%)
Literacy: 90%
Capital: Nassau, 141,000
Government: Parliamentary state
Languages: English, Creole
Ethnic Groups: Black 85%, white 15%
Religions: Baptist 29%, Anglican 23%,
  Roman Catholic 22%
Currency: Dollar
Tel. Area Code: 809

## Bahrain (Al-Bahrayn)

Location: Southwestern Asian islands (in
  Persian Gulf)
Area: 267 mi$^2$ (691 km$^2$)
Population: 546,000 (Urban: 83%)
Literacy: 77%
Capital: Al-Manāmah (Manama), 115,054
Government: Monarchy
Languages: Arabic, English, Farsi, Urdu
Ethnic Groups: Bahraini 63%, Asian 13%,
  other Arab 10%
Religions: Shiite Muslim 70%, Sunni
  Muslim 30%
Currency: Dinar
Tel. Area Code: 973

## Bangladesh

Location: Southern Asia
Area: 55,598 mi$^2$ (143,998 km$^2$)
Population: 118,000,000 (Urban: 14%)
Literacy: 35%
Capital: Dhaka, 2,365,695
Government: Islamic republic
Languages: Bangla, English
Ethnic Groups: Bengali 98%
Religions: Muslim 83%, Hindu 16%
Currency: Taka
Tel. Area Code: 880

## Barbados

Location: Caribbean island
Area: 166 mi$^2$ (430 km$^2$)
Population: 257,000 (Urban: 45%)
Literacy: 99%
Capital: Bridgetown, 7,466
Government: Parliamentary state
Languages: English
Ethnic Groups: Black 92%, white 3%,
  mixed 3%, East Indian 1%
Religions: Anglican 40%, Pentecostal 8%,
  Methodist 7%, Roman Catholic 4%

Currency: Dollar
Tel. Area Code: 809

## Belarus (Byelarus')

Location: Eastern Europe, landlocked
Area: 80,155 mi² (207,600 km²)
Population: 10,390,000 (Urban: 65%)
Literacy: 99%
Capital: Minsk, 1,633,600
Government: Republic
Languages: Belorussian, Russian
Ethnic Groups: Belorussian 78%,
Russian 13%, Polish 4%
Religions: Eastern Orthodox, Roman
Catholic
Currency: Ruble
Tel. Area Code: 7

## Belgium (Belgique, België)

Location: Western Europe
Area: 11,783 mi² (30,518 km²)
Population: 9,932,000 (Urban: 97%)
Literacy: 99%
Capital: Bruxelles (Brussels), 136,920
Government: Constitutional monarchy
Languages: Dutch (Flemish), French,
German
Ethnic Groups: Fleming 55%, Walloon 33%,
mixed and others 12%
Religions: Roman Catholic 75%
Currency: Franc
Tel. Area Code: 32

## Belize

Location: Central America
Area: 8,866 mi² (22,963 km²)
Population: 232,000 (Urban: 52%)
Literacy: 91%
Capital: Belmopan, 5,256
Government: Parliamentary state
Languages: English, Spanish, Garifuna,
Mayan
Ethnic Groups: Creole 40%, mestizo 33%,
Amerindian 16%
Religions: Roman Catholic 62%,
Anglican 12%, Methodist 6%,
Mennonite 4%
Currency: Dollar
Tel. Area Code: 501

## Benin (Bénin)

Location: Western Africa
Area: 43,475 mi² (112,600 km²)
Population: 4,914,000 (Urban: 42%)
Literacy: 23%
Capital: Porto-Novo (designated), 164,000;
Cotonou (de facto), 478,000
Government: Republic
Languages: French, Fon, Adja, indigenous
Ethnic Groups: Fon 39%, Yoruba 12%,
Adja 10%, others
Religions: Fetishism 70%, Muslim 15%,
Christian 15%
Currency: CFA franc
Tel. Area Code: 229

## Bhutan (Druk-Yul)

Location: Southern Asia, landlocked
Area: 17,954 mi² (46,500 km²)
Population: 1,614,000 (Urban: 5%)
Capital: Thimphu, 12,000
Government: Monarchy (Indian protection)
Languages: Dzongkha, Tibetan and
Nepalese dialects
Ethnic Groups: Bhotia 60%, Nepalese 25%,
indigenous 15%
Religions: Buddhist 75%, Hindu 25%
Currency: Ngultrum, Indian rupee
Tel. Area Code: 975

## Bolivia

Location: Central South America,
landlocked
Area: 424,165 mi² (1,098,581 km²)
Population: 7,243,000 (Urban: 51%)
Literacy: 78%
Capital: La Paz (seat of government),
1,125,600; Sucre (seat of judiciary),
101,400
Government: Republic
Languages: Aymara, Quechua, Spanish
Ethnic Groups: Quechua 30%, Aymara 25%,
mixed 25-30%, European 5-15%
Religions: Roman Catholic 95%, Methodist
and other Protestant
Currency: Boliviano
Tel. Area Code: 591

## Bosnia and Herzegovina (Bosna i Hercegovina)

Location: Eastern Europe
Area: 19,741 mi² (51,129 km²)
Population: 4,519,000 (Urban: 36%)
Literacy: 86%
Capital: Sarajevo, 341,200

**Government:** Republic
**Languages:** Serb, Croat, Albanian
**Ethnic Groups:** Bosnian, Serbian, Croatian
**Religions:** Serbian Orthodox, Muslim,
Roman Catholic
**Currency:** Yugoslavian dinar
**Tel. Area Code:** 38

## Botswana

**Location:** Southern Africa, landlocked
**Area:** 224,711 mi$^2$ (582,000 km$^2$)
**Population:** 1,345,000 (Urban: 24%)
**Literacy:** 23%
**Capital:** Gaborone, 133,791
**Government:** Republic
**Languages:** English, Tswana
**Ethnic Groups:** Tswana 95%; Kalanga,
Baswara, and Kgalagadi 4%; white 1%
**Religions:** Tribal religionist 50%, Roman
Catholic and other Christian 50%
**Currency:** Pula
**Tel. Area Code:** 267

## Brazil (Brasil)

**Location:** Eastern South America
**Area:** 3,286,488 mi$^2$ (8,511,965 km$^2$)
**Population:** 156,750,000 (Urban: 77%)
**Literacy:** 81%
**Capital:** Brasília, 1,567,709
**Government:** Republic
**Languages:** Portuguese, Spanish, English,
French
**Ethnic Groups:** White 55%, mixed 38%,
black 6%
**Religions:** Roman Catholic 96%
**Currency:** Cruzeiro
**Tel. Area Code:** 55

## Brunei

**Location:** Southeastern Asia (island of
Borneo)
**Area:** 2,226 mi$^2$ (5,765 km$^2$)
**Population:** 411,000 (Urban: 58%)
**Literacy:** 78%
**Capital:** Bandar Seri Begawan, 22,777
**Government:** Monarchy
**Languages:** Malay, English, Chinese
**Ethnic Groups:** Malay 65%, Chinese 20%,
indigenous 8%, Tamil 3%
**Religions:** Muslim 63%, Buddhist 14%,
Roman Catholic and other Christian 10%
**Currency:** Dollar
**Tel. Area Code:** 673

## Bulgaria (Bâlgarija)

**Location:** Eastern Europe
**Area:** 42,823 mi$^2$ (110,912 km$^2$)
**Population:** 8,902,000 (Urban: 70%)
**Literacy:** 93%
**Capital:** Sofija (Sofia), 1,136,875
**Government:** Republic
**Languages:** Bulgarian
**Ethnic Groups:** Bulgarian (Slavic) 85%,
Turkish 9%, Gypsy 3%, Macedonian 3%
**Religions:** Bulgarian Orthodox, Muslim
**Currency:** Lev
**Tel. Area Code:** 359

## Burkina Faso

**Location:** Western Africa, landlocked
**Area:** 105,869 mi$^2$ (274,200 km$^2$)
**Population:** 9,510,000 (Urban: 9%)
**Literacy:** 18%
**Capital:** Ouagadougou, 441,514
**Government:** Provisional military
government
**Languages:** French, indigenous
**Ethnic Groups:** Mossi 30%, Fulani, Lobi,
Malinke, Bobo, Senufo, Gurunsi, others
**Religions:** Animist 65%, Muslim 25%,
Roman Catholic and other Christian
**Currency:** CFA franc
**Tel. Area Code:** 226

## Burundi

**Location:** Eastern Africa, landlocked
**Area:** 10,745 mi$^2$ (27,830 km$^2$)
**Population:** 5,924,000 (Urban: 7%)
**Literacy:** 50%
**Capital:** Bujumbura, 226,628
**Government:** Republic
**Languages:** French, Kirundi, Swahili
**Ethnic Groups:** Hutu 85%, Tutsi 14%,
Twa 1%
**Religions:** Roman Catholic 62%,
Animist 32%, Protestant 5%, Muslim 1%
**Currency:** Franc
**Tel. Area Code:** 257

## Cambodia (Kâmpŭchéa)

**Location:** Southeastern Asia
**Area:** 69,898 mi$^2$ (181,035 km$^2$)
**Population:** 8,543,000 (Urban: 12%)
**Literacy:** 35%
**Capital:** Phnum Pénh (Phnom Penh),
477,874
**Government:** Socialist republic
**Languages:** Khmer, French
**Ethnic Groups:** Khmer 90%, Chinese 5%

**Religions:** Buddhist 95%, Animist, Muslim
**Currency:** Riel
**Tel. Area Code:** 855

## Cameroon (Cameroun)

**Location:** Central Africa
**Area:** 183,569 mi$^2$ (475,442 km$^2$)
**Population:** 11,550,000 (Urban: 49%)
**Literacy:** 54%
**Capital:** Yaoundé, 653,670
**Government:** Republic
**Languages:** English, French, indigenous
**Ethnic Groups:** Cameroon Highlander 31%, Equatorial Bantu 19%, Kirdi 11%, Fulani 10%
**Religions:** Animist 51%, Christian 33%, Muslim 16%
**Currency:** CFA franc
**Tel. Area Code:** 237

## Canada

**Location:** Northern North America
**Area:** 3,849,674 mi$^2$ (9,970,610 km$^2$)
**Population:** 26,985,000 (Urban: 76%)
**Literacy:** 99%
**Capital:** Ottawa, 300,763
**Government:** Parliamentary state
**Languages:** English, French
**Ethnic Groups:** British origin 40%, French origin 27%, other European 23%, native Canadian 2%
**Religions:** Roman Catholic 47%, United Church 16%, Anglican 10%, other Christian
**Currency:** Dollar

## Cape Verde (Cabo Verde)

**Location:** Western African islands
**Area:** 1,557 mi$^2$ (4,033 km$^2$)
**Population:** 393,000 (Urban: 52%)
**Literacy:** 66%
**Capital:** Praia, 61,797
**Government:** Republic
**Languages:** Portuguese, Crioulo
**Ethnic Groups:** Creole (mulatto) 71%, African 28%, European 1%
**Religions:** Roman Catholic, Nazarene and other Protestant
**Currency:** Escudo
**Tel. Area Code:** 238

## Central African Republic (République centrafricaine)

**Location:** Central Africa, landlocked
**Area:** 240,535 mi$^2$ (622,984 km$^2$)
**Population:** 2,990,000 (Urban: 47%)
**Literacy:** 27%
**Capital:** Bangui, 473,817
**Government:** Republic
**Languages:** French, Sango, Arabic, indigenous
**Ethnic Groups:** Baya 34%, Banda 27%, Mandja 21%, Sara 10%
**Religions:** Protestant 25%, Roman Catholic 25%, Animist 24%, Muslim 15%
**Currency:** CFA franc
**Tel. Area Code:** 236

## Chad (Tchad)

**Location:** Central Africa, landlocked
**Area:** 495,755 mi$^2$ (1,284,000 km$^2$)
**Population:** 5,178,000 (Urban: 33%)
**Literacy:** 30%
**Capital:** N'Djamena, 500,000
**Government:** Republic
**Languages:** Arabic, French, indigenous
**Ethnic Groups:** Sara and other African, Arab
**Religions:** Muslim 44%, Christian 33%, Animist 23%
**Currency:** CFA franc
**Tel. Area Code:** 235

## Chile

**Location:** Southern South America
**Area:** 292,135 mi$^2$ (756,626 km$^2$)
**Population:** 13,395,000 (Urban: 86%)
**Literacy:** 93%
**Capital:** Santiago, 232,667
**Government:** Republic
**Languages:** Spanish
**Ethnic Groups:** White and mestizo 95%, Amerindian 3%
**Religions:** Roman Catholic 89%, Pentecostal and other Protestant 11%
**Currency:** Peso
**Tel. Area Code:** 56

## China (Zhongguo)

**Location:** Eastern Asia
**Area:** 3,689,631 mi$^2$ (9,556,100 km$^2$)
**Population:** 1,181,580,000 (Urban: 21%)
**Literacy:** 73%
**Capital:** Beijing (Peking), 6,710,000
**Government:** Socialist republic
**Languages:** Chinese dialects

**Ethnic Groups:** Han Chinese 93%, Zhuang, Hui, Uygur, Yi, Miao, Manchu, Tibetan, others
**Religions:** Confucian, Taoist, Buddhist, Muslim
**Currency:** Yuan
**Tel. Area Code:** 86

## Colombia
**Location:** Northern South America
**Area:** 440,831 mi$^2$ (1,141,748 km$^2$)
**Population:** 33,170,000 (Urban: 70%)
**Literacy:** 87%
**Capital:** Santa Fe de Bogotá, 3,982,941
**Government:** Republic
**Languages:** Spanish
**Ethnic Groups:** Mestizo 58%, white 20%, mulatto 14%, black 4%
**Religions:** Roman Catholic 95%
**Currency:** Peso
**Tel. Area Code:** 57

## Comoros (Al-Qumur, Comores)
**Location:** Southeastern African islands
**Area:** 863 mi$^2$ (2,235 km$^2$)
**Population:** 484,000 (Urban: 28%)
**Literacy:** 48%
**Capital:** Moroni, 23,432
**Government:** Islamic republic
**Languages:** Arabic, French, Shaafi Islam (Swahili), Malagasy
**Ethnic Groups:** African-Arab descent (Antalote, Cafre, Makua, Oimatsaha, Sakalava)
**Religions:** Sunni Muslim 86%, Roman Catholic 14%
**Currency:** Franc
**Tel. Area Code:** 269

## Congo
**Location:** Central Africa
**Area:** 132,047 mi$^2$ (342,000 km$^2$)
**Population:** 2,344,000 (Urban: 42%)
**Literacy:** 57%
**Capital:** Brazzaville, 585,812
**Government:** Socialist republic
**Languages:** French, Lingala, Kikongo, indigenous
**Ethnic Groups:** Kongo 48%, Sangho 20%, Bateke 17%, Mbochis 12%
**Religions:** Christian 50%, Animist 48%, Muslim 2%
**Currency:** CFA franc
**Tel. Area Code:** 242

## Costa Rica
**Location:** Central America
**Area:** 19,730 mi$^2$ (51,100 km$^2$)
**Population:** 3,151,000 (Urban: 54%)
**Literacy:** 93%
**Capital:** San José, 278,600
**Government:** Republic
**Languages:** Spanish
**Ethnic Groups:** White and mestizo 96%, black 3%, Amerindian 1%
**Religions:** Roman Catholic 95%
**Currency:** Colon
**Tel. Area Code:** 506

## Cote d'Ivoire
**Location:** Western Africa
**Area:** 124,518 mi$^2$ (322,500 km$^2$)
**Population:** 13,240,000 (Urban: 47%)
**Literacy:** 54%
**Capital:** Abidjan (de facto), 1,950,000; Yamoussoukro (future), 80,000
**Government:** Republic
**Languages:** French, indigenous
**Ethnic Groups:** Baule 23%, Bete 18%, Senoufou 15%, Malinke 11%, other African
**Religions:** Animist 63%, Muslim 25%, Christian 12%
**Currency:** CFA franc
**Tel. Area Code:** 225

## Croatia (Hrvatska)
**Location:** Eastern Europe
**Area:** 21,829 mi$^2$ (56,538 km$^2$)
**Population:** 4,800,000 (Urban: 51%)
**Literacy:** 92%
**Capital:** Zagreb, 697,925
**Government:** Republic
**Languages:** Croatian, Serbian
**Ethnic Groups:** Croatian, Serbian
**Religions:** Roman Catholic
**Currency:** Yugoslavian dinar
**Tel. Area Code:** 38

## Cuba
**Location:** Caribbean island
**Area:** 42,804 mi$^2$ (110,861 km$^2$)
**Population:** 10,785,000 (Urban: 75%)
**Literacy:** 94%
**Capital:** La Habana (Havana), 2,119,059
**Government:** Socialist republic
**Languages:** Spanish
**Ethnic Groups:** White 66%, mixed 22%, black 12%

**Religions:** Roman Catholic, Pentecostal,
Baptist
**Currency:** Peso

## Cyprus (Kípros, Kıbrıs)

**Location:** Southern part of the island of
Cyprus
**Area:** 2,276 mi$^2$ (5,896 km$^2$)
**Population:** 713,000 (Urban: 53%)
**Literacy:** 90%
**Capital:** Nicosia (Levkosía), 48,221
**Government:** Republic
**Languages:** Greek, English
**Ethnic Groups:** Greek
**Religions:** Greek Orthodox
**Currency:** Pound
**Tel. Area Code:** 357

## Czech Republic (Česká Republika)

**Location:** Eastern Europe, landlocked
**Area:** 30,450 mi$^2$ (78,864 km$^2$)
**Population:** 10,335,000
**Capital:** Prague (Praha), 1,215,656
**Government:** Republic
**Languages:** Czech, Slovak
**Ethnic Groups:** Czech, Slovak
**Religions:** Roman Catholic, Evangelical,
Hussite, Uniate
**Currency:** Koruna
**Tel. Area Code:** 42

## Denmark (Danmark)

**Location:** Northern Europe
**Area:** 16,638 mi$^2$ (43,093 km$^2$)
**Population:** 5,154,000 (Urban: 86%)
**Literacy:** 99%
**Capital:** København (Copenhagen), 466,723
**Government:** Constitutional monarchy
**Languages:** Danish
**Ethnic Groups:** Danish (Scandinavian),
German
**Religions:** Lutheran 90%
**Currency:** Krone
**Tel. Area Code:** 45

## Djibouti

**Location:** Eastern Africa
**Area:** 8,958 mi$^2$ (23,200 km$^2$)
**Population:** 351,000 (Urban: 81%)
**Literacy:** 48%
**Capital:** Djibouti, 120,000
**Government:** Republic
**Languages:** French, Somali, Afar, Arabic
**Ethnic Groups:** Somali (Issa) 60%, Afar 35%
**Religions:** Muslim 94%, Christian 6%

**Currency:** Franc
**Tel. Area Code:** 253

## Dominica

**Location:** Caribbean island
**Area:** 305 mi$^2$ (790 km$^2$)
**Population:** 87,000 (Urban: 27%)
**Literacy:** 94%
**Capital:** Roseau, 9,348
**Government:** Republic
**Languages:** English, French
**Ethnic Groups:** Black 91%, mixed 6%, West
Indian 2%
**Religions:** Roman Catholic 77%,
Methodist 5%, Pentecostal 3%
**Currency:** East Caribbean dollar
**Tel. Area Code:** 809

## Dominican Republic (República Dominicana)

**Location:** Caribbean island (eastern
Hispaniola)
**Area:** 18,704 mi$^2$ (48,442 km$^2$)
**Population:** 8,124,000 (Urban: 60%)
**Literacy:** 83%
**Capital:** Santo Domingo, 2,411,900
**Government:** Republic
**Languages:** Spanish
**Ethnic Groups:** Mulatto 73%, white 16%,
black 11%
**Religions:** Roman Catholic 95%
**Currency:** Peso
**Tel. Area Code:** 809

## Ecuador

**Location:** Western South America
**Area:** 109,484 mi$^2$ (283,561 km$^2$)
**Population:** 10,880,000 (Urban: 57%)
**Literacy:** 86%
**Capital:** Quito, 1,094,318
**Government:** Republic
**Languages:** Spanish, Quechua, indigenous
**Ethnic Groups:** Mestizo 65%,
Amerindian 25%, white 7%, black 10%
**Religions:** Roman Catholic 95%
**Currency:** Sucre
**Tel. Area Code:** 593

## Egypt (Misr)

**Location:** Northeastern Africa
**Area:** 386,662 mi$^2$ (1,001,449 km$^2$)
**Population:** 55,105,000 (Urban: 49%)
**Literacy:** 48%
**Capital:** Al-Qāhirah, 6,052,836

**Government:** Socialist republic
**Languages:** Arabic
**Ethnic Groups:** Egyptian (Eastern Hamitic) 90%
**Religions:** Muslim 94%, Coptic Christian and others 6%
**Currency:** Pound
**Tel. Area Code:** 20

## El Salvador

**Location:** Central America
**Area:** 8,124 mi$^2$ (21,041 km$^2$)
**Population:** 5,473,000 (Urban: 44%)
**Literacy:** 73%
**Capital:** San Salvador, 462,652
**Government:** Republic
**Languages:** Spanish, Nahua
**Ethnic Groups:** Mestizo 89%, Amerindian 10%, white 1%
**Religions:** Roman Catholic 97%
**Currency:** Colon
**Tel. Area Code:** 503

## Equatorial Guinea (Guinea Ecuatorial)

**Location:** Central Africa
**Area:** 10,831 mi$^2$ (28,051 km$^2$)
**Population:** 384,000 (Urban: 65%)
**Literacy:** 50%
**Capital:** Malabo, 31,630
**Government:** Republic
**Languages:** Spanish, indigenous, English
**Ethnic Groups:** Fang 80%, Bubi 15%
**Religions:** Roman Catholic 83%, other Christian, tribal religionist
**Currency:** CFA franc
**Tel. Area Code:** 240

## Eritrea

**Location:** Eastern Africa
**Area:** 36,170 mi$^2$ (93,679 km$^2$)
**Population:** 3,425,000 (Urban: 15%)
**Capital:** Asmera, 319,353
**Government:** Republic
**Languages:** Tigringa, Tigre, Arabic, Saho, Agau
**Ethnic Groups:** Tigre, Afar, Beja, Saho, Agau, others
**Religions:** Coptic Christian 50%, Muslim 50%

## Estonia (Eesti)

**Location:** Eastern Europe
**Area:** 17,413 mi$^2$ (45,100 km$^2$)
**Population:** 1,606,000 (Urban: 72%)
**Literacy:** 99%

**Capital:** Tallinn, 481,500
**Government:** Republic
**Languages:** Estonian, Russian
**Ethnic Groups:** Estonian 62%, Russian 30%, Ukrainian 3%
**Religions:** Lutheran
**Currency:** Ruble
**Tel. Area Code:** 372

## Ethiopia (Ītyop'iya)

**Location:** Eastern Africa
**Area:** 446,953 mi$^2$ (1,157,603 km$^2$)
**Population:** 51,715,000 (Urban: 13%)
**Literacy:** 62%
**Capital:** Adis Abeba (Addis Ababa), 1,686,300
**Government:** Transitional military government
**Languages:** Amharic, Tigrinya, Orominga, Arabic
**Ethnic Groups:** Oromo (Galla) 40%, Amhara and Tigrean 32%, Sidamo 9%, Shankella 6%, Somali 6%
**Religions:** Muslim 45%, Ethiopian Orthodox 35%, Animist 15%
**Currency:** Birr
**Tel. Area Code:** 251

## Fiji (Viti)

**Location:** South Pacific islands
**Area:** 7,078 mi$^2$ (18,333 km$^2$)
**Population:** 747,000 (Urban: 44%)
**Literacy:** 86%
**Capital:** Suva, 69,665
**Government:** Republic
**Languages:** English, Fijian, Hindustani
**Ethnic Groups:** Indian 49%, Fijian 46%
**Religions:** Methodist and other Christian 53%, Hindu 38%, Muslim 8%
**Currency:** Dollar
**Tel. Area Code:** 679

## Finland (Suomi)

**Location:** Northern Europe
**Area:** 130,559 mi$^2$ (338,145 km$^2$)
**Population:** 5,001,000 (Urban: 68%)
**Literacy:** 100%
**Capital:** Helsinki, 489,965
**Government:** Republic
**Languages:** Finnish, Swedish
**Ethnic Groups:** Finnish (mixed Scandinavian and Baltic), Swedish, Lappic, Gypsy, Tatar
**Religions:** Jehova's Witness, Free Church, Adventist, Confessional Lutheran

**Currency:** Markka
**Tel. Area Code:** 358

## France

**Location:** Western Europe
**Area:** 211,208 mi$^2$ (547,026 km$^2$)
**Population:** 57,010,000 (Urban: 74%)
**Literacy:** 99%
**Capital:** Paris, 2,152,423
**Government:** Republic
**Languages:** French
**Ethnic Groups:** French (mixed Celtic, Latin, and Teutonic)
**Religions:** Roman Catholic 90%, Protestant 2%, Jewish 1%, Muslim 1%
**Currency:** Franc
**Tel. Area Code:** 33

## French Guiana (Guyane)

**Location:** Northeastern South America
**Area:** 35,135 mi$^2$ (91,000 km$^2$)
**Population:** 104,000 (Urban: 75%)
**Literacy:** 82%
**Capital:** Cayenne, 38,091
**Government:** Overseas department (France)
**Languages:** French
**Ethnic Groups:** Black or mulatto 66%; white 12%; East Indian, Chinese, and Amerindian 12%
**Religions:** Roman Catholic
**Currency:** French franc
**Tel. Area Code:** 594

## French Polynesia (Polynésie française)

**Location:** South Pacific islands
**Area:** 1,544 mi$^2$ (4,000 km$^2$)
**Population:** 198,000 (Urban: 65%)
**Literacy:** 98%
**Capital:** Papeete, 23,555
**Government:** Overseas territory (France)
**Languages:** French, Tahitian, Chinese
**Ethnic Groups:** Polynesian 69%, European 12%, Chinese 10%
**Religions:** Evangelical and other Protestant 55%, Roman Catholic 32%
**Currency:** CFP franc
**Tel. Area Code:** 689

## Gabon

**Location:** Central Africa
**Area:** 103,347 mi$^2$ (267,667 km$^2$)
**Population:** 1,088,000 (Urban: 46%)
**Literacy:** 61%
**Capital:** Libreville, 235,700

**Government:** Republic
**Languages:** French, Fang, indigenous
**Ethnic Groups:** Fang, Eshira, Bapounou, Teke
**Religions:** Roman Catholic and other Christian 55-75%, Fetishism, Muslim
**Currency:** CFA franc
**Tel. Area Code:** 241

## Gambia

**Location:** Western Africa
**Area:** 4,127 mi$^2$ (10,689 km$^2$)
**Population:** 889,000 (Urban: 23%)
**Literacy:** 27%
**Capital:** Banjul, 44,188
**Government:** Republic
**Languages:** English, Malinke, Wolof, Fula, indigenous
**Ethnic Groups:** Malinke 40%, Fulani 19%, Wolof 15%, Jola 10%, Serahuli 8%
**Religions:** Muslim 90%, Christian 9%, tribal religionist 1%
**Currency:** Dalasi
**Tel. Area Code:** 220

## Georgia (Sakartvelo)

**Location:** Southwestern Asia
**Area:** 26,911 mi$^2$ (69,700 km$^2$)
**Population:** 5,550,000 (Urban: 56%)
**Literacy:** 99%
**Capital:** Tbilisi, 1,279,000
**Government:** Provisional military government
**Languages:** Georgian, Russian, Armenian
**Ethnic Groups:** Georgian 70%, Armenian 8%, Russian 6%
**Religions:** Christian
**Currency:** Ruble
**Tel. Area Code:** 7

## Germany (Deutschland)

**Location:** Northern Europe
**Area:** 137,822 mi$^2$ (356,955 km$^2$)
**Population:** 79,710,000 (Urban: 84%)
**Literacy:** 99%
**Capital:** Berlin (designated), 3,409,737; Bonn (de facto), 287,117
**Government:** Republic
**Languages:** German
**Ethnic Groups:** German (Teutonic)
**Religions:** Evangelical and other Protestant 45%, Roman Catholic 37%
**Currency:** Mark
**Tel. Area Code:** 49

## Ghana

**Location:** Western Africa
**Area:** 92,098 mi$^2$ (238,533 km$^2$)
**Population:** 15,865,000 (Urban: 33%)
**Literacy:** 60%
**Capital:** Accra, 949,113
**Government:** Provisional military government
**Languages:** English, Akan, indigenous
**Ethnic Groups:** Akan 44%, Moshi-Dagomba 16%, Ewe 13%, Ga 8%
**Religions:** Tribal religionist 38%, Muslim 30%, Christian 24%
**Currency:** Cedi
**Tel. Area Code:** 233

## Greece (Ellás)

**Location:** Southeastern Europe
**Area:** 50,962 mi$^2$ (131,990 km$^2$)
**Population:** 10,285,000 (Urban: 63%)
**Literacy:** 93%
**Capital:** Athínai (Athens), 748,110
**Government:** Republic
**Languages:** Greek
**Ethnic Groups:** Greek 98%, Turkish 1%
**Religions:** Greek Orthodox 98%, Muslim 1%
**Currency:** Drachma
**Tel. Area Code:** 30

## Greenland (Kalaallit Nunaat, Grønland)

**Location:** North Atlantic island
**Area:** 840,004 mi$^2$ (2,175,600 km$^2$)
**Population:** 57,000 (Urban: 78%)
**Capital:** Godthåb, 12,217
**Government:** Self-governing territory (Danish protection)
**Languages:** Danish, Greenlandic, Inuit dialects
**Ethnic Groups:** Greenlander (Inuit and native-born whites) 86%, Danish 14%
**Religions:** Lutheran
**Currency:** Danish krone
**Tel. Area Code:** 299

## Grenada

**Location:** Caribbean island
**Area:** 133 mi$^2$ (344 km$^2$)
**Population:** 98,000 (Urban: 15%)
**Literacy:** 98%
**Capital:** St. George's, 4,788
**Government:** Parliamentary state
**Languages:** English, French
**Ethnic Groups:** Black 82%, mixed 13%, East Indian 3%
**Religions:** Roman Catholic 59%, Anglican 17%, Seventh Day Adventist 6%
**Currency:** East Caribbean dollar
**Tel. Area Code:** 809

## Guatemala

**Location:** Central America
**Area:** 42,042 mi$^2$ (108,889 km$^2$)
**Population:** 9,386,000 (Urban: 42%)
**Literacy:** 55%
**Capital:** Guatemala, 1,057,210
**Government:** Republic
**Languages:** Spanish, indigenous
**Ethnic Groups:** Ladino (mestizo and westernized Maya) 56%, Maya 44%
**Religions:** Roman Catholic, Protestant, tribal religionist
**Currency:** Quetzal
**Tel. Area Code:** 502

## Guinea (Guinée)

**Location:** Western Africa
**Area:** 94,926 mi$^2$ (245,857 km$^2$)
**Population:** 7,553,000 (Urban: 26%)
**Literacy:** 24%
**Capital:** Conakry, 800,000
**Government:** Provisional military government
**Languages:** French, indigenous
**Ethnic Groups:** Fulani, Malinke, Susu, others
**Religions:** Muslim 85%, Christian 10%, Animist 5%
**Currency:** Franc
**Tel. Area Code:** 224

## Guinea-Bissau (Guiné-Bissau)

**Location:** Western Africa
**Area:** 13,948 mi$^2$ (36,125 km$^2$)
**Population:** 1,036,000 (Urban: 31%)
**Literacy:** 36%
**Capital:** Bissau, 125,000
**Government:** Republic
**Languages:** Portuguese, Crioulo, indigenous
**Ethnic Groups:** Balanta 30%, Fulani 20%, Manjaca 14%, Malinke 13%, Papel 7%
**Religions:** Tribal religionist 65%, Muslim 30%, Christian 5%
**Currency:** Peso
**Tel. Area Code:** 245

## Guyana

**Location:** Northeastern South America
**Area:** 83,000 mi$^2$ (214,969 km$^2$)
**Population:** 748,000 (Urban: 35%)

**Literacy:** 95%
**Capital:** Georgetown, 78,500
**Government:** Republic
**Languages:** English, indigenous
**Ethnic Groups:** East Indian 51%, black 30%, mixed 11%, Amerindian 5%
**Religions:** Anglican and other Christian 57%, Hindu 33%, Muslim 9%
**Currency:** Dollar
**Tel. Area Code:** 592

## Haiti (Haïti)

**Location:** Caribbean island (western Hispaniola)
**Area:** 10,714 mi$^2$ (27,750 km$^2$)
**Population:** 6,361,000 (Urban: 30%)
**Literacy:** 53%
**Capital:** Port-au-Prince, 797,000
**Government:** Provisional military government
**Languages:** Creole, French
**Ethnic Groups:** Black 95%, mulatto and white 5%
**Religions:** Roman Catholic 80%, Baptist 10%, Pentecostal 4%
**Currency:** Gourde
**Tel. Area Code:** 509

## Honduras

**Location:** Central America
**Area:** 43,277 mi$^2$ (112,088 km$^2$)
**Population:** 5,342,000 (Urban: 44%)
**Literacy:** 73%
**Capital:** Tegucigalpa, 551,606
**Government:** Republic
**Languages:** Spanish, indigenous
**Ethnic Groups:** Mestizo 90%, Amerindian 7%, black 2%, white 1%
**Religions:** Roman Catholic 97%
**Currency:** Lempira
**Tel. Area Code:** 504

## Hong Kong (Xianggang)

**Location:** Eastern Asia (islands and mainland area on China's southeastern coast)
**Area:** 414 mi$^2$ (1,072 km$^2$)
**Population:** 5,874,000 (Urban: 93%)
**Literacy:** 77%
**Capital:** Victoria (Hong Kong), 1,250,993
**Government:** Chinese territory under British administration
**Languages:** Chinese (Cantonese), English
**Ethnic Groups:** Chinese 95%

**Religions:** Buddhist and Taoist 90%, Christian 10%
**Currency:** Dollar
**Tel. Area Code:** 852

## Hungary (Magyarország)

**Location:** Eastern Europe, landlocked
**Area:** 35,920 mi$^2$ (93,033 km$^2$)
**Population:** 10,555,000 (Urban: 60%)
**Literacy:** 99%
**Capital:** Budapest, 2,018,035
**Government:** Republic
**Languages:** Hungarian
**Ethnic Groups:** Hungarian (Magyar) 99%
**Religions:** Roman Catholic 68%, Calvinist 20%, Lutheran 5%
**Currency:** Forint
**Tel. Area Code:** 36

## Iceland (Ísland)

**Location:** North Atlantic island
**Area:** 39,769 mi$^2$ (103,000 km$^2$)
**Population:** 261,000 (Urban: 91%)
**Literacy:** 100%
**Capital:** Reykjavík, 97,569
**Government:** Republic
**Languages:** Icelandic
**Ethnic Groups:** Icelander (mixed Norwegian and Celtic)
**Religions:** Lutheran 95%, other Christian 3%
**Currency:** Krona
**Tel. Area Code:** 354

## India (Bharat)

**Location:** Southern Asia
**Area:** 1,237,062 mi$^2$ (3,203,975 km$^2$)
**Population:** 874,150,000 (Urban: 28%)
**Literacy:** 48%
**Capital:** New Delhi, 294,149
**Government:** Republic
**Languages:** English, Hindi, Telugu, Bengali, indigenous
**Ethnic Groups:** Indo-Aryan 72%, Dravidian 25%, Mongoloid and other 3%
**Religions:** Hindu 80%, Muslim 11%, Christian 2%, Sikh 2%
**Currency:** Rupee
**Tel. Area Code:** 91

## Indonesia

**Location:** Southeastern Asian islands
**Area:** 752,410 mi$^2$ (1,948,732 km$^2$)
**Population:** 195,300,000 (Urban: 29%)
**Literacy:** 77%
**Capital:** Jakarta, 9,200,000

**Government:** Republic
**Languages:** Indonesian, Javanese,
Sundanese, Madurese, other indigenous
**Ethnic Groups:** Javanese 45%,
Sundanese 14%, Madurese 8%, coastal
Malay 8%
**Religions:** Muslim 87%, Protestant 7%,
Catholic 3%, Hindu 2%
**Currency:** Rupiah
**Tel. Area Code:** 62

## Iran (Īrān)

**Location:** Southwestern Asia
**Area:** 632,457 mi$^2$ (1,638,057 km$^2$)
**Population:** 60,000,000 (Urban: 55%)
**Literacy:** 54%
**Capital:** Tehrān, 6,042,584
**Government:** Islamic republic
**Languages:** Farsi, Turkish, Kurdish, Arabic,
English, French
**Ethnic Groups:** Persian 63%, Turkish 18%,
other Iranian 13%, Kurdish 3%
**Religions:** Shiite Muslim 93%, Sunni
Muslim 5%
**Currency:** Rial
**Tel. Area Code:** 98

## Iraq (Al-'Irāq)

**Location:** Southwestern Asia
**Area:** 169,235 mi$^2$ (438,317 km$^2$)
**Population:** 19,915,000 (Urban: 74%)
**Literacy:** 60%
**Capital:** Baghdād, 3,841,268
**Government:** Republic
**Languages:** Arabic, Kurdish, Assyrian,
Armenian
**Ethnic Groups:** Arab 75%-80%; Kurdish 15-
20%; Turkoman, Assyrian, or other 5%
**Religions:** Shiite Muslim 60-65%, Sunni
Muslim 32-37%, Christian and others 3%
**Currency:** Dinar
**Tel. Area Code:** 964

## Ireland (Éire)

**Location:** Northwestern European island
(five-sixths of island of Ireland)
**Area:** 27,137 mi$^2$ (70,285 km$^2$)
**Population:** 3,484,000 (Urban: 59%)
**Literacy:** 98%
**Capital:** Dublin, 502,749
**Government:** Republic
**Languages:** English, Irish Gaelic
**Ethnic Groups:** Irish (Celtic), English
**Religions:** Roman Catholic 93%, Church of
Ireland 3%

**Currency:** Pound (punt)
**Tel. Area Code:** 353

## Israel (Yisra'el, Isrā'īl)

**Location:** Southwestern Asia
**Area:** 8,019 mi$^2$ (20,770 km$^2$)
**Population:** 4,393,000 (Urban: 92%)
**Literacy:** 92%
**Capital:** Yerushalayim (Jerusalem), 524,500
**Government:** Republic
**Languages:** Hebrew, Arabic, Yiddish
**Ethnic Groups:** Jewish 83%, Arab and
others 17%
**Religions:** Jewish 82%, Muslim 14%,
Christian 2%, Druze 2%
**Currency:** Shekel
**Tel. Area Code:** 972

## Italy (Italia)

**Location:** Southern Europe
**Area:** 116,324 mi$^2$ (301,277 km$^2$)
**Population:** 57,830,000 (Urban: 69%)
**Literacy:** 97%
**Capital:** Roma (Rome), 2,815,457
**Government:** Republic
**Languages:** Italian
**Ethnic Groups:** Italian (Latin)
**Religions:** Roman Catholic 99%
**Currency:** Lira
**Tel. Area Code:** 39

## Jamaica

**Location:** Caribbean island
**Area:** 4,244 mi$^2$ (10,991 km$^2$)
**Population:** 2,501,000 (Urban: 52%)
**Literacy:** 98%
**Capital:** Kingston, 646,400
**Government:** Parliamentary state
**Languages:** English, Creole
**Ethnic Groups:** Black 75%, mixed 13%, East
Indian 1%
**Religions:** Church of God and other
Protestant, Anglican, Roman Catholic
**Currency:** Dollar
**Tel. Area Code:** 809

## Japan (Nihon)

**Location:** Eastern Asian islands
**Area:** 145,870 mi$^2$ (377,801 km$^2$)
**Population:** 124,270,000 (Urban: 77%)
**Literacy:** 99%
**Capital:** Tōkyō, 8,163,127
**Government:** Constitutional monarchy
**Languages:** Japanese
**Ethnic Groups:** Japanese 99%, Korean

Religions: Buddhist and Shinto
Currency: Yen
Tel. Area Code: 81

## Jordan (Al-Urdun)

Location: Southwestern Asia
Area: 35,135 mi$^2$ (91,000 km$^2$)
Population: 3,485,000 (Urban: 68%)
Literacy: 80%
Capital: 'Ammān, 936,300
Government: Constitutional monarchy
Languages: Arabic
Ethnic Groups: Arab 98%, Circassian 1%,
Armenian 1%
Religions: Sunni Muslim 95%, Christian 5%
Currency: Dinar
Tel. Area Code: 962

## Kazakhstan

Location: Central Asia, landlocked
Area: 1,049,156 mi$^2$ (2,717,300 km$^2$)
Population: 16,880,000 (Urban: 57%)
Literacy: 98%
Capital: Almaty, 1,156,200
Government: Republic
Languages: Kazakh, Russian, German,
Ukrainian
Ethnic Groups: Kazakh 40%, Russian 38%,
German 6%
Religions: Muslim
Currency: Ruble
Tel. Area Code: 7

## Kenya

Location: Eastern Africa
Area: 224,961 mi$^2$ (582,646 km$^2$)
Population: 25,695,000 (Urban: 24%)
Literacy: 69%
Capital: Nairobi, 1,505,000
Government: Republic
Languages: English, Swahili, indigenous
Ethnic Groups: Kikuyu 21%, Luhya 14%,
Luo 13%, Kamba 11%, Kalenjin 11%,
Kisii 6 %, Meru 5%
Religions: Protestant 38%, Roman
Catholic 28%, Animist 26%, Muslim 6%
Currency: Shilling
Tel. Area Code: 254

## Kiribati

Location: Central Pacific islands
Area: 313 mi$^2$ (811 km$^2$)
Population: 72,000 (Urban: 36%)
Capital: Bairiki, 2,226
Government: Republic

Languages: English, Gilbertese
Ethnic Groups: Kiribatian (Micronesian)
98%
Religions: Roman Catholic 53%,
Congregationalist 39%, Bahai 2%
Currency: Australian dollar
Tel. Area Code: 686

## Korea, North (Chosŏn-minjujuŭi-inmīn-konghwaguk)

Location: Eastern Asia
Area: 46,540 mi$^2$ (120,538 km$^2$)
Population: 22,250,000 (Urban: 67%)
Capital: P'yŏngyang, 1,283,000
Government: Socialist republic
Languages: Korean
Ethnic Groups: Korean 100%
Religions: Shamanist, Chondoist, Buddhist
Currency: Won

## Korea, South (Taehan-min'guk)

Location: Eastern Asia
Area: 38,230 mi$^2$ (99,016 km$^2$)
Population: 43,305,000 (Urban: 72%)
Literacy: 96%
Capital: Sŏul (Seoul), 10,627,790
Government: Republic
Languages: Korean
Ethnic Groups: Korean
Religions: Buddhist 20%, Roman
Catholic 16%, Protestant 5%,
Confucian 1%
Currency: Won
Tel. Area Code: 82

## Kuwait (Al-Kuwayt)

Location: Southwestern Asia
Area: 6,880 mi$^2$ (17,818 km$^2$)
Population: 2,244,000 (Urban: 96%)
Literacy: 74%
Capital: Al-Kuwayt (Kuwait), 44,335
Government: Constitutional monarchy
Languages: Arabic, English
Ethnic Groups: Kuwaiti 40%, other
Arab 39%, Southern Asian 9%, Iranian 4%
Religions: Sunni Muslim 45%, Shiite
Muslim 30%, Christian 6%
Currency: Dinar
Tel. Area Code: 965

## Kyrgyzstan

Location: Central Asia, landlocked
Area: 76,641 mi$^2$ (198,500 km$^2$)
Population: 4,385,000 (Urban: 38%)

**Literacy:** 97%
**Capital:** Biškek (Frunze), 631,300
**Government:** Republic
**Languages:** Kirghiz, Russian, Uzbek
**Ethnic Groups:** Kirghiz 52%, Russian 21%, Uzbek 13%
**Religions:** Muslim
**Currency:** Ruble
**Tel. Area Code:** 7

## Laos (Lao)
**Location:** Southeastern Asia, landlocked
**Area:** 91,429 mi$^2$ (236,800 km$^2$)
**Population:** 4,158,000 (Urban: 19%)
**Literacy:** 84%
**Capital:** Viangchan (Vientiane), 377,409
**Government:** Socialist republic
**Languages:** Lao, French, Thai, indigenous
**Ethnic Groups:** Lao 50%; Thai 20%; Phoutheung 15%; Miao, Hmong, Yao, and others 15%
**Religions:** Buddhist 85%, Animist and others 15%
**Currency:** Kip
**Tel. Area Code:** 856

## Latvia (Latvija)
**Location:** Eastern Europe
**Area:** 24,595 mi$^2$ (63,700 km$^2$)
**Population:** 2,737,000 (Urban: 71%)
**Literacy:** 99%
**Capital:** Rīga, 910,200
**Government:** Republic
**Languages:** Latvian, Russian
**Ethnic Groups:** Latvian 52%, Russian 34%, Belorussian 5%
**Religions:** Roman Catholic, Lutheran
**Currency:** Ruble
**Tel. Area Code:** 371

## Lebanon (Lubnān)
**Location:** Southwestern Asia
**Area:** 4,015 mi$^2$ (10,400 km$^2$)
**Population:** 3,409,000 (Urban: 84%)
**Literacy:** 80%
**Capital:** Bayrūt (Beirut), 509,000
**Government:** Republic
**Languages:** Arabic, French, Armenian, English
**Ethnic Groups:** Arab 93%, Armenian 6%
**Religions:** Muslim 75%, Christian 25%, Jewish
**Currency:** Pound
**Tel. Area Code:** 961

## Lesotho
**Location:** Southern Africa, landlocked
**Area:** 11,720 mi$^2$ (30,355 km$^2$)
**Population:** 1,824,000 (Urban: 20%)
**Literacy:** 59%
**Capital:** Maseru, 109,382
**Government:** Constitutional monarchy
**Languages:** English, Sesotho, Zulu, Xhosa
**Ethnic Groups:** Sotho 99%
**Religions:** Roman Catholic and other Christian 80%, tribal religionist 20%
**Currency:** Loti
**Tel. Area Code:** 266

## Liberia
**Location:** Western Africa
**Area:** 38,250 mi$^2$ (99,067 km$^2$)
**Population:** 2,776,000 (Urban: 44%)
**Literacy:** 40%
**Capital:** Monrovia, 465,000
**Government:** Republic
**Languages:** English, indigenous
**Ethnic Groups:** Indigenous black 95%, descendants of freed American slaves 5%
**Religions:** Animist 70%, Muslim 20%, Christian 10%
**Currency:** Dollar
**Tel. Area Code:** 231

## Libya (Lībiyā)
**Location:** Northern Africa
**Area:** 679,362 mi$^2$ (1,759,540 km$^2$)
**Population:** 4,416,000 (Urban: 70%)
**Literacy:** 64%
**Capital:** Ṭarābulus (Tripoli), 591,062
**Government:** Socialist republic
**Languages:** Arabic
**Ethnic Groups:** Arab-Berber 97%
**Religions:** Sunni Muslim 97%
**Currency:** Dinar
**Tel. Area Code:** 218

## Liechtenstein
**Location:** Central Europe, landlocked
**Area:** 62 mi$^2$ (160 km$^2$)
**Population:** 28,000 (Urban: 26%)
**Literacy:** 100%
**Capital:** Vaduz, 4,874
**Government:** Constitutional monarchy
**Languages:** German
**Ethnic Groups:** Liechtensteiner (Alemannic) 66%, Swiss 15%, Austrian 7%, German 4%
**Religions:** Roman Catholic 85%, Protestant 9%

Currency: Swiss franc
Tel. Area Code: 41

## Lithuania (Lietuva)

Location: Eastern Europe
Area: 25,174 mi² (65,200 km²)
Population: 3,767,000 (Urban: 68%)
Literacy: 99%
Capital: Vilnius, 582,000
Government: Republic
Languages: Lithuanian, Russian, Polish
Ethnic Groups: Lithuanian 80%,
Russian 9%, Polish 7%
Religions: Roman Catholic
Currency: Ruble
Tel. Area Code: 370

## Luxembourg (Lezebuurg)

Location: Western Europe, landlocked
Area: 998 mi² (2,586 km²)
Population: 390,000 (Urban: 84%)
Literacy: 100%
Capital: Luxembourg, 75,622
Government: Constitutional monarchy
Languages: French, Luxembourgish,
German
Ethnic Groups: Luxembourger (mixed
Celtic, French, and German)
Religions: Roman Catholic 97%, Jewish and
Protestant 3%
Currency: Franc
Tel. Area Code: 352

## Macao (Macau)

Location: Eastern Asia (islands and
peninsula on China's southeastern coast)
Area: 6.6 mi² (17 km²)
Population: 448,000 (Urban: 99%)
Literacy: 90%
Capital: Macau, 429,000
Government: Chinese territory under
Portuguese administration
Languages: Portuguese, Chinese (Cantonese)
Ethnic Groups: Chinese 95%, Portuguese 3%
Religions: Buddhist 45%, Roman
Catholic 16%, other Christian 3%
Currency: Pataca
Tel. Area Code: 853

## Macedonia (Makedonija)

Location: Eastern Europe
Area: 9,928 mi² (25,713 km²)
Population: 2,120,000 (Urban: 54%)
Literacy: 89%

Capital: Skopje, 444,900
Government: Republic
Languages: Macedonian, Albanian
Ethnic Groups: Macedonian, Albanian
Religions: Orthodox, Muslim
Currency: Yugoslavian dinar

## Madagascar (Madagasikara)

Location: Southeastern African island
Area: 226,658 mi² (587,041 km²)
Population: 12,380,000 (Urban: 25%)
Literacy: 80%
Capital: Antananarivo, 1,250,000
Government: Republic
Languages: Malagasy, French
Ethnic Groups: Merina 15%,
Betsimisaraka 9%, Betsileo 7%,
Tsimihety 4%, Antaisaka 4 %, other tribes
Religions: Animist 52%, Christian 41%,
Muslim 7%
Currency: Franc

## Malawi (Malaŵi)

Location: Southern Africa, landlocked
Area: 45,747 mi² (118,484 km²)
Population: 9,523,000 (Urban: 15%)
Literacy: 22%
Capital: Lilongwe, 233,973
Government: Republic
Languages: Chichewa, English, Tombuka
Ethnic Groups: Chewa, Nyanja, Tumbuka,
Yao, Lomwe, others
Religions: Protestant 55%, Roman
Catholic 20%, Muslim 20%
Currency: Kwacha
Tel. Area Code: 265

## Malaysia

Location: Southeastern Asia (includes part
of the island of Borneo)
Area: 129,251 mi² (334,758 km²)
Population: 18,200,000 (Urban: 42%)
Literacy: 78%
Capital: Kuala Lumpur, 919,610
Government: Constitutional monarchy
Languages: Malay, Chinese dialects,
English, Tamil
Ethnic Groups: Malay and other
indigenous 61%, Chinese 30%, Indian 8%
Religions: Muslim 53%, Buddhist 17%,
Chinese religions 12%, Hindu 7%
Currency: Ringgit
Tel. Area Code: 60

## Maldives

**Location:** Indian Ocean islands
**Area:** 115 mi$^2$ (298 km$^2$)
**Population:** 230,000 (Urban: 21%)
**Literacy:** 92%
**Capital:** Male, 46,334
**Government:** Republic
**Languages:** Divehi
**Ethnic Groups:** Maldivian (mixed Sinhalese, Dravidian, Arab, and black)
**Religions:** Sunni Muslim
**Currency:** Rufiyaa
**Tel. Area Code:** 960

## Mali

**Location:** Western Africa, landlocked
**Area:** 478,767 mi$^2$ (1,240,000 km$^2$)
**Population:** 8,438,000 (Urban: 19%)
**Literacy:** 32%
**Capital:** Bamako, 658,275
**Government:** Republic
**Languages:** French, Bambara, indigenous
**Ethnic Groups:** Malinke 50%, Fulani 17%, Voltaic 12%, Songhai 6%
**Religions:** Sunni Muslim 90%, Animist 9%, Christian 1%
**Currency:** CFA franc
**Tel. Area Code:** 223

## Malta

**Location:** Mediterranean island
**Area:** 122 mi$^2$ (316 km$^2$)
**Population:** 357,000 (Urban: 87%)
**Literacy:** 84%
**Capital:** Valletta, 9,199
**Government:** Republic
**Languages:** English, Maltese
**Ethnic Groups:** Maltese (mixed Arab, Sicilian, Norman, Spanish, Italian, and English)
**Religions:** Roman Catholic 98%
**Currency:** Lira
**Tel. Area Code:** 356

## Mauritania (Mūrītāniyā, Mauritanie)

**Location:** Western Africa
**Area:** 395,956 mi$^2$ (1,025,520 km$^2$)
**Population:** 2,028,000 (Urban: 42%)
**Literacy:** 34%
**Capital:** Nouakchott, 285,000
**Government:** Provisional military government
**Languages:** Arabic, French, indigenous

**Ethnic Groups:** Mixed Moor and black 40%, Moor 30%, black 30%
**Religions:** Sunni Muslim 100%
**Currency:** Ouguiya
**Tel. Area Code:** 222

## Mauritius

**Location:** Indian Ocean island
**Area:** 788 mi$^2$ (2,040 km$^2$)
**Population:** 1,085,000 (Urban: 42%)
**Literacy:** 61%
**Capital:** Port Louis, 141,870
**Government:** Parliamentary state
**Languages:** English, Creole, Bhojpuri, Hindi
**Ethnic Groups:** Indo-Mauritian 68%, Creole 27%, Sino-Mauritian 3%, Franco-Mauritian 2%
**Religions:** Hindu 31%, Muslim 13%, Sanatanist 10%
**Currency:** Rupee
**Tel. Area Code:** 230

## Mexico (México)

**Location:** Southern North America
**Area:** 756,066 mi$^2$ (1,958,201 km$^2$)
**Population:** 91,000,000 (Urban: 73%)
**Literacy:** 87%
**Capital:** Ciudad de México (Mexico City), 8,831,079
**Government:** Republic
**Languages:** Spanish, indigenous
**Ethnic Groups:** Mestizo 60%, Amerindian 30%, white 9%
**Religions:** Roman Catholic 97%, Protestant 3%
**Currency:** Peso

## Moldova

**Location:** Eastern Europe, landlocked
**Area:** 13,012 mi$^2$ (33,700 km$^2$)
**Population:** 4,440,000 (Urban: 47%)
**Literacy:** 99%
**Capital:** Chişinău, 676,700
**Government:** Republic
**Languages:** Romanian (Moldovan), Russian, Ukrainian
**Ethnic Groups:** Moldovan 64%, Ukrainian 14%, Russian 13%
**Currency:** Ruble
**Tel. Area Code:** 373

## Monaco

**Location:** Southern Europe (on the southeastern coast of France)
**Area:** 0.7 mi$^2$ (1.9 km$^2$)

**Population:** 30,000 (Urban: 100%)
**Capital:** Monaco, 30,000
**Government:** Constitutional monarchy
**Languages:** French, English, Italian, Monegasque
**Ethnic Groups:** French 47%, Monegasque 17%, Italian 16%, English 4%, Belgian 2 %, Swiss 1%
**Religions:** Roman Catholic 95%
**Currency:** French franc
**Tel. Area Code:** 33

## Mongolia (Mongol Uls)

**Location:** Central Asia, landlocked
**Area:** 604,829 mi$^2$ (1,566,500 km$^2$)
**Population:** 2,278,000 (Urban: 51%)
**Literacy:** 90%
**Capital:** Ulaanbaatar (Ulan Bator), 548,400
**Government:** Socialist republic
**Languages:** Khalkha Mongol, Kazakh, Russian, Chinese
**Ethnic Groups:** Mongol 90%, Kazakh 4%, Chinese 2%, Russian 2%
**Religions:** Shamanic, Tibetan Buddhist, Muslim
**Currency:** Tughrik
**Tel. Area Code:** 976

## Morocco (Al-Magrib)

**Location:** Northwestern Africa
**Area:** 172,414 mi$^2$ (446,550 km$^2$)
**Population:** 26,470,000 (Urban: 49%)
**Literacy:** 50%
**Capital:** Rabat, 518,616
**Government:** Constitutional monarchy
**Languages:** Arabic, Berber dialects, French
**Ethnic Groups:** Arab-Berber 99%
**Religions:** Sunni Muslim 99%
**Currency:** Dirham
**Tel. Area Code:** 212

## Mozambique (Moçambique)

**Location:** Southern Africa
**Area:** 308,642 mi$^2$ (799,380 km$^2$)
**Population:** 15,460,000 (Urban: 27%)
**Literacy:** 33%
**Capital:** Maputo, 1,069,727
**Government:** Republic
**Languages:** Portuguese, indigenous
**Ethnic Groups:** Makua, Lomwe, Thonga, others
**Religions:** Tribal religionist 60%, Roman Catholic and other Christian 30%, Muslim
**Currency:** Metical
**Tel. Area Code:** 258

## Myanmar

**Location:** Southeastern Asia
**Area:** 261,228 mi$^2$ (676,577 km$^2$)
**Population:** 42,615,000 (Urban: 25%)
**Literacy:** 81%
**Capital:** Rangoon (Yangon), 2,705,039
**Government:** Provisional military government
**Languages:** Burmese, indigenous
**Ethnic Groups:** Bamar (Burmese) 69%, Shan 9%, Kayin 6%, Rakhine 5%
**Religions:** Buddhist 89%, Muslim 4%, Christian 5%
**Currency:** Kyat
**Tel. Area Code:** 95

## Namibia

**Location:** Southern Africa
**Area:** 318,254 mi$^2$ (824,272 km$^2$)
**Population:** 1,626,000 (Urban: 57%)
**Literacy:** 38%
**Capital:** Windhoek, 114,500
**Government:** Republic
**Languages:** Afrikaans, English, German, indigenous
**Ethnic Groups:** Ovambo 49%, Kavango 9%, Damara 8%, Herero 7%, white 7%, mixed 7 %
**Religions:** Lutheran and other Protestant, Roman Catholic, Animist
**Currency:** South African rand
**Tel. Area Code:** 264

## Nepal (Nepāl)

**Location:** Southern Asia, landlocked
**Area:** 56,827 mi$^2$ (147,181 km$^2$)
**Population:** 19,845,000 (Urban: 10%)
**Literacy:** 26%
**Capital:** Kāṭmāṇḍaū (Kathmandu), 235,160
**Government:** Constitutional monarchy
**Languages:** Nepali, Maithali, Bhojpuri, other indigenous
**Ethnic Groups:** Newar, Indian, Tibetan, Gurung, Magar, Tamang, Bhotia, others
**Religions:** Hindu 90%, Buddhist 5%, Muslim 3%
**Currency:** Rupee
**Tel. Area Code:** 977

## Netherlands (Nederland)

**Location:** Western Europe
**Area:** 16,133 mi$^2$ (41,785 km$^2$)
**Population:** 15,065,000 (Urban: 89%)

**Literacy:** 99%
**Capital:** Amsterdam (designated), 702,686;
The Hague (seat of government), 444,256
**Government:** Constitutional monarchy
**Languages:** Dutch
**Ethnic Groups:** Dutch (mixed Scandinavian,
French, and Celtic) 99%, Indonesian and
others 1%
**Religions:** Roman Catholic 36%, Dutch
Reformed 19%, Calvinist 8%
**Currency:** Guilder
**Tel. Area Code:** 31

## New Caledonia (Nouvelle-Calédonie)

**Location:** South Pacific islands
**Area:** 7,358 mi$^2$ (19,058 km$^2$)
**Population:** 174,000 (Urban: 81%)
**Literacy:** 91%
**Capital:** Nouméa, 65,110
**Government:** Overseas territory (France)
**Languages:** French, Malay-Polynesian
languages
**Ethnic Groups:** Melanesian 43%,
French 37%, Wallisian 8%, Polynesian 4%,
Indonesian 4 %, Vietnamese 2%
**Religions:** Roman Catholic 60%,
Protestant 30%
**Currency:** CFP franc
**Tel. Area Code:** 687

## New Zealand

**Location:** South Pacific islands
**Area:** 103,519 mi$^2$ (268,112 km$^2$)
**Population:** 3,463,000 (Urban: 84%)
**Literacy:** 99%
**Capital:** Wellington, 137,495
**Government:** Parliamentary state
**Languages:** English, Maori
**Ethnic Groups:** European origin 86%,
Maori 9%, Samoan and other Pacific
islander 3%
**Religions:** Anglican 24%, Presbyterian 18%,
Roman Catholic 15%, Methodist 5%
**Currency:** Dollar
**Tel. Area Code:** 64

## Nicaragua

**Location:** Central America
**Area:** 50,054 mi$^2$ (129,640 km$^2$)
**Population:** 3,805,000 (Urban: 60%)
**Literacy:** 57%
**Capital:** Managua, 682,000
**Government:** Republic
**Languages:** Spanish, English, indigenous

**Ethnic Groups:** Mestizo 69%, white 17%,
black 9%, Amerindian 5%
**Religions:** Roman Catholic 95%
**Currency:** Cordoba
**Tel. Area Code:** 505

## Niger

**Location:** Western Africa, landlocked
**Area:** 489,191 mi$^2$ (1,267,000 km$^2$)
**Population:** 8,113,000 (Urban: 20%)
**Literacy:** 28%
**Capital:** Niamey, 398,265
**Government:** Provisional military
government
**Languages:** French, Hausa, Djerma,
indigenous
**Ethnic Groups:** Hausa 56%, Djerma 22%,
Fulani 9%, Taureg 8%, Beriberi 4%
**Religions:** Muslim 80%, Animist and
Christian 20%
**Currency:** CFA franc
**Tel. Area Code:** 227

## Nigeria

**Location:** Western Africa
**Area:** 356,669 mi$^2$ (923,768 km$^2$)
**Population:** 124,300,000 (Urban: 35%)
**Literacy:** 51%
**Capital:** Lagos (de facto), 1,213,000; Abuja
(future)
**Government:** Provisional military
government
**Languages:** English, Hausa, Fulani, Yoruba,
Ibo, indigenous
**Ethnic Groups:** Hausa, Fulani, Yoruba, Ibo,
others
**Religions:** Muslim 50%, Christian 40%,
Animist 10%
**Currency:** Naira
**Tel. Area Code:** 234

## Norway (Norge)

**Location:** Northern Europe
**Area:** 149,412 mi$^2$ (386,975 km$^2$)
**Population:** 4,286,000 (Urban: 74%)
**Literacy:** 99%
**Capital:** Oslo, 452,415
**Government:** Constitutional monarchy
**Languages:** Norwegian, Lapp
**Ethnic Groups:** Norwegian (Scandinavian),
Lappic
**Religions:** Lutheran 94%, other Protestant
and Roman Catholic 4%
**Currency:** Krone
**Tel. Area Code:** 47

## Oman ('Umān)

**Location:** Southwestern Asia
**Area:** 82,030 mi$^2$ (212,457 km$^2$)
**Population:** 1,562,000 (Urban: 11%)
**Capital:** Muscat, 30,000
**Government:** Monarchy
**Languages:** Arabic, English, Baluchi, Urdu, Indian dialects
**Ethnic Groups:** Arab, Baluchi, Zanzibari, Indian
**Religions:** Ibadite Muslim 75%, Sunni Muslim, Shiite Muslim, Hindu
**Currency:** Rial
**Tel. Area Code:** 968

## Pakistan (Pākistān)

**Location:** Southern Asia
**Area:** 339,732 mi$^2$ (879,902 km$^2$)
**Population:** 119,000,000 (Urban: 32%)
**Literacy:** 35%
**Capital:** Islāmābād, 204,364
**Government:** Islamic republic
**Languages:** English, Urdu, Punjabi, Pashto, Sindhi, Saraiki
**Ethnic Groups:** Punjabi, Sindhi, Pathan, Baluchi
**Religions:** Sunni Muslim 77%, Shiite Muslim 20%, Christian 1%, Hindu 1%
**Currency:** Rupee
**Tel. Area Code:** 92

## Panama (Panamá)

**Location:** Central America
**Area:** 29,157 mi$^2$ (75,517 km$^2$)
**Population:** 2,503,000 (Urban: 55%)
**Literacy:** 88%
**Capital:** Panamá, 411,549
**Government:** Republic
**Languages:** Spanish, English, indigenous
**Ethnic Groups:** Mestizo 70%, West Indian 14%, white 10%, Amerindian 6%
**Religions:** Roman Catholic 93%, Protestant 6%
**Currency:** Balboa
**Tel. Area Code:** 507

## Papua New Guinea

**Location:** South Pacific islands
**Area:** 178,704 mi$^2$ (462,840 km$^2$)
**Population:** 3,960,000 (Urban: 16%)
**Literacy:** 52%
**Capital:** Port Moresby, 193,242
**Government:** Parliamentary state
**Languages:** English, Motu, Pidgin, indigenous
**Ethnic Groups:** Melanesian, Papuan, Negrito, Micronesian, Polynesian
**Religions:** Roman Catholic 35%, Lutheran 26%, United Church 13%, Evangelical 9%
**Currency:** Kina
**Tel. Area Code:** 675

## Paraguay

**Location:** Central South America, landlocked
**Area:** 157,048 mi$^2$ (406,752 km$^2$)
**Population:** 4,871,000 (Urban: 48%)
**Literacy:** 90%
**Capital:** Asunción, 477,100
**Government:** Republic
**Languages:** Spanish, Guarani
**Ethnic Groups:** Mestizo 95%, white and Amerindian 5%
**Religions:** Roman Catholic 90%, Mennonite and other Protestant
**Currency:** Guarani
**Tel. Area Code:** 595

## Peru (Perú)

**Location:** Western South America
**Area:** 496,225 mi$^2$ (1,285,216 km$^2$)
**Population:** 22,585,000 (Urban: 70%)
**Literacy:** 85%
**Capital:** Lima, 371,122
**Government:** Republic
**Languages:** Quechua, Spanish, Aymara
**Ethnic Groups:** Amerindian 45%, mestizo 37%, white 15%
**Religions:** Roman Catholic 89%, Protestant 5%
**Currency:** Inti
**Tel. Area Code:** 51

## Philippines (Pilipinas)

**Location:** Southeastern Asian islands
**Area:** 115,831 mi$^2$ (300,000 km$^2$)
**Population:** 62,380,000 (Urban: 42%)
**Literacy:** 90%
**Capital:** Manila, 1,587,000
**Government:** Republic
**Languages:** English, Pilipino, Tagalog
**Ethnic Groups:** Christian Malay 92%, Muslim Malay 4%, Chinese 2%
**Religions:** Roman Catholic 83%, Protestant 9%, Muslim 5%, Buddhist and others 3%

Currency: Peso
Tel. Area Code: 63

## Poland (Polska)

Location: Eastern Europe
Area: 120,728 mi$^2$ (312,683 km$^2$)
Population: 37,840,000 (Urban: 63%)
Literacy: 99%
Capital: Warszawa (Warsaw), 1,655,700
Government: Republic
Languages: Polish
Ethnic Groups: Polish (mixed Slavic and
    Teutonic) 99%, Ukrainian, Byelorussian
Religions: Roman Catholic 95%
Currency: Zloty
Tel. Area Code: 48

## Portugal

Location: Southwestern Europe
Area: 35,516 mi$^2$ (91,985 km$^2$)
Population: 10,410,000 (Urban: 33%)
Literacy: 85%
Capital: Lisbon, 807,167
Government: Republic
Languages: Portuguese
Ethnic Groups: Portuguese (Mediterranean),
    black
Religions: Roman Catholic 81%,
    Protestant 1%
Currency: Escudo
Tel. Area Code: 351

## Puerto Rico

Location: Caribbean island
Area: 3,515 mi$^2$ (9,104 km$^2$)
Population: 3,528,000 (Urban: 74%)
Literacy: 89%
Capital: San Juan, 426,832
Government: Commonwealth (U.S.
    protection)
Languages: Spanish
Ethnic Groups: Puerto Rican (mixed
    Spanish and black)
Religions: Roman Catholic 85%
Currency: U.S. dollar

## Qatar

Location: Southwestern Asia
Area: 4,416 mi$^2$ (11,437 km$^2$)
Population: 532,000 (Urban: 90%)
Literacy: 76%
Capital: Ad-Dawḥah (Doha), 217,294
Government: Monarchy
Languages: Arabic, English

Ethnic Groups: Arab 40%, Pakistani 18%,
    Indian 18%, Iranian 10%
Religions: Muslim 95%
Currency: Riyal
Tel. Area Code: 974

## Romania (România)

Location: Eastern Europe
Area: 91,699 mi$^2$ (237,500 km$^2$)
Population: 23,465,000 (Urban: 50%)
Literacy: 96%
Capital: Bucureşti (Bucharest), 2,036,894
Government: Republic
Languages: Romanian, Hungarian, German
Ethnic Groups: Romanian (mixed Latin,
    Thracian, Slavic, and Celtic) 89%,
    Hungarian 8%, German 2%
Religions: Romanian Orthodox 80%, Roman
    Catholic 6%
Currency: Leu
Tel. Area Code: 40

## Russia (Rossija)

Location: Eastern Europe and Northern
    Asia
Area: 6,592,849 mi$^2$ (17,075,400 km$^2$)
Population: 150,505,000 (Urban: 74%)
Literacy: 99%
Capital: Moskva (Moscow), 8,801,500
Government: Republic
Languages: Russian, Tatar, Ukrainian
Ethnic Groups: Russian 82%, Tatar 4%,
    Ukrainian 3%
Religions: Russian Orthodox
Currency: Ruble
Tel. Area Code: 7

## Rwanda

Location: Eastern Africa, landlocked
Area: 10,169 mi$^2$ (26,338 km$^2$)
Population: 8,053,000 (Urban: 8%)
Literacy: 50%
Capital: Kigali, 181,600
Government: Provisional military
    government
Languages: French, Kinyarwanda
Ethnic Groups: Hutu 89%, Tutsi 10%, Twa
Religions: Roman Catholic 52%,
    Protestant 21%, Animist 9%
Currency: Franc
Tel. Area Code: 250

## St. Kitts and Nevis

Location: Caribbean islands
Area: 104 mi$^2$ (269 km$^2$)

**Population:** 42,000 (Urban: 49%)
**Literacy:** 98%
**Capital:** Basseterre, 14,725
**Government:** Parliamentary state
**Languages:** English
**Ethnic Groups:** Black 94%, mixed 3%, white 1%
**Religions:** Anglican 33%, Methodist 29%, Moravian 9%, Roman Catholic 7%
**Currency:** East Caribbean dollar
**Tel. Area Code:** 809

### St. Lucia

**Location:** Caribbean island
**Area:** 238 mi$^2$ (616 km$^2$)
**Population:** 155,000 (Urban: 46%)
**Literacy:** 67%
**Capital:** Castries, 53,933
**Government:** Parliamentary state
**Languages:** English, French
**Ethnic Groups:** Black 87%, mixed 9%, East Indian 3%
**Religions:** Roman Catholic 86%, Seventh Day Adventist 4%, Anglican 3%
**Currency:** East Caribbean dollar
**Tel. Area Code:** 809

### St. Vincent and the Grenadines

**Location:** Caribbean islands
**Area:** 150 mi$^2$ (388 km$^2$)
**Population:** 115,000 (Urban: 21%)
**Literacy:** 96%
**Capital:** Kingstown, 19,028
**Government:** Parliamentary state
**Languages:** English, French
**Ethnic Groups:** Black 82%, mixed 14%, East Indian 2%, white 1%
**Religions:** Anglican 42%, Methodist 21%, Roman Catholic 12%, Baptist 6%
**Currency:** East Caribbean dollar
**Tel. Area Code:** 809

### Sao Tome and Principe (São Tomé e Príncipe)

**Location:** Western African islands
**Area:** 372 mi$^2$ (964 km$^2$)
**Population:** 130,000 (Urban: 42%)
**Literacy:** 57%
**Capital:** São Tomé, 17,380
**Government:** Republic
**Languages:** Portuguese, Fang
**Ethnic Groups:** Black, mixed black and Portuguese, Portuguese
**Religions:** Roman Catholic, African Protestant, Seventh Day Adventist

**Currency:** Dobra
**Tel. Area Code:** 239

### Saudi Arabia (Al-'Arabīyah as-Su'ūdīyah)

**Location:** Southwestern Asia
**Area:** 830,000 mi$^2$ (2,149,690 km$^2$)
**Population:** 16,690,000 (Urban: 77%)
**Literacy:** 62%
**Capital:** Ar-Riyāḍ (Riyadh), 1,250,000
**Government:** Monarchy
**Languages:** Arabic
**Ethnic Groups:** Arab 90%, Afro-Asian 10%
**Religions:** Muslim 100%
**Currency:** Riyal
**Tel. Area Code:** 966

### Senegal (Sénégal)

**Location:** Western Africa
**Area:** 75,951 mi$^2$ (196,712 km$^2$)
**Population:** 7,569,000 (Urban: 38%)
**Literacy:** 38%
**Capital:** Dakar, 1,490,450
**Government:** Republic
**Languages:** French, Wolof, Fulani, Serer, indigenous
**Ethnic Groups:** Wolof 44%, Fulani 23%, Serer 15%, Diola 6%, Malinke 5%
**Religions:** Muslim 94%, Christian 5%
**Currency:** CFA franc
**Tel. Area Code:** 221

### Seychelles

**Location:** Indian Ocean islands
**Area:** 175 mi$^2$ (453 km$^2$)
**Population:** 69,000 (Urban: 59%)
**Literacy:** 58%
**Capital:** Victoria, 23,000
**Government:** Republic
**Languages:** English, French, Creole
**Ethnic Groups:** Seychellois (mixed Asian, African, and European)
**Religions:** Roman Catholic 90%, Anglican 8%
**Currency:** Rupee
**Tel. Area Code:** 248

### Sierra Leone

**Location:** Western Africa
**Area:** 27,925 mi$^2$ (72,325 km$^2$)
**Population:** 4,330,000 (Urban: 32%)
**Literacy:** 21%
**Capital:** Freetown, 469,776
**Government:** Republic

**Languages:** English, Krio, indigenous
**Ethnic Groups:** Temne 30%, Mende 30%, Creole 2%, other African
**Religions:** Muslim 30%, Animist 30%, Christian 10%
**Currency:** Leone
**Tel. Area Code:** 232

## Singapore

**Location:** Southeastern Asian island
**Area:** 246 mi$^2$ (636 km$^2$)
**Population:** 3,062,000 (Urban: 100%)
**Literacy:** 88%
**Capital:** Singapore, 3,062,000
**Government:** Republic
**Languages:** Chinese (Mandarin), English, Malay, Tamil
**Ethnic Groups:** Chinese 76%, Malay 15%, Indian 6%
**Religions:** Taoist 29%, Buddhist 27%, Muslim 16%, Christian 10%, Hindu 4%
**Currency:** Dollar
**Tel. Area Code:** 65

## Slovakia (Slovensko)

**Location:** Eastern Europe, landlocked
**Area:** 18,933 mi$^2$ (49,035 km$^2$)
**Population:** 5,287,000
**Capital:** Bratislava, 444,482
**Government:** Republic
**Languages:** Slovak, Hungarian
**Ethnic Groups:** Slovak, Hungarian
**Religions:** Roman Catholic, Hussite, Uniate, Orthodox
**Currency:** Koruna
**Tel. Area Code:** 42

## Slovenia (Slovenija)

**Location:** Eastern Europe
**Area:** 7,819 mi$^2$ (20,251 km$^2$)
**Population:** 1,989,000 (Urban: 49%)
**Literacy:** 99%
**Capital:** Ljubljana, 233,200
**Government:** Republic
**Languages:** Slovene
**Ethnic Groups:** Slovene, Italian, Hungarian
**Religions:** Roman Catholic
**Currency:** Tolar, Yugoslavian dinar
**Tel. Area Code:** 38

## Solomon Islands

**Location:** South Pacific islands
**Area:** 10,954 mi$^2$ (28,370 km$^2$)
**Population:** 353,000 (Urban: 11%)
**Capital:** Honiara, 30,413

**Government:** Parliamentary state
**Languages:** English, Malay-Polynesian languages
**Ethnic Groups:** Melanesian 93%, Polynesian 4%, Micronesian 2%
**Religions:** Church of Melanesia 34%, Roman Catholic 19%, South Sea Evangelical 17%
**Currency:** Dollar
**Tel. Area Code:** 677

## Somalia (Soomaaliya)

**Location:** Eastern Africa
**Area:** 246,201 mi$^2$ (637,657 km$^2$)
**Population:** 6,823,000 (Urban: 36%)
**Literacy:** 24%
**Capital:** Mogadishu, 600,000
**Government:** Provisional military government
**Languages:** Arabic, Somali, English, Italian
**Ethnic Groups:** Somali 85%
**Religions:** Sunni Muslim
**Currency:** Shilling

## South Africa (Suid-Afrika)

**Location:** Southern Africa
**Area:** 471,090 mi$^2$ (1,220,118 km$^2$)
**Population:** 42,224,000 (Urban: 59%)
**Literacy:** 76%
**Capital:** Pretoria (administrative), 443,059; Cape Town (legislative), 776,617; Bloemfontein (judicial), 104,381
**Government:** Republic
**Languages:** Afrikaans, English, Xhosa, Zulu, Swazi, other indigenous
**Ethnic Groups:** Black 70%, white 16%, mulatto (coloured) 10%, Indian 3%
**Religions:** Black Independent 19%, Dutch Reformed 14%, Roman Catholic 10%
**Currency:** Rand
**Tel. Area Code:** 27

## Spain (España)

**Location:** Southwestern Europe
**Area:** 194,885 mi$^2$ (504,750 km$^2$)
**Population:** 39,465,000 (Urban: 78%)
**Literacy:** 95%
**Capital:** Madrid, 3,102,846
**Government:** Constitutional monarchy
**Languages:** Spanish (Castilian), Catalan, Galician, Basque
**Ethnic Groups:** Spanish (mixed Mediterranean and Teutonic)
**Religions:** Roman Catholic 99%

Currency: Peseta
Tel. Area Code: 34

## Sri Lanka

Location: Southern Asian island
Area: 24,962 mi$^2$ (64,652 km$^2$)
Population: 17,530,000 (Urban: 21%)
Literacy: 87%
Capital: Colombo (de facto), 683,000; Sri Jayawardenapura (future), 104,000
Government: Socialist republic
Languages: English, Sinhala, Tamil
Ethnic Groups: Sinhalese 74%, Ceylon Tamil 10%, Ceylon Moor 7%, Indian Tamil 6%
Religions: Buddhist 69%, Hindu 15%, Muslim 8%, Christian 7%
Currency: Rupee
Tel. Area Code: 94

## Sudan (As-Sūdān)

Location: Eastern Africa
Area: 967,500 mi$^2$ (2,505,813 km$^2$)
Population: 27,630,000 (Urban: 22%)
Literacy: 27%
Capital: Al-Kharṭūm (Khartoum), 476,218
Government: Provisional military government
Languages: Arabic, indigenous, English
Ethnic Groups: Black 52%, Arab 39%, Beja 6%
Religions: Sunni Muslim 70%, indigenous 20%, Christian 5%
Currency: Pound

## Suriname

Location: Northeastern South America
Area: 63,251 mi$^2$ (163,820 km$^2$)
Population: 405,000 (Urban: 48%)
Literacy: 95%
Capital: Paramaribo, 241,000
Government: Republic
Languages: Dutch, Sranan Tongo, English, Hindustani, Javanese
Ethnic Groups: East Indian 37%, Creole 31%, Javanese 15%, black 10%, Amerindian 3 %, Chinese 2%
Religions: Hindu 27%, Protestant 25%, Roman Catholic 23%, Muslim 20%
Currency: Guilder
Tel. Area Code: 597

## Swaziland

Location: Southern Africa, landlocked
Area: 6,704 mi$^2$ (17,364 km$^2$)
Population: 875,000 (Urban: 33%)
Literacy: 64%
Capital: Mbabane (de facto), 38,290; Lobamba (future)
Government: Monarchy
Languages: English, siSwati
Ethnic Groups: Swazi 95%, European 2%, Zulu 1%
Religions: African Protestant and other Christian 57%, tribal religionist 43%
Currency: Lilangeni
Tel. Area Code: 268

## Sweden (Sverige)

Location: Northern Europe
Area: 173,732 mi$^2$ (449,964 km$^2$)
Population: 8,581,000 (Urban: 84%)
Literacy: 99%
Capital: Stockholm, 674,452
Government: Constitutional monarchy
Languages: Swedish
Ethnic Groups: Swedish (Scandinavian) 92%, Finnish, Lappic
Religions: Lutheran (Church of Sweden) 94%, Roman Catholic 2%
Currency: Krona
Tel. Area Code: 46

## Switzerland (Schweiz, Suisse, Svizzera)

Location: Central Europe, landlocked
Area: 15,943 mi$^2$ (41,293 km$^2$)
Population: 6,804,000 (Urban: 60%)
Literacy: 99%
Capital: Bern, 134,393
Government: Republic
Languages: German, French, Italian, Romansch
Ethnic Groups: German 65%, French 18%, Italian 10%, Romansch 1%
Religions: Roman Catholic 48%, Protestant 44%
Currency: Franc
Tel. Area Code: 41

## Syria (Sūrīyah)

Location: Southwestern Asia
Area: 71,498 mi$^2$ (185,180 km$^2$)
Population: 13,210,000 (Urban: 52%)
Literacy: 64%
Capital: Dimashq (Damascus), 1,326,000
Government: Socialist republic
Languages: Arabic, Kurdish, Armenian, Aramaic, Circassian
Ethnic Groups: Arab 90%, Kurdish, Armenian, and others 10%

**Religions:** Sunni Muslim 74%, other
 Muslim 16%, Christian 10%
**Currency:** Pound
**Tel. Area Code:** 963

## Taiwan (T'aiwan)
**Location:** Eastern Asian island
**Area:** 13,900 mi² (36,002 km²)
**Population:** 20,785,000 (Urban: 66%)
**Literacy:** 91%
**Capital:** T'aipei, 2,719,659
**Government:** Republic
**Languages:** Chinese dialects
**Ethnic Groups:** Taiwanese 84%,
 Chinese 14%, aborigine 2%
**Religions:** Buddhist, Confucian, and
 Taoist 93%, Christian 5%
**Currency:** Dollar
**Tel. Area Code:** 886

## Tajikistan
**Location:** Central Asia, landlocked
**Area:** 55,251 mi² (143,100 km²)
**Population:** 5,210,000 (Urban: 33%)
**Literacy:** 96%
**Capital:** Dušanbe, 582,400
**Government:** Republic
**Languages:** Tajik, Uzbek, Russian
**Ethnic Groups:** Tajik 62%, Uzbek 24%,
 Russian 8%
**Religions:** Muslim
**Currency:** Ruble
**Tel. Area Code:** 7

## Tanzania
**Location:** Eastern Africa
**Area:** 364,900 mi² (945,087 km²)
**Population:** 27,325,000 (Urban: 33%)
**Literacy:** 46%
**Capital:** Dar es Salaam (de facto),
 1,300,000; Dodoma (designated), 54,000
**Government:** Republic
**Languages:** English, Swahili, indigenous
**Ethnic Groups:** African 99%
**Religions:** Animist 35%, Muslim 35%,
 Christian 30%
**Currency:** Shilling
**Tel. Area Code:** 255

## Thailand (Prathet Thai)
**Location:** Southeastern Asia
**Area:** 198,115 mi² (513,115 km²)
**Population:** 57,200,000 (Urban: 23%)
**Literacy:** 93%
**Capital:** Krung Thep (Bangkok), 5,845,152

**Government:** Constitutional monarchy
**Languages:** Thai, indigenous
**Ethnic Groups:** Thai 84%, Chinese 12%
**Religions:** Buddhist 98%, Muslim 1%
**Currency:** Baht
**Tel. Area Code:** 66

## Togo
**Location:** Western Africa
**Area:** 21,925 mi² (56,785 km²)
**Population:** 3,880,000 (Urban: 26%)
**Literacy:** 43%
**Capital:** Lomé, 500,000
**Government:** Provisional military
 government
**Languages:** French, indigenous
**Ethnic Groups:** Ewe, Mina, Kabye, others
**Religions:** Animist 70%, Christian 20%,
 Muslim 10%
**Currency:** CFA franc
**Tel. Area Code:** 228

## Tonga
**Location:** South Pacific islands
**Area:** 290 mi² (750 km²)
**Population:** 103,000 (Urban: 21%)
**Literacy:** 100%
**Capital:** Nuku'alofa, 21,265
**Government:** Constitutional monarchy
**Languages:** Tongan, English
**Ethnic Groups:** Tongan (Polynesian) 98%
**Religions:** Methodist 47%, Roman
 Catholic 16%, Free Church 14%, Church
 of Tonga 9%
**Currency:** Pa'anga
**Tel. Area Code:** 676

## Trinidad and Tobago
**Location:** Caribbean islands
**Area:** 1,980 mi² (5,128 km²)
**Population:** 1,293,000 (Urban: 69%)
**Literacy:** 95%
**Capital:** Port of Spain, 50,878
**Government:** Republic
**Languages:** English, Hindi, French, Spanish
**Ethnic Groups:** Black 41%, East Indian 41%,
 mixed 16%, white 1%
**Religions:** Roman Catholic 33%, Anglican
 and other Protestant 29%, Hindu 25%
**Currency:** Dollar
**Tel. Area Code:** 809

## Tunisia (Tunisie, Tunis)
**Location:** Northern Africa
**Area:** 63,170 mi² (163,610 km²)

**Population:** 8,367,000 (Urban: 54%)
**Literacy:** 65%
**Capital:** Tunis, 596,654
**Government:** Republic
**Languages:** Arabic, French
**Ethnic Groups:** Arab 98%, European 1%
**Religions:** Muslim 98%, Christian 1%
**Currency:** Dinar
**Tel. Area Code:** 216

## Turkey (Türkiye)

**Location:** Southeastern Europe and southwestern Asia
**Area:** 300,948 mi$^2$ (779,452 km$^2$)
**Population:** 58,850,000 (Urban: 48%)
**Literacy:** 81%
**Capital:** Ankara, 2,559,471
**Government:** Republic
**Languages:** Turkish, Kurdish, Arabic
**Ethnic Groups:** Turkish 85%, Kurdish 12%
**Religions:** Muslim 98%
**Currency:** Lira
**Tel. Area Code:** 90

## Turkmenistan

**Location:** Central Asia, landlocked
**Area:** 188,456 mi$^2$ (488,100 km$^2$)
**Population:** 3,615,000 (Urban: 45%)
**Literacy:** 97%
**Capital:** Ašhabad, 412,200
**Government:** Republic
**Languages:** Turkmen, Russian, Uzbek, Kazakh
**Ethnic Groups:** Turkmen 72%, Russian 9%, Uzbek 9%
**Religions:** Muslim
**Currency:** Ruble
**Tel. Area Code:** 7

## Uganda

**Location:** Eastern Africa, landlocked
**Area:** 93,104 mi$^2$ (241,139 km$^2$)
**Population:** 18,485,000 (Urban: 10%)
**Literacy:** 48%
**Capital:** Kampala, 773,463
**Government:** Republic
**Languages:** English, Luganda, Swahili, indigenous
**Ethnic Groups:** Ganda, Nkole, Gisu, Soga, Turkana, Chiga, Lango, Acholi
**Religions:** Roman Catholic 33%, Protestant 33%, Muslim 16%, Animist
**Currency:** Shilling
**Tel. Area Code:** 256

## Ukraine (Ukrayina)

**Location:** Eastern Europe
**Area:** 233,090 mi$^2$ (603,700 km$^2$)
**Population:** 52,800,000 (Urban: 67%)
**Literacy:** 97%
**Capital:** Kyyiv (Kiev), 2,635,000
**Government:** Republic
**Languages:** Ukrainian, Russian
**Ethnic Groups:** Ukrainian 73%, Russian 22%
**Religions:** Eastern Orthodox, Roman Catholic
**Currency:** Ruble, hryvnia
**Tel. Area Code:** 7

## United Arab Emirates (Al-Imārāt al-'Arabīyah al-Muttahidah)

**Location:** Southwestern Asia
**Area:** 32,278 mi$^2$ (83,600 km$^2$)
**Population:** 2,459,000 (Urban: 78%)
**Literacy:** 68%
**Capital:** Abū Ẓaby (Abu Dhabi), 242,975
**Government:** Federation of monarchs
**Languages:** Arabic, English, Farsi, Hindi, Urdu
**Ethnic Groups:** South Asian 50%, native Emirian 19%, other Arab 23%
**Religions:** Muslim 89%, Christian 6%
**Currency:** Dirham
**Tel. Area Code:** 971

## United Kingdom

**Location:** Northwestern European islands
**Area:** 94,248 mi$^2$ (244,100 km$^2$)
**Population:** 57,630,000 (Urban: 93%)
**Literacy:** 99%
**Capital:** London, 6,574,009
**Government:** Constitutional monarchy
**Languages:** English, Welsh, Gaelic
**Ethnic Groups:** English 82%, Scottish 10%, Irish 2%, Welsh 2%
**Religions:** Anglican 45%, Roman Catholic 9%, Presbyterian 3%, Methodist 1%
**Currency:** Pound sterling
**Tel. Area Code:** 44

## United States

**Location:** Central North America
**Area:** 3,787,425 mi$^2$ (9,809,431 km$^2$)
**Population:** 253,510,000 (Urban: 74%)
**Literacy:** 97%
**Capital:** Washington, 606,900
**Government:** Republic
**Languages:** English, Spanish

**Ethnic Groups:** White 85%, black 12%
**Religions:** Baptist and other Protestant 56%, Roman Catholic 28%, Jewish 2%
**Currency:** Dollar

## Uruguay
**Location:** Eastern South America
**Area:** 68,500 mi$^2$ (177,414 km$^2$)
**Population:** 3,130,000 (Urban: 86%)
**Literacy:** 96%
**Capital:** Montevideo, 1,251,647
**Government:** Republic
**Languages:** Spanish
**Ethnic Groups:** White 88%, mestizo 8%, black 4%
**Religions:** Roman Catholic 66%, Protestant 2%, Jewish 2%
**Currency:** Peso
**Tel. Area Code:** 598

## Uzbekistan (Ŭzbekiston)
**Location:** Central Asia, landlocked
**Area:** 172,742 mi$^2$ (447,400 km$^2$)
**Population:** 20,325,000 (Urban: 41%)
**Literacy:** 97%
**Capital:** Taškent, 2,113,300
**Government:** Republic
**Languages:** Uzbek, Russian, Kazakh, Tajik, Tatar
**Ethnic Groups:** Uzbek 71%, Russian 8%, Tajik 5%
**Religions:** Muslim
**Currency:** Ruble
**Tel. Area Code:** 7

## Vanuatu
**Location:** South Pacific islands
**Area:** 4,707 mi$^2$ (12,190 km$^2$)
**Population:** 153,000 (Urban: 30%)
**Literacy:** 53%
**Capital:** Port-Vila, 18,905
**Government:** Republic
**Languages:** Bislama, English, French
**Ethnic Groups:** Ni-Vanuatu 92%, European 2%, other Pacific Islander 2%
**Religions:** Presbyterian 37%, Anglican 15%, Roman Catholic 15%, other Protestant
**Currency:** Vatu
**Tel. Area Code:** 678

## Vatican City (Città del Vaticano)
**Location:** Southern Europe, landlocked (within the city of Rome, Italy)
**Area:** 0.2 mi$^2$ (0.4 km$^2$)
**Population:** 800 (Urban: 100%)
**Literacy:** 100%
**Capital:** Città del Vaticano, 800
**Government:** Ecclesiastical city-state
**Languages:** Italian, Latin
**Ethnic Groups:** Italian, Swiss
**Religions:** Roman Catholic
**Currency:** Lira
**Tel. Area Code:** 39

## Venezuela
**Location:** Northern South America
**Area:** 352,145 mi$^2$ (912,050 km$^2$)
**Population:** 20,430,000 (Urban: 91%)
**Literacy:** 85%
**Capital:** Caracas, 1,816,901
**Government:** Republic
**Languages:** Spanish, indigenous
**Ethnic Groups:** Mestizo 67%, white 21%, black 10%, Indian 2%
**Religions:** Roman Catholic 96%, Protestant 2%
**Currency:** Bolivar
**Tel. Area Code:** 58

## Vietnam (Viet Nam)
**Location:** Southeastern Asia
**Area:** 128,066 mi$^2$ (331,689 km$^2$)
**Population:** 68,310,000 (Urban: 22%)
**Literacy:** 88%
**Capital:** Ha Noi, 905,939
**Government:** Socialist republic
**Languages:** Vietnamese, French, Chinese, English, Khmer, indigenous
**Ethnic Groups:** Kinh 87%, Hao 2%, Tay 2%
**Religions:** Buddhist, Chondoist, Roman Catholic, Animist, Muslim, Confucian
**Currency:** Dong
**Tel. Area Code:** 84

## Western Samoa (Samoa i Sisifo)
**Location:** South Pacific islands
**Area:** 1,093 mi$^2$ (2,831 km$^2$)
**Population:** 192,000 (Urban: 23%)
**Literacy:** 98%
**Capital:** Apia, 33,170
**Government:** Constitutional monarchy
**Languages:** English, Samoan
**Ethnic Groups:** Samoan, mixed European and Polynesian
**Religions:** Congregational 50%, Roman Catholic 22%, Methodist 16%, Mormon 8%
**Currency:** Tala
**Tel. Area Code:** 685

## Yemen (Al-Yaman)

**Location:** Southwestern Asia
**Area:** 205,356 mi$^2$ (531,869 km$^2$)
**Population:** 11,825,000 (Urban: 24%)
**Literacy:** 38%
**Capital:** Șan'ā', 427,150
**Government:** Republic
**Languages:** Arabic
**Ethnic Groups:** Arab, Afro-Arab
**Religions:** Muslim, Christian, Hindu
**Currency:** Dinar and Riyal
**Tel. Area Code:** 967

## Yugoslavia (Jugoslavija)

**Location:** Eastern Europe
**Area:** 39,449 mi$^2$ (102,173 km$^2$)
**Population:** 10,622,000 (Urban: 50%)
**Literacy:** 90%
**Capital:** Beograd (Belgrade), 1,130,000
**Government:** Socialist republic
**Languages:** Serbian, Montenegrin, Albanian, Macedonian, Bulgarian, Hungarian
**Ethnic Groups:** Serbian, Montenegrin, Albanian, Macedonian, Bulgarian, Hungarian
**Religions:** Eastern Orthodox, Muslim, Roman Catholic, Protestant
**Currency:** Dinar
**Tel. Area Code:** 38

## Zaire

**Location:** Central Africa
**Area:** 905,446 mi$^2$ (2,345,095 km$^2$)
**Population:** 38,475,000 (Urban: 40%)
**Literacy:** 72%
**Capital:** Kinshasa, 3,000,000
**Government:** Republic
**Languages:** French, Kikongo, Lingala, Swahili, Tshiluba
**Ethnic Groups:** Kongo, Luba, Mongo, Mangbetu-Azande, others
**Religions:** Roman Catholic 50%, Protestant 20%, Kimbanguist 10%, Muslim 10%
**Currency:** Zaire
**Tel. Area Code:** 243

## Zambia

**Location:** Southern Africa, landlocked
**Area:** 290,586 mi$^2$ (752,614 km$^2$)
**Population:** 8,201,000 (Urban: 56%)
**Literacy:** 73%
**Capital:** Lusaka, 921,000
**Government:** Republic
**Languages:** English, Tonga, Lozi, other indigenous
**Ethnic Groups:** African 99%, European 1%
**Religions:** Christian 70%, tribal religionist 29%, Muslim and Hindu 1%
**Currency:** Kwacha
**Tel. Area Code:** 260

## Zimbabwe

**Location:** Southern Africa, landlocked
**Area:** 150,873 mi$^2$ (390,759 km$^2$)
**Population:** 9,748,000 (Urban: 28%)
**Literacy:** 67%
**Capital:** Harare, 681,000
**Government:** Republic
**Languages:** English, ChiShona, SiNdebele
**Ethnic Groups:** Shona 71%, Ndebele 16%, white 1%
**Religions:** Animist, Roman Catholic, Apostolic and other Protestant
**Currency:** Dollar
**Tel. Area Code:** 263

# Traveler's Personal Diary

## Contents

## Calendar

### 1993

**January**

| S | M | T | W | T | F | S |
|---|---|---|---|---|---|---|
|  |  |  |  |  | 1 | 2 |
| 3 | 4 | 5 | 6 | 7 | 8 | 9 |
| 10 | 11 | 12 | 13 | 14 | 15 | 16 |
| 17 | 18 | 19 | 20 | 21 | 22 | 23 |
| 24 | 25 | 26 | 27 | 28 | 29 | 30 |
| 31 |  |  |  |  |  |  |

**February**

| S | M | T | W | T | F | S |
|---|---|---|---|---|---|---|
|  | 1 | 2 | 3 | 4 | 5 | 6 |
| 7 | 8 | 9 | 10 | 11 | 12 | 13 |
| 14 | 15 | 16 | 17 | 18 | 19 | 20 |
| 21 | 22 | 23 | 24 | 25 | 26 | 27 |
| 28 |  |  |  |  |  |  |

**March**

| S | M | T | W | T | F | S |
|---|---|---|---|---|---|---|
|  | 1 | 2 | 3 | 4 | 5 | 6 |
| 7 | 8 | 9 | 10 | 11 | 12 | 13 |
| 14 | 15 | 16 | 17 | 18 | 19 | 20 |
| 21 | 22 | 23 | 24 | 25 | 26 | 27 |
| 28 | 29 | 30 | 31 |  |  |  |

**April**

| S | M | T | W | T | F | S |
|---|---|---|---|---|---|---|
|  |  |  |  | 1 | 2 | 3 |
| 4 | 5 | 6 | 7 | 8 | 9 | 10 |
| 11 | 12 | 13 | 14 | 15 | 16 | 17 |
| 18 | 19 | 20 | 21 | 22 | 23 | 24 |
| 25 | 26 | 27 | 28 | 29 | 30 |  |

**May**

| S | M | T | W | T | F | S |
|---|---|---|---|---|---|---|
|  |  |  |  |  |  | 1 |
| 2 | 3 | 4 | 5 | 6 | 7 | 8 |
| 9 | 10 | 11 | 12 | 13 | 14 | 15 |
| 16 | 17 | 18 | 19 | 20 | 21 | 22 |
| 23 | 24 | 25 | 26 | 27 | 28 | 29 |
| 30 | 31 |  |  |  |  |  |

**June**

| S | M | T | W | T | F | S |
|---|---|---|---|---|---|---|
|  |  | 1 | 2 | 3 | 4 | 5 |
| 6 | 7 | 8 | 9 | 10 | 11 | 12 |
| 13 | 14 | 15 | 16 | 17 | 18 | 19 |
| 20 | 21 | 22 | 23 | 24 | 25 | 26 |
| 27 | 28 | 29 | 30 |  |  |  |

**July**

| S | M | T | W | T | F | S |
|---|---|---|---|---|---|---|
|  |  |  |  | 1 | 2 | 3 |
| 4 | 5 | 6 | 7 | 8 | 9 | 10 |
| 11 | 12 | 13 | 14 | 15 | 16 | 17 |
| 18 | 19 | 20 | 21 | 22 | 23 | 24 |
| 25 | 26 | 27 | 28 | 29 | 30 | 31 |

**August**

| S | M | T | W | T | F | S |
|---|---|---|---|---|---|---|
| 1 | 2 | 3 | 4 | 5 | 6 | 7 |
| 8 | 9 | 10 | 11 | 12 | 13 | 14 |
| 15 | 16 | 17 | 18 | 19 | 20 | 21 |
| 22 | 23 | 24 | 25 | 26 | 27 | 28 |
| 29 | 30 | 31 |  |  |  |  |

**September**

| S | M | T | W | T | F | S |
|---|---|---|---|---|---|---|
|  |  |  | 1 | 2 | 3 | 4 |
| 5 | 6 | 7 | 8 | 9 | 10 | 11 |
| 12 | 13 | 14 | 15 | 16 | 17 | 18 |
| 19 | 20 | 21 | 22 | 23 | 24 | 25 |
| 26 | 27 | 28 | 29 | 30 |  |  |

**October**

| S | M | T | W | T | F | S |
|---|---|---|---|---|---|---|
|  |  |  |  |  | 1 | 2 |
| 3 | 4 | 5 | 6 | 7 | 8 | 9 |
| 10 | 11 | 12 | 13 | 14 | 15 | 16 |
| 17 | 18 | 19 | 20 | 21 | 22 | 23 |
| 24 | 25 | 26 | 27 | 28 | 29 | 30 |
| 31 |  |  |  |  |  |  |

**November**

| S | M | T | W | T | F | S |
|---|---|---|---|---|---|---|
|  | 1 | 2 | 3 | 4 | 5 | 6 |
| 7 | 8 | 9 | 10 | 11 | 12 | 13 |
| 14 | 15 | 16 | 17 | 18 | 19 | 20 |
| 21 | 22 | 23 | 24 | 25 | 26 | 27 |
| 28 | 29 | 30 |  |  |  |  |

**December**

| S | M | T | W | T | F | S |
|---|---|---|---|---|---|---|
|  |  |  | 1 | 2 | 3 | 4 |
| 5 | 6 | 7 | 8 | 9 | 10 | 11 |
| 12 | 13 | 14 | 15 | 16 | 17 | 18 |
| 19 | 20 | 21 | 22 | 23 | 24 | 25 |
| 26 | 27 | 28 | 29 | 30 | 31 |  |

### 1994

**January**

| S | M | T | W | T | F | S |
|---|---|---|---|---|---|---|
|  |  |  |  |  |  | 1 |
| 2 | 3 | 4 | 5 | 6 | 7 | 8 |
| 9 | 10 | 11 | 12 | 13 | 14 | 15 |
| 16 | 17 | 18 | 19 | 20 | 21 | 22 |
| 23 | 24 | 25 | 26 | 27 | 28 | 29 |
| 30 | 31 |  |  |  |  |  |

**February**

| S | M | T | W | T | F | S |
|---|---|---|---|---|---|---|
|  |  | 1 | 2 | 3 | 4 | 5 |
| 6 | 7 | 8 | 9 | 10 | 11 | 12 |
| 13 | 14 | 15 | 16 | 17 | 18 | 19 |
| 20 | 21 | 22 | 23 | 24 | 25 | 26 |
| 27 | 28 |  |  |  |  |  |

**March**

| S | M | T | W | T | F | S |
|---|---|---|---|---|---|---|
|  |  | 1 | 2 | 3 | 4 | 5 |
| 6 | 7 | 8 | 9 | 10 | 11 | 12 |
| 13 | 14 | 15 | 16 | 17 | 18 | 19 |
| 20 | 21 | 22 | 23 | 24 | 25 | 26 |
| 27 | 28 | 29 | 30 | 31 |  |  |

**April**

| S | M | T | W | T | F | S |
|---|---|---|---|---|---|---|
|  |  |  |  |  | 1 | 2 |
| 3 | 4 | 5 | 6 | 7 | 8 | 9 |
| 10 | 11 | 12 | 13 | 14 | 15 | 16 |
| 17 | 18 | 19 | 20 | 21 | 22 | 23 |
| 24 | 25 | 26 | 27 | 28 | 29 | 30 |

**May**

| S | M | T | W | T | F | S |
|---|---|---|---|---|---|---|
| 1 | 2 | 3 | 4 | 5 | 6 | 7 |
| 8 | 9 | 10 | 11 | 12 | 13 | 14 |
| 15 | 16 | 17 | 18 | 19 | 20 | 21 |
| 22 | 23 | 24 | 25 | 26 | 27 | 28 |
| 29 | 30 | 31 |  |  |  |  |

**June**

| S | M | T | W | T | F | S |
|---|---|---|---|---|---|---|
|  |  |  | 1 | 2 | 3 | 4 |
| 5 | 6 | 7 | 8 | 9 | 10 | 11 |
| 12 | 13 | 14 | 15 | 16 | 17 | 18 |
| 19 | 20 | 21 | 22 | 23 | 24 | 25 |
| 26 | 27 | 28 | 29 | 30 |  |  |

**July**

| S | M | T | W | T | F | S |
|---|---|---|---|---|---|---|
|  |  |  |  |  | 1 | 2 |
| 3 | 4 | 5 | 6 | 7 | 8 | 9 |
| 10 | 11 | 12 | 13 | 14 | 15 | 16 |
| 17 | 18 | 19 | 20 | 21 | 22 | 23 |
| 24 | 25 | 26 | 27 | 28 | 29 | 30 |
| 31 |  |  |  |  |  |  |

**August**

| S | M | T | W | T | F | S |
|---|---|---|---|---|---|---|
|  | 1 | 2 | 3 | 4 | 5 | 6 |
| 7 | 8 | 9 | 10 | 11 | 12 | 13 |
| 14 | 15 | 16 | 17 | 18 | 19 | 20 |
| 21 | 22 | 23 | 24 | 25 | 26 | 27 |
| 28 | 29 | 30 | 31 |  |  |  |

**September**

| S | M | T | W | T | F | S |
|---|---|---|---|---|---|---|
|  |  |  |  | 1 | 2 | 3 |
| 4 | 5 | 6 | 7 | 8 | 9 | 10 |
| 11 | 12 | 13 | 14 | 15 | 16 | 17 |
| 18 | 19 | 20 | 21 | 22 | 23 | 24 |
| 25 | 26 | 27 | 28 | 29 | 30 |  |

**October**

| S | M | T | W | T | F | S |
|---|---|---|---|---|---|---|
|  |  |  |  |  |  | 1 |
| 2 | 3 | 4 | 5 | 6 | 7 | 8 |
| 9 | 10 | 11 | 12 | 13 | 14 | 15 |
| 16 | 17 | 18 | 19 | 20 | 21 | 22 |
| 23 | 24 | 25 | 26 | 27 | 28 | 29 |
| 30 | 31 |  |  |  |  |  |

**November**

| S | M | T | W | T | F | S |
|---|---|---|---|---|---|---|
|  |  | 1 | 2 | 3 | 4 | 5 |
| 6 | 7 | 8 | 9 | 10 | 11 | 12 |
| 13 | 14 | 15 | 16 | 17 | 18 | 19 |
| 20 | 21 | 22 | 23 | 24 | 25 | 26 |
| 27 | 28 | 29 | 30 |  |  |  |

**December**

| S | M | T | W | T | F | S |
|---|---|---|---|---|---|---|
|  |  |  |  | 1 | 2 | 3 |
| 4 | 5 | 6 | 7 | 8 | 9 | 10 |
| 11 | 12 | 13 | 14 | 15 | 16 | 17 |
| 18 | 19 | 20 | 21 | 22 | 23 | 24 |
| 25 | 26 | 27 | 28 | 29 | 30 | 31 |

## 1995

**January**
```
S  M  T  W  T  F  S
1  2  3  4  5  6  7
8  9 10 11 12 13 14
15 16 17 18 19 20 21
22 23 24 25 26 27 28
29 30 31
```

**February**
```
S  M  T  W  T  F  S
         1  2  3  4
5  6  7  8  9 10 11
12 13 14 15 16 17 18
19 20 21 22 23 24 25
26 27 28
```

**March**
```
S  M  T  W  T  F  S
         1  2  3  4
5  6  7  8  9 10 11
12 13 14 15 16 17 18
19 20 21 22 23 24 25
26 27 28 29 30 31
```

**April**
```
S  M  T  W  T  F  S
                  1
2  3  4  5  6  7  8
9 10 11 12 13 14 15
16 17 18 19 20 21 22
23 24 25 26 27 28 29
30
```

**May**
```
S  M  T  W  T  F  S
1  2  3  4  5  6
7  8  9 10 11 12 13
14 15 16 17 18 19 20
21 22 23 24 25 26 27
28 29 30 31
```

**June**
```
S  M  T  W  T  F  S
            1  2  3
4  5  6  7  8  9 10
11 12 13 14 15 16 17
18 19 20 21 22 23 24
25 26 27 28 29 30
```

**July**
```
S  M  T  W  T  F  S
                  1
2  3  4  5  6  7  8
9 10 11 12 13 14 15
16 17 18 19 20 21 22
23 24 25 26 27 28 29
30 31
```

**August**
```
S  M  T  W  T  F  S
      1  2  3  4  5
6  7  8  9 10 11 12
13 14 15 16 17 18 19
20 21 22 23 24 25 26
27 28 29 30 31
```

**September**
```
S  M  T  W  T  F  S
                1  2
3  4  5  6  7  8  9
10 11 12 13 14 15 16
17 18 19 20 21 22 23
24 25 26 27 28 29 30
```

**October**
```
S  M  T  W  T  F  S
1  2  3  4  5  6  7
8  9 10 11 12 13 14
15 16 17 18 19 20 21
22 23 24 25 26 27 28
29 30 31
```

**November**
```
S  M  T  W  T  F  S
         1  2  3  4
5  6  7  8  9 10 11
12 13 14 15 16 17 18
19 20 21 22 23 24 25
26 27 28 29 30
```

**December**
```
S  M  T  W  T  F  S
               1  2
3  4  5  6  7  8  9
10 11 12 13 14 15 16
17 18 19 20 21 22 23
24 25 26 27 28 29 30
31
```

## 1996

**January**
```
S  M  T  W  T  F  S
   1  2  3  4  5  6
7  8  9 10 11 12 13
14 15 16 17 18 19 20
21 22 23 24 25 26 27
28 29 30 31
```

**February**
```
S  M  T  W  T  F  S
            1  2  3
4  5  6  7  8  9 10
11 12 13 14 15 16 17
18 19 20 21 22 23 24
25 26 27 28 29
```

**March**
```
S  M  T  W  T  F  S
                1  2
3  4  5  6  7  8  9
10 11 12 13 14 15 16
17 18 19 20 21 22 23
24 25 26 27 28 29 30
31
```

**April**
```
S  M  T  W  T  F  S
   1  2  3  4  5  6
7  8  9 10 11 12 13
14 15 16 17 18 19 20
21 22 23 24 25 26 27
28 29 30
```

**May**
```
S  M  T  W  T  F  S
         1  2  3  4
5  6  7  8  9 10 11
12 13 14 15 16 17 18
19 20 21 22 23 24 25
26 27 28 29 30 31
```

**June**
```
S  M  T  W  T  F  S
                  1
2  3  4  5  6  7  8
9 10 11 12 13 14 15
16 17 18 19 20 21 22
23 24 25 26 27 28 29
30
```

**July**
```
S  M  T  W  T  F  S
1  2  3  4  5  6
7  8  9 10 11 12 13
14 15 16 17 18 19 20
21 22 23 24 25 26 27
28 29 30 31
```

**August**
```
S  M  T  W  T  F  S
            1  2  3
4  5  6  7  8  9 10
11 12 13 14 15 16 17
18 19 20 21 22 23 24
25 26 27 28 29 30 31
```

**September**
```
S  M  T  W  T  F  S
1  2  3  4  5  6  7
8  9 10 11 12 13 14
15 16 17 18 19 20 21
22 23 24 25 26 27 28
29 30
```

**October**
```
S  M  T  W  T  F  S
      1  2  3  4  5
6  7  8  9 10 11 12
13 14 15 16 17 18 19
20 21 22 23 24 25 26
27 28 29 30 31
```

**November**
```
S  M  T  W  T  F  S
               1  2
3  4  5  6  7  8  9
10 11 12 13 14 15 16
17 18 19 20 21 22 23
24 25 26 27 28 29 30
```

**December**
```
S  M  T  W  T  F  S
1  2  3  4  5  6  7
8  9 10 11 12 13 14
15 16 17 18 19 20 21
22 23 24 25 26 27 28
29 30 31
```

## 1997

**January**
```
S  M  T  W  T  F  S
         1  2  3  4
5  6  7  8  9 10 11
12 13 14 15 16 17 18
19 20 21 22 23 24 25
26 27 28 29 30 31
```

**February**
```
S  M  T  W  T  F  S
                  1
2  3  4  5  6  7  8
9 10 11 12 13 14 15
16 17 18 19 20 21 22
23 24 25 26 27 28
```

**March**
```
S  M  T  W  T  F  S
                  1
2  3  4  5  6  7  8
9 10 11 12 13 14 15
16 17 18 19 20 21 22
23 24 25 26 27 28 29
30 31
```

**April**
```
S  M  T  W  T  F  S
      1  2  3  4  5
6  7  8  9 10 11 12
13 14 15 16 17 18 19
20 21 22 23 24 25 26
27 28 29 30
```

**May**
```
S  M  T  W  T  F  S
            1  2  3
4  5  6  7  8  9 10
11 12 13 14 15 16 17
18 19 20 21 22 23 24
25 26 27 28 29 30 31
```

**June**
```
S  M  T  W  T  F  S
1  2  3  4  5  6  7
8  9 10 11 12 13 14
15 16 17 18 19 20 21
22 23 24 25 26 27 28
29 30
```

**July**
```
S  M  T  W  T  F  S
      1  2  3  4  5
6  7  8  9 10 11 12
13 14 15 16 17 18 19
20 21 22 23 24 25 26
27 28 29 30 31
```

**August**
```
S  M  T  W  T  F  S
               1  2
3  4  5  6  7  8  9
10 11 12 13 14 15 16
17 18 19 20 21 22 23
24 25 26 27 28 29 30
31
```

**September**
```
S  M  T  W  T  F  S
   1  2  3  4  5  6
7  8  9 10 11 12 13
14 15 16 17 18 19 20
21 22 23 24 25 26 27
28 29 30
```

**October**
```
S  M  T  W  T  F  S
      1  2  3  4
5  6  7  8  9 10 11
12 13 14 15 16 17 18
19 20 21 22 23 24 25
26 27 28 29 30 31
```

**November**
```
S  M  T  W  T  F  S
                  1
2  3  4  5  6  7  8
9 10 11 12 13 14 15
16 17 18 19 20 21 22
23 24 25 26 27 28 29
30
```

**December**
```
S  M  T  W  T  F  S
1  2  3  4  5  6
7  8  9 10 11 12 13
14 15 16 17 18 19 20
21 22 23 24 25 26 27
28 29 30 31
```

## 1998

**January**
```
S  M  T  W  T  F  S
            1  2  3
4  5  6  7  8  9 10
11 12 13 14 15 16 17
18 19 20 21 22 23 24
25 26 27 28 29 30 31
```

**February**
```
S  M  T  W  T  F  S
1  2  3  4  5  6  7
8  9 10 11 12 13 14
15 16 17 18 19 20 21
22 23 24 25 26 27 28
```

**March**
```
S  M  T  W  T  F  S
1  2  3  4  5  6  7
8  9 10 11 12 13 14
15 16 17 18 19 20 21
22 23 24 25 26 27 28
29 30 31
```

**April**
```
S  M  T  W  T  F  S
         1  2  3  4
5  6  7  8  9 10 11
12 13 14 15 16 17 18
19 20 21 22 23 24 25
26 27 28 29 30
```

**May**
```
S  M  T  W  T  F  S
               1  2
3  4  5  6  7  8  9
10 11 12 13 14 15 16
17 18 19 20 21 22 23
24 25 26 27 28 29 30
31
```

**June**
```
S  M  T  W  T  F  S
   1  2  3  4  5  6
7  8  9 10 11 12 13
14 15 16 17 18 19 20
21 22 23 24 25 26 27
28 29 30
```

**July**
```
S  M  T  W  T  F  S
         1  2  3  4
5  6  7  8  9 10 11
12 13 14 15 16 17 18
19 20 21 22 23 24 25
26 27 28 29 30 31
```

**August**
```
S  M  T  W  T  F  S
                  1
2  3  4  5  6  7  8
9 10 11 12 13 14 15
16 17 18 19 20 21 22
23 24 25 26 27 28 29
30 31
```

**September**
```
S  M  T  W  T  F  S
      1  2  3  4  5
6  7  8  9 10 11 12
13 14 15 16 17 18 19
20 21 22 23 24 25 26
27 28 29 30
```

**October**
```
S  M  T  W  T  F  S
            1  2  3
4  5  6  7  8  9 10
11 12 13 14 15 16 17
18 19 20 21 22 23 24
25 26 27 28 29 30 31
```

**November**
```
S  M  T  W  T  F  S
1  2  3  4  5  6  7
8  9 10 11 12 13 14
15 16 17 18 19 20 21
22 23 24 25 26 27 28
29 30
```

**December**
```
S  M  T  W  T  F  S
      1  2  3  4  5
6  7  8  9 10 11 12
13 14 15 16 17 18 19
20 21 22 23 24 25 26
27 28 29 30 31
```

## Weights, Measures, and Formulas

### Distance

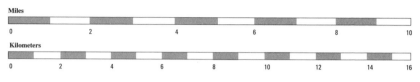

Miles to Kilometers: Multiply number of miles by 1.6
Kilometers to Miles: Multiply number of kilometers by .6

### Liquid Measurement

### Temperature

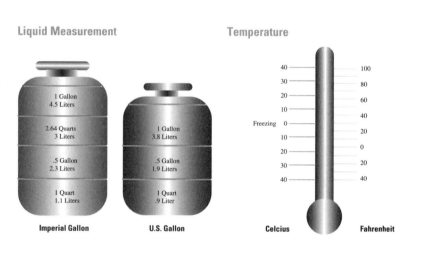

| Imperial Gallon | U.S. Gallon | Celcius | Fahrenheit |

The Imperial/Canadian gallon is based on the Imperial quart, which is approximately one-fifth larger than the U.S. quart.

The following measurements are approximate for easy conversion.

1 Imperial gallon = 4.5 liters
1 Imperial gallon = 1.2 U.S. gallons
1 liter = .22 Imperial gallon
5 Imperial gallons = 6 U.S. gallons

**Comparative Thermometer Readings**

Fahrenheit to Celsius:
Subtract 32 from the number of Fahrenheit, then multiply by 5/9.

Celsius to Fahrenheit:
Multiply the number of Celsius by 9/5 and add 32.

## Speed

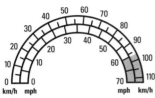

30 mph is maximum speed limit in most U.S. towns. The metric equivalent is 50 km/h.

50 mph is maximum speed limit on many rural two-lane roads in U.S. In metrics, 80 km/h.

55 mph is maximum speed limit on U.S. interstate highways. In metrics, 90 km/h.

60 mph is maximum speed allowed on access-controlled highways in Canada. The metric equivalent is 100 km/h.

## Measures

### Linear
1 inch = 2.540 centimeters
1 foot = .305 meter
1 yard = .914 meter
1 mile = 1.609 kilometers
1 meter = 39.37 inches
1 meter = 3.28 feet = 1.094 yards
1 kilometer = .621 mile
1 mile = 1,760 yards = 5,280 feet
1 yard = 36 inches = 3 feet
1 foot = 12 inches
1 span = 9 inches
1 hand = 4 inches
1 mile = 8 furlongs
1 furlong = 220 yards
1 nautical mile (knot) = 1.152 statute miles = 1.853 kilometers

### Square/Area
1 sq. inch = 6.451 sq. centimeters
1 sq. foot = .093 sq. meter
1 sq. yard = .836 sq. meter
1 sq. centimeter = .155 sq. inch
1 sq. meter = 10.764 sq. feet = 1.196 sq. yards
1 sq. foot = 144 sq. inches
1 sq. yard = 9 sq. feet
An acre is equal to a square, the side of which is 208.7 feet
1 acre = 4,840 sq. yards = 43,560 sq. feet
1 sq. mile = 640 acres
1 sq. mile = 2.59 sq. kilometers
1 sq. kilometer = .386 sq. mile

### Cubic/Volume
1 cu. inch = 16.387 cu. centimeters
1 cu. foot = .028 cu. meter
1 cu. yard = .765 cu. meter
1 cu. centimeter = .061 cu. inch
1 cu. meter = 35.314 cu. feet
1 cu. meter = 1.308 cu. yards
1 cu. yard = 27 cu. feet
1 cu. foot = 1,728 cu. inches
1 cord of wood = 4 x 4 x 8 feet = 128 cu. feet

### Dry Measure (U.S.)
1 bushel = 1.245 cu. feet = 2,150.42 cu. inches
1 bushel = 4 pecks = 32 quarts = 64 pints
1 peck = 8 quarts = 16 pints

### Liquid Measure (U.S.)
1 pint = 16 ounces = .473 liter
1 quart = 2 pints = 32 ounces
1 quart = .946 liter
1 gallon = 4 quarts = 3.785 liters
1 liter = 1.057 quarts

### Miscellaneous
1 great gross = 12 gross = 144 dozen
1 gross = 12 dozen = 144 units
1 dozen = 12 units
1 score = 20 units
1 quire = 24 sheets
1 ream = 20 quires = 480 sheets
1 ream printing paper = 500 sheets

### Weights

#### Avoirdupois
1 ounce = 28.35 grams
1 pound = .453 kilograms = 16 ounces
1 gram = .035 ounce
1 kilogram = 2.205 pounds
1 short ton = 2,000 pounds
1 short ton = .907 metric tons
1 long ton = 2,240 pounds
1 long ton = 1.016 metric tons
1 stone = 14 pounds

#### Troy
1 ounce = 20 pennyweights = 480 grains
1 pound = 12 ounces = 5,760 grains
1 carat = 3.086 grains
1 pennyweight = 24 grains = .05 ounce
1 grain troy = 1 grain avoirdupois = 1 grain apothecaries' weight

### Mathematical Formulas
Diameter of Circle: circumference divided by 3.1416
Circumference of Circle: diameter multiplied by 3.1416
Area of Circle: square of radius multiplied by 3.1416 or square of diameter multiplied by .7854
Area of Triangle: base multiplied by ½ of height
Area of Parallelogram (including square): base multiplied by height
Surface Area of Sphere: square of diameter multiplied by 3.1416
Volume of Sphere: cube of diameter multiplied by .5236
Volume of Prism or Cylinder: area of base multiplied by height
Volume of Pyramid or Cone: area of base multiplied by ⅓ of height
Amount of Simple Interest: principle multiplied by rate of interest multiplied by time (in terms of years or fractions thereof)

### Clothing Size Equivalents

#### Men's Suits and Overcoats
American: 36, 38, 40, 42, 44, 46
British: 36, 38, 40, 42, 44, 46
European: 46, 48, 51, 54, 56, 59

#### Women's Suits and Dresses
America: 8, 10, 12, 14, 16, 18
British: 10, 12, 14, 16, 18, 20
European: 38, 40, 42, 44, 46, 48

#### Shirts
American: 14, 14½, 15, 15½, 16, 16½. 17
British: 14, 14½, 15, 15½, 16, 16½, 17
European: 36, 37, 38, 39, 41, 42, 43

#### Men's Shoes
American: 7½, 8, 8½, 9½, 10½, 11½
British: 7, 7½, 8, 9, 10, 11
European: 40½, 41, 42, 43, 44½, 46

#### Women's Shoes
American: 6, 6½, 7, 7½, 8, 8½
British: 4½, 5, 5½, 6, 6½, 7
European: 37½, 38, 39, 39½, 40, 40½

#### Children's Clothes
American: 4, 6, 8, 10, 12, 14
British: Height (in) 43, 48, 55, 58, 60, 62
Age 4-5, 6-7, 9-10, 11, 12, 13
European Height (cm) 125, 135, 150, 155, 160, 165
Age 7, 9, 12, 13, 14, 15

## Names and Addresses

Name

Address

City State Zip

Country

Telephone    (       )

FAX    (       )


Name

Address

City State Zip

Country

Telephone    (       )

FAX    (       )


Name

Address

City State Zip

Country

Telephone    (       )

FAX    (       )


Name

Address

City State Zip

Country

Telephone    (       )

FAX    (       )


Name

Address

City State Zip

Country

Telephone    (       )

FAX    (       )


Name

Address

City State Zip

Country

Telephone    (       )

FAX    (       )


Name

Address

City State Zip

Country

Telephone    (       )

FAX    (       )


Name

Address

City State Zip

Country

Telephone    (       )

FAX    (       )


Name

Address

City State Zip

Country

Telephone    (       )

FAX    (       )


Name

Address

City State Zip

Country

Telephone    (       )

FAX    (       )

Name

Address

City State Zip

Country

Telephone    (        )

FAX    (        )

Name

Address

City State Zip

Country

Telephone    (        )

FAX    (        )

Name

Address

City State Zip

Country

Telephone    (        )

FAX    (        )

Name

Address

City State Zip

Country

Telephone    (        )

FAX    (        )

Name

Address

City State Zip

Country

Telephone    (        )

FAX    (        )

Name

Address

City State Zip

Country

Telephone    (        )

FAX    (        )

Name

Address

City State Zip

Country

Telephone    (        )

FAX    (        )

Name

Address

City State Zip

Country

Telephone    (        )

FAX    (        )

Name

Address

City State Zip

Country

Telephone    (        )

FAX    (        )

Name

Address

City State Zip

Country

Telephone    (        )

FAX    (        )

**Travel Notes**

**Travel Notes**

## Travel Notes

## Itinerary

| Date | Destination | Lodging | Address | Phone/FAX # |
|------|-------------|---------|---------|-------------|
| | | | | |
| | | | | |
| | | | | |
| | | | | |
| | | | | |
| | | | | |
| | | | | |
| | | | | |
| | | | | |
| | | | | |
| | | | | |
| | | | | |
| | | | | |
| | | | | |
| | | | | |
| | | | | |
| | | | | |
| | | | | |
| | | | | |
| | | | | |
| | | | | |

## Financial Worksheet

**Date:**

**Travel Fares**

**Meals**

**Lodging**

**Tips**

**Entertainment**

**Gifts**

**Other**

**Total**

**Currency Exchanged**

**Exchange Rate**

## Personal Information

Name

Street

City State Zip

Country

Home Telephone (    )

Home FAX  (    )

Company

Street

City State Zip

Country

Company Telephone

Company FAX (    )

Social Security No.

Passport No.

Passport Expiration Date

Driver's License No.

Other ID Nos:

Automobile Model & Year

Automobile License

Vehicle Serial

Emergency Road Service

Insurance Policies:

Company Name

Policy Number

Type

Amount

Expiration Date

Company Name

Policy Number

Type

Amount

Expiration Date

In Case of Emergency, Notify:

Name

Relationship

Street

City State Zip

Telephone (    )

FAX (    )

Emergency Medical Instructions:

Medic Alert

Blood Type

Allergies

Prescriptions

Glasses

Physician

Office Telephone (    )

FAX (    )

Home Telephone (    )

Pharmacist

Telephone (    )

FAX (    )

Religious Affiliation

Financial Accounts:

Institution

Address

Telephone (    )

Account #

Institution

Address

Telephone (    )

Account #

Traveler's Cheque Numbers